WRITING & Grammar 12

Third Edition

Elizabeth Rose
Kimberly Y. Stegall

bju press
Greenville, South Carolina

NOTE: The fact that materials produced by other publishers may be referred to in this volume does not constitute an endorsement by BJU Press of the content or theological position of materials produced by such publishers. Any references and ancillary materials are listed as an aid to the student or the teacher and in an attempt to maintain the accepted academic standards of the publishing industry.

WRITING AND GRAMMAR 12
Third Edition

Coordinating Writers
Judith W. Lanier, MA
Elizabeth Rose, MEd, MA
Kimberly Y. Stegall, MEd

Contributing Writers
Eileen M. Berry, MA
Seth W. Carper
Glenda H. Guthrie
Maisie E. Douglas Hansen
Erin Harper
Sarah Abigail Stahl Mattos
Shelby J. Morris, MA
Rebecca A. Osborne, MEd
Michael Pope, MA
Greta Forman Rohrer, MEd
Rachel Maes Stewart
Dawn L. Watkins, MEd, MA

Project Coordinator
Benjamin Sinnamon

Consultants
Will Gray
Grace Collins Hargis, PhD
Chairman Emeritus of the Department of English Education and Chairman of the Department of Linguistics, Bob Jones University

Bible Integration
Bryan Smith, PhD
Mark L. Ward Jr., PhD

Editors
Rebecca S. Moore
Virginia M. Nutz

Page Layout
Kelley Moore
Bonnijean Marley

Cover Designer
Drew Fields

Designers
Christy Matias
US Color

Permissions
Sylvia Gass
Brenda Hansen
Ashley Hobbs

Illustrators
Matthew Bjerk
Aaron Dickey
Johanna Ehnis
Cory Godbey
Preston Gravely Jr.
Dyke Habegger
John Roberts

Acknowledgments and Photograph Credits begin on page xi, which is an extension of this copyright page.

All trademarks are the registered and unregistered marks of their respective owners. BJU Press is in no way affiliated with these companies. No rights are granted by BJU Press to use such marks, whether by implication, estoppel, or otherwise.

© 2013, 2020 BJU Press
Greenville, South Carolina 29609
First Edition © 1985 BJU Press
Second Edition © 2004 BJU Press

Printed in the United States of America
All rights reserved

ISBN 978-1-60682-381-1

15 14 13 12 11 10 9 8 7 6 5 4 3 2 1

TABLE OF CONTENTS

Acknowledgments	xi
To the Student	xiii

CHAPTER 1

Composition: The Writing Process — 1

- Planning — 1
  - Choosing Your Topic — 1
  - Narrowing Your Topic — 4
  - Considering Your Audience — 4
  - Determining Your Purpose — 4
  - Gathering Information — 5
  - Outlining the Paper — 6
- Drafting — 8
  - Writing Exposition — 8
    - Mode — 9
    - Thesis Statements — 10
    - Introductions — 10
    - Paragraph Development — 11
    - Paragraph Organization — 14
    - Conclusions — 19
  - Writing Essays — 19
- Revising — 20
  - Revising for Ideas — 20
  - Revising for Style — 22
  - Revising for Correctness: Proofreading — 23
- Publishing — 24
  - Choosing a Title — 24
  - Making a Neat Copy — 24

History of the English Language: Language Differences — 26

CHAPTER 2

- Excerpt from "The Encantadas" — 29

Writing: Descriptive Essay — 30

Grammar: Parts of Speech — 35

- Nouns — 35
- Pronouns — 37
  - Personal Pronouns — 37
  - Indefinite Pronouns — 38
  - Demonstrative Pronouns — 39
  - Relative Pronouns — 39
  - Interrogative Pronouns — 40
  - Reflexive and Intensive Pronouns — 40
  - Reciprocal Pronouns — 40
- Verbs — 42
  - Intransitive Verbs — 43
  - Transitive Verbs — 44

Linking Verbs	44
Auxiliaries	44
Verb-Adverb Combinations	45
Adjectives	48
Determiners	48
Modifying Nouns	50
Proper Adjectives	50
Adverbs	50
Qualifiers	50
Conjunctive Adverbs	51
Relative Adverbs	51
Interrogative Adverbs	51
Prepositions	53
Conjunctions	54
Interjections	55

From the Written Word:
Recognizing the Truth — 59

CHAPTER 3

"Grant and Lee: A Study in Contrasts"	61
Writing: Comparison-and-Contrast Essay	63
Grammar: Sentences	69
Defining Sentences	69
Kinds of Sentences	69
Finding Subjects and Predicates	70
Basic Sentence Patterns	74
S-InV	75
S-LV-PN	75
S-LV-PA	75
S-*be*-AdvI	76
S-TrV-DO	76
S-TrV-IO-DO	76
S-TrV-DO-OC	77

Think About It:
Thinking Skills — 80

CHAPTER 4

Excerpt from *By the Light of a Thousand Stars*	83
Writing: Interior Monologue	84
Grammar: Phrases	88
Nonverbal Phrases	88
Prepositional Phrases	88
Absolute Phrases	88
Appositive Phrases	89
Verbal Phrases	92
Participles and Participial Phrases	92
Gerunds and Gerund Phrases	96
Infinitives and Infinitive Phrases	101

From the Written Word:
Formulating the Details — 107

CHAPTER 5

"Signs of the Times: Littering the Verbal Landscape" — 109
Writing: Persuasive Essay — 110
Grammar: Clauses — 116
   Identifying Kinds of Dependent Clauses — 116
      Adjective Clauses — 116
      Adverb Clauses — 122
      Noun Clauses — 126
   Using Independent and Dependent Clauses — 132
   Avoiding Sentence Errors — 135
      Fragment — 135
      Comma Splice and Fused Sentence — 137
Think About It:
Authorial Intention — 141

CHAPTER 6

Excerpt from *This Same Jesus* — 143
Writing: Dramatic Scene — 144
Usage: Agreement — 148
   Subject-Verb Agreement — 148
      Subjects and Predicates — 148
      Subject Identification — 150
      Problem Nouns and Pronouns — 153
      Compound Subjects — 161
   Pronoun-Antecedent Agreement — 163
      Nouns as Antecedents — 163
      Indefinite Pronouns as Antecedents — 167
From the Written Word:
Presenting an Argument — 171

CHAPTER 7

"A Record of Our Journeys" — 173
Writing: Extemporaneous Essay — 174
Usage: Verb Use — 177
   Principal Parts — 178
   Tenses — 178
      Simple Tenses — 178
      Perfect Tenses — 179
      Progressive Tenses — 180
      Consistency and Sequence of Tenses — 184
   Voice — 187
      Using Active and Passive Sentences — 188
      Revising Active and Passive Sentences — 188
   Mood — 192
      Forms of the Subjunctive — 192
      Uses of the Subjunctive — 193
Think About It:
Subjectivity and Objectivity; Fact and Opinion — 196

CHAPTER 8

"Invest in Teens"	199
Writing: Video Report	200
Usage: Pronoun Use	203
Pronoun Case	203
General Principles	204
Appositives	206
Comparisons Using *Than* or *As*	206
"Subjects" and Objects of Verbals	209
Who and *Whom*	210
Pronoun Courtesy Order	213
Reflexive and Intensive Pronouns	213
Pronoun Shift	215
Shifts in Person	216
Shifts in Number	216
From the Written Word:	
Recognizing the Differences	219

CHAPTER 9

"New Heights"	221
Writing: College Application Essay	222
Usage: Pronoun Reference	225
Clear Reference	226
Reference to a Noun, Not an Implied Noun	229
Reference to a Noun That Is Not a Modifier	229
Definite Reference of Personal Pronouns	232
Indefinite *They*	232
Indefinite *It*	232
Indefinite *You*	232
Reference to a Noun, Not a Broad Idea	233
Think About It:	
Truth and Validity	237

CHAPTER 10

Sonnet 34	239
Writing: Sonnet	240
Usage: Adjective and Adverb Use	243
Showing Comparison with Modifiers	243
Regular Comparison of Adjectives and Adverbs	244
Absolute Comparative and Superlative of Adjectives	244
Irregular Comparison of Adjectives and Adverbs	244
Problems with Modifiers	247
Modifiers That Cannot Be Compared	247
Double Comparisons	247
Double Negatives	247
Placement of Modifiers	250
Misplaced Modifiers	250
Two-Way Modifiers	251
Modifiers That Split Infinitives	251
Dangling Modifiers	252

From the Written Word:
Analyzing the Cause 257

CHAPTER 11

"Piltdown Chicken" 259
Writing: Research Report 262
Usage: Capitalization 270
   Personal Names, Religions, Nationalities, and
      Proper Adjectives 270
   Place Names, Transportation, and Astronomy Terms 274
   Businesses and Organizations, Cultural and Historical
      Terms 277
   Titles 282
   First Words and Single Letters 285
Think About It:
Examine the Evidence! 289

CHAPTER 12

"Bringing Some Sanity to Airport Security" 291
Writing: Issue Analysis Essay 292
Usage: Punctuation 296
   Exclamation Point 296
   Question Mark 296
   Period 296
      In Sentences 296
      For Initials and Abbreviations 297
      In Outlines and Lists 297
      For Decimals 298
   Comma 301
      In a Series 301
      After Introductory Elements 304
      To Set Off Elements 307
      In Letters and with Quotations, Dates, and
         Addresses 310
      To Signal Special Constructions 311
      Incorrect Commas 311
   Semicolon 315
      Between Two Independent Clauses 315
      Before a Conjunction in a Long Compound
         Sentence 315
      Between Word Groups Containing Commas 315
   Colon 315
      In Bible References and Expressions of Time 316
      After a Salutation of a Business Letter 316
      Between a Book Title and Subtitle 316
      Before a Series at the End of a Sentence 316
      Before a Long or Formal Direct Quotation 316
      Between Two Independent Clauses 316
From the Written Word:
Developing a Plan 321

CHAPTER 13

"Infected Minds" ... 323
Writing: Response to Dramatic Scene ... 324
Usage: More Punctuation ... 329
- Quotation Marks ... 329
  - Direct Quotations ... 329
  - Dialogue ... 330
  - Titles of Short Works ... 330
  - Words Used in a Special Sense ... 331
  - Quotation Marks and Other Punctuation ... 331
  - Single Quotation Marks ... 332
- Ellipses ... 335
  - Omission of Words in a Quotation ... 335
  - Halting or Unfinished Speech ... 335
- Brackets ... 335
  - Insertion or Replacement in a Quotation ... 336
  - Replacing Parentheses Inside Other Parentheses ... 336
  - Error in Original ... 336
- Underlining for Italics ... 336
  - Titles of Long Works ... 337
  - Works of Art ... 337
  - Large Vehicles ... 337
  - Words, Letters, and Numerals Being Discussed ... 337
  - Foreign Words and Phrases ... 337
  - Special Emphasis ... 338
- Apostrophe ... 341
  - Omission ... 341
  - Possession ... 341
  - Special Plurals ... 342
- Hyphen ... 342
  - Omission of Connecting Words ... 342
  - Word Division at the End of a Line ... 342
  - Compound Constructions ... 343
  - Words with a Common Element ... 343
- Dash ... 347
  - Certain Sentence Elements ... 347
  - Emphasis ... 347
  - Interrupted Speech ... 347
- Parentheses ... 348
  - Supplementary Elements ... 348
  - Placement of Other Punctuation with Parentheses ... 348
  - Numbers or Letters That Identify Divisions ... 348
  - Comparison of Parentheses with Pairs of Commas and Dashes ... 348

Think About It:
Problem Solving ... 353

CHAPTER 14

Composition: Writing Strategies — 355

Sentence Variety and Emphasis — 355
- Achieving Emphasis — 355
- Varying Sentence Length and Complexity — 358
- Varying Sentence Patterns — 359
- Varying Sentence Beginnings — 359
- Choosing Between Constructions — 361
- Using Coordination and Subordination — 363

Sentence Energy — 366
- Action Verbs — 366
- Details — 367
- Accuracy — 367
- Pauses for Breath — 368
- Figurative Language — 368

Sentence Expansion and Reduction — 371
- Expansion of Sentences — 371
- Reduction of Sentences — 373

Parallelism — 379
- Using Parallelism Only for Parallel Ideas — 380
- Using the Same Part of Speech — 380
- Using the Same Type of Structure — 380
- Clarifying Parallelism — 381

Sentence Logic — 383
- Saying Things Directly — 383
- Saying What You Mean — 384
- Saying Things Consistently — 384
- Making Clear and Logical Comparisons — 384
- Using Noun Clauses When Needed — 386
- Placing Words in the Sentence — 387

Biased Language — 390

History of the English Language: Continual Small Changes — 393

CHAPTER 15

Reference: Library Skills — 395

The Arrangement of Library Materials — 395
- Fiction — 396
- Nonfiction — 396

Search Tools and Strategies — 399
- Library Website — 399
- Library Stacks — 399
- Library Catalog — 399
- Specialized Indexes — 400

Reference Works — 403
- Almanacs and Yearbooks — 403
- Atlases and Gazetteers — 403
- Bible Commentaries and Concordances — 404
- Biographical Sources — 404
- Dictionaries — 404

Encyclopedias	404
Literary Sources	405
Thesauruses	405
History of the English Language:	
Great Vowel Shift	407

CHAPTER 16

Reference: Study Skills — 409

Developing Good Study Skills	409
Using the Parts of a Book	410
Improving Reading Comprehension	413
Context Clues	413
Word Parts	415
Using Memory Techniques	417
Taking Tests	417
Classroom Tests	417
Essay Tests	419
Standardized Tests	420
History of the English Language:	
Rules for Modern English	425

APPENDIX: SPELLING

Spelling Hints	426
Spelling Singular Present-Tense Verbs and Plural Nouns	427
General Principles	427
Plurals of Proper Nouns	428
Plurals of Compounds	428
Spelling with *ie* and *ei*	429
Adding Suffixes	429
Doubling a Final Consonant	429
Changing the Final *y* to *i*	430
Dropping the Final Silent *e*	430

CHAPTER REVIEWS

Chapter 2 Review	431
Chapter 3 Review	433
Chapter 4 Review	435
Chapter 5 Review	437
Chapter 6 Review	439
Chapter 7 Review	443
Chapter 8 Review	445
Chapter 9 Review	449
Chapter 10 Review	453
Chapter 11 Review	457
Chapter 12 Review	459
Chapter 13 Review	463

INDEX — 465

ACKNOWLEDGMENTS

A careful effort has been made to trace the ownership of selections included in this textbook in order to secure permission to reprint copyrighted material and to make full acknowledgment of their use. If any error or omission has occurred, it is unintentional and will be corrected in subsequent editions, provided written notification is made to the publisher.

CHAPTER 3
U.S. Capitol Historical Society: "Grant and Lee: A Study in Contrasts" by Bruce Catton. Copyright © U.S. Capitol Historical Society. Used by permission.

CHAPTER 4
Jamie Langston Turner: Excerpt from *By the Light of a Thousand Stars* by Jamie Langston Turner. Copyright © 1999 Jamie Langston Turner. Bethany House Publishers, a division of Baker Publishing Group. Used by permission of the author.

CHAPTER 5
McGraw-Hill Companies, Inc.: "Signs of the Times: Littering the Verbal Landscape" by Charlotte K. Frank. Copyright © 2002 Charlotte K. Frank. As first appeared in *Education Week*, September 4, 2002. Used by permission. © McGraw-Hill Companies, Inc.

CHAPTER 6
Bob Jones University Museum & Gallery: Excerpt from *This Same Jesus* by David Burke. Copyright © 2002 Bob Jones University Museum & Gallery. Used by permission.

CHAPTER 11
***FrontLine* Magazine:** "Piltdown Chicken" by Stephen Caesar. Copyright © 2002 *FrontLine* Magazine. Used by permission from FrontLine magazine.

CHAPTER 12
Peter Shawn Taylor: "Bringing Some Sanity to Airport Security" by Peter Shawn Taylor from *Maclean's* Magazine, May 7, 2012. Used by permission of the author.

PHOTOGRAPH CREDITS

Cover
©iStockphoto.com/Sara Winter

Front Matter
i ©iStockphoto.com/Sara Winter; **xiv** (both) PhotoDisc/Getty Images

xvi, 2, 3, 10, 13, 14, 15, 16, 28, 40, 41, 42, 44, 46, 47, 48, 51, 53, 54, 56, 63, 64, 65, 69, 72, 74, 75, 76, 77, 79, 81, 82, 83, 86, 92, 94, 95, 96, 100, 102, 106, 113, 114, 115, 116, 118, 122, 132, 133, 136 (both), **137, 140, 151, 153, 161, 166, 167, 175, 193, 206, 207, 208, 210, 222, 228, 232, 233, 237** (both), **238, 239, 240, 241, 243, 251, 265, 267, 268, 274, 276, 279, 280, 282, 293, 299, 302, 303, 304, 317, 323, 331, 333, 335, 346, 348, 350, 355, 361, 368, 376, 379, 387, 395, 396, 404, 406, 408, 421, 422** ©2003 Hemera Technologies, Inc. All Rights Reserved; **1, 189, 367** Getty Images/Ron Chapple Studios RF/Thinkstock; **4, 35, 49, 101, 108, 173, 178, 187, 195, 227, 229** (b), **256, 269, 290, 294, 300, 306, 377, 383, 394** Getty Images/iStockphoto/Thinkstock; **7, 59** (t), **98, 329, 401, 411** Brenda Hansen; **8, 34, 36, 38, 39, 43, 52, 55, 59** (b), **70, 71, 78, 89, 104, 105, 107** (b), **107** (t), **109, 112, 125, 142, 145, 147, 154, 158, 171, 179, 180, 197, 202, 212, 214, 217, 218, 219, 252, 257, 259, 286, 287, 295, 301, 305, 307, 308, 309, 312** (all), **313, 320, 321, 325, 330, 334, 337, 340, 342, 343, 349, 354, 362, 363, 364, 369, 375, 378, 380, 386, 398, 409, 415, 416, 417, 418, 420, 424** PhotoDisc/Getty Images; **12, 20** www.arttoday.com; **19** ©Yuri Arcurs-Fotolia.com; **22** ©iStockphoto.com/Rich Legg; **25, 26, 61, 129, 157, 198, 221, 322, 356, 393, 407** (t), **425** (b) Unusual Films; **29** Digital Vision; **31** ©iStockphoto.com/Claudia Dewald; **33** Getty Images/Hemera/Thinkstock; **50** ©iStockphoto.com/dirkr; **57, 68** NOAA; **58** Unusual Films/From the Isabella Stuart Gardener Museum, Boston; **60, 67** National Park Service; **73** ©iStockphoto.com/VikramRaghuvanshi; **80** (t) Unusual Films/From the Bob Jones University Collection; **80** (b), **91, 130, 139, 141, 152, 156, 163, 169, 182, 186, 196** (both), **225, 231, 235, 242, 246, 262, 275, 283, 289, 297, 310, 339, 344, 345, 352, 353, 358, 371, 384, 405, 407** (b) ©2003-www.arttoday.com; **85** ©iStockphoto.com/Catherine Yeulet; **90** Hemera Technologies/Ablestock.com/Thinkstock; **99** Carl Abrams; **110** White House/Tina Hager; **117** www.sporting-heroes.net; **119** (both) National Archives; **138** BJU Press Files; **143** Getty Images/Photodisc/Buccina Studios/Thinkstock; **146, 162, 165, 254, 403** BJU Photo Services; **155** (t) Unusual Films/From the Metropolitan Museum of Art, New York; **155** (b) ©iStockphoto.com/Suprijono Suharjoto; **172** ©iStockphoto.com/kristian sekulic; **174** Getty Images/Brand X/Thinkstock; **177** ©iStockphoto.com/Roberto A Sanchez; **181** Western Union; **192** Getty Images/Photodisc/Thinkstock; **201** ©iStockphoto.com/Wittelsbach bernd; **205** Greg Moss; **213, 229** (t) Getty Images/Digital Vision/Thinkstock; **220** COREL Corporation; **264** ©iStockphoto.com/antony spencer; **271** National Anthropological Archives, Smithsonian Institution 07194100; **273** Richard Lancelyn Green; **284, 390** NASA; **291** Getty Images/Creatas RF/Thinkstock; **311** ©iStockphoto.com/YinYang; **315** ©iStockphoto.com/Nikola Milijkovic; **316** Photo Courtesy of Natasha Vins; **327** Joyce Landis; **328** Corbis; **341** Getty Images/Zoonar RF/Thinkstock; **360** Marian Anderson Collection, Rare Book and Manuscript Library, University of Pennsylvania; **366** ©iStockphoto.com/vichie81; **370** U.S. Navy Photo/Jason Jacobowitz; **372** Ed Richards; **391** Imfolds/Bigstock.com; **397** White House Photo/David Johnson; **399** Bryan Smith; **423** ©iStockphoto.com/EdStock2; **425** (t) ©iStockphoto.com/asiseeit

TO THE STUDENT

Do you ever wonder why you need to study writing and grammar? People study language for varying reasons—to make good grades, to secure a better-paying job, to impress people, or even for fun! But Christians have an even greater reason to study language.

Christians should study any subject seriously because of who God is. As Creator, He made humans in His image, gave us many gifts, and told us to exercise dominion over the earth (Gen. 1:27–28). Language, one such gift, can help accomplish this goal (Gen. 2:19–20).

Serious language study also makes us better communicators, which helps us obey God's most important commands to "love the Lord thy God with all thy heart, and with all thy soul, and with all thy mind, and with all thy strength" and "love thy neighbor as thyself" (Mark 12:30–31).

One of the most exciting benefits of developing language skills is that God can use our words to further His plan of redeeming the world to Himself (John 1:1–18; Rom. 10:14–17). He used language to generate the universe (Gen. 1:3) and called Christ "the Word" (John 1:1, 14) to reveal Christ's deity and ownership of the same transformative power. Articulate and kind speech can open hearts to Christ's beauty and love; fictional works that handle life's conflicts biblically can draw people to God's ways; and even blogging on cultural issues from a biblical worldview can declare God's truth.

WRITING AND GRAMMAR 12, Third Edition, offers you opportunities to polish your language skills. To familiarize yourself with its features, see the box below.

Combine the Skills icons in the margin direct you to pages in the text with more information on a topic. Each icon highlights the category of materials that icon references.

- A **grammar** icon refers you to material from Chapters 2 through 5.

- A **usage** icon sends you to material in Chapters 6 through 13 discussing correct usage or mechanics.

- A **writing** icon indicates material reflecting an important writing concept discussed in Chapter 1 or 14 or in one of the book's writing activities.

- A **reference** icon refers you to the library skills and study skills in Chapters 15 and 16 or to the special information at the end of a chapter.

ESL notes explain in detail concepts that can be difficult for students from another language background (ESL stands for English as a Second Language). Many native English speakers may also benefit from these helpful explanations.

Tips offer advice about using the grammar and usage concepts you are studying to improve your writing.

Your grammar and writing studies this year can help you appreciate the beauty and complexity of language and improve your communication. Both of these results can allow you to better know the Creator and share the good news of His loving, redemptive work.

RESEARCH REPORT Writing
CAPITALIZATION Usage
11

Learning about something that interests you can be both enjoyable and educational. After reading about an unfamiliar topic in an article or coming across a new idea in a novel, have you ever taken the next step and looked up information on that topic or idea? If you have, you took a step into the research process. You probably found your "research" to be enjoyable and rewarding. Researching various sources, gathering information, and formulating this information into an outline and report can be an exciting and rewarding experience.

In "Piltdown Chicken," scientist Stephen Caesar refutes the supposed evidence of a "link" between dinosaurs and birds. After a brief introduction regarding the finding, he moves to his main idea: "The fossil was a fraud." Notice that Caesar focuses on his main idea and incorporates a number of varied sources into his writing.

Piltdown Chicken *by Stephen Caesar*

In November 1999, *National Geographic* published photographs of what it claimed was incontrovertible proof that birds evolved from dinosaurs. In an article titled "Feathers for T. Rex?" the magazine announced, "New Birdlike Fossils Are Missing Links in Dinosaur Evolution" (Sloan 99). The article featured a photograph, taken under ultraviolet light, of a creature "[w]ith arms of a primitive bird and the tail of a dinosaur" (Ibid. 100). The fossil, named *Archaeoraptor*, was discovered in Liaoning Province, China, and was trumpeted as "a true missing link in the complex chain that connects dinosaurs to birds" (Ibid.). The photo was accompanied by a quotation in large letters by Stephen Czerkas, who led the study of the fossil: "IT'S A MISSING LINK between terrestrial dinosaurs and birds that could actually fly" (Ibid. [emphasis original]). Czerkas also commented, "This fossil is perhaps the best evidence since *Archaeopteryx* that birds did, in fact, evolve from certain types of carnivorous dinosaurs" (Ibid. 101).

Eventually, the word got out—like so many other "proofs" of Darwinism, the fossil was a fraud. In the "Letters to the Editor" section of the March 2000 issue of *National Geographic*, Xu Xing of the Institute of Vertebrate Paleontology and Paleoanthropology (Chinese Academy of Sciences) wrote: "I have concluded that *Archaeoraptor* is a composite. . . . Though I do not want to believe it,

> A sample from a professional or student composition begins each chapter, orienting you to the type of writing covered in the chapter and providing you with a model.

> Labeled examples help to illustrate certain grammar principles.

Who and Whom

The pronouns *who* and *whom* follow the same principles as personal pronouns do. The subjective case pronouns *who* and *whoever* function as subjects or predicate nouns. Use the objective case pronouns *whom* and *whomever* as objects. When the pronoun appears in a dependent clause, the case of the pronoun is determined by its function within the clause, not by the function of the dependent clause.

S LV PN
Who is the new president of the youth group?

S LV PN DO S TrV
He is the one *whom* we met at camp last week.

S InV (OP) S TrV DO
Sam voted for *whoever* would do the best job.

(OP) S TrV DO
For *whom* did you cast your vote?

S TrV DO DO S TrV
My friends will support *whomever* the youth group elected.

In sentences with parenthetical expressions such as *do you think*, *I believe*, or *did they say*, ignore the parenthetical expression when you determine the function and case of *who/whom*.

DO S LV TrV
Whom do you think he will choose as his assistant? (He will choose *whom*?)

S LV PN S LV PN
He is the one *who* I believe is the better choice (*who* is the better choice).

S LV PA
Who did they say is most capable to lead the group? (*Who* is most capable?)

As you may have noticed, in colloquial English (informal conversation) there is a strong tendency to use *who* at the beginning of all questions, regardless of its function. In written and formal use, however, you should follow the rules stated here in the text.

INFORMAL | Who did you meet?
FORMAL | Whom did you meet?

Pronouns pp. 37–38

Clauses pp. 126–28

ESL

> In Summary sections provide an immediate review of new material.

in SUMMARY

Use a possessive case pronoun as the **"subject"** of a gerund. Use an objective case pronoun as the **object of a gerund**.

A pronoun that follows a linking verb infinitive must be in the same case as the earlier word that it is renaming.

Use *who* and *whoever* for subjects and predicate nouns.

Use *whom* and *whomever* for direct objects, indirect objects, and objects of prepositions.

When *who* or *whom* appears in a dependent clause, the case of the pronoun is determined by its function within the clause, not by the function of the dependent clause.

Ignore parenthetical expressions when you determine the function and case of *who* and *whom*.

Pronoun Use | Chapter 8 **211**

Exercises provide you with the opportunity to practice and review the grammar skills you are acquiring.

PRACTICE the skill

8.5 Underline the correct pronoun from the choices in parentheses.

1. A teen (*who, whom*) attends a Christian camp often makes life-changing decisions.
2. Parents may pray for the teen, (*who, whom*) they hope will serve the Lord.
3. (*Him, His*) being set apart from the distractions of home, school, and friends helps him to focus on spiritual issues.
4. Spiritual messages challenge (*whoever, whomever*) the Holy Spirit convicts.
5. Giving (*they, them*) a chance to focus on Christ is the purpose of setting aside time for campers to read the Bible and pray.
6. As a result of Christ-honoring preaching, many teens purpose to serve (*He, Him*).
7. God directs (*whoever, whomever*) is willing to be a missionary, a preacher, a teacher, or a Christian lay worker.
8. (*They, Their*) serving God requires eliminating habits that would hamper their testimonies.
9. Many teens are helped by those to (*who, whom*) they go for counsel and prayer.
10. After a teen's week at a Christian camp, (*him, his*) following through on a decision to yield his life to Christ is most important.

REVIEW the skill

8.6 Underline each pronoun that represents a case error in "subjects" or objects of verbals or in *who* and *whom*. Write the correction in the blank. If the sentence is already correct, write *C* in the blank.

_____ 1. Recreational vehicles vary in purpose and design in order to meet the needs of whomever wants one of them.

_____ 2. After talking with some families, a salesperson often expects they to choose a conversion van.

_____ 3. Us considering a camper is a big step for our family.

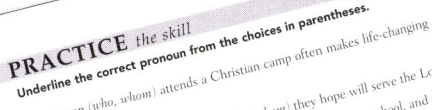

FROM THE WRITTEN WORD

Analyzing the Cause

Perhaps you have discussed with a friend why a particular college basketball team did not make the NCAA Final Four, or perhaps you have debated whether the three-point shot line for basketball should be moved. Or maybe you have discussed why the girls' soccer team lost in overtime last week. As you talk about these ideas, you are commenting on the causes for these particular results. Analyzing a subject to identify its causes or effects is another rhetorical strategy.

The Scriptures abound with this rhetorical strategy. Why did God send the Flood? The cause is evident: man was wicked.

> And God saw that the wickedness of man was great in the earth, and that every imagination of the thoughts of his heart was only evil continually. And the Lord said, I will destroy man whom I have created from the face of the earth;... for it repenteth me that I have made them. (Gen. 6:5, 7)

You might think about what caused Job's testing or Israel's captivity or Ruth's allegiance to her mother-in-law.

Consider Numbers 20:2–12. Moses, the leader of Israel, heard perhaps the most disappointing declaration of his lifetime. Although Moses had led Israel through many hardships and trials, Moses was not to bring the Israelites into the land of promise. The evident cause was Moses' disobedience. But what other causes do you read about in this passage? The people had complained to Moses and Aaron because there was no water. They had even questioned why Moses had brought them to such a place. Perhaps their harsh complaints caused Moses to doubt God's leading. Standing before this multitude, Moses may have lost his temper, or he might have thought that speaking would not be enough to cause water to come from the rock. Moses' failure to recognize God's power and presence must also have contributed to his disobedience.

Personal Response

Read Judges 8:1–4. As Gideon and his three hundred were returning from battle with the Midianites, the men of Ephraim complained to Gideon. Gideon may have had cause to answer the men of Ephraim with harsh words. Do you think that he did have a cause to? What was the effect of his answer and his manner in answering them?

Now read Proverbs 15:1–2. From your personal experience, write a paragraph that illustrates cause and effect in either a positive or a negative way.

---

8. What is the elevation of Great Salt Lake in Utah?

_____

9. In what year did Queen Victoria of England marry Prince Albert, and how many children did they have?

_____

10. What novel contains a character named Peggotty?

_____

HISTORY OF THE ENGLISH LANGUAGE

Great Vowel Shift

The American English that you speak today developed from Early Modern English, the language of Queen Elizabeth I, of William Shakespeare, and of the King James Version of the Bible. Late in the Middle English period (in the 1400s), a phenomenon known as the Great Vowel Shift (GVS) began to alter greatly the vowel system of English. Because the GVS was a gradual, multistep process, scholars vary on the exact dates of the shift, but most agree that the changes occurred mainly in the fifteenth and sixteenth centuries.

This "shift" in vowels refers to the area of the mouth where English vowels are articulated. Today when you say the vowel sound of the word *feet* (the so-called long /ē/ sound), your tongue is high and forward in your mouth. Now say *foam* (long /ō/ sound); your tongue lowers and moves ("shifts") to the back of your mouth. In Old and Middle English, however, the sounds indicated by the same spellings were somewhat different. For example, the word *feet* probably sounded much more like the long /ā/ of today's *fate*. Therefore, the GVS refers to changes in the long vowels of English. It affected only the vowels that were literally long (held out longer). In the GVS most long vowels were raised in the mouth, one was also fronted, and some became diphthongs. We still call these our "long vowels," even though the term does not apply literally today.

We can thank the GVS for many of the complexities of and exceptions to our English spelling and pronunciation. Have you ever wondered why words spelled with *ea* can be pronounced with a long /ē/ (*glean, leaf, speak*) or a long /ā/ (*break, great, steak*)? Blame the Great Vowel Shift!

Enrichment sections highlight critical-thinking skills, rhetorical strategies used in Scripture, and the changing nature of the English language.

The Writing Process | 1
History of the English Language | 26

THE WRITING PROCESS Composition 1

You have not come this far in your academic career without learning at least a little about writing. Essays, reports, and letters are all examples of the types of writing you have most likely already worked on. For some students writing seems to come naturally, as if the words flow from somewhere inside and pour out onto the page (or screen). For others, writing is arduous and therefore something that they dread. Whether writing comes easily or as the result of much labor, the process itself is similar for everyone. It follows a natural progression from the idea to the finished work.

As you have no doubt noticed, the writing process is not strictly linear. In other words, very rarely does a writer complete his research (*planning*), proceed to writing his thoughts (*drafting*), look over what he has written (*revising*), and then submit his work (*publishing*). Rather, the writer does a little research, jots some thoughts down, remembers something he forgot to look up, writes a little more, rereads the first part and crosses most of it out, writes again, reads again, and so on until he arrives at a finished product.

This text will give instruction in the four stages of the writing process (*planning, drafting, revising, publishing*) just described. For each writing project you tackle, you will move through the four steps. Varying amounts of time will be spent on each step, depending on the assignment. That is, some assignments will require extensive planning; some will require very little. Some may be revised repeatedly; others may require only minimal revision. In any case, you, the writer, will follow the four-stage writing process until it becomes second nature, until you are comfortable when you encounter the words "Today's test will be entirely essay."

Thinking Biblically

The *New York Times* website is one of the most visited in the world, let alone the United States. Statistics also reveal that its readers tend to have college and graduate degrees. And what do these accomplished people like to read? The opinion pages are consistently found among the top ten most shared articles on the site. Read a little about the current roster of opinion writers. Check out the opinion pages and see what they say. These are people who can write—but what kinds of ideas are they spreading? Write a comment on one of the articles and share the results with your class. Unless Christians can write and write well, false ideas on the prominent opinion pages of the world will go unchallenged. Writing is an extremely important tool. It is the most prominent tool God Himself chose to communicate truth.

Planning

For most of the writing tasks you will tackle, the planning stage will be the most important. Work done at the outset will reward the writer later. Planning can involve everything from selecting a topic to interviewing experts in the field to deciding exactly who your audience will be. Remember that the amount of planning you do varies greatly with the task at hand. The following sections will give you plenty of strategies to choose from when planning a piece of writing.

Choosing Your Topic

Some writers know immediately what they will write about. If you are one who has difficulty deciding what course to take, some of the methods listed below may help you find inspiration.

Listing

Keep a running list of ideas and topics in a journal or on your computer. Add to the list whenever you think of a new idea that interests you and consult the list whenever you need inspiration for a writing assignment. Newspapers, magazines, and online articles may also suggest writing ideas to you. Listening to and observing those around you will add many items to your list as well.

palaces of Europe

light bulbs—technology/history

brand/branding (as in advertising)

Bible prophecy

Creationism

popcorn

hairstyles

Questioning

Ask yourself the six journalist's questions *(who? what? where? when? why? how?)* before you start writing. These questions will help you not only to include the important information about your topic but also to expand your ideas as they generate other questions.

- Who/what is in the news right now?
- What issues affect me and my future?
- Where would I like to serve as a missionary, should the Lord send me?
- When is _____ a good idea? When is this same thing a bad idea?
- Why should/shouldn't someone participate in _____?
- How should I handle _____ (person, situation, conflict)?

Going forward or backward in time from the event or item being considered can be another helpful questioning technique. For example, an essay on hairstyles might examine the powdered wigs and intricately woven hairpieces of the past or predict the hairstyles of the future, given trends and the cyclical nature of fashion.

Brainstorming

Brainstorming techniques are used by businesses and organizations when they attempt to create slogans or revamp strategies. Writers use brainstorming to generate ideas for writing. Working alone or in a group, a writer records everything he can think of about a topic. For a Christian, the ideas generated during a brainstorming session should meet the criteria set down in Philippians 4:8. Within those biblical guidelines, a writer should consider no idea unworkable or inane.

> **tip**
> Finally, brethren, whatsoever things are true, whatsoever things are honest, whatsoever things are just, whatsoever things are pure, whatsoever things are lovely, whatsoever things are of good report; if there be any virtue, and if there be any praise, think on these things. (Phil. 4:8)

One brainstorming session produced the following ideas about light bulbs.
- frosted light bulbs
- filaments
- types of bulbs
- Edison
- flashbulbs
- history of streetlights, stoplights, flashlights, refrigerator lights, headlights
- lamps—from gas to electric
- dependence upon
- power outages
- cost of electricity
- ultra long-lasting bulbs
- wattage

Eliminate items from the list that are too far afield (like *Edison* or *cost of electricity*) or re-brainstorm about one of the items (*types of bulbs—incandescent, halogen, fluorescent, black light, infrared*).

Freewriting

Writing on a topic without concern for precise wording, punctuation, or other grammatical issues is called **freewriting.** This technique will enable you to explore aspects of a subject that you have never considered before. To engage in freewriting, set a time limit of four to five minutes and begin writing. Challenge yourself to write without stopping for the time you have. Below is an example of one person's freewriting attempt.

> I have always wanted to learn to scuba dive. I enjoy hearing about the sea adventures of Jacques Cousteau. To me it would be fascinating to see the beautifully colored fish and the intriguing coral formations. A person has to wear a wetsuit, to learn to use oxygen tanks and to function in deep water. Oxygen tanks must be heavy to hold on your back. One danger is going too deep and surfacing too quickly. I have heard that people get the "bends" when this happens. What exactly is the bends? I wonder where there is a good place to learn to scuba dive. Then I wonder where a person would go to dive. The lakes around here are not very clear and I doubt that you would see very many pretty colored fish. I suspect that a person would have to go to the ocean to be able to see the beautiful fish and coral. I wonder how expensive scuba equipment and training is? Then I wonder how much it would cost to go scuba diving at the Great Barrier Reef or in the Cayman Islands.

Freewriting can be an effective way to develop fluency—a free flow—in writing English. Your goal should be to write out your thoughts without worrying about grammar or word choice. You can edit your writing later, after you have recorded on paper what you want to say about your topic.

Interviewing

For firsthand knowledge about a subject, conduct an **interview** of someone who is an expert in your field of interest. Contact your interview subject and state the purpose of your interview and propose a time to meet. Before meeting your subject, find out as much as possible about him so that you will be able to express interest in him and so that you will not waste time asking questions concerning matters of common knowledge.

Come up with a list of questions that require extended answers (e.g., *How were your findings different each time you conducted the experiment?* is a better question than *How many times did you conduct the experiment?*). Be prepared to use spontaneous follow-up questions in response to the answers given. Consider the following faulty interview:

INTERVIEWER	You conduct fitness seminars in the summer. Tell me about them.
SUBJECT	Over 100,000 people have come to our one- and two-week summer fitness camps.
INTERVIEWER	Why do you prefer ultradistance events to others?

This interviewer should have followed up his first question with another about where the camps are held, what happens at the camps, how campers are challenged, and so on. Instead, the interviewer plowed ahead to the next question on the list and missed an opportunity for more (and better) information.

Narrowing Your Topic

Often you will need to narrow an idea to make it adhere to the length requirements of an assignment or to make it more manageable. As you consider your topic, ask yourself these questions: *What is the length requirement of my paper? Is the topic that I have chosen too broad to be covered adequately in the assigned length?* If you answered yes to the second question, force yourself to focus on one aspect of the topic.

TOPIC TOO BROAD	Light Bulbs: Then and Now
TOPIC TOO LIMITED	Uses for Old Light Bulbs
APPROPRIATE TOPIC FOR BRIEF PAPER	Advances in Light-Emitting Diode (LED) Technology

Use the ideas generated by listing, questioning, brainstorming, freewriting, and interviewing as you seek to narrow your topic. Sometimes an idea you rejected at first will work well after all.

Considering Your Audience

Before you begin writing, you will need to know more about those to whom you are writing. Are they well educated? Are they adults/children/teens? Are they already familiar with your topic, or are they totally unacquainted with it? A well-educated electrical engineer would not need an explanation of what LED technology is. By the same token, most young children would be unprepared and perhaps unable to read anything more than a very simple explanation of LEDs. In academic writing, you will often be assigned an audience; however, your real-world writing (application essays, school newspaper articles, yearbook copy, letters, e-mails) will require that you choose for whom you write and publish.

Determining Your Purpose

After considering your audience, you will need to determine a purpose for writing. The standard purposes are *to analyze, to describe, to entertain, to inform,* and *to persuade*. Although a single piece of writing may have several purposes within it, the paper's main purpose should be a single one. For example, one student wrote *to inform* his audience of advances in LED technology. As a means of informing the audience of the many uses of LED, the writer told a brief anecdote meant *to entertain*. Another student in the class wrote an article *to persuade* companies to switch to LED lighting as a cost-cutting measure. In order to do this, the writer needed *to analyze* data about traditional fluorescent and incandescent lighting costs versus LED costs. Your answer to the question *What is my purpose?* will narrow your field of inquiry as you begin gathering information and later serve as the basis for your thesis statement. (See page 10.)

tip — Force yourself to state your purpose in a single declarative sentence. Then ask the question *What information will best help me accomplish that purpose?*

Gathering Information

In this stage of the process, you will build upon your writing purpose to gather further information about your topic. Writers typically use one of three sources: (1) themselves—by writing about something they already know; (2) others—by interviewing people knowledgeable about their topic; (3) reference materials—by researching books, magazines, newspapers, almanacs, the Internet, and other sources.

Search Tools
pp. 399–401

Internet Precaution

Remember that a source is only as reliable as its author; therefore, a good researcher investigates the credentials of any author whose information he chooses to include. Before you use information from a website, investigate the website as thoroughly as possible. Look for information at the top, bottom, or sides of the screen or in a section titled "About This Site" or "Mission Statement." If the site provides a site map or a table of contents, explore it for further information. Try to answer the following questions about each website you visit:

- Who runs the site? Is it a respected academic institution? A government agency? A well-known business? A qualified individual? An interested but possibly uninformed amateur?
- Who wrote the content on the website? What are the author's qualifications? Is he an expert? Does he have experience in this field?
- Are both the sponsoring organization and the author unbiased and trustworthy? Or do they have a financial interest in the subject the website discusses?
- Where did the author get his information? Are his sources reliable?
- Is the information current? Or does the author include outdated information that no longer applies or has since been proved untrue?
- Is the information presented clearly and understandably?
- Do other experts value this website? Does it include links to other respected organizations? Does it display an icon indicating approval from a respected expert or organization?

Thinking Biblically

Overwhelming amounts of information flood us each day. As a result, we need information filters to help us sort the wheat from the chaff and tell us which news is fit to print and which is not worth knowing. We use news sites and search engines for this purpose. But a biblically wise Internet user will understand that every information filter has a bias. A search engine's bias is popularity: sites rise to the top if a lot of people link to them. What does this say about the validity of the information found through a search engine? Does popular equal true? Biblical discernment in an information age requires the ability to evaluate not just information but even the services that filter it for us.

Before you begin your research, list questions that you hope to answer about your topic. These questions should both relate to your purpose and address the needs of your audience. The following questions are one student's list about hair ironing, a topic narrowed from hairstyles under "Listing" above. The student wants to inform his audience, which consists primarily of teenagers in America, about the phenomenon of hair ironing, a process by which a person with curly hair would attempt to straighten his or her hair.

- *What is hair ironing? How was it done?*
- *Were there any harmful effects from hair ironing?*
- *Why would a person iron his hair? How did this relate to his status (perceived or otherwise) in society?*
- *During what period was hair ironing popular?*
- *In what places was hair ironing most popular?*
- *Was hair ironing done only among certain groups or classes of people?*
- *How long did the effects of the ironing last?*
- *Did one need any special equipment for hair ironing?*

1.1 PRACTICE *the skill*

Read the following paragraph and answer the questions at the end.

I've never enjoyed eating liver, for I find it difficult to ingest something an animal uses during its digestive process. As I was growing up, my mom served liver on a bimonthly basis. We were always required to eat at least five silver-dollar-sized pieces of liver, and we received extra pieces if we complained about the chunks of liver already on our plates. I believe I never would have survived the ordeal if my mom had not also served mashed potatoes. Five pieces of liver required two large heaps of mashed potatoes; I was always really full at the end of this meal. As we willed down our five pieces, my mom always reviewed the benefits of liver: first, that it was packed full of nutrition and second, that it would put hair on our chests (not a desirable thing for a third-grade girl). Because my mother always told us how good liver is for us, I wonder now why we no longer eat it. Surely if it was good for me when I was in elementary school, it is still beneficial to my health now that I am in high school! I have come to believe that the real reason we ate liver was not because of its nutrition or because of its hair-growing abilities but because eating it instilled character in us—character to endure those things we find unpleasant. It seems to me that my mom could have just made us chop wood.

1. Who is the audience for this paragraph? _____

2. What is the purpose of this paragraph? _____

3. What kind of person probably wrote this paragraph? _____

Outlining the Paper

Often the nature of your writing will necessitate an outline. An outline is simply an organizational plan for your writing. Research reports or essays, issue analyses, and in-class essays require the structure that an outline provides. Perhaps most important, an outline forces the writer to organize his thoughts into a logical sequence, eliminate unnecessary points, and identify any omissions before he begins drafting.

Sometimes it will be useful for you to write a tentative outline—for brief, informal pieces of writing. A **tentative outline** is one in which the writer does not use numerals or letters and is unconcerned about parallelism of points or making sure that the points are fully developed. Tentative outlines are helpful when jotting down ideas and organization strategies for an in-class essay or a letter. However, if your outline will be published as part of your paper or will be turned in as a separate assignment, you should follow proper outline form. Two forms of outline are considered acceptable: the topic outline and the sentence outline. Although either is correct, you should use the form that your teacher or publication guidelines specify.

A **topic outline** uses only words or phrases—no complete sentences and no verbs except verbals. Within a numbered or lettered series, each point should have the same grammatical form (e.g., participles or prepositional phrases); that is, all points should be parallel.

Periods in Outlines pp. 297–98

Parallelism pp. 379–80

Popcorn
  I. Ways to prepare popcorn
     A. Air popper
     B. Microwave
     C. Oil popper
  II. Varieties of popcorn
     A. Regular
        1. Low fat
        2. Extra butter
        3. Low sodium
     B. Caramel
     C. Cheddar cheese
  III. Uses for popcorn
     A. Popcorn balls
     B. Healthful snack
     C. Stay-awake mechanism
     D. Holiday decorations

In a **sentence outline,** every point is a complete sentence.

European Palaces
  I. Royalty built many of the European palaces.
     A. After Maria Theresa established her residence at Schönbrunn, she added many of the 1,440 rooms in existence today.
     B. Louis XIV built Versailles, the largest palace in Europe.
     C. King Ludwig II of Bavaria built many fancy and extravagant castles; his most famous is Neuschwanstein.
     D. The Duke of Buckingham built the original Buckingham House; George IV commissioned a new palace to be built around the old Buckingham House.
  II. Some original palaces were more than a monarch's official residence.
     A. The Schönbrunn location was originally a hunting estate.
     B. Versailles, originally a hunting lodge, was Louis XIV's escape from the rebellious people of Paris.
     C. Neuschwanstein was Ludwig's place to escape reality.
  III. European palaces displayed various artistic accents.
     A. Most palace areas have beautifully landscaped gardens.
     B. Many palaces have unique structural features.
        1. Schönbrunn exemplifies Baroque architecture.
        2. Versailles is famous for its Hall of Mirrors.
        3. Neuschwanstein exhibits a fancy design with multiple turrets.
     C. Many palaces display beautiful sculptures and priceless paintings.

> **tip**
> When writing an outline, remember two things: (1) use the same form consistently and (2) be sure that every *I* has a *II* (and every *A* a *B*, and so on).

1.2 PRACTICE *the skill*

Arrange the following list of topics into an outline with three main points. Group the items logically. One item will be the heading for the outline.

pollution of environment
deserts
conservation of environment
endangered wildlife
environmentalism
endangered ecosystems
preservation of environment
rainforests
trash
oceans
acid rain
chemicals

_____

_____

_____

_____

_____

_____

_____

_____

_____

_____

_____

_____

_____

Drafting

Once the planning is behind you, it is time to put your thoughts and ideas down. The first draft should never be thought of as a finished work: it is rather a work in progress, a preliminary version. The first draft should be written without overmuch concern for grammar, usage, or punctuation. (Do not forget, however, that the work you do now in these areas will save work later in the revision process.) When beginning your draft, try to sustain your writing long enough to get a sense of flow.

> **tip**
> Try writing through an entire point in your outline at one sitting.

Writing Exposition

Much of the writing that you will do, not only for the assignments in this text but also for real-life writing, will be expository writing. **Expository writing** is writing that systematically explains, analyzes, or informs about a subject. Most nonfiction is expository in nature. Narrative or **creative writing** is writing that is characterized by expressiveness, imagination, and originality. Most fiction is considered creative writing. (Of course, as with any dichotomy, exceptions abound. Some expository writing may be quite imaginative; a piece of creative writing may be very informative.) Creative writing does not follow the same set of "rules" that expository writing usually does. For example, the sonnet that you write in Chapter 10 and the interior monologue that you write in Chapter 4 will probably not follow the methods of paragraph development and organization that we will discuss in this chapter. We will focus mainly on writing exposition since you will likely use it most as you continue your education. The individual creative writing assignments in this book will discuss elements of more imaginative writing.

Mode

Mode is the term given to the form or method of writing that you choose. You will study four basic modes: descriptive, expository, narrative, and persuasive. (**Note:** Two of the terms for the modes overlap with the two types of writing described above. These are standard terms, so you should learn to differentiate between type and mode to avoid confusion.) Your stated topic and purpose will influence the mode you choose for your writing, and each has style and organizational patterns particular to it. As you complete the writing assignments in this book, you will note that every piece of writing will fit into one of these modes. For example, the comparison/contrast essay in Chapter 12 will be written in the expository mode. Chapter 4's interior monologue will be written in narrative mode. Sometimes, several modes will be used within one piece of writing, as with the college application you will write for Chapter 9. Often, writers select the mode (or have it selected for them) at the beginning of the writing process; however, some writers wait to see where their research leads them before deciding on a mode. The following chart shows the four basic modes of writing, the purpose of each mode, and an example taken from the literature pieces in this book.

Mode	Purpose	Example
Descriptive	Describes an object, person, or place	"The Encantadas" by Herman Melville
Expository	Informs about a topic; explains or analyzes a process; defines or classifies a topic	"Piltdown Chicken" by Stephan Caesar
Narrative	Relates a story or an event	Sonnet 34 by William Shakespeare
Persuasive	Persuades readers to take action or to change their position on a topic	"Signs of the Times" by Charlotte K. Frank

This writing and grammar series includes two additional modes: academic and personal. Both could be considered subcategories of the four basic modes listed above but have instead been listed separately because of their importance.

Academic	Focuses on demonstrating a specific academic skill	"A Record of Our Journeys" by Ilana Sibley
Personal	Tells an individual's own thoughts or feelings	excerpt from *By the Light of a Thousand Stars* by Jamie Langston Turner

Thesis Statements

In the planning stage you asked yourself *What is my purpose?* Your answer to that question will become the basis of the thrust of your writing. That thrust, or main idea, is called the **thesis statement.** The thesis statement is usually expressed in a single declarative sentence. As the term implies, it makes a statement rather than posing a real or rhetorical question. The thesis statement should also be verifiable. In other words, your point should be something that can be substantiated with evidence. In addition, the thesis may indicate what your approach, point of view, and organizational style will be.

In answering the question *What is my purpose?* about an essay on Creationism, one student came up with the following statement:

> My purpose is to inform people about some of the recent scientific findings that support Creationism.

The student researched her topic and interviewed several Creationist scientists doing current research in the field. She found the topic of an ice age particularly interesting. For example, she found that the effects of the Genesis flood could have caused an ice age to occur. This information led her to write the thesis statement below.

> Although it goes almost unnoticed by the media at large, evolutionists cannot adequately explain the causes of the multiple ice ages they posit.

After looking back over her research and her preliminary topic outline, the student realized that her thesis statement did not adequately communicate the approach or the emphasis of her writing. She also wondered whether her opening dependent clause might be unnecessarily inflammatory or might better fit at the end of her piece. She then revised her thesis to read as follows:

> The Genesis flood provides a probable stimulus for a single Temperate Zone ice age and thereby establishes an upper bound on its duration.

The new thesis statement tells how the Genesis flood relates to the ice age, and, further, it gives the implications of that statement.

Thinking Biblically

Even the Bible has thesis statements. Proverbs 1:7 is the thesis of the book: "The fear of the Lord is the beginning of knowledge." Likewise, Romans 1:16–18 can be called the thesis statement of Paul's letter to the church at Rome. To clearly communicate your main idea, state your thesis succinctly in a key place in your composition. Placing the thesis statement toward the beginning of your piece, as Solomon and Paul did in the two examples, can be especially helpful to the reader.

Introductions

Writers typically use introductions to accomplish several purposes: to capture reader interest, to introduce a topic, and to draw attention to the main idea, the thesis statement. The introduction may be a complete paragraph (as in a research report or a comparison/contrast essay), or the introduction may be a single sentence (as in an in-class essay). Whatever the length, introductions usually accomplish the purposes mentioned above by employing one (or more) of the following methods:

- analogy
- anecdote
- fact or statistic
- question
- quotation

Read the examples of effective introductions below.

FACT | No event could have filled me with greater anxieties than that of which the notification was transmitted by your order, and received on the fourteenth day of the present month. On the one hand, I was summoned by my Country, whose voice I can never hear but with veneration and love, from a retreat which I had chosen. . . . On the other hand, the magnitude and difficulty of the trust to which the voice of my Country called me . . . could not but overwhelm . . . one, who inheriting inferior endowments from nature and unpractised in the duties of civil administration, ought to be peculiarly conscious of his own deficiencies. (The introduction of Washington's inaugural address of 1789)

ANECDOTE | Have you seen the effects of HIV? A local islander who had been saved during his twenties was at thirty-five years of age training at a Bible college and planning to assume the pastorate of the local island church that the missionary had established. While trying to study and fulfill his work responsibilities at school, he began to feel ill. After consultation with several physicians, he was diagnosed with AIDS and died within a year. For sixteen years the virus had been dormant, but eventually HIV ravaged his body. The effects of HIV are not always immediate, but they are always devastating.

It should be noted that not all writers write their introductions first. Sometimes a writer will save his introduction for the end of his drafting process and will save an effective quotation or statistic to use in drawing the reader into his piece.

Paragraph Development

Most writing is composed of a series of **paragraphs,** groups of sentences closely related to one another and to the main idea of the piece. Provided you have well-documented research and a well-organized outline, you should be prepared to draft the body of your paper. Your outline from the planning stage should serve as the basis for your paper: Each paragraph will cover one division of your outline.

Topic Sentences

In academic writing, many of the paragraphs you write will contain topic sentences. A **topic sentence** expresses the main idea of a paragraph in a single sentence. Most often, topic sentences are found at the beginnings of paragraphs; however, they may occur anywhere in the paragraph. An opening topic sentence lays the groundwork for what will come next in the paragraph; an ending topic sentence summarizes or reinforces what was said earlier in the paragraph.

The main points of your outline will become the topic sentences of your paragraphs. Of course, you may need to rework the words and phrases (from a topic outline) into complete sentences or to recast the sentences (from a sentence outline) for appropriate transitional expressions and logic.

ESL

Good writing in your native language may follow different patterns and techniques from the ones described here. For effectiveness, observe and use those patterns and techniques when you write in that language.

When you write in English, do your best to follow the patterns and techniques of English writing. For example, English readers will expect to find your main idea (your thesis) stated at the end of your introductory paragraph. Look for these patterns as you read.

1.3 USE the skill

Write a good beginning topic sentence for the following paragraph. The sentence should express the main idea of the paragraph and indicate what will be said later about the main idea.

Dumas lived in France and wrote several historical romances based on French history. He used many characters that are familiar to us from the study of history, characters such as Louis XIV and other French monarchs. Generally, the characters in his works are somewhat larger than life—men who overcome hundreds of guards to gain their freedom and who perform other amazing and heroic feats. Although these and other characters in his stories did exist, most of the events in Dumas's stories never happened. Despite the inaccuracies of Alexandre Dumas's history, his fiction is well written and has captivated audiences from the 1800s until today. Some of his most popular works are *The Three Musketeers*, *The Man in the Iron Mask*, and *The Count of Monte Cristo*.

Supporting Sentences

As you move through your outline, write each paragraph so that it develops its topic sentence and supports the overall thesis. **Supporting sentences** develop, or support, the topic sentence. Facts and statistics, details and anecdotes—these are some of the ways writers support topic sentences and build paragraphs. Of course, certain types of writing lend themselves to certain strategies. For example, an issue analysis may be best developed using facts and statistics, whereas a personal response essay may draw on sensory details for paragraph development. The chart below shows the various kinds of developmental strategies for supporting sentences.

Developmental Strategy	Definition
Comparison/Contrast	The similarities and differences between two things
Example	An instance or an event that illustrates a point
Fact	A statement that can be proved
Incident/Anecdote	A brief personal account that illustrates a topic
Quotation	The copied words of another person, usually an expert in the field being discussed
Reasons	The explanation of a truth
Sensory Details	The use of sense words—sight, sound, smell, etc.
Statistic	A fact expressed in numbers
Visual Aid	A graphic or pictorial representation of a fact or statistic

tip
Sometimes a combination of several developmental strategies works best for crafting a particular paragraph.

Concluding Sentences

Once you have developed a paragraph with a topic sentence and supporting sentences, you are ready to write a **concluding sentence.** If the paragraph is to stand alone (or if it ends a multiparagraph essay), the concluding sentence should summarize your main idea, give a solution to a problem addressed in your paragraph, ask a question of the audience, or make a prediction about an outcome. If the paragraph is to be followed by another paragraph, the concluding sentence should tie the ideas in the paragraph together and provide a transition to the next paragraph. The purpose and the mode of writing you chose to use determine whether your conclusion will describe (descriptive), explain (expository), persuade (persuasive), or relate a story (narrative).

1.4 PRACTICE the skill

Identify the type of paragraph development the author used in the following paragraph.

An essential element in maintaining teamwork is trust. Members of a team must trust one another in order to accomplish their goals or assignments successfully. One type of team that particularly needs this element of trust is the military team. Soldiers must be able to trust those with whom they work and fight. They must especially be able to trust their commander, the person who gives them instructions and to whom they must be completely obedient. The commander of a military group makes the final call in every decision. It is he who decides when to wait and when to advance into battle. The soldiers under his command must trust him, or they may hesitate in obeying him. They must be convinced that he has the skills and knowledge to lead them in the right course. Trust is essential for the success of our military.

_____

1.5 REVIEW the skill

Identify the type of paragraph development the author used in the following paragraph.

For the businessperson who works in New York City, the resident who shops in the city, or the tourist who visits the city, the New York subway system, also called the train system, provides the most efficient means of transportation. Scattered throughout the five boroughs of the city are 468 train stations. In many cases these stations are easily accessible to the five million who commute daily on the trains. Traveling by train eliminates several problems that would be associated with driving a car: commuters avoid bumper-to-bumper traffic, a high risk of accidents on crowded streets, and increased stress levels before the workday begins. The daily commuter can purchase a Metrocard that is both cost-effective and convenient, and the commuter can travel as far as thirty-eight miles one way into the city. The system provides clean stations, well-maintained cars, and safe surroundings for those who choose to commute by train. Certainly, the subway system provides the most efficient means of transportation in and out of New York City.

_____

1.6 USE *the skill*

Write an appropriate concluding sentence for the following paragraph.

It was dark outside, and rain fell in icy torrents. Inside, the three children sat around their grandfather, the only light in the room coming from an old lantern that sat on the rough, wooden table. The children were captivated by his every word as his low voice poured out tales of pirates, treasure, and the sea. They were certain they could hear the sound of the rough wind hurling the surf against the rocks. Though it was cold and wet outside and in their imaginations, inside it was warm and dry, and one by one the children's eyes began to droop. With gentle hands, the grandfather carried them up to their beds and tucked them in.

_____

_____

Paragraph Organization

Organizing your ideas within a paragraph is much like organizing your entire paper. You must decide how best to accomplish your purpose using the information that you have gathered. Obviously, certain types of writing lend themselves best to certain organizational methods. For example, news stories most often use chronological order to depict events in the order of their occurrence. The chart below lists the five major methods of paragraph organization as well as the types of writing in which the various methods are used.

Note how the following examples use different organizational methods to achieve different purposes.

Paragraph Organization

Method	Definition	Used most often in
Chronological Order	A presentation of events in order of their occurrence	Stories, biographies, news reports, process or historical writing
Spatial Order	A description according to how something is arranged in physical layout	Description of places or objects
Order of Importance	A move from least important to most important or vice versa	Persuasive, informative, or descriptive writing
Cause-and-Effect Order	An explanation of a cause and its effects or of an effect and its causes	Persuasive or informative writing
Comparison-and-Contrast Order	A description of two or more people or things that emphasizes points of similarity and points of difference	Persuasive, informative, or descriptive writing

Chronological Order

One of the most common ordering techniques for writing both expository and creative pieces is chronological order. Writers use words and phrases such as *earlier, not long after,* and *later that afternoon* to indicate that events are being presented in the order of their occurrence. The following paragraph uses chronological order:

> The military career of Colin Powell reveals determination and success. After he graduated from New York City College in 1958, Powell received a commission as an army second lieutenant. He served in Vietnam from 1962 to 1963 and again from 1968 to 1969. Powell received numerous military decorations and civilian awards, including honorary knighthood from the queen of England. Not long after, in 1973, Powell served as battalion commander in Korea. During the interim years from 1974 to 1987, Colin Powell served as a commander in Europe and on bases in the United States. Late in 1987 he became the Assistant to the President for National Security Affairs. In 1989, prior to the first Gulf War, he accepted the appointment as the Chairman of the Joint Chiefs of Staff. Following his retirement from the military in 1993, Colin Powell served as Secretary of State from 2001 to 2004. In his role as chief foreign affairs officer, Powell again worked closely with military leaders.

A variation of the chronological order technique is called flashback. In **flashback**, a writer inserts events out of sequence in order to recall a past event in the middle of narration. The following paragraph uses flashback to tell of Rudi's remembrance of his mother.

> His eyes [Rudi's eyes] eventually came to rest on one cathedral. He then thought back to the first moment he had noticed it. It was on his seventh birthday, the day that he received his mother's first letter. When Rudi's mother had found out that she was dying, Rudi was too young to store up memories of her. So she had decided to write as many letters to him as she could. He had already received five of the seven that she had completed.
> (From *A Father's Promise* by Donnalynn Hess)

Spatial Order

Sometimes a writer wants a reader to visualize the layout of a room or the placement of objects. When such a description is needed, one should write from a single point of view to prevent reader confusion. That single point of view may be from left to right or right to left, top to bottom or bottom to top, or some other system that gives the reader a logical order to follow as he attempts to visualize what the writer is describing.

> The young pastor walked through the center double doors that led into the auditorium. Before him stretched a blue-carpeted aisle that led to the platform where the white wooden pulpit stood. On the left side of the platform was a grand piano and to the right was a large electric organ. Several feet behind the pulpit, forty-eight blue upholstered chairs filled the choir chancel. His eyes looked beyond the chancel to the baptismal pool. The young pastor then observed the rest of the room. On either side of the auditorium were matching stained glass windows that allowed some sunlight to brighten the room. Overhead, track lights and chandeliers provided more light. Twenty rows of white wooden pews with blue upholstered seats were grouped in four sections across the auditorium. As the young pastor assimilated what he saw, he prayed that he would be able to minister to those who would sit in this auditorium.

Order of Importance

Moving from most important information to least important information (or vice versa) is called order-of-importance writing. Journalists hoping to relay information to readers who have only enough time to scan daily headlines and one or two opening sentences move from most important facts to least important facts (often called the inverted pyramid). Other writers build a case by moving to increasingly important points, building support as they go, thus moving the reader to action. Order-of-importance writing uses terms such as *first, most important,* and *last* to signal what is important to the author.

> In the 1760s and 1770s the emergence of the term *American* reflected a spirit of nationalism among the colonists. One important factor that contributed to an independent spirit was the geographic separation from the Old World. The colonists had to defend themselves; thus they learned self-reliance and independence. In addition to the separation, settlers had the opportunity to own property in this New World, something they had not been able to do in their homeland. Another factor contributing to the development of an American spirit was the diverse backgrounds of the settlers. They had to learn to live together and to blend their cultures. While all of these factors were important, one of the most important influences in the development of nationalism was strong self-government. The colonists were determined to make their own laws, and strong political leaders emerged. These newly named Americans possessed confidence in their role in the New World.

Cause-and-Effect Order

Some writers organize their writing according to a cause-and-effect relationship. Causes and effects create a chain of events: a cause leads to an effect, and then that effect becomes the cause leading to another effect, and so on. For example, neglecting to apply sunscreen can lead to sunburn, which could lead to sun poisoning or even skin cancer. Of course, one cause could have multiple effects: not getting enough sleep might affect your motor skills, your thinking skills, and your general health. The reverse could also be true; that is, one effect could have multiple causes.

> Upon reflection, Charisse discovered that her less-than-desirable chemistry test score resulted from of a variety of causes. During the week before the test, she had missed an important chapter review lesson because of her basketball tournament; she had failed to seek out a study partner or to obtain a copy of the review worksheet. Then, because her tournament game marked the end of a successful basketball season, Charisse celebrated with her teammates by eating all the pizza, sweets, and sodas they had avoided during the sports season. To make matters worse, she tried to compensate for her junk food binge by not eating breakfast the morning of her test. Besides, she felt too exhausted to eat because she had not slept well the night before. While turning in her chemistry test, Charisse realized she had failed to pray for wisdom in preparing for and in taking the test. A lack of academic, physical, and spiritual preparation for her chemistry test resulted in Charisse's poor performance.

Comparison-and-Contrast Order

Comparison and Contrast
pp. 61–63, 66

To show similarities and/or differences between two things, writers use comparison-and-contrast order. In this type of order, two arrangements are possible: the block and the point-by-point arrangement. In **block arrangement** the author devotes one paragraph to the characteristics of one item being compared and another paragraph to the characteristics of the second item. **Point-by-point arrangement** makes statements about one item and immediately follows them with statements about the second item—within the same paragraph. The paragraph below shows point-by-point arrangement.

> Hotels and motels evidence certain similarities as well as differences. Both provide overnight lodging for travelers. Both target business travelers as well as families. And both may be found in bustling cities and near airports. On the other hand, the word *motel,* a combination of the words *motor* and *hotel,* explains one key difference between these types of accommodations. Motels were first founded in the 1940s and 1950s to meet the lodging needs of American families traversing the new national highway system. Motels therefore have traditionally sought to provide budget lodging with convenient access to parking lots and interstate highways. Hotels, however, with their valet services, on-site restaurants, and conference rooms, appeal to a different clientele. Patrons of hotels can expect a more resortlike atmosphere: services such as complimentary toiletries, room service, and activities for children help the patrons justify spending the extra money required for a hotel stay. As motels and hotels vie for customers, they both tend to offer such amenities as swimming pools and continental breakfasts. How interesting it then appears when these similar yet different institutions try to attract new patrons by advertising to each other's customers!

Note that the paragraph includes terms such as *on the other hand, however, likewise, in the same way,* and so on. Words and phrases like these can tell the reader whether a similarity or a difference is being presented.

1.7 PRACTICE *the skill*

Underline the words or phrases that indicate the type of order used for the following paragraph. In the blank write the type of paragraph organization used.

Although rice is a staple food eaten in almost every country of the world, some people are not aware that white rice and brown rice are different. White rice, the most common type of rice, is milled and polished to produce the shiny white layer. During the milling process the hull or husk is removed. The core is primarily carbohydrate with a lower fiber and oil content. White rice is not a highly nutritious food; therefore, white rice is often enriched to heighten its nutritional value. Brown rice, on the other hand, is the least favorite of the rice varieties. Brown rice is not milled and retains its darker color. The hull or husk has a bran layer of minerals and complex carbohydrates such as fiber and oil. It is not necessary to enrich brown rice since it is a naturally nutritious food. Despite the differences of the varieties, rice remains a food staple for millions of people.

_____

1.8 REVIEW *the skill*

Underline the words or phrases that indicate the type of order. In the blank write the type of paragraph organization used in the following paragraph.

Judges 7 presents Gideon's preparation for battle against the Midianites. God spoke to Gideon and told him that thirty-two thousand men were too many for the army and that Gideon needed to reduce the number of soldiers. First, Gideon told the people that those who were fearful should leave. At this point twenty-two thousand men left the army. Second, Gideon brought the army to water. God commanded that those who knelt down on their knees to drink should not be part of the army, but those who lapped the water from their hands would remain. Gideon retained an army of three hundred men. Next, Gideon divided the three hundred men into three companies and gave each man a trumpet for his right hand and a pitcher containing a lamp for his left hand. When Gideon gave the signal, the men blew their trumpets, broke their pitchers, held their lamps in the air, and cried, "The sword of the Lord, and of Gideon." The Midianites fled from the presence of the army, and God gave the army of three hundred the victory.

_____

1.9 USE *the skill*

Write a paragraph using one of the types of paragraph organization discussed in this chapter. Then identify the type of organization you used. Be prepared to explain your reasons for selecting the type of organization you did.

_____
_____
_____
_____
_____
_____
_____
_____
_____
_____

Conclusions

Strong conclusions are critical to the success of any piece of writing. A conclusion should pull together all of the ideas presented and give the reader a sense of closure on the topic. Several methods for conclusions are listed below.

- call to action
- prediction
- question
- quotation/anecdote
- restatement of thesis
- summary

Each day the sick and shut-in senior citizens in your community face needless hardships in preparing their own meals. Tasks such as cutting, measuring, and cooking basic ingredients present insurmountable odds for hands crippled with arthritis, eyes dimmed by cataracts, and legs unaccustomed to standing independently. But you can help. Many senior citizens in your community would benefit from an hour or two of your time each week. By agreeing to deliver hot, nutritious meals to these individuals, you can join a community-wide network of people dedicated to strengthening and supporting our community. Won't you invest a few hours each week in serving others by helping our senior citizens maintain the quality of life they enjoy?

In the paragraph above, a call to action concludes a discussion about sick and shut-in senior citizens and their need for hot, nutritious meals. Note how the writer appealed to the reader by employing visual imagery, personal pronouns, and rhetorical questioning. Of course, the purpose of your piece will determine how you conclude your composition.

Writing Essays

Having studied the modes of writing and paragraph development and organization, we turn our attention to the essay form. An **essay** is a composition usually of several paragraphs, all of which deal with the same idea. Similar in form to an individual paragraph, the essay usually contains three parts: introduction, body, and conclusion. A thesis proposes the main idea of the piece and generally appears at the end of the introduction (the major exception being the in-class essay, studied later). Supporting paragraphs develop the thesis statement, and the concluding paragraph unifies the essay, often by a restatement of the thesis.

As you further your academic career this year and in college, you will most likely encounter several types of essay, the most common being the three- and five-paragraph essays and the in-class essay (which you will write in Chapter 7). The form for each type of essay is similar, with the body paragraphs expanding from one to three paragraphs and the introduction and conclusions ranging from a single sentence (in the in-class essay) to a full paragraph (in the three- and five-paragraph essays). In the three-paragraph essay, each part consists of one paragraph: introductory paragraph, body paragraph, and concluding paragraph. In the five-paragraph essay, the body of the piece is expanded to three paragraphs.

The **in-class essay,** which you will use often in your academic career, may consist of several paragraphs or, sometimes, a single paragraph. In traditional in-class essay form, the thesis and the concluding statements become the first and last sentences of the essay. The thesis begins the first paragraph of the essay, which is followed immediately by the first topic sentence and then the supporting sentences. If the essay consists of multiple paragraphs, the first sentence of each subsequent paragraph is a topic sentence. The conclusion follows the last supporting sentence in the last paragraph. The following example is of a one-paragraph in-class essay.

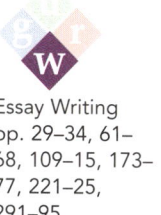

Essay Writing
pp. 29–34, 61–68, 109–15, 173–77, 221–25, 291–95

In Tennyson's "The Lady of Shalott," the mirror into which the isolated woman continually gazes symbolizes her idealized view of life. Daily she weaves and watches the outside world from her island tower, and, while peering into her mirror, she surveys an enchanting cross section of life. Such brilliant and enchanting reflections cause the Lady of Shalott to yearn for life outside of her ivory tower. She cries, "I am half sick of shadows" and takes matters into her own hands. Upon her decision to forsake her dream world, the mirror cracks "from side to side," and the lady senses a deep sense of foreboding. With the mirror ruined, the lady's idealism goes too, leaving a harsh view of life and ultimately leading to tragedy for the Lady of Shalott.

Revising

Thomas Jefferson once wrote, "No [style] of writing is so delightful as that which is all pith, which never omits a necessary word, nor uses an unnecessary one." But few writers compose a perfect draft on the first attempt. Revision is the writer's opportunity to make his writing a delight to read.

The revision stage may well be the most important stage in the writing process. No doubt you did some minor revising—crossing out words, leaving gaps—as you wrote. Now is your chance to look again at the goals you set for yourself in the planning stage: Have you accomplished your purpose for writing? Remember that even professional writers revise—deleting large portions of text or moving paragraphs around. Some writers work directly at the keyboard; others prefer to work from the printed page. However you choose to revise, consider three main areas: ideas, style, and correctness.

Revising for Ideas

Revising for ideas requires that you rethink certain aspects of your paper. The following chart summarizes four specific areas that you need to consider as you revise.

Areas to Consider	Actions to Take
Clarity of Purpose Is your purpose clear from your topic sentence or thesis statement?	Focus on the main idea; eliminate irrelevant information. Check organization.
Interest Does the beginning grab the reader's attention? Do details throughout the piece make the reader want to continue reading?	Change the beginning. Use an interesting fact, question, or anecdote that will interest your audience.
Unity of Ideas Is everything included that needs to be included? Is there anything unnecessary in the piece?	Rewrite or eliminate sentences that do not relate to the topic of the paragraph.
Coherence Is the relationship among ideas, sentences, and paragraphs obvious and logical?	Include transitional expressions to link the various parts of the paper together.

The following paragraphs show how careful revision corrects problems of clarity, interest, unity, and coherence.

First Draft

Numerous psychology books discuss color preferences. There are personality tests based on color preferences. Are such tests reliable? Color psychologists generally ascribe outgoing, adventurous, and competitive personalities to those who prefer bold, bright colors. Do these generalizations apply to you? Of course, colors are frequently classified into two broad groups, warm and cool colors. People who prefer softer tones are more likely to exhibit quieter, gentler personas. What about someone whose favorite color is black or white? People from various backgrounds and experiences will gravitate to certain colors and be repelled by others. Color psychology proves an interesting field of study.

Second Draft

What do color preferences say about people? Some psychologists actually use personality tests based on color preferences. These color psychologists have generally observed that outgoing, adventurous, and competitive people prefer bold, bright colors. Conversely, people who prefer softer tones are more likely to exhibit quieter, gentler personas. While considering such assumptions, one should remember that people from various backgrounds and experiences will gravitate to certain colors and be repelled by others. Therefore, color psychology, although interesting, provides only broad generalizations in analyzing personality types.

Writer's Toolbox

1.10 USE *the skill*

Revise the following paragraph using the checklist on page 20.

In the United States photography has been used for many things through the years. Photography began in the early eighteenth century in Europe with the creation of a photosensitive compound. Almost one hundred years later the idea of a photo studio became reality in Paris. In the United States photography was not popularized until the second half of the nineteenth century. The Civil War was the first major war to be photographed. This fact has contributed greatly to historians' knowledge. There were some seven thousand negatives of the Civil War. Shortly after the Civil War, photographers made their way west to document the expansion of the West. Since that time, photography has grown into a major art form, providing a historic treasure trove. Photographs were taken when mankind fought two great world wars and when man walked in space and landed on the moon. Photography enabled man to capture moments in time on film, preserved for generations.

Revising for Style

As you read the literature pieces that open the chapters in this book, you will find that good writers use emphasis to make certain messages more noticeable to the reader. Manipulating sentence length, type, and structure affects what stands out to a reader and therefore what a reader finds important. Specific, concise words as well as natural expression also influence how a reader interprets a piece of writing. The chart below lists problems and solutions for common stylistic errors. Use these troubleshooting tips as you revise your own writing for style.

Emphasis and Energy pp. 355–69

Areas to Consider	Actions to Take
Emphasis Are the important ideas central or emphasized? Do wrong or unimportant ideas stand out?	Place important ideas at the beginning or end of sentences. (The end is the strongest position in a sentence or paragraph.)
Precise Words Have you chosen nouns and verbs that are imprecise or general? *(The asparagus was not good.)*	Choose specific words. Your thesaurus contains precise words. *(The asparagus was tasteless.)*
Conciseness Is your writing redundant? Are there too many cumbersome dependent clauses?	Use fewer words. Reduce dependent clauses to shorter, simpler phrases.
Smoothness Does your writing contain awkward or rough parts?	Rewrite using language that sounds natural.
Fresh Words Is your writing full of overused words and phrases?	Replace clichéd words and phrases with new comparisons.

 **1.11**

REVIEW *the skill*

Rewrite the following paragraph, correcting any problems of emphasis, precision, conciseness, smoothness, and word choice.

Finding a job can often be a real hassle. Sometimes the only jobs available are the ones that not many people want to do. There is definitely an art to finding jobs. You have to be nice to the person interviewing you, and you have to have a good handshake. Otherwise he might not hire you, and if he doesn't hire you, you'll have to work somewhere else. Sometimes people can get good jobs, even though they're only in high school, but other times, they can't. Popular jobs for high schoolers are things like working at grocery stores and restaurants and things like that. The discipline and experience can't hurt even if you aren't pulling down big bucks.

_____
_____
_____
_____

Revising for Correctness: Proofreading

Proofreading is the final step in the revision process. As you revise for correctness, you will have the opportunity to rid your paper of grammatical and mechanical errors. The chart below presents areas for consideration as you look for specific problems.

Areas to Consider	Actions to Take
Sentence Structure Does your paper contain sentence errors?	Correct comma splices, fused sentences, and all nonstylistic fragments.
Usage Do any subjects and verbs or pronouns and antecedents disagree? Have you used correct pronoun case and reference?	Correct usage problems and agreement—both subject-verb and pronoun-antecedent agreement.
Spelling, Punctuation, Capitalization Do you have any spelling errors? Are sentences punctuated and capitalized correctly?	Use both your computer's spell checker and your own check for spelling errors. Correct punctuation and capitalization errors.

Proofreading skills must be developed. Even professional proofreaders miss errors in the first read-through. The chart of strategies below gives ideas for becoming a better proofreader.

Proofreading Strategies
Read a piece several times. No one finds every error the first time he reads a piece. Read yours three or more times through.
Read slowly. Consider using a blank sheet of paper to cover what you have not read yet so that it does not distract you.
Read aloud. Your ear may hear an error that your eye missed.
Read backwards. This strategy forces you to look at words individually.
Read specifically. Look for a specific error on each read-through. For example, read through once looking only for spelling errors.

Use careful proofreading to make your paper the best it can be. After all, the results affect not only your grade but also your effectiveness and your audience's impression of you.

Publishing

After drafting and revising your work, you are ready for the last step in the writing process. **Publishing** is the act of sharing your work with others: fellow students, teachers, friends, or the public at large. In the publishing stage, you may submit your work to someone who will put it in print in a medium such as a periodical or newspaper. More often perhaps, you will publish by allowing someone else to read your work, or you may read it aloud to a group. In any case, you must choose a title and make a neat final copy before you publish in any form.

Choosing a Title

Title selection may affect your reader more than any other writing decision you make. The title of an academic paper, one written primarily for school or for submission to a scholarly publication, should suggest to the reader the subject as well as the approach of the paper (such as "A Dialogue Concerning Heresies and Matters of Religion" by Sir Thomas More). "Signs of the Times," the title of Charlotte K. Frank's persuasive article on the decay of spelling as seen in modern signage, is a clever play on a well-known phrase. Such titles are often appropriate for informal expository writing.

Titles for creative writing assignments differ somewhat from those for academic ones. Creative titles often name the subject directly (as with George Eliot's *Silas Marner*); other titles may merely suggest a topic, prompting the reader to wonder what the title could mean (as with Jamie Langston Turner's *By the Light of a Thousand Stars*).

tip
Titles for academic papers may need to be longer than those for creative works since the writer must give more advance information to the reader.

Making a Neat Copy

Out of respect for your reader, your published work should be as nearly perfect as you can make it. From a technical standpoint no handwritten corrections are acceptable: reprint a single page or the whole piece if need be. For all submissions, pay attention to the accuracy of bibliographic information, margins, and spacing as well as to title page requirements.

For pieces submitted for outside publication, acquaint yourself with the publication guidelines of the journal, newspaper, or magazine to which you are submitting. Follow the guidelines exactly. Not only does this carefulness show respect for the publisher, but it also gives you a better chance of being published, since most publishers immediately reject any piece that does not meet their submission requirements.

1.12 USE *the skill*

Write an appropriate title for each of the paragraphs below. The first is a creative paragraph, and the second is an academic one. Make sure that each title fits the description for a good title as given above.

    The angry mob surged toward the platform, every face twisted with livid rage and hatred. The multitude of voices rose and combined into one thunderous cry, "Crucify him!" Soldiers stood on either side of the drooping figure that stood before the throng of people. The Roman governor Pilate stood beside Christ and offered a choice to the people. "Will you have me release the King of the Jews?" As he said this, several voices cried out, their voices dripping with hatred, "Release unto us Barabbas!" The crowd took up the cry and began chanting it over and over again, the sound of it like the ocean hurling itself furiously against a rocky shore. "What will you have me do with the King of the Jews?" shouted Pilate over the noise of the people. Before his words had died away, they were drowned in cries of "Crucify him!"

_____

    Matthew, Mark, Luke, and John present four separate accounts of the trial and crucifixion of Christ. Although each Gospel presents a different perspective, each recounts the major events accurately as they appear in the other Gospels, the four together providing a perfect portrayal of the Passion of Christ. This lack of discrepancies among the Gospel accounts reminds us that our Bible is infallible and inerrant. Both together and separately, the Gospels provide us with a vivid picture of the sufferings of our God for His people. The true believer cannot help being stirred as he reads of Christ's sufferings that sinners might be saved from the wrath to come.

_____

HISTORY OF THE ENGLISH LANGUAGE

Thinking Biblically

The King James Version was translated between 1607 and 1611. (It was updated in 1769.) No one alive today speaks or writes English in quite the same way the King James translators did, but the KJV definitely belongs to the Modern English period. (If you try to read English from 100 years before the KJV, you will find it very difficult if not impossible.) English has changed even in the modern period, however, and some words now mean the opposite of what they did in 1611. One well-known example is "he who now letteth" (2 Thess. 2:7), which then meant "he who now restrains" and now means "he who now allows." Can you think of any more examples of how language has changed since the King James Version?

Language Differences

Have you ever wondered why there are so many languages and just how many languages there are? Actually, no one knows for sure how many languages exist, partly because some areas of the world are still not very well known. Careful surveys are needed to determine whether certain people speak dialects of the same language or separate languages. We estimate that at least five or six thousand languages are spoken today. Below, John 1:1 is given in a few of these languages, as well as some languages of earlier centuries. Example 3.3 is in Early Modern English, the language of the King James Version of the Bible. The languages are in groups as shown by their first numbers—with all of the languages originating from the same language having the same first number and a different second number: 1.1, 1.2; 2.1, 2.2, 2.3, and so on. Notice what is the same and what is different in each group of languages. (Try to pick out the words for *God* and for *Word* in the verses.)

John 1:1

1.1 Original Greek

En archē ēn ho logos, kai ho logos ēn pros ton theon, kai theos ēn ho logos.

1.2 Modern Greek translation

En archē ēto ho Logos, kai ho Logos ēto para tō theō, kai theos ēto ho Logos.

2.1 Latin translation

In principio erat Verbum, et Verbum erat apud Deum, et Deus erat Verbum.

2.2 Spanish translation

En el principio era el Verbo, y el Verbo era con Dios, y el Verbo era Dios.

2.3 Portuguese translation

No principio era o Verbo, e o Verbo estava com Deus, e o Verbo era Deus.

2.4 French translation

Au commencement était le Verbe; et le Verbe était avec Dieu; et le Verbe était Dieu.

3.1 Old English (Anglo-Saxon) translation

On frymthe wæs Word, and thæt Word wæs mid Gode, and God wæs thæt Word.

3.2 Middle English translation

In the bygynnynge was the worde (that is goddis sone) and the worde was at god, and god was the worde.

3.3 Early Modern English translation

In the beginning was the Word, and the Word was with God, and the Word was God.

3.4 German translation

Im Anfang war das Wort, und das Wort war bei Gott, und Gott war das Wort.

3.5 Yiddish translation

In anhēb iz givēn das vart, un das vart iz givēn bai gott, un das vart iz givēn gott.

4.1 Welsh translation

In y dechreuad yr oedd y Gair, a'r Gair oedd gyd â Duw, a Duw oedd y Gair.

5.1 Armenian translation

Sgizpēn ēr panə, u panə asdudzo kovn ēr, yev panə asdvadz ēr.

6.1 Hebrew translation

Bərē'shīth hāyāh haddābār, wəhaddābār hāyāh 'eth ha'əlōhīm, wəhū' haddābār hāyāh ə'lōhīm.

6.2 Arabic translation

Fi 'elbed'i kāna 'elkelima, wa 'elkelima kāna ʕanda 'allāh, wa kāna 'elkelimatu 'allāh.

7.1 Tagalog translation

Sa pasimula pa ay naroroon na ang Salita. Ang Salita ay sumasa Diyos at ang Salita ay Diyos.

Notice that some of the languages are very much like one another, and others seem very different. There are two basic reasons for those differences: (1) the confusion of languages at the Tower of Babel as recorded in Genesis 11 and (2) the changeable character of spoken languages. These reasons also explain why there are so many different languages. Over the years, as a language changes differently in its various geographical areas, regional dialect differences develop. Over several centuries these regional differences can become numerous enough to prevent communication. At that point different dialects have become different languages. In Chapter 14 you will learn more about this process.

Descriptive Essay | 30
Parts of Speech | 35
From the Written Word | 59

DESCRIPTIVE ESSAY Writing
PARTS OF SPEECH Grammar

Before cameras were invented, moments and places could be preserved for posterity only by artists of the brush and of the pen. Great painters captured the sunsets and faces of times past for us with skillful strokes. These masters of the visual arts did not labor alone to record the past, however. Writers painted too, only with words.

Herman Melville, for example, painted a place for us—a place that we will likely never see with our own eyes (today we call this place the Galápagos Islands). He introduces us to this chain of volcanic islands with this description: "Take five-and-twenty heaps of cinders dumped here and there in an outside city lot; imagine some of them magnified into mountains, and the vacant lot the sea; and you will have a fit idea of the general aspect of the Encantadas, or Enchanted Isles."

Do you already "see" this place?

The Encantadas *by Herman Melville*

Take five-and-twenty heaps of cinders dumped here and there in an outside city lot; imagine some of them magnified into mountains, and the vacant lot the sea; and you will have a fit idea of the general aspect of the Encantadas, or Enchanted Isles. . . .

It is to be doubted whether any spot of earth can, in desolateness, furnish a parallel to this group. Abandoned cemeteries of long ago, old cities by piecemeal tumbling to their ruin, these are melancholy enough; but, like all else which has but once been associated with humanity they still awaken in us some thoughts of sympathy, however sad. Hence, even the Dead Sea, along with whatever other emotions it may at times inspire, does not fail to touch in the pilgrim some of his less unpleasurable feelings. . . .

But the special curse, as one may call it, of the Encantadas, that which exalts them in desolation above Idumea and the Pole, is that to them change never comes; neither the change of seasons nor of sorrows. Cut by the Equator, they know not autumn and they know not spring; while already reduced to the lees of fire, ruin itself can work little more upon them. The showers refresh the deserts, but in these isles, rain never falls. Like split Syrian gourds, left withering in the sun, they are cracked by an everlasting drought beneath a torrid sky. "Have mercy upon me," the wailing spirit of the Encantadas seems to cry, "and send Lazarus that he may dip the tip of his finger in water and cool my tongue, for I am tormented in this flame."

Another feature in these isles is their emphatic uninhabitableness. It is deemed a fit type of all-forsaken overthrow, that the jackal should den in the wastes of weedy Babylon; but the Encantadas refuse to harbor even the outcasts of the beasts. Man and

wolf alike disown them. Little but reptile life is here found:—tortoises, lizards, immense spiders, snakes, and that strangest anomaly of outlandish Nature, the *aguano*. No voice, no low, no howl is heard; the chief sound of life here is a hiss.

On most of the isles where vegetation is found at all, it is more ungrateful than the blankness of Aracama. Tangled thickets of wiry bushes, without fruit and without a name, springing up among deep fissures of calcined rock, and treacherously masking them; or a parched growth of distorted cactus trees.

In many places the coast is rock-bound, or more properly, clinker-bound; tumbled masses of blackish or greenish stuff like the dross of an iron-furnace, forming dark clefts and caves here and there, into which a ceaseless sea pours a fury of foam; overhanging them with a swirl of grey, haggard mist, amidst which sail screaming flights of unearthly birds heightening the dismal din. However calm the sea without, there is no rest for these swells and those rocks, they lash and are lashed, even when the outer ocean is most at peace with itself. On the oppressive, clouded days such as are peculiar to this part of the watery Equator, the dark vitrified masses, many of which raise themselves among white whirlpools and breakers in detached and perilous places off the shore, present a most Plutonian sight. In no world but a fallen one could such lands exist.

DESCRIPTIVE ESSAY

 **Thinking Biblically**

When you think of how writing and grammar fit into the life of a Christian, you should think of the word *tool*. But do not think of the rarely used tools that migrate to the bottom of a toolbox; think hammer and screwdriver, the essential tools used daily. But even these common tools have no value apart from the purposes for which they are used. Hammers help build houses and sheds and a million other useful things. What purposes—and what Christian purposes—can writing and grammar serve? The power of astute description helped Flannery O'Connor, for example, become a memorable and persuasive writer. She seemed incapable of making God's amazing world a boring place through bland writing.

And when these days were expired, the king made a feast unto all the people that were present in Shushan the palace, both unto great and small, seven days, in the court of the garden of the king's palace;

Where were white, green, and blue, hangings, fastened with cords of fine linen and purple to silver rings and pillars of marble: the beds were of gold and silver, upon a pavement of red, and blue, and white, and black, marble.

Esther 1:5–6

Why describe a place? What do you think Melville's purpose was in describing so fully the Encantadas? Why do you think the Bible records in such detail the décor of Ahasuerus's garden court?

Sometimes description serves a scientific purpose, detailing specific features of a place. Sometimes it serves a literary purpose: we have a much better understanding of the power and wealth of the king whom Esther must later petition for the lives of her people. If we had been told only that the king was wealthy and powerful, we might not feel the time and place as strongly and thus would not be as moved by the account.

Sometimes description can serve multiple purposes—but only if it is well done. What makes Melville's description vivid? He appeals to the senses: "like split Syrian gourds, left withering in the sun, they [the islands] are cracked by an everlasting drought beneath a torrid sky"; "tumbled masses of blackish or greenish stuff like the dross of an iron-furnace, forming dark clefts and caves here and there, into which a ceaseless sea pours a fury of foam."

Melville also uses beautiful language. His words sound like poetry, enhancing the meaning. The phrase "ceaseless sea" actually sounds like the hiss of the waves washing a rocky shore. And he chooses keen verbs and adjectives: "swirl of gray, haggard mist" and "they [the swells and the rocks] lash and are lashed."

Whether the purpose is to inform, record, entertain, inspire, or support a theme or a setting, description must be specific, precisely expressed, clear, and engaging.

Choose a place and write a descriptive essay about it.

Planning

✓ **Choose what you will describe.** Where can you get ideas for this assignment? Perhaps from your memory—is there a place that you like to visit or remember vividly? Perhaps from a picture—did someone send you a postcard from his travels? Perhaps from your everyday surroundings—is there a place you pass going to church that catches your attention? There are advantages to describing a place with which you are quite familiar: you are aware of all of the details and subtleties of the place. On the other hand, a new place offers opportunities to give your initial impressions of a locale, what one sees with fresh eyes.

✓ **Make a list.** Try to account for all of the senses. Are there smells that define this place? What would the description of the corner bakery be without some mention of the aroma of freshly baked bread? What sounds and sights are there? Is it hot? Cold? Mild? Is there a salty taste to the air?

Here is a list one writer made about a trip to the bakery.

irregular brick floor—watch your step!

large brick oven

huge flat wooden paddles for putting bread in oven

clouds of flour

smell of rosemary, yeast, crusty bread

stronger blast of heat the closer you stand to oven

brewing coffee—almost taste the bitter beans

array of creamers, flavors, sugars, condiments for breads

people reading newspapers—business people in suits, folks in exercise clothes, some barely awake

scrape of wooden stools on brick floor

art for sale

✓ **Consider your audience.** When you think first about your audience, you help yourself focus on exactly what kinds of details you should include and which ones you can omit. Will your audience be persons familiar with the place you are describing—like regulars at the bakery described above? Or will they be first-timers entering the place? The two types of audiences will want to know very different things about the place. Remember that looking at a place from a different point of view from your own will help bring different details to your attention.

✓ **Decide how you will organize your description.** Some descriptions are spatially organized; that is, they follow the path your eye would take as you see something for the first time. For example, as you enter a bakery, you might look toward the counter and then toward the board listing the day's specials and then around at the other people and the display cases.

Paragraph Organization pp. 14–17

Other descriptions are organized by the order in which your senses respond (chronological order). Entering a bakery, you would doubtless first be struck by the wonderful smell. Then you might notice the light coming through the

Descriptive Essay | Chapter 2 31

windows and hear the chatter of the customers or the sounds of pans sliding on metal racks. You might notice a baker slicing bread. He might even hand you a piece to taste.

Still other writers arrange the details to produce a single effect (a type of order of importance). They place the details carefully, letting them accrue through the paragraph to achieve a goal. Melville, for example, brings his readers to the Encantadas to overwhelm them with the sublime desolation of the islands.

✔ **Freewrite about your place.** Set a time limit for yourself and write about your topic without stopping. Write whatever comes to your mind—provided it is reasonably on topic and shows biblical restraint. Allow yourself the freedom to write unpolished text; that is, write without worrying about the finer points of grammar or spelling . . . for now. Your freewriting can give you options that might be useful for further exploration or development. Or it may make you realize that you have chosen a topic about which you have little or nothing to say. It is better to find that out now, in the planning stage, than in the middle of a draft. The paragraph below is the result of one writer's freewriting.

> When you enter the bakery, you've gotta watch your step because the floor is made up of irregularly shaped and placed old bricks—red ones that are chipped and flawed and therefore nearly perfect for such a place. If you manage to get yourself two steps inside, you'll *feel* bread baking. I mean, there's flour in the air—not like dust or anything—but like a fine smoky mist. And you smell at once the yeast and flour and coffee beans. Sometimes, if someone's just ground them, the beans are so strong you can taste them. If you're there early enough, the baker is still stoking the brick ovens with wood, and the wood smell mixes with the other smells and seems like winter at my grandparents' cabin. At least, that's what I think of. The baker uses huge wooden paddles, faded and bleached (with flour?) and scorched in places to slide lumps of dough speckled with rosemary—or if you've been especially fortunate, cranberry and white chocolate, into the oven. You can hear the paddles whoosh and scrape against the oven bottom. The ovens cover one whole side of the bakery. Scones fresh from the oven sparkle with sugar. Sometimes I pour cream from the coffee station onto a scone. Yum. At the coffee station there are four flavors of creamer and three types of sugar. Some people use them all. Some don't use any. Matt says people who drink their coffee black have just given up on life.

tip
Let the time limit you set for yourself in freewriting be the minimum amount of time you will spend writing—if you're still inspired at the end of the time, keep writing!

Tentative Outline
p. 6

Developmental Strategies
pp. 12–13

✔ **List your details in an order appropriate to your organization.** Using the results of your freewriting or your list of details, draft a tentative outline. Be ready to drop some details and add others. After making the outline below, the writer of the bakery piece realized that he needed to include more details on taste. After all, it's a bakery! He also wanted to think more about the senses of touch and hearing, adding information about the sound of beans grinding and coffee perking and people talking in hushed tones.

The Bakery and Senses
    Sight
        bricks
        oven
        paddles
        lumps of dough, scones

Smell
    flour
    yeast
    coffee

Touch
    tripping on bricks?
    flour

Hearing
    scrape of paddles

Taste
    scones
    coffee

Drafting

✓ **Scan your outline for figurative possibilities.** Melville, for instance, compares the islands to cinder heaps. Is there something in your chosen place that reminds you of something quite different? Do the white crumbs on the bakery counter look like snow? Do the pans going in and out of the oven seem like ships coming and going in a busy harbor? Does the sample of a cinnamon roll taste like Christmas? Avoid the use of clichéd expressions. Try to think of new ways to express your comparisons.

tip
Do not overplay a comparison. Choose appropriate, believable comparisons and use them sparingly.

✓ **Identify the primary impression you have of this place.** Choose some detail or figure of speech that will set the tone for your description. Melville decided that the Encantadas were sere and uninhabitable. He then began his account with a comparison that was not only easy to visualize but also evocative of the emotion he felt as he looked at the islands.

✓ **Draft an opening.** Write your introductory paragraph, keeping in mind the impression you wish to create. Remember that your first paragraph should not only introduce your place but also spark your readers' interest in your description and draw attention to your main idea. Melville immediately draws a brief picture of his place so that we see a generalized picture of the Encantadas as he proceeds with further details. Depending on the length of your essay, you may or may not have a fully developed thesis statement: You may instead just launch into your description. However, some sort of statement of controlling purpose may help your readers adjust to your topic.

tip
Consider placing a thesis statement at the end of your description—especially if you are writing a brief description.

✓ **Write your description in one sitting.** Write with purpose and direction. You can go back later and refine the essay. Keep in mind the overall tone and organization you have chosen. Always be envisioning the place as you write. Try to make the reader feel that he has been there himself.

Descriptive Essay | Chapter 2

Revising

✓ **Set your writing aside for a while.** If you leave your writing for a few hours or a day, you can get a fresh perspective on it when you return to it. Then pick it up again as though you had not written it. If it were someone else's, what would you think of it? What would you tell him to change? What would you tell him to keep? Take your advice.

✓ **Read your description aloud.** Does anything sound confusing? Do the sounds of the words help support your meaning in some places? (Remember the "ceaseless sea"?) Do the figures of speech seem appropriate, and do they make your account clearer? If not, you may need to drop them or rework them. The writer of the bakery description eventually dropped his reference to a "fine smoky mist" because he realized that many people would conjure up a negative association with a room filled with cigarette smoke. Be sure that you think about how someone else would read your description.

✓ **Ask a second reader.** Ask him what his main impression is. Is it the one you intended? Ask him what part was clearest. Ask him whether anything confused him. Ask him whether he can sense this place in his imagination. Use his feedback to make revisions.

✓ **Make changes to your essay.** You and your reader have implemented revisions for ideas and style. Now proofread the essay for correctness. Check for mistakes in grammar, usage, and spelling. Look also for coherence of transitions, especially if your essay is a chronological one.

Publishing

✓ **Hold a contest.** Post your essay along with the other essays and ask everyone to vote on which essay is most effective in portraying an impression.

✓ **Create a travel magazine.** Using computer images or photos or sketches, design a magazine of interesting places to visit.

✓ **Draw a picture.** Put your own artistic skills to work to illustrate your piece. If you feel you cannot adequately draw or paint your place, take a photograph or make a collage of the impressions you included in your descriptive essay.

✓ **Send the essay to the owner of the place you described.** The owner of the bakery or produce stand or the pastor of the church—whoever has a special interest in the place you wrote about will certainly appreciate a copy of your work.

Some Ideas to Consider

History
- Write a description as if from a window overlooking a famous place, such as the palace of Versailles.

Literature
- Find good descriptions of places in classic novels or well-known essays. Study the authors' styles and try to use similar techniques in your description.

Science
- Find a factual account of the details of a certain place. Rewrite the information in an expressive way, using figurative language.

Palace of Versailles

Parts of Speech

Words are the means by which we express our thoughts, both spoken and written. The Scriptures give many references concerning words: words that are powerful, words that are comforting, words that are well spoken. Choosing words accurately and correctly depends upon an understanding of the classification of words. In English, words are classified into one of eight parts of speech. However, correct usage goes beyond mere knowledge of the eight parts of speech and includes the understanding that the form and function of a given word can change. In the following sentences, observe how the word *chair* functions and how the form of the word changes.

NOUN	His small *chair* remained in good repair.
	Dining room *chairs* come in many different designs.
	Chairing the committee requires many hours of preparation.
ADJECTIVE	After years of extended use, the *chair* back broke.
	Chairing the sports committee, he excused himself from participation in the game.
VERB	The senior senator *chairs* the influential committee.
	Tenured congress members *chair* many of the committees.
	His predecessor was *chairing* the committee before he was forced to resign.
ADVERB	Because of his leadership ability, he was chosen *to chair* the sports committee.

Determine part of speech by the way the word functions in the sentence.

Nouns

A **noun** names a person, place, or thing. In fact, a noun is the name of anything. A noun can be singular or plural. Nouns function as subjects, direct objects, indirect objects, objects of prepositions, predicate nouns, nouns of direct address, appositives, and objective complements. Notice the first two sentences in the group of example sentences above. In the first sentence *chair* is singular, and in the second sentence *chair* is made plural. Nouns can be made to show possession as well, by adding an apostrophe or an apostrophe plus an *s*.

The *chair's* decorative carving is intricate and beautiful.

The two *chairs'* upholstery matched the décor of the room.

Notice that the first sentence indicates singular possession and the second sentence indicates plural possession.

Nouns are either common or proper. A **common noun** names any person, place, or thing. A **proper noun** names a specific item in one of these categories.

The antique green *chair* broke when the workman dropped it.

Thomasville Chairs manufactures many styles of chairs.

Common nouns can be count nouns or noncount nouns. A **count noun** can be singular or plural (countable). A **noncount noun**, sometimes called a *mass noun,* is singular in form and cannot be counted.

COUNT	chair, chairs
NONCOUNT	furniture

  Use a determiner, such as an article, before a singular count noun. (See pages 48–49 for more information about determiners.)

WRONG	George returned ~~book~~ to ~~library~~.
RIGHT	George returned **a** book to **the** library.

Because noncount nouns represent something that cannot be broken up into individual parts, they cannot be preceded by number words such as *a, an,* or *one* or by other determiners that imply counting rather than amount.

WRONG	Would you like ~~a rice~~ with your meal?
RIGHT	Would you like *rice* with your meal?
	Would you like **some** *rice* with your meal?
	Would you like **a serving of** *rice* with your meal?
WRONG	This pitcher holds ~~fewer water~~ than the other pitcher holds.
RIGHT	This pitcher holds **less** *water* than the other pitcher holds.

A common mistake is to use modifiers for noncount nouns as modifiers for count nouns. A list of modifiers for count and noncount nouns appears below.

SINGULAR COUNT NOUNS ONLY	*Each, every, either, neither*
	Each cow produces milk.
PLURAL COUNT NOUNS ONLY	*Many, few/fewer/fewest, a few, several*
	Several gallons of milk are produced.
NONCOUNT NOUNS ONLY	*Much, little/less/least, a little*
WRONG	Much ~~cows~~ produce milk.
RIGHT	Much milk is produced.

Compound nouns combine two or more words in one of three ways: as a closed compound (one word), as an open compound (two words), or as a hyphenated compound (one word).

CLOSED COMPOUND	wheelchair
OPEN COMPOUND	rocking chair
HYPHENATED COMPOUND	sister-in-law

  Notice the intonation difference between compound nouns and adjectives describing nouns.

- Compound nouns in English have their main stress (their loudest syllable) in the first part of the compound: **high**chair, **blue**bird.
- However, when the same two words appear as an adjective and a noun, the noun receives the main stress: high **chair**, blue **bird**.

COMPOUND NOUN	Little Dannie is in his highchair eating cereal.
ADJECTIVE AND NOUN	A double-bass player usually uses a high chair or a high stool.

Collective nouns are words like *majority, crowd,* and *audience* that refer to a group. A collective noun, although singular in form, can be considered plural when the individuals of the group act separately.

SINGULAR | The *audience* assumed **its** place near the front of the auditorium.

PLURAL | The *audience* took **their** seats before the orchestra members were seated.

Agreement p. 154

> A number of expressions that name groups of people come from adjectives (including participles): *the talented, the wealthy, the blind.* The following guidelines apply only to collective nouns made from adjectives or participles.
>
> 1. Always use the definite article **the** before this kind of collective noun.
>   Some members of our church minister to **the** homeless at the local rescue mission.
>
> 2. Always use a plural verb when this kind of collective noun is the subject.
>   The educated **are** likely to obtain good jobs.
>
> 3. Use this kind of expression only in reference to a group. To refer to just one such person, use an adjective + noun construction instead.
>   A **visually impaired student** faces challenges different from those of other students.

Common nouns are either concrete or abstract in meaning. **Concrete nouns**, most of which are count nouns, refer to material things which usually can be experienced by at least one of the five senses. **Abstract nouns**, most of which are non-count nouns, refer to abstract ideas.

CONCRETE NOUNS | apple, flame, rose, bell

ABSTRACT NOUNS | loyalty, truth, purity

Some adjectives may form abstract nouns by the addition of certain noun suffixes, such as *ness, ty,* or *th: goodness, sweetness, purity, sincerity, truth.*

Pronouns

A **pronoun** substitutes for a noun or for a noun and its modifiers. The use of pronouns allows a writer or speaker to employ variety and avoids repetition. The **antecedent** is the word to which the pronoun refers. It usually appears earlier in the sentence or paragraph.

The strict soccer coach said that *he* benched the star player for being late.

The remaining soccer players determined that *they* would be on time.

Personal Pronouns

Personal pronouns are the most common kind of pronoun. They name **three grammatical persons:** first person (the speaker or writer); second person (the person spoken or written to); and third person (any other person or thing). Personal pronouns have three additional characteristics: number, gender, and case. **Number** indicates whether the pronoun is singular or plural. **Gender** indicates whether the pronoun is masculine, feminine, or neuter. **Case** indicates the form of the pronoun based upon its use in the sentence. Personal pronouns have three cases: subjective, objective, and possessive.

The professional soccer player played *his* best game in the World Cup championship. *(third person singular, masculine, possessive case)*

His teammates did *their* part in passing the ball effectively. *(third person plural, possessive case)*

He trapped, dribbled, and shot the ball. *(third person singular, masculine, subjective case)*

Did *you* see the ball go in? *(second person singular or plural, subjective case)*

The team congratulated *him* at the end of the game. *(third person singular, masculine, objective case)*

Agreement pp. 148–49

Pronoun Use pp. 203–5

Pronoun Reference pp. 226, 229, 232–33

Singular

	Subjective	Objective	Possessive
First person	I	me	my, mine
Second person	you	you	your, yours
Third person			
Neuter	it	it	its
Masculine	he	him	his
Feminine	she	her	her, hers

Plural

	Subjective	Objective	Possessive
First person	we	us	our, ours
Second person	you	you	your, yours
Third person	they	them	their, theirs

Indefinite Pronouns

Unlike personal pronouns that refer to specific persons, places, or things, **indefinite pronouns** refer to nonspecific persons, places, or things. For this reason indefinite pronouns do not usually have antecedents.

Agreement pp. 157–59

all	anything	everyone	none	some
any	both	everything	no one	somebody
anybody	each	most	nothing	someone
anyone	everybody	nobody	one	something

38 Chapter 2 | Parts of Speech

Most of the indefinite pronouns shown above are always used with singular verbs.

> Anybody *is* able to come.
>
> Each *brings* his own pencil to class.

However, some are always used with plural verbs.

> All *are* able to come.
>
> Both *bring* their own pencils to class.

Some indefinite pronouns may be singular or plural, depending on context.

> None *is* able to come.
>
> None but her friends *are* here.

ESL

Indefinite pronouns are different from nouns in several ways. Nouns, but not indefinite pronouns, can be made plural and can be preceded by determiners and adjectives. We do not say "somebodies" or "a nice somebody." However, sometimes one of these words can be used idiomatically as a noun: "She thinks that he is **an absolute nobody**." (She thinks that he is not important.) "The coach asked each player to give **his all**." (The coach asked each player to give all of his effort.)

Demonstrative Pronouns

Demonstrative pronouns point out specific persons, places, or things. *This* (singular) and *these* (plural) refer to things that are near. *That* (singular) and *those* (plural) refer to things that are farther away.

> *That* was a well-executed goal by the front line.
>
> The goals scored all season were not as well executed as *these*.

When demonstrative pronouns are used as modifiers, they are determiners, not pronouns.

Relative Pronouns

A **relative pronoun** (*who, whom, whose, which, that*) appears in an adjective clause and shows a relationship between itself and its antecedent. The pronouns *who* and *whom* refer to people; *whose* can refer to people, animals, or things; the pronoun *which* refers to things and most animals; the pronoun *that* refers to any type of word. The relative pronoun has a noun function within the adjective clause.

> The goalkeeper was the one *who* stopped all the penalty kicks.
>
> The goals *that* were scored by the opposition came from corner kicks.

An **indefinite relative pronoun** (*who, whom, whose, which, what, whoever, whomever, whosoever, whichever,* and *whatever*) does not occur in an adjective clause and does not have an antecedent. Indefinite relative pronouns usually appear in noun clauses. Occasionally, an indefinite relative pronoun will be part of an adverb clause.

> [*Whatever* team scores the most goals] will win the game. (*noun clause*)
>
> [*Whoever* comes,] our players will play their very best. (*adverb clause*)
>
> I know [*what* will happen next.] (*noun clause*)

Determiners
pp. 48–49

Adjective
Clauses
pp. 116–19

Pronoun-
Antecedent
Agreement
pp. 163–68

Interrogative Sentences p. 69

Question Marks p. 296

Appositives p. 206

Commas with Appositives p. 307

Interrogative Pronouns

An **interrogative pronoun** (*who, whom, whose, which, what*) asks a question to which a noun or pronoun is the answer. For special emphasis, *ever* may be added to the basic interrogative pronouns.

Who is goalkeeper for the soccer team?

To *whom* did the coach direct his encouraging remarks?

Whatever made you think that you could win a game without practice?

Someone left equipment on the field. *Whose* is it?

Reflexive and Intensive Pronouns

Reflexive and intensive pronouns end in *self* or *selves*. **Reflexive pronouns** are used as objects but refer to the same person or thing as the subject of the sentence. **Intensive pronouns** emphasize a noun or pronoun that is already present in the sentence. Grammatically, an intensive pronoun functions as an appositive; therefore, it can be removed from the sentence without changing the meaning of the sentence. The intensive pronoun may appear at some place in the sentence other than immediately after the noun or pronoun it emphasizes.

REFLEXIVE	The goalkeeper injured *himself* on the corner brace of the goal box.
INTENSIVE	The goalkeeper *himself* stopped the quick, difficult corner kick.
	The goalkeeper stopped the quick, difficult corner kick *himself*.

Reciprocal Pronouns

Reciprocal pronouns express a mutual relationship between or among the persons mentioned in the subject of the sentence. The two reciprocal pronouns, *each other* and *one another,* cannot be separated and usually function as direct objects. Less frequently they function as indirect objects or objects of prepositions.

DIRECT OBJECT	Defensive players on the soccer team supported *one another* as they practiced for the game.
INDIRECT OBJECT	The team members gave *each other* encouragement as they jogged their miles in practice.
OBJECT OF THE PREPOSITION	Both offensive and defensive players gave encouraging words to *each other*.

Reciprocal pronouns can be made into possessive determiners.

Both defensive and offensive players enjoyed playing *one another's* positions during practice.

in SUMMARY

Nouns name persons, places, or things. Nouns can be singular or plural, and they may be made possessive.

Common nouns name any person, place, or thing. **Proper nouns** name specific persons, places, or things.

Count nouns can be singular or plural. **Noncount nouns** are always singular in form and cannot be counted.

Compound nouns are a combination of two or more words.

Collective nouns refer to a group. A collective noun, although singular in form, can usually be considered plural when the individuals of the group act separately.

Concrete nouns, most of which are count nouns, refer to material things that can be experienced by at least one of the five senses. **Abstract nouns**, most of which are noncount nouns, refer to abstract ideas.

Pronouns substitute for nouns or for a noun and its modifiers. The **antecedent** is the word that a pronoun replaces.

Personal pronouns show **person**, **number**, **gender**, and **case**.

Indefinite pronouns refer to nonspecific persons, places, or things.

Demonstrative pronouns point out specific persons, places, or things.

Relative pronouns show a relationship between themselves and another word in the sentence. **Indefinite relative pronouns** do not have antecedents.

Interrogative pronouns ask a question.

Reflexive pronouns are used as objects but refer to the same person or thing as the subject of the sentence. **Intensive pronouns** emphasize a noun or pronoun that is already present in the sentence.

Reciprocal pronouns express a mutual relationship between or among the persons mentioned in the subject of the sentence.

2.1 PRACTICE *the skill*

Underline each noun once and each pronoun twice. For each pronoun, write the type in the blank (interrogative, indefinite, etc.). If there is no pronoun in the sentence, write *none* in the blank.

_____ 1. I stood watching as the wind tore the remaining leaves from the branches of the oak tree.

_____ 2. Like a gymnastics team in slow motion, they tumbled through the air before coming to rest on the cold earth.

_____ 3. The tree stood, devoid of leaves, silhouetted starkly against a sky that was a somber gray.

_____ 4. Icy rain began to fall lightly from the sky. Who knew how long it would last?

_____ 5. The air itself grew colder as the rain fell.

_____ 6. Rain began to freeze on the tree and on all of the bushes.

_____ 7. As the ice thickened on the tree, the branches began creaking and groaning beneath the weight.

_____ 8. Ice-laden branches rubbed against each other as the wind tossed them about.

_____ 9. Bushes and tree branches, especially those that were delicate, were sagging with the weight of the ice.

_____ 10. Cautiously, I walked back the way I had come, back to the warm fire and hot chocolate made by Aunt Julie.

2.2 USE *the skill*

Write an appropriate noun or pronoun to complete each sentence.

_____ 1. The beach glistened, spread like a blanket before ?. (*personal pronoun*)

_____ 2. The ? slowly and rhythmically washed over the sand. (*singular noun*)

_____ 3. Shells and rocks in abundance were piled on ? . (*reciprocal pronoun*)

_____ 4. As the ? swept over the sand, it left behind beautiful patterns. (*noncount noun*)

_____ 5. ? took a few steps forward, looked backwards, and saw footprints. (*indefinite pronoun*)

_____ 6. Some shells sparkled beneath the incoming tide ?. (*intensive pronoun*)

_____ 7. ? steps on the shells will not be happy with the result. (*indefinite relative pronoun*)

_____ 8. ? scuttled across the sand with its claws waving in the air? (*interrogative pronoun*)

_____ 9. The crab ? glared angrily at me dodged beneath a rock. (*relative pronoun*)

_____ 10. ? was a good visit to the beach. (*demonstrative pronoun*)

Verbs

The **verb** is the backbone of a sentence. Verbs combine with nouns and pronouns to form sentences. An **action verb** expresses either an external, observable action that can be perceived by the senses or an inward action that cannot be perceived by the senses. A **state-of-being verb** expresses a state of being or a condition of the subject and is often followed by a complement.

ACTION	The missionaries *began* a youth group for teenagers in the area.
	The young people's spiritual growth *encouraged* the missionaries.
STATE OF BEING	Activities for the teenagers *are* unique.
	The youth group members *remain* fervent in their outreach to friends and other teenagers.

Understanding verbs and their relationships with other words is vital to understanding the meaning of a sentence. Sentence analysis often requires that you identify a verb by one or more of its characteristics. You can determine the person, number, tense, voice, and mood of a verb by examining the verb and its subject.

The muddy *children* **had played** with the new puppy all afternoon.

(third person plural, past perfect, active, indicative)

You can also write a sentence using a verb with certain characteristics.

First person plural, past, linking of *were*:

We **were** sure of the new puppy's welcome.

Verb Use
pp. 178–93

Characteristic	Meaning	Examples
Tense	Time (past, present, future, and so on)	The scavenger *hunt* **begins** at 3:00 p.m. Last month's *activity* **began** too late. Future *activities* **will begin** earlier.
Person	Agreement with the person of the subject	Each *program* **begins** with a time for games. *You* **begin** with opening prayer.
Number	Singular or plural (agreement with the number of the subject)	*Softball* **begins** with one team in the field. Other *games* **begin** after the softball game.
Voice	Active or passive	*All* of the teens **began** the capture-the-flag game. The capture-the-flag *game* **was begun** by all of the teens.
Mood	Indicative, imperative, or subjunctive	*I* **began** that game. If *I* **were beginning** again, I would try harder.

In addition to these characteristics of verbs, verbs can be identified according to the sentence pattern in which they appear. Each sentence pattern has one kind of verb.

Intransitive Verbs

An **intransitive verb** is a verb that, with its subject, is complete in meaning; it has no complement. However, the subject and verb may have modifiers.

Intransitive Verbs
p. 75

Teenagers from the youth group **worked** hard during the car wash.

They **were working** in teams of two or three.

Parts of Speech | Chapter 2   **43**

Sentence Patterns pp. 76–77

Transitive Verbs

A **transitive verb** is a verb that has a receiver of action to complete the meaning of the verb. The receiver of the action (the complement) is a **direct object**. Some transitive verbs have an additional complement, the **indirect object**, which tells to whom or for whom the verb's action was done. Occasionally, a transitive verb will have an **objective complement** that renames or describes the direct object.

DIRECT OBJECT	Teenagers and their sponsors *washed* fifty **cars** that Saturday morning.
INDIRECT OBJECT	Those at the car wash *gave* the mission **fund** their tips.
OBJECTIVE COMPLEMENT	The youth group *considered* the car wash a successful **outreach** to the community.

Sentence Patterns pp. 75–76

Linking Verbs

A **linking verb** joins the subject with a complement that either renames the subject—a predicate noun—or describes the subject—a predicate adjective. The most common linking verbs are the forms of *be*.

PREDICATE NOUN	Another successful outreach *was* the community **cleanup**.
PREDICATE ADJECTIVE	Learning to help others *was* **good** for the teens.

Auxiliaries

Auxiliaries, also called helping verbs, combine with the main verb to form the complete verb. They come before the main verb. Forms of *be, have,* and *do* can be used as main verbs or auxiliary verbs. When these are auxiliaries, they will be followed by a main verb.

MAIN VERB	A youth-group mission trip *is* another outreach.
	The teenagers *have* the opportunity to minister in a different culture.
	In preparation, the teens *do* extensive verse memorization.
AUXILIARY	They **are** *learning* verses to help them be good witnesses.
	The teenagers **have** *worked* hard to earn their support for the trip.
	A mission trip **does** *give* the youth group an opportunity to grow spiritually.

Modal auxiliaries indicate something about the speaker's attitude toward the action or state he is talking about. Standard English uses only one modal at a time. A modal auxiliary comes first in the complete verb before any other auxiliaries or the main verb. The common modal auxiliaries are *can, could, may, might, should, would, must,* and *ought (to)*.

NONSTANDARD	Parents *might could* help with the finances for the trip.
STANDARD	Parents *could* possibly help with the finances for the trip.

44 Chapter 2 | Parts of Speech

Modal auxiliaries are different from other auxiliaries.

- Modals never have an *s* suffix.

  WRONG | Takeshi ~~cans~~ run faster than anyone else on the team.
  RIGHT | Takeshi **can run** faster than anyone else on the team.

- Except for *ought*, modals are never followed by the *to* of the infinitive.

  WRONG | Vivica must not ~~to~~ be late for her appointment.
  RIGHT | Vivica **must** not **be** late for her appointment.
  Vivica **ought** not **to be** late for her appointment.
  Vivica **ought** not **be** late for her appointment.

Verb-Adverb Combinations

A **verb-adverb combination (VAC)** consists of two words, a verb and a following adverb. The verb and the adverb combine to function as the simple predicate in a clause. Often, the two words together produce a meaning different from the meaning of the two words individually. Many VACs are transitive and are followed by direct objects.

Adverbs
pp. 50–51

In a verb-adverb combination, the adverb may remain with the verb or may move to a position after the direct object. If the meaning of the sentence changes when the adverb is moved, the word is not an adverb but is a preposition instead.

Several teenagers *made up* new games to play with the children.

Several teenagers *made* new games *up* to play with the children.

Because the meaning of a VAC is often different from the meanings of the two words by themselves, be sure you understand the meaning of a VAC before you use it in your writing. Look in an ESL dictionary or ask your teacher or another native speaker of English for help if necessary.

Your ESL dictionary will probably call VACs *phrasal verbs*. It will include them alphabetically at the end of the verb entry. For example, *make up* will be near the end of the entry for *make*; *make up* will have its own meaning and sample sentence.

in SUMMARY

A **verb** expresses action or state of being. **Action verbs** express an action by the subject. **State of being verbs** express a state of being or condition of the subject. Verbs have **tense**, **person**, **number**, **voice**, and **mood**.

An **intransitive verb** is complete in meaning with its subject and does not have a complement. A **transitive verb** has a receiver of action to complete the meaning of the verb: the direct object. Transitive verbs may also have an additional complement, either an indirect object or an objective complement.

A **linking verb** links the subject with a complement that either renames the subject or describes the subject.

Auxiliaries combine with the main verb to form the complete verb. **Modal auxiliaries** often indicate the speaker's attitude toward the action or state of being he is relating.

A **verb-adverb combination** consists of a verb and a following adverb. Together these two words produce a meaning different from the meaning of the same two words used individually.

2.3 PRACTICE the skill

Underline each main verb once and each auxiliary twice. Place parentheses around each verb-adverb combination. In the blank identify each main verb as action (A) or state-of-being (S).

_____ 1. Dark thunderclouds had ominously blotted out the blue of the summer sky.

_____ 2. Moving the fields of tall grass like a turbulent sea, the warm winds were blowing over the meadow.

_____ 3. The sky grew bright with flashing bolts of lightning.

_____ 4. Like the sounds of cannon fire, the thunder rumbled across the plains.

_____ 5. Pouring mercilessly out of the sky, the rain was cold against our skin.

_____ 6. To the left and just over the hill, the trees bent and swayed violently in the wind.

_____ 7. The pond in the middle of the field appeared to boil from the multitude of raindrops.

_____ 8. The farmer looked over the meadow drenched with rain and strewn with hailstones.

_____ 9. After the rain had become less severe, the sky became brighter.

_____ 10. When the storm is over, sunlight will be beaming on the wet ground below.

2.4 USE the skill

Answer each question and respond to each statement by writing a sentence using the kind of verb indicated in parentheses. Try to use verbs other than *be* verbs.

1. Describe the worst storm that you have experienced. (*third person singular, past, active*)

   _____

   _____

2. Has your family ever been in a tornado or a hurricane? (*first person plural, present perfect, active*)

   _____

   _____

3. What is the present weather forecast for your area? *(third person singular, present, active)*

   _____
   _____

4. Describe the process of erosion. *(third person plural, present, verb-adverb combination, active)*

   _____
   _____

5. What is one way to prevent erosion? *(second person, modal auxiliary, present, active)*

   _____
   _____

6. How could the weather damage agricultural crops in ways other than by erosion? *(third person singular, modal auxiliary, present, active)*

   _____
   _____

7. Have lightning and thunder ever scared you? *(first person singular, past, passive)*

   _____
   _____

8. How has God used weather to bless your life? *(third person singular, past, linking)*

   _____
   _____

9. How did God use weather in the Bible? *(third person singular, past, active)*

   _____
   _____

10. Give another example of God's using weather in the Bible. *(third person singular, past, active)*

    _____
    _____

Adjectives

Adjectives expand, limit, or describe nouns or pronouns. Most adjectives will answer one of the following questions: *which one? what kind? how many? how much? whose?* Adjectives that answer these questions are called descriptive adjectives. Any word that fits into the following test frame can be used as an adjective.

The _____ thing (or person) is very _____.

The *tall* building is very *tall*.

The *feeble* man is very *feeble*.

> **ESL** Adjectives cannot be made plural in English.
> **WRONG** | Patricia picked several ~~fragrants~~ flowers.
> | The garden has two ~~elegants~~ gates.
> **RIGHT** | Patricia picked several **fragrant** flowers.
> | The garden has two **elegant** gates.

Adjectives can occur in various positions within a sentence. Most adjectives come somewhere before the nouns they modify. An adjective that modifies an indefinite pronoun, however, will appear after the pronoun.

Brian is a *successful* businessman.

His presentation emphasized everything *positive* about the plan.

An adjective that is part of a longer modifying phrase comes after the noun it modifies.

After the meeting, he needed ideas *helpful* for his clients.

Two adjectives joined by a conjunction can come either before or after the noun.

Quiet and *determined*, the businessman planned his strategy.

The client, *calm* and *confident*, waited for the presentation.

A predicate adjective comes after a linking verb and describes the subject. An objective complement follows a direct object and describes the direct object.

Sentence Patterns
pp. 75, 77

PREDICATE ADJECTIVE | He was *cautious* about his choice of ideas.

OBJECTIVE COMPLEMENT | He considered his plan *workable* for his clients.

Determiners

A **determiner** is an adjective that points out or limits a following noun. Determiners come before other adjectives that may modify the noun. Unlike descriptive adjectives, determiners do not fit into the adjective test frame and cannot be compared using *er/est* or *more/most*.

48 Chapter 2 | Parts of Speech

Articles

Articles are the most common determiners. *A* and *an* are indefinite articles, used to modify general nouns or nouns that have not been previously mentioned. *The* is the only definite article and is used to modify specific nouns or nouns already mentioned.

> Brian prepared *a* portfolio for everyone in attendance.
> *The* portfolio explained the retirement benefits.

> **ESL**
> Use *a* before a word beginning with a **consonant sound**; use *an* before a word beginning with a **vowel sound**: *a* tree, *a* university (begins with a *y* sound), *an* olive, *an* hour (the *h* is silent).

Possessives

Independent Possessives
p. 204

Possessive nouns or pronouns are determiners when they modify nouns. Possessives always modify a following noun and show ownership or another close relationship. When a possessive noun is modified by at least one other adjective, the possessive and its modifiers form a **possessive phrase**. An **independent possessive** is a possessive that functions as a noun or a pronoun rather than as a modifier.

POSSESSIVE NOUN	*Brian's* presentation was very informative.
POSSESSIVE PRONOUN	I could appreciate *his* preparation for the seminar.
POSSESSIVE PHRASE	The growing *company's* focus was on the individual.
INDEPENDENT POSSESSIVE	*Theirs* was the most comprehensive of the three plans.

Demonstratives

Demonstratives (*this, that, these, those*) can be used as determiners. Demonstrative determiners have the same form and meaning as demonstrative pronouns, but they function as modifiers, not as subjects or objects.

PRONOUN	*That* was the most convincing part of the presentation.
DETERMINER	*That* part of the presentation was the most convincing.

Interrogatives

Interrogative Sentences
p. 69

Interrogatives (*what, which, whose*), like demonstratives, can be used as determiners when they modify nouns. They are pronouns when they appear alone.

PRONOUN	*What* is the strongest point of the argument?
DETERMINER	*What* program will you choose to follow?

Indefinites

Question Marks
p. 296

Indefinites, like possessives, demonstratives, and interrogatives, can function either as pronouns or as determiners. An indefinite is a determiner when it modifies a noun.

PRONOUN	*Some* doubted the success of the program.
DETERMINER	*Some* workers chose plans to fit their needs.

Modifying Nouns

A **modifying noun** is a noun used to modify another noun. A modifying noun follows any other adjectives and appears directly before the noun that it modifies.

NOUN	I attended the *seminar* to learn about the new program.
MODIFYING NOUN	I learned about the new program through the *seminar* presentation.

Proper Adjectives

Proper adjectives are formed from proper nouns. Like the proper nouns, proper adjectives must be capitalized.

> The seminar took place in Philadelphia, where we bought *Philly* steak-and-cheese sandwiches from a street vendor.
>
> His ancient portable shop seemed almost *Victorian*.

Proper Adjectives pp. 270–71

Adverbs

Adverbs modify verbs, adjectives, or other adverbs. Most adverbs show one of the following meanings: manner (including extent and number), place (including direction and order), time (including frequency), result and logical conclusion, and cause. The adverb *not* has a purely negative meaning.

Adverbs appear in various positions within sentences. An adverb that affects the meaning of the verb is usually movable, able to appear in several positions within the sentence. The negative adverb *not* always appears after the first auxiliary. Furthermore, *not* can be joined to the auxiliary *can* to form a whole word (*cannot*) or to an auxiliary to form a contraction (*haven't, didn't, weren't,* etc.).

> *Outside,* the rain fell.
>
> The rain fell *outside*.
>
> We were *not* prepared for this spring storm.
>
> There was*n't* time to protect the young plants.

Although many adverbs end in *ly*, not all *ly* words are adverbs. Other kinds of words can end in *ly* as well.

ADVERB	Gray clouds formed *rapidly* in the sky.
ADJECTIVE	The *untimely* storm brought a downpour of chilling rain.
NOUN	The *lily* next to the front door couldn't stand up to the force of the rain.

Qualifiers

A **qualifier** is an adverb that modifies an adjective or another adverb. Qualifiers usually appear directly before the adjectives or adverbs that they modify and strengthen or weaken them.

MODIFYING AN ADJECTIVE	During the day *really* cold air blew against our skin.
MODIFYING A PREDICATE ADJECTIVE	The rainfall was *slightly* heavy at times.
MODIFYING AN ADVERB	The rain changed to snow *very* soon.

Conjunctive Adverbs

A **conjunctive adverb** shows a meaning connection between two independent clauses that are separated by a period or a semicolon. The conjunctive adverb usually, but not always, appears at the beginning of the second independent clause.

> A spring snowstorm in our area is highly unlikely; *nevertheless,* our three-state area had a severe one last year.
>
> A spring snowstorm in our area is highly unlikely. *Nevertheless,* our three-state area had a severe one last year.
>
> A spring snowstorm in our area is highly unlikely; our three-state area, *nevertheless,* had a severe one last year.

Some common conjunctive adverbs are listed below.

also	however	then
besides	in fact	therefore
for example	instead	
furthermore	nevertheless	

Relative Adverbs

A **relative adverb** (*when, where,* or *why*) introduces an adjective clause and relates that dependent clause to the rest of the sentence. An **indefinite relative adverb** introduces a noun clause or, occasionally, an adverb clause. The indefinite relative adverbs *when, where, why,* and *how* introduce noun clauses; *whenever, wherever,* and *however* introduce adverb clauses.

ADJECTIVE CLAUSE	During a spring snowstorm, peach farmers spend time in the orchards, *where* they check fragile blossoms.
NOUN CLAUSE	Peach farmers know *where* they need to check for damage.
ADVERB CLAUSE	The peach farmers realize that a portion of their crop is damaged *whenever* they experience such a storm.

Interrogative Adverbs

An **interrogative adverb** (*when, where, why,* or *how*) asks a question.

> *How* much of the crop was damaged?

---

in SUMMARY

Adjectives expand, limit, or describe nouns or pronouns.

A **determiner** is an adjective that points out or limits a following noun and comes before other adjectives that modify the same noun.

Articles (*a, an,* and *the*) are the most common determiners.

Possessives are nouns or pronouns that modify nouns and show ownership or another close relationship. **Independent possessives** function as nouns or pronouns rather than as modifiers.

Demonstratives, **interrogatives**, and **indefinites** retain their pronoun form but function as determiners when used to modify nouns.

A **modifying noun** is a noun used to modify another noun.

Proper adjectives are formed from proper nouns.

Adverbs modify verbs, adjectives, or other adverbs.

A **qualifier** is an adverb that modifies an adjective or another adverb, either strengthening or weakening its meaning.

A **conjunctive adverb** shows a meaning connection between two independent clauses that are separated by a period or a semicolon.

A **relative adverb** introduces an adjective clause. An **indefinite relative adverb** usually introduces a noun clause.

Interrogative adverbs ask questions.

2.5 PRACTICE *the skill*

Underline each adjective once and each adverb twice. Do not underline articles except in a possessive phrase.

1. The tremendous weather elements that accompany hurricanes can cause catastrophic damage to the landscape.

2. Some specialists refer to hurricanes as typhoons or tropical cyclones; however, these terms usually describe less violent storms.

3. Whenever a hurricane reaches land, heavy winds can uproot large trees and can create excessive debris.

4. The hurricane's center, calm and free from clouds, is called the eye.

5. Outside the eye, however, the most violent part of the storm rages.

6. Hurricanes produce abundant rainfall that causes a great risk for flooding.

7. One might wonder how often a hurricane creates favorable conditions for tornadoes.

8. In the coastal regions of the United States, homeowners evacuate quickly whenever hurricane warnings are issued.

9. Tropical storms that become hurricanes usually develop shortly after the peak of summer, when the ocean's waters are the warmest.

10. During these times, advanced technology helps scientists, but sometimes they find accurate prediction difficult.

2.6 REVIEW *the skill*

Underline each adjective once and each adverb twice. Do not underline articles. Then draw an arrow from each adjective or adverb to the word it modifies.

1. When do forest fires usually occur?

2. During the summer months, forest fires can cause damage terrible to see.

3. Often fires are the result of a lengthy drought, but some fires are caused by something tragic—arson or carelessness.

4. These fires begin a process of rebirth; new life springs up in their wake.

5. Some trees produce seedpods that break open and release their seeds in the middle of a raging fire.

6. Which seeds survive the fire and spring up, bringing life to the blackened wilderness, is always an enigma.

7. The Yellowstone National Park fire of 1988 was one event when progress came from apparent destruction.

8. Fighting forest fires is a very dangerous occupation that includes many risks.

9. Firefighters are always extremely careful as they seek to control the inferno.

10. Eventually the firefighters bring the fire under control; then the forest is free to begin rebuilding.

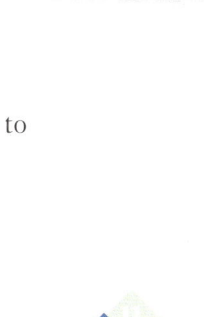

Prepositions

A **preposition** is a word that shows a relationship between its object (usually a noun or pronoun) and another word in the sentence. The **object of a preposition** follows the preposition. A **prepositional phrase** is made up of the preposition, its object, and any modifiers of the object.

Early American settlers used pumpkins (*in* two different **ways**.)

Although there are many one-word prepositions, nine of them occur most frequently: *of, in, to, for, with, on, at, by,* and *from*. In addition to one-word prepositions, multiword prepositions also exist. Some common multiword prepositions are *according to, along with, as well as, because of,* and *in spite of*.

American settlers used pumpkins for food (*as well as* decorative **purposes**.)

Noun Clauses
pp. 126–28

Prepositional
Phrases
p. 88

Prepositions indicate a variety of meanings; here are some examples.

LOCATION	above, across, against, around, at, behind, below, beneath, beside, between, beyond, by, in, in front of, inside, on, outside, over, past, toward(s), under, upon, within
DIRECTION	down, from, into, off, onto, out, out of, through, to, up (*see also* Location)
TIME	after, at, before, between, by, during, for, in, on, past, since, until, till, up to
AGENCY OR MEANS	by, by means of, of (*archaic*), with
CAUSE	because of, due to, in view of, on account of
ASSOCIATION	about, according to, along with, among, around, as for, besides, for, like, of, with
OPPOSITION OR EXCEPTION	against, apart from, but (*meaning* "except"), despite, except, except for, in spite of, instead of, without

Prepositional phrases function like adjectives and adverbs to modify another word in the sentence.

ADJECTIVAL	Pumpkins (*with* hard **shells** and a bright orange **color**) are ready for harvesting.
ADVERBIAL	(*During* the harvesting **stage**,) one must be sure not to damage or break the pumpkin's stem.

Writer's Toolbox

Many verbs and adjectives and some nouns must be followed by specific prepositions. English speakers and writers usually learn these combinations as they learn the language. However, some of these combinations can cause problems and can be found in dictionary entries that illustrate certain meanings.

Pumpkin farmers *agreed to* the planting proposal for the ten acres. (*to consent*)

Pumpkin farmers *agreed with* the agricultural department about the planting time. (*to be in agreement about an opinion*)

Pumpkin farmers *agreed on* a plan that would produce the most pumpkins. (*to come to terms*)

Conjunctions

Conjunctions connect words or groups of words in a sentence. **Coordinating conjunctions** join sentence elements of the same type. The coordinating conjunctions are *and, but, or, nor, for, yet,* and *so*.

SUBJECTS	A *maggot*, a *beetle*, **or** a *bore* can damage a pumpkin.
DIRECT OBJECTS	Pumpkins require *direct sunlight* **and** *well-drained soil*.
DEPENDENT CLAUSES	A pumpkin farmer considers his yield to be very good *when a small variety yields seven tons per acre* **and** *when a large variety yields thirty tons per acre*.
INDEPENDENT CLAUSES	*Connecticut Field pumpkins average about sixteen pounds,* **but** *the Big Mac pumpkins average more than twenty pounds.*

Compound and Compound-Complex Sentences pp. 132–33

Comma and Semicolon pp. 302, 315

A comma usually precedes a coordinating conjunction that joins two or more independent clauses.

Correlative conjunctions are coordinating conjunctions that occur in pairs and join equal sentence parts. Correlative conjunctions provide emphasis, let the reader know that a second idea will be added to the first, and make clear the ideas being joined in the sentence. The correlative conjunctions are *either—or, neither—nor, both—and,* and *not only—but also.*

> **Either** *we will go to the pumpkin farm tomorrow,* **or** *we will go on Tuesday.*
>
> **Neither** *the Jack Be Little variety* **nor** *the Munchkin variety grows much bigger than one pound.*
>
> **Both** *the Autumn Gold* **and** *the Jackpot weigh about twelve pounds.*
>
> *The farmers enjoy* **not only** *planting the pumpkins* **but also** *harvesting a bountiful crop.*

Subordinating conjunctions join dependent clauses to independent clauses. A subordinating conjunction is part of the dependent clause and functions as the introductory word for that clause. The following are some common subordinating conjunctions: *after, although, as, because, before, if, once, since, that, unless, until, when, where, while.* Phrasal subordinating conjunctions include *as if, even though,* and *so that.*

> *If it is not raining, we will visit the pumpkin stand tonight.*
>
> *We will visit the pumpkin stand tomorrow even though it may still be raining.*

Dependent Clauses pp. 116–28

Don't confuse **because** (a subordinating conjunction followed by a subject and a verb) with **because of** (a preposition followed by a noun or pronoun object.)

| SUBORDINATING CONJUNCTION | Lester went to the library **because** his book was due. |
| PREPOSITION | He avoided a late fine **because of** his carefulness. |

ESL

Interjections

An **interjection** is a word that can stand alone, punctuated as a sentence, or that can appear along with a sentence in which it takes no real part. Interjections express various meanings, such as strong feeling, agreement or disagreement, greeting or leave-taking, politeness, hesitation, or introduction of a subject.

> *Wow!* That pumpkin weighs more than one hundred pounds.
>
> *Yes,* my mother could make many delicious pumpkin pies from that pumpkin.
>
> I cannot eat another piece of that delicious pie. *Thank you.*

Phrases such as *good morning, thank you,* and *you know* may function in the same way as a single-word interjection. An interjection can be followed by a comma, an exclamation point, or a period.

Exclamation Points and Commas pp. 296, 307

---

in SUMMARY

A **preposition** shows a relationship between its object and another word in the sentence.

The **object of the preposition** is a noun or pronoun that follows the preposition.

A **conjunction** connects words or groups of words in a sentence.

A **coordinating conjunction** joins sentence elements of the same grammatical type.

Correlative conjunctions occur in pairs and join grammatically equal sentence parts.

A **subordinating conjunction** joins a dependent clause to an independent clause.

An **interjection** can stand alone as a sentence or can be part of a regular sentence in which it takes no real part.

2.7 PRACTICE *the skill*

Place parentheses around each prepositional phrase and underline the preposition once. Underline each conjunction twice. Identify each conjunction as *coordinating*, *correlative*, or *subordinating*. Some sentences may not have both a preposition and a conjunction.

1. In the distance a large funnel cloud moved across the dark sky.
2. Bright flashes of light were distinguishable as it approached the farm.
3. The neat rows of corn started waving noticeably, as if they were fearful.
4. Not only were the objects flying around the outer rim identifiable, but they were also dangerous.
5. Wood, metal, and vegetation whirled wildly.
6. The deafening sound was like the sound of roaring freight trains or fighter planes.
7. The tornado also ripped stalks from the ground, flinging corn everywhere.
8. Then the tornado began tossing cars into the air, letting them lie where they fell.
9. When the storm began to weaken, it dropped its contents over the area.
10. The funnel disappeared quickly yet left a disturbed calm behind.

2.8 USE the skill

Combine each set of ideas to form one sentence, using the type of conjunction specified in parentheses. In your answers underline each conjunction and circle each interjection.

1. The Cape Hatteras Lighthouse was built on the Outer Banks of North Carolina. It could warn ships of the barrier islands. (*subordinating*)

2. The treacherous waters along the barrier islands are called "the graveyard of the Atlantic." The "graveyard" entombs thousands of seamen and vessels. (*subordinating*)

3. Erosion had destroyed 1,300 feet of the beach in front of the lighthouse. In the 1900s the lighthouse was within 150 feet of the water. (*subordinating*)

4. In 1999 the lighthouse was moved a quarter of a mile inland. It may still be plagued by coastal erosion. (*coordinating*)

5. Wow! Beaches and houses are disappearing and cliffs are disintegrating along the coast. Erosion is threatening other parts of the coast. (*correlative*)

6. Some erosion is desirable. We would have no dunes, bays, or barrier beaches without erosion. (*subordinating*)

7. Many factors contribute to beach erosion. One major factor is that many people want to live near the sea. (*subordinating*)

Parts of Speech | Chapter 2

8. Major erosion problems must be addressed. New Orleans, already several feet below sea level, could eventually be surrounded by water. (correlative)

9. Efforts have been made to protect the Hamptons in New York from erosion. They could be destroyed if the sea level rises only three feet. (coordinating)

10. Oh, no! They are pumping sand from one location to another. Corrections to the erosion problem are not always helpful. (coordinating)

2.9 REVIEW the skill

Identify each italicized word or phrase as a noun, pronoun, verb, adjective, adverb, preposition, conjunction, or interjection.

1. Three New Testament Gospels *record* the events of a storm on the Sea of Galilee.
2. Often intense storms came up *fast* on the Sea of Galilee.
3. In addition to the strong *wind* and large waves, there may have been a heavy rainstorm.
4. The disciples rowed a certain distance *into* the strong wind but were unable to reach their destination.
5. The ship *may have had* sails, but the disciples were unable to unfurl the sails because of the strong wind.
6. The disciples feared for their lives and their faith failed them *when* shipwreck seemed the certain outcome.
7. After the disciples woke Christ, who had been asleep, He spoke, and *all* of the elements of the storm subsided.
8. Christ showed His *great* power and authority over all creation.
9. *Have* you ever *faced* storms of persecution or rejection in your life?
10. *Yes*, you can rely on the authority of His words, "Peace, be still."

BJU Living Gallery presentation of the painting *Christ on the Sea of Galilee* by Rembrandt, The Isabella Stewart Gardner Museum, Boston. Photo by Unusual Films.

FROM THE WRITTEN WORD

Recognizing the Truth

God uses a variety of rhetorical strategies to communicate truth. God chose the paradox to convey some of the most profound ideas and comforting promises found in the Bible. Have you considered the idea that a person must kneel to conquer? Our initial reaction may be that a person who kneels before another has given up freedom. On the contrary, the person who kneels before God conquers sin and the distresses of this world. Or have you thought about the person who experiences true freedom under the law of God? Often we think of being under the law as a hindrance. Yet the psalmist declared, "So shall I keep thy law continually for ever and ever. And I will walk at liberty: for I seek thy precepts" (Ps. 119:44–45). Law and liberty seem to be opposites, yet here they are not.

God uses what appears to be a contradiction to teach truth. Consider Isaiah 40:29–30.

> He giveth power to the faint; and to them that have no might he increaseth strength. Even the youths shall faint and be weary, and the young men shall utterly fall.

Perhaps you are asking yourself how someone who has fainted or lacks physical strength can have power. Consider the house-church pastor in Russia who was dragged off to prison because he refused to stop holding meetings and preaching the gospel. He endured persecution, separation from his family, dark solitary confinement, and months of malnutrition. In the midst of these circumstances he sang hymns, prayed for his enemies, encouraged other believers, and scratched portions of Bible verses on his prison walls for future prisoners. He experienced power in the midst of weakness. Even in death the house-church pastor was victorious.

Personal Response

Psalm 78 recounts the sinfulness and rebellion of the children of Israel in the wilderness. Read Psalm 78:19. Think about this paradox in relation to your life. Write about a personal experience that illustrates the paradox in this verse.

Comparison-and-Contrast Essay	63
Sentences	69
Think About It	80

COMPARISON-AND-CONTRAST ESSAY Writing
SENTENCES Grammar
3

Bruce Catton, a noted Civil War historian, won both the Pulitzer Prize and the National Book Award for history. The title "Grant and Lee: A Study in Contrasts" reveals the author's purpose. As you read his essay, look for words or phrases that indicate contrast and transition.

Grant and Lee: A Study in Contrasts *by Bruce Catton*

When Ulysses S. Grant and Robert E. Lee met in the parlor of a modest house at Appomattox Court House, Virginia, on April 9, 1865, to work out the terms for the surrender of Lee's Army of Northern Virginia, a great chapter in American life came to a close, and a great new chapter began.

These men were bringing the Civil War to its virtual finish. To be sure, other armies had yet to surrender, and for a few days the fugitive Confederate government would struggle desperately and vainly, trying to find some way to go on living now that its chief support was gone. But in effect it was all over when Grant and Lee signed the papers. And the little room where they wrote out the terms was the scene of one of the poignant, dramatic contrasts in American history.

They were two strong men, these oddly different generals, and they represented the strengths of two conflicting currents that, through them, had come into final collision.

Back of Robert E. Lee was the notion that the old aristocratic concept might somehow survive and be dominant in American life.

Lee was tidewater Virginia, and in his background were family, culture, and tradition . . . the age of chivalry transplanted to a New World which was making its own legends and its own myths. He embodied a way of life that had come down through the age of knighthood and the English country squire. America was a land that was beginning all over again, dedicated to nothing much more complicated than the rather hazy belief that all men had equal rights, and should have an equal chance in the world. In such a land Lee stood for the feeling that it was somehow of advantage to human society to have a pronounced inequality in the social structure. There should be a leisure class, backed by ownership of land; in turn, society itself should be keyed to the land as the chief source of wealth and influence. It would bring forth (according to this ideal) a class of men with a strong sense of obligation to the community; men who lived not to gain advantage for themselves, but to meet the solemn obligations which had been laid on them by the very fact that they were privileged. From them the country would get its leadership; to them it could look for the higher values—of thought, of conduct, of personal deportment— to give it strength and virtue.

Lee embodied the noblest elements of this aristocratic ideal. Through him, the landed nobility justified itself. For four years, the Southern states had fought a desperate war to uphold the ideals for which Lee stood. In the end, it almost seemed as if the Confederacy fought for Lee; as if he himself was the Confederacy . . . the best thing that the way of life for which the Confederacy stood could ever have to offer. He had passed into legend before Appomattox. Thousands of tired, underfed, poorly clothed Confederate soldiers, long-since past the simple enthusiasm of the early days of the struggle, somehow considered Lee the symbol of everything for which they had been willing to die. But they could not quite put this feeling into words. If the Lost Cause, sanctified by so much heroism and so many deaths, had a living justification, its justification was General Lee.

Grant, the son of a tanner on the Western frontier, was everything Lee was not. He had come up the hard way, and embodied nothing in particular except the eternal toughness and sinewy fiber of the men who grew up beyond the mountains. He was one of a body of men who owed reverence and obeisance to no one, who were self-reliant to a fault, who cared hardly anything for the past but who had a sharp eye for the future.

These frontier men were the precise opposites of the tidewater aristocrats. Back of them, in the great surge that had taken people over the Alleghenies and into the opening Western country, there was a deep, implicit dissatisfaction with a past that had settled into grooves. They stood for democracy, not from any reasoned conclusion about the proper ordering of human society, but simply because they had grown up in the middle of democracy and knew how it worked. Their society might have privileges, but they would be privileges each man had won for himself. Forms and patterns meant nothing. No man was born to anything, except perhaps to a chance to show how far he could rise. Life was competition.

Yet along with this feeling had come a deep sense of belonging to a national community. The Westerner who developed a farm, opened a shop or set up in business as a trader, could hope to prosper only as his own community prospered—and his community ran from the Atlantic to the Pacific and from Canada down to Mexico. If the land was settled, with towns and highways and accessible markets, he could better himself. He saw his fate in terms of the nation's own destiny. As its horizons expanded, so did his. He had, in other words, an acute dollars-and-cents stake in the continued growth and development of his country.

And that, perhaps, is where the contrast between Grant and Lee becomes most striking. The Virginia aristocrat, inevitably, saw himself in relation to his own region. He lived in a static society which could endure almost anything except change. Instinctively, his first loyalty would go to the locality in which that society existed. He would fight to the limit of endurance to defend it, because in defending it he was defending everything that gave his own life its deepest meaning.

The Westerner, on the other hand, would fight with an equal tenacity for the broader concept of society. He fought so because everything he lived by was tied to growth, expansion, and a constantly widening horizon. What he lived by would survive or fall with the nation itself. He could not possibly stand by unmoved in the face of an attempt to destroy the Union. He would combat it with everything he had, because he could only see it as an effort to cut the ground out from under his feet.

So Grant and Lee were in complete contrast, representing two diametrically opposed elements in American life. Grant was the modern man emerging; beyond him, ready to come on the stage, was the great age of steel and machinery, of crowded cities and a restless, burgeoning vitality. Lee might have ridden down from the old age of chivalry, lance in hand, silken banner fluttering over his head. Each man was the perfect champion of his cause, drawing both his strengths and his weaknesses from the people he led.

Yet it was not all contrast, after all. Different as they were—in background, in personality, in underlying aspiration—these two great soldiers had much in common.

Thinking Biblically

Every comparison and contrast you make is made against some standard. When writing for public consumption, Christians may be tempted to write to the lowest common denominator—to leave God and the Bible out in order to be more persuasive to non-Christians. Of course, the Bible need not make an appearance in everything you write; for instance, when writing an op-ed in the local newspaper about the proposed placement of a new sewer line, you may choose to leave the Bible out altogether. But when writing on public issues with strong connections to ultimate questions, Christians cannot afford to leave God out. Neither can they afford to abuse the Bible to support their point. Christians have the right and duty to appeal—carefully—to the eternal, fixed, objective standard of Scripture in public debates. Who else will?

Under everything else, they were marvelous fighters. Furthermore, their fighting qualities were really very much alike.

Each man had, to begin with, the great virtue of utter tenacity and fidelity. Grant fought his way down the Mississippi Valley in spite of acute personal discouragement and profound military handicaps. Lee hung on in the trenches at Petersburg after hope itself had died. In each man there was an indomitable quality . . . the born fighter's refusal to give up as long as he can still remain on his feet and lift his two fists.

Daring and resourcefulness they had, too; the ability to think faster and move faster than the enemy. These were the qualities which gave Lee the dazzling campaigns of Second Manassas and Chancellorsville and won Vicksburg for Grant.

Lastly, and perhaps greatest of all, there was the ability, at the end, to turn quickly from war to peace once the fighting was over. Out of the way these two men behaved at Appomattox came the possibility of a peace of reconciliation. It was a possibility not wholly realized, in the years to come, but which did, in the end, help the two sections to become one nation again . . . after a war whose bitterness might have seemed to make such a reunion wholly impossible. No part of either man's life became him more than the part he played in their brief meeting in the McLean house at Appomattox. Their behavior there put all succeeding generations of Americans in their debt. Two great Americans, Grant and Lee—very different, yet under everything very much alike. Their encounter at Appomattox was one of the great moments of American history.

COMPARISON-AND-CONTRAST ESSAY

A soft answer turneth away wrath: but grievous words stir up anger.
Proverbs 15:1

The goal of Christian writers should be to learn various kinds of writing techniques and to use their writing skills to good advantage. Comparison-and-contrast writing is a valuable technique to know. When you are determining the ways in which two subjects are alike or different, you are comparing or contrasting based upon certain facts or characteristics. When you make a decision about the purchase of one item over another, you are using comparison or contrast. Comparison shows how two subjects are alike, or similar; contrast, on the other hand, shows how two subjects are different.

Writer's Toolbox

Comparison
pp. 243–44

The Scriptures contain many examples of comparison and contrast. In Psalm 1:1, the blessed man is compared to "a tree planted by the rivers of water." The middle chapters of Proverbs focus entirely on a contrast of good and evil by using the word *but*. "A faithful witness will not lie: but a false witness will utter lies" (Prov. 14:5). In the New Testament, Mark 4:30–31 compares the kingdom of God to a mustard seed, and in Galatians 5:19–23 Paul contrasts the "works of the flesh" and the "fruit of the Spirit." In each of these, specific truths are revealed through the method of comparison and contrast.

In the sample essay, Catton uses words such as *contrasts*, *different*, and *opposites* to describe Lee's and Grant's characteristics and qualities. In his organization, Catton parallels the points of contrast and the organization of the contrasting points. At the end of the essay, however, Catton acknowledges several similarities between the two men.

Plan and write a two- or four-paragraph comparison or contrast essay on the subjects of your choice.

Planning

Choosing Your Topic pp. 1–4

✓ **Choose your subjects.** As you begin thinking about this assignment, be sure to consider two subjects that are somewhat related and with which you are familiar. Consider your personal interests, or think about articles or stories that you have read, or ask yourself questions about pertinent topics. From these sources determine the subjects for your assignment. You might choose to compare two candidates within the same political party or two candidates from different political parties, two styles of preaching, or two careers. You would not, for example, choose to compare a professional baseball player and a sports car. Although both of these could be temperamental and quite expensive to secure, they are not closely related. As you look back at Catton's essay, notice that he focuses on two related subjects: two men who were both accomplished Civil War leaders and responsible for bringing the war to an end.

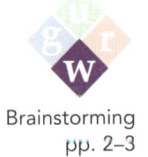

Brainstorming pp. 2–3

✓ **Brainstorm on what you know about each topic.** After you have chosen the subjects for the assignment, write them at the top of a piece of paper. On the rest of the paper, write down what you know about each of the subjects, both general and specific ideas. Then sort your ideas according to the subjects they belong with and identify each idea as a similarity or a difference. Some of your ideas will not be relevant and can be eliminated.

Wooden Roller Coaster		Steel Roller Coaster
looping	speed	height
swaying	drops	hills
steep	long runs	fun
scary	above the rail	locations
below the rail	rough	smooth
colors	kinds of seats	sound
single track	double track	

64   Chapter 3 | Comparison-and-Contrast Essay

✓ **Determine your purpose.** Ask yourself *why* you are writing this essay. Do you propose to show the differences between two subjects such as two modes of transportation, two kinds of cars, or two different sports? Or do you intend to inform your reader about the similarities between two relatives or two concepts by comparing the one to the other one? Catton reveals his purpose when he describes the meeting between Grant and Lee as "one of the . . . dramatic contrasts in American history." Catton's purpose was to show the differences between Grant and Lee.

Determining Your Purpose p. 4

✓ **State your purpose in a single sentence.** At this point, you are ready to write a statement of your purpose. As you formulate this statement, ask yourself what you wish to accomplish in your essay. Here are some ideas you might consider.

What is my purpose?
- To change the reader's opinion about an idea or a product
- To compare solutions to a problem
- To contrast two specific products
- To show readers that one opinion is better than another

Without a clear purpose, your writing assignment may remain a list of facts without any clear direction. Include in this statement of purpose the names of both subjects and the point of comparison or contrast. Catton writes that Grant and Lee were "different generals . . . [who] represented the strengths of two conflicting currents."

✓ **Choose an order for the points of comparison.** Read through your ideas from the Brainstorm step and begin to organize these ideas. Perhaps some of the ideas will fall into a group of observable physical characteristics. Others may form a group of quality characteristics.

Outlining the Paper pp. 6–8

roller coasters

wooden		steel
physical characteristics		
sway		tight
rough		smooth
no loops		loops
above the rail		above and below the rail
176 feet	*longest drop*	418 feet
197 feet	*highest*	456 feet
7,359 feet	*longest*	8,133 feet
70 mph	*fastest*	149 mph
77 degrees	*steepest angle*	121 degrees
quality characteristics		
loud		quiet
nostalgia (old coasters)		
scary		scary
fun		fun

Notice that there are some ideas from the Brainstorm step that were not used.

Comparison-and-Contrast Essay | Chapter 3

✔ **Put your most important ideas in the position of strength.** Ordering the facts about your topics is very important. Remember to build the reader's interest. A contrast of wooden and steel roller coasters would capitalize on the difference in their physical characteristics, particularly the height, length, and speed. Therefore, these ideas should be last in the contrast. That way, your reader will remember them best.

In the essay on Lee and Grant, notice the clear organization of ideas as Catton contrasts each man's background and relationship to his country. The point of Catton's essay is to show how the essential qualities of character that Lee and Grant shared outweighed their striking contrasts. Therefore, for Catton, the similarities of the two men are the strongest point. He leaves the men's shared vision for the future to conclude the essay.

Drafting

✔ **Choose a method of organization.** Suppose you intend to show the differences between two brothers, Sam and Joel. Two methods of organization are available to you. The **block arrangement** devotes one paragraph to Sam's characteristics and another paragraph to Joel's characteristics. If you make a statement about Sam's feelings toward motorcycles, you must make a related statement in the next paragraph about Joel's feelings about motorcycles. Both paragraphs should include the same type of information and should follow the same order of discussion. The **point-by-point arrangement**, however, first makes a statement about one of Sam's characteristics and then immediately makes a statement to show a difference in Joel. This point-by-point contrast continues throughout the paragraph. The same principles apply in this arrangement as in the block arrangement. If you make a statement about Sam's characteristics, you must make a related statement about the difference in Joel's characteristics and maintain the same order in your discussion.

Catton's essay follows the block arrangement. Paragraphs 4–6 and 10 present the characteristics and qualities of General Lee. Then in paragraphs 7–9 and 11 he describes General Grant. As you survey these paragraphs, you will see that Catton was consistent in the organization of his ideas about each man.

✔ **Construct a thesis.** Using the single sentence that stated the purpose for your writing, develop a thesis statement. The thesis for your assignment will provide organization and give specific direction to your writing. In the thesis statement, state each subject and the point of comparison. Are you going to show that these two subjects are alike or different?

POOR THESIS STATEMENTS	I am going to discuss the differences between white sauce vegetable lasagna and red sauce meat lasagna. (*The thesis statement should not announce what you intend to do.*)
	Did you know that the 1927 Cyclone at Coney Island is similar to the 1995 Viper at Six Flags, Great America? (*A thesis should be a statement, not a question.*)
GOOD THESIS STATEMENTS	White sauce vegetable lasagna is quite different from red sauce meat lasagna.
	The 1927 Cyclone at Coney Island and the 1995 Viper at Six Flags, Great America, are similar.

✓ **Write a rough draft.** Set aside an amount of time that would allow you to complete the first draft in one sitting. You may wish to postpone writing the introduction and the conclusion until you have written the middle paragraphs of the assignment. Each middle paragraph should have a topic sentence, the main idea of the paragraph. Using your list of organized ideas, compare or contrast the two subjects by using specific details or examples. A variety of transitional elements, both words and phrases, will clarify the points you are making about each subject. Some useful transitional words and phrases follow.

on the other hand	however	also	both
although	similarly	whereas	

tip
Many writers complete the middle paragraphs of an essay before writing the introduction and conclusion.

✓ **Write the introduction and the conclusion of your essay.** The introduction should introduce the two subjects of the paper and should end with the thesis statement. Attention-getting introductions often use quotations or facts and statistics to get the reader thinking about the topic. A conclusion, on the other hand, should begin with a restatement of the thesis. Then make any general closing comments about the two subjects to clinch the main idea and to add finality to the essay.

Introductions pp. 10–11

✓ **Consider incorporating both similarities and differences into your essay.** Catton's essay first describes the differences between the two generals. Yet in the closing paragraphs Catton concedes that both Lee and Grant were "marvelous fighters" who had "fighting qualities [that] were really very much alike." He compares their equally successful military skills and emphasizes their similar conduct in their meeting at Appomattox. You may want to both compare and contrast your topics, perhaps in separate paragraphs.

Conclusions pp. 13

Revising

✓ **Let your essay rest.** Allow yourself adequate time, overnight or perhaps a day or two, to put your writing aside before you begin the revising step. When you return to your writing, you will have a fresh perspective from which to evaluate what you have written.

✓ **Read your essay carefully and mark places that need revision.** Think about the purpose and organization of your comparison. Have you maintained your focus on either the similarities or the differences of the two subjects? Have you included specific details that show similarities or differences? Have you incorporated transitional elements that help the reader shift smoothly from one subject to another?

Revising pp. 20–24

Proofreading
pp. 23–24

✔ **Revise for correctness.** At this point you are carefully checking for accurate sentence structure, for proper usage, and for correct spelling, capitalization, and punctuation. You may use the spell checker on your computer; however, you must remember that the spell checker will not flag all errors. Remember that grammar, spelling, and mechanical errors will distract the reader from the message as well as injure your credibility.

✔ **Rewrite your assignment.** Now you are ready to incorporate the improvements and corrections you have made to your final essay. Before you submit the essay for a grade, be sure to proofread again.

Publishing

Publishing
p. 24

✔ **Choose a title.** The title should reveal to the reader the idea of the essay. Be sure that the title is not longer than five or six words.

✔ **Post your essay on a bulletin board entitled "Comparisons and Contrasts."** Your teacher may ask for volunteers to have their works posted in the classroom.

✔ **Submit your essay to the school newspaper.** If the topic of your essay is relevant to a particular section of the school newspaper, the newspaper may want to print it.

✔ **Bind your work for a class display.** Create an attractive cover for your essay and display it in the classroom.

✔ **Read your essay aloud to your family.** If you have chosen to compare or contrast two family members, your family might especially enjoy hearing your essay.

Some Ideas to Consider

History
- Consider a contrast between women of the frontier West and women of the aristocratic South.
- Consider a comparison of the contribution of Chinese immigrants to the building of the transcontinental railroad and the contribution of African Americans to the building of the agricultural South.

Statistics
- Consider a comparison or contrast between essay and objective tests.

Physical Education
- Consider a comparison or contrast of two team sports or two individual sports.

Geography
- Consider a comparison or contrast of the geographic features of the islands of Hawaii and Oahu.

Home Economics
- Consider a comparison or contrast of two diets or cooking styles.

Chapter 3 | Comparison-and-Contrast Essay

SENTENCES

The expression of a complete idea requires more than a random arrangement of words, and successful communication is more than choosing the right kinds of words. Successful communication results from correctly placed and properly related words that create understandable thoughts. In the group of words *the golf course in the mountains,* the words are related but do not express a complete idea. What is there to know about the golf course in the mountains? However, the group of words *The golf course in the mountains presents a challenge to the accomplished golfer* creates a complete thought, a sentence. Successful communication, both spoken and written, depends upon the correct formation of sentences.

Defining Sentences

A **sentence** is a group of related words that has a **subject** (person, place, thing, or idea that the sentence is about) and a **predicate** (a verb and perhaps other words that tell what the subject is doing or what the subject is). A sentence **fragment** is a group of words that may have a subject but no verb, a verb but no subject, or neither a subject nor a verb; or it may have both a subject and a verb but may contain an additional word that makes the thought incomplete. *Because I played the course carefully* has both a subject and a verb, but it does not express a complete thought and is not a sentence. In this example the first word, *Because,* creates a fragment. A sentence, therefore, is a group of words that has a subject and a verb and nothing that makes it a dependent part of a sentence.

Kinds of Sentences

Sentences can be classified according to purpose. A **declarative sentence** makes a statement and ends with a period. An **interrogative sentence** asks a question and ends with a question mark. An **imperative sentence** gives a command or a request and usually ends with a period. An imperative sentence can end with an exclamation point when it expresses strong emotion. An **exclamatory sentence** shows strong emotion and ends with an exclamation point.

End Marks
p. 296

Quotation Marks
pp. 331–32

DECLARATIVE	The mountaintop golf course provides long fairways and difficult greens.
INTERROGATIVE	Have you scored par on a round of golf there?
IMPERATIVE	Take your turn last.
	Watch out for that large rock!
EXCLAMATORY	He made a hole in one on the eighteenth green!

Imperatives are used in emergencies or with people from whom you expect cooperation or obedience. Requests are often stated as polite questions, not as imperatives.

PLAIN COMMAND	Call an ambulance! (emergency)
POLITE COMMAND	Please repeat your name.
POLITE REQUEST	Could you please repeat your name.

ESL

> **ESL**
>
> In spoken English, one of the major differences in the types of sentences is rising and falling pitch, called **intonation**. The intonation of a sentence can be a hint about what type the sentence is.
> - Declarative sentences have falling intonation at the end.
> - Interrogative sentences that expect a *yes* or *no* answer have rising intonation at the end.
> - Interrogative sentences that ask for information (using question words like *who, how, where,* and *why*) have falling intonation at the end.
> - Imperative sentences have falling intonation at the end.
> - Exclamatory sentences are stated at a higher pitch than other sentences or with a greater difference between the high and the low pitches.

Finding Subjects and Predicates

Because sentences have two basic parts, the subject and the predicate, knowing how to identify these parts correctly is important in sentence analysis. The first step is to locate the verb or **predicate**. The predicate tells something about the subject and may include auxiliaries. The **complete predicate** includes the **simple predicate** (or the complete verb) and all other words that relate to the verb.

SIMPLE PREDICATE	The breathtaking panoramic view from the fairway *has drawn* our attention away from the game many times.
COMPLETE PREDICATE	The breathtaking panoramic view from the fairway *has drawn our attention away from the game many times.*

Gerund and Infinitive Phrases pp. 98–99, 101–3

The second step in sentence analysis is to locate the subject of the sentence. Usually, the subject will tell who or what did the action of the verb or who or what was described. The **simple subject** is a noun or a pronoun or a group of words functioning as a noun. The **complete subject** includes the simple subject and any modifiers of the simple subject.

SIMPLE SUBJECT	The breathtaking panoramic *view* from the fairway has drawn our attention away from the game many times.
COMPLETE SUBJECT	*The breathtaking panoramic view from the fairway* has drawn our attention away from the game many times.

> **ESL**
>
> In English, the subject of a clause usually comes before the verb (the simple predicate).
>
>   S   V
> When the golfers reached the final hole, the rain began.

Although the subject usually comes before the predicate, the subject of a request or a command may be omitted. In such cases the subject is the **understood subject *you***; the meaning is clearly understood.

    (You) Give me my putter, please.

    (You) Take your turn at putting.

The subject *you* can be used with a command for clarity.

    Miho, *you* go first.

It can also be used for emphasis, making the command stronger. For example, a mother might say to her careless child, "*You* shut the door right now."

Sentences
p. 69

The subject in some sentences may not be immediately apparent because the subject and the verb are in **inverted order**. The inverted order places the verb or a part of the verb before the subject. An interrogative sentence places the subject between the parts of the verb. Inverted order often occurs in sentences that begin with *there* or *here*. (*There* and *here* are almost never the subject of a sentence.)

    V   V   S
Standing at the tee box *was* my chief **rival**.

  V S V
Did **he** *hit* the ball in the fairway?

     V   S
There *are* two **couples** in the foursome today.

   V   S
Here *are* the **scores** for today.

S/V Agreement,
Inverted Order
pp. 150–51

When English inverts the normal word order to form a question (an interrogative sentence), the complete subject changes places with the auxiliary verb, not with the main verb.

| STATEMENT | **Grant** and **Lee** *were bringing* the Civil War to its end. |
| QUESTION | *Were* **Grant** and **Lee** *bringing* the Civil War to its end? |

If there are two or more auxiliaries, only the first one occurs before the subject.

| STATEMENT | **He** *has been examining* the similarities and differences between these two men. |
| QUESTION | *Has* **he** *been examining* the similarities and differences between these two men? |

Subjects and verbs may be compound. **Compound subjects** share the same verb and **compound predicates** share the same subject.

COMPOUND SUBJECTS	My **brother** and **I** *enjoy* playing golf together.
	The **selection** of the club and the **approach** to the tee *are* two important aspects of any golf game.
COMPOUND PREDICATES	The golf **instructor** *encouraged* me to practice putting and *showed* me how to hold my club.
	James *practiced* his swing and *improved* his game by six strokes.

Kinds of
Sentences
pp. 132–33

Sentences | Chapter 3

in SUMMARY

A **sentence** is a group of related words with a subject and a predicate and nothing that makes it dependent on another sentence.

A **fragment** may have a subject but no verb, a verb but no subject, or neither a subject nor a verb. A fragment also may have both a subject and a verb but contain a word that makes it a dependent part of a sentence.

A **subject** is the topic of the sentence. The **predicate** is a verb and perhaps other words that tell what the subject is doing or what the subject is.

A **declarative sentence** makes a statement and is followed by a period. An **interrogative sentence** asks a question and is followed by a question mark. An **imperative sentence** gives a command or a request and is followed by a period. An **exclamatory sentence** shows strong feeling or emotion and is followed by an exclamation point.

The **complete predicate** includes the **simple predicate** (or complete verb) and all other words that relate to the verb. The **complete subject** includes the **simple subject** and any modifiers of the simple subject.

The subject of a request or a command may be the **understood subject *you***.

Inverted order places the subject after the verb or between the parts of the verb.

Compound subjects share the same verb and **compound predicates** share the same subject.

3.1 PRACTICE *the skill*

Identify each sentence as *declarative, interrogative, imperative,* or *exclamatory*. Place an appropriate punctuation mark at the end of each sentence.

_____ 1. Although some cultures approach meal times as a social experience, others view food simply as a necessity

_____ 2. Japanese culture has developed unique dining traditions

_____ 3. The Japanese do not talk while eating or drinking

_____ 4. Did you know that the Japanese frequently lift their plates or bowls to their mouths when they are eating rice or miso soup

_____ 5. Watch out for etiquette violations when dining with the emperor

_____ 6. Never lick your fingers when you are eating a meal in Japan

_____ 7. Although Korean chopsticks are metal and American chopsticks are plastic, Japanese chopsticks are wooden

_____ 8. Why should you learn about Japanese dining

_____ 9. Knowing some social graces will enhance your Japanese dining experience

_____ 10. I'm very eager to try these tips when I visit Japan

3.2 PRACTICE the skill

Underline the simple subject once and the simple predicate twice. If the subject is understood, write *you* in the blank.

_____ 1. Compare the family values of different cultures with your own.

_____ 2. Mexicans give their families priority over work.

_____ 3. Unlike people of other cultures, Americans typically concentrate on the nuclear family.

_____ 4. Members of extended families often demonstrate their loyalty and help relatives in need.

_____ 5. The Hawaiian term for the extended family is *o'hana*.

_____ 6. Filipino children and teens are expected to behave well and therefore rarely receive praise in public.

_____ 7. Notice older Asian children caring for younger siblings.

_____ 8. Native Americans respect elderly family members for their wisdom.

_____ 9. Youthfulness, a quality valued by American culture, receives more respect and attention than age.

_____ 10. There are differences in family relationships from culture to culture.

3.3 REVIEW the skill

Underline the simple subject once and the simple predicate twice. If the subject is understood, write *you* in the blank.

_____ 1. Acadian culture thrives and flourishes in Louisiana.

_____ 2. The French originally settled in an area of Nova Scotia called Acadia.

_____ 3. Did the British king fear the French Acadians?

_____ 4. When did deportees exiled by the British travel to and settle in Louisiana?

_____ 5. Here is a copy of Longfellow's poem *Evangeline*, telling of the struggles and sorrows of a pair of Nova Scotia exiles.

_____ 6. Why is Evangeline's beloved Gabriel forced to leave Acadia?

_____ 7. *Cajun* became the shortened version of *Acadian* and is now the better-known term.

_____ 8. Creole cooking, based on grand cuisine, and Cajun cooking, based on common ingredients, are not the same.

_____ 9. Watch out for the strong seasoning in Cajun cooking!

_____ 10. Found in Cajun cooking is a memorable flavoring: pepper sauce!

Basic Sentence Patterns

All English sentences contain at least a **subject** (sometimes understood *you* in an imperative sentence) and a **verb**. Some sentences need only these two components, but others require more. The kind of verb in the sentence determines whether it will be followed by a complement. A **complement** ("completer") is a word or phrase that completes the thought of the sentence; along with the verb, it is part of the complete predicate. To locate a complement, say the subject and verb of the sentence and then ask yourself *whom?* or *what?* If there is a reasonable answer, then you will have identified a complement. If there is no reasonable answer, then the sentence is probably complete without one. These different combinations of words can be expressed as the **basic sentence patterns** of English. All simple sentences are based upon these patterns, and all other sentences are formed from simple sentences.

Verbs
pp. 43–44

WITHOUT COMPLEMENT	The beautiful oak tree *stands* in the middle of the front yard.
WITH COMPLEMENT	The leaves of the beautiful oak tree *are* bright **orange** and subtle **gold**.
	The artist *drew* a beautiful oak **tree** with orange and gold leaves.

S-InV

The **S-InV** pattern has a subject (S) and an intransitive verb (InV). This pattern does not have a complement. The sentence is complete with only a subject and a verb. Remember, however, that other modifying words may be present in the sentence in addition to the subject and the verb.

        S   **V**
The children played.

             S   **InV**
The enthusiastic children played in the orange and yellow leaves.

The phrase *in the orange and yellow leaves* modifies the verb *played*, but the phrase is not a complement because it does not receive the action of the verb (i.e., it does not complete the verb).

S-LV-PN

The **S-LV-PN** pattern uses a linking verb (LV) to link the subject (S) with the complement of the sentence, the **predicate noun** (PN). The predicate noun renames or identifies the subject. The forms of the verb *be* are the most common linking verbs when they are used as the main verb in a sentence.

         S   **LV**   **PN**
The apple orchard is my favorite place on the farm.

       S   **LV**   **PN**
Apple cider became a popular drink at the store.

S-LV-PA

The pattern **S-LV-PA** also uses a linking verb to link the subject with the complement. In this pattern, however, the complement is a word that describes the subject, a **predicate adjective** (PA). Common linking verbs that are completed by

predicate adjectives are *be, appear, become, grow, remain, seem, stay, look, feel, smell, sound,* and *taste.* The last five verbs refer to the five senses.

```
         S  LV     PA
The apple yield was very large in October.
```

```
    S                       LV       PA
My investment in an apple orchard became very profitable.
```

```
   S                          LV PA
The samples of ripe red apples tasted good to the shoppers in the store.
```

Either a predicate noun or a predicate adjective can be called a *subjective complement* because either one completes the meaning of the subject.

S-*be*-Advl

Adverbs
pp. 50–51

The sentence pattern **S-*be*-Advl** uses only forms of the verb *be*. The complement of the verb is an adverb or an adverbial prepositional phrase showing place or time. The complement is called an **adverbial** (Advl) to show its adverb-like qualities.

```
     S     be  Advl
The best apples are there.
```

```
     S              be    Advl
Baskets of ripe apples were in the orchard.
```

Adverbial
Prepositional
Phrases
p. 54

This pattern often occurs in sentences with inverted order. The interrogative adverbs *where* and *when* may be a part of this pattern as well as other patterns.

The ripened apples are *where?*   *Where* are the ripened apples?

The sale is *when?*   *When* is the sale?

Interrogative
Sentences
p. 69

Some sentences use the placeholder *there* to stand in the subject position. In these sentences, *there* is an **expletive** and is not an adverbial. The verb *be* follows the expletive, which is followed by the subject and then the adverbial. Sentences with the expletive *there* typically introduce new topics.

There are twenty bushels of apples in the storage shed.

Twenty bushels of apples are in the storage shed.

Agreement
pp. 150–51

S-TrV-DO

Some sentences have a complement that is a receiver of the action of the verb. In the pattern **S-TrV-DO**, the **direct object** (DO) receives the action of the verb and refers to something different from the subject (except when the direct object is a reflexive pronoun). A **transitive verb** (TrV) expresses action that is transferred from the doer (*subject*) to the receiver of action (*direct object*).

Reflexive
Pronouns
pp. 213–14

```
        S       S   TrV     DO
My brothers and I gathered apples from the orchard.
```

```
         S   TrV    DO
Sometimes we ate too many apples.
```

S-TrV-IO-DO

A transitive verb may have another complement in the sentence in addition to the direct object. An **indirect object** (IO) comes between the verb and the direct object and tells *to whom* or *for whom* the action is done. The indirect object does not follow a preposition. The verb in the **S-TrV-IO-DO** pattern is a transitive verb.

```
         S    TrV   IO      DO
```
The customers gave Mother the money for the bushel of apples.

```
         S     TrV      IO     DO
```
Many tourists brought their friends apples from the mountains.

If the indirect object is replaced by a prepositional phrase, the sentence pattern changes. The object of a preposition cannot function as anything else at the same time.

```
         S   TrV   IO      DO
```
The store clerk took Dad the money for the bushel of apples.

```
         S    TrV        DO
```
The store clerk took the money for the bushel of apples to Dad.

S-TrV-DO-OC

Some sentences with a direct object may have an additional complement that renames or describes the direct object. An **objective complement** (OC) is usually a noun or an adjective that completes the idea of what the verb does to the direct object. The **S-TrV-DO-OC** pattern would, of course, have a transitive verb.

```
         S         TrV        DO      OC
```
The researcher considered our apples the best in the county.

```
         S       TrV    DO    OC
```
The local farmers elected Dad president of the organization.

Indirect objects and objective complements never occur in the same sentence pattern.

> **ESL**
>
> Notice the close relationship between the direct object and the objective complement. You can usually imagine that there is a form of *be* between them.
>
> ```
>          S      TrV  DO           OC
> ```
> The farmers elected Dad (to be) president.
>
> Dad *is* president because the farmers elected him.

in SUMMARY

An **intransitive verb** is a verb that does not have a complement.

A **linking verb** serves as a link, or equal sign, between the subject and a subjective complement.

A **predicate noun** renames or identifies the subject and follows a linking verb.

A **predicate adjective** describes the subject and follows a linking verb.

An **adverbial** is an adverb or adverbial prepositional phrase of time or place that completes the verb *be* in the sentence pattern S-*be*-Advl.

A **transitive verb** has a complement that receives the action of the verb.

A **direct object** receives the action of a transitive verb.

An **indirect object** comes between the verb and the direct object and tells *to whom* or *for whom* the action of the verb is done.

An **objective complement** is a noun or an adjective that follows the direct object and renames or describes the direct object because of the action of the verb.

3.4 PRACTICE *the skill*

Label the sentence patterns *S-InV*, *S-LV-PN*, *S-LV-PA*, *S-be-Advl*, *S-TrV-DO*, *S-TrV-IO-DO*, or *S-TrV-DO-OC*. If the adverbial is a prepositional phrase, underline it.

1. Within a particular region, various social norms exist.
2. Travel guides give tourists help with cultural transitions.
3. Native American cultures exhibit infrequent use of hand gestures.
4. However, storytellers are skillful with gestures as a means of communicating with their audiences.
5. A Native American storyteller was in the auditorium last night.
6. The handshake is the traditional American greeting.
7. Some cultures include more formal greetings such as bowing or hugging.
8. Direct eye contact is disrespectful in many Hispanic cultures.
9. Europeans consider eye contact during a conversation a sign of respect.
10. Eye contact in Japan and China depends largely on social status.

3.5 USE *the skill*

Use the given information to write a sentence that has the sentence pattern indicated in parentheses. The new sentence does not need to include all the words from the original sentence(s). You may need to use a new subject or verb.

1. There are two areas where the Inuit live. They live in arctic and subarctic regions. (*S-TrV-DO*)

   _____

2. Alaska, Canada, Greenland, and Russia have Inuit communities. (*S-be-Advl*)

   _____

3. They are stereotyped as living in igloos; however, this is not the case for most Inuit people. (S-InV)

4. Except for winter hunts, the Inuit rarely use igloos. (S-InV)

5. Today, many Inuit live in modern houses with heating systems. (S-TrV-IO-DO)

6. When it comes to hunting, the Inuit are excellent. (S-LV-PN)

7. The Inuit often get skins and meat from caribou for protection and nourishment. (S-TrV-IO-DO)

8. The Inuit believe in sharing food and labor with family and friends. (S-LV-PN)

9. The Inuit religion says that humanity's harmony with nature is a primary concern. (S-TrV-DO-OC)

10. As they progress through the new millennium, the Inuit depend less and less on the land for their needs. (S-LV-PA)

3.6 CUMULATIVE *review*

Label the sentence patterns *S-InV, S-LV-PN, S-LV-PA, S-be-Advl, S-TrV-DO, S-TrV-IO-DO,* or *S-TrV-DO-OC*. If the adverbial is a prepositional phrase, underline it. In the blank, identify the part of speech of each italicized word.

_____ 1. The regional conflict between the Jews *and* the Samaritans was evident in Christ's encounter with the Samaritan woman at the well.

_____ 2. She may have called Jesus a Jew because of His *manner* of dress.

_____ 3. *Consequently*, she questioned Jesus' request for water.

_____ 4. Jesus then *gave* the woman a surprising truth.

_____ 5. The water of *this* well was not a permanent satisfaction for her thirst.

_____ 6. However, Jesus *could* give the woman the satisfying gift of God, forgiveness and eternal life.

_____ 7. *In spite of* the conflict between the Jews and the Samaritans, Jesus freely gave.

_____ 8. Jesus' gift of *salvation* continues today.

_____ 9. Salvation is from God and for *anyone*.

_____ 10. *Yes*, we can experience the same gift of God, everlasting and abundant life.

BJU Living Gallery presentation of the painting *Christ and the Samaritan Woman* by Francois de Troy, the Bob Jones University Collection. Photo by Unusual Films.

THINK ABOUT IT

Thinking Skills

Critical thinking, creative thinking, higher-order thinking—professional educators routinely use these terms to describe what they want their students to be able to do. But what do these terms mean? What do educators mean when they refer to "thinking skills"?

In the broadest sense, these terms identify not what someone thinks but rather how he thinks. In other words, someone's thinking skills are the procedures that he or she uses to process information. Does he accept the information unquestioningly? Or does he evaluate statements to judge their validity? Does he consider alternatives in order to solve a problem? Is he able to make connections, draw conclusions, and apply what he has learned for use in real-life situations?

Many people focus on what to think. Students want to know what they will be tested over so that they can learn the answers to likely questions. They want to know what they will need to know in order to survive and even prosper in life outside the classroom. Employees may wonder what they are supposed to learn from a presentation or a report. A promotion, a raise, perhaps even job security itself may depend on gleaning the right information. New parents want to know what traits and behaviors they can expect their child to display at every stage of life.

Scripture tells us that God considers what we think to be important too. In fact, the Bible is full of commands about what we are to think on, commands such as Philippians 4:8.

> Finally, brethren, whatsoever things are true, whatsoever things are honest, whatsoever things are just, whatsoever things are pure, whatsoever things are lovely, whatsoever things are of good report; if there be any virtue, and if there be any praise, think on these things.

Clearly, God wants us to know what to think. However, He also wants us to know how to think. Specifically, God wants us to think as He thinks. In Romans 12:2, Paul admonishes other Christians: "And be not conformed to this world: but be ye transformed by the renewing of your mind, that ye may prove what is that good, and acceptable, and perfect, will of God." In this verse and many others, the Bible teaches that true wisdom—both what to think and how to think—is impossible without God.

Of course, an ungodly person can master human reasoning skills. History proves that men and women throughout history have used appeals to logic and emotion in order to sway people toward evil. Human wisdom, nevertheless, can never measure up to God's highest standard. Notice the contrast in these Scripture passages.

> For the wisdom of this world is foolishness with God. (1 Cor. 3:19)

> The fear of the Lord is the beginning of wisdom: a good understanding have all they that do his commandments: his praise endureth for ever. (Ps. 111:10)

Likewise, a Christian who knows what to think (scriptural truths) but does not know how to think (proper reasoning) may be unable to counter the arguments of one who disagrees with God. Each Christian is to "be ready always to give an answer to every man that asketh [him] a reason of the hope that is in [him] with meekness and fear" (1 Pet. 3:15). For the Christian, then, what to think and how to think are equally important because both are important to God.

Thinking Biblically

The very structure of Bible books like Romans says something about the kind of critical thinking God wants to encourage. God could have just handed out a perfect list of rules or a detailed doctrinal statement, but instead He inspired letters. And these letters force you to reason, to push your mind through multiple steps of logic, to draw conclusions. Books like Romans are in the Bible not merely to teach you what to think but also to teach you how to think.

Thinking It Through

Read Mark 12:30 and Acts 18:4. Then write a paragraph concerning what these verses teach about what Christians should think and how they should think.

Interior Monologue	84
Phrases	88
From the Written Word	107

INTERIOR MONOLOGUE Writing
PHRASES Grammar
4

In the novel By the Light of a Thousand Stars, *the main character, Catherine, is a self-absorbed wife and mother who is more interested in the décor of her home than in the welfare of her family. This excerpt follows her after she finds a door open when she returns from shopping. Her son, Hardy, is downstairs listening to loud music and does not know that an intruder could be in the house. In this interior monologue from the book, notice how Catherine's thoughts give us insight into her character. And notice, too, how the monologue builds suspense, although it appears to be only random thinking.*

By the Light of a Thousand Stars *by Jamie Langston Turner*

[Catherine] yanked a paper towel from the roller, then stooped to pick up the peach with one hand and swipe at the floor with the other. Sparkle Flynn, the cleaning woman she hired once a week, would be in on Friday to do the floors, so a quick wipe-up would do for now. She threw away the paper towel, set the damaged peach on the counter next to the sink, then retrieved her keys from the floor and tossed them on top of her purse.

She had half expected to hear voices coming from the living room or den, but the only thing she heard as she stood in the middle of the kitchen with her hands on her hips was the muffled racket of Hardy's music coming from downstairs. From the kitchen she could see into the dining room, and she moved so that she could admire the new floral table runner with its heavy blue tassels on the mahogany sideboard. She still wondered, though, if burgundy tassels would have looked better with the wallpaper.

She walked from the kitchen through the hallway and into the den. No one was there. She turned and looked across the hallway into the living room. It, too, was empty. She scowled at the open front door, then walked over and closed it firmly. That eucalyptus wreath had cost a small fortune to put together, and it was all for nothing if it couldn't be seen from the street. She had kept telling the floral designer to add another couple of silk roses here, then a few more sprigs of berries there, and then some curly willows, and when she heard the final cost, Catherine had said, "Well, my word, you'd think that stuff was made out of solid gold!"

She moved now toward the draperies and adjusted a tieback, then noticing that a sofa cushion was out of place, she straightened it. Catching sight of herself in the mirror above the fireplace, Catherine turned her head from side to side. Dottie Puckett really knew how to fix hair, she thought.

It suddenly dawned on her that it hadn't even entered her mind to be afraid. Here she was going from room to room, looking for a stranger! She was alone in the house for all practical purposes, since Hardy sure couldn't be counted on to be of any help, even when he was home. Well, she *wasn't* afraid. Nobody with ulterior motives was going to leave his umbrella in plain sight and forget to close the front door. Still, she paused and laid a hand across her chest. She briefly imagined herself on stage—the heroine in a suspense drama, unsuspecting of imminent danger.

WRITING

INTERIOR MONOLOGUE

For out of the abundance of the heart the mouth speaketh.
Matthew 12:34

Pronouns pp. 37–38

Thinking Biblically

Controlling your inner thoughts is very difficult. They grow from what you love (out of the abundance of the heart the mind thinks! [cf. Matt. 12:34]), and what you love can't be turned on or off with a switch. But God has given you something to chew on that can renovate your heart and therefore your thoughts: Scripture. This idea sounds ridiculous to people who consider the Bible boring, but to someone who relishes God's words as David did, meditation on the Bible is not a chore. "O how love I thy law! it is my meditation all the day," David said (Ps. 119:97). His thinking was a fruit of his loving.

Your brain is never silent. Even when you are sleeping, it continues to generate thoughts and images. It is the part of us that allows us to "talk to ourselves." The psalmist David speaks to himself in Psalm 42:11: "Why art thou cast down, O my soul? And why art thou disquieted within me? hope thou in God: for I shall yet praise him, who is the health of my countenance, and my God."

The **interior monologue** is a narrative technique that presents a character's thoughts and feelings in a way that makes the reader feel that he is seeing the person's true inner self. Of course, the writer controls the monologue and the impressions given to the reader. Interior monologue may be written in either first or third person, depending on the point of view used in the rest of the piece. Interior monologue is closely related to dramatic monologue (poetry) and to soliloquy (drama). Sometimes an author chooses to write in stream of consciousness form. Similar to interior monologue and, in fact, often overlapping and merging with it, **stream of consciousness** is a technique that attempts to record uninterrupted thought. Stream of consciousness writing usually seems irrational and spontaneous, jumpy and disjointed, whereas interior monologue generally flows meaningfully—albeit meanderingly—from point to point. To compose such a monologue, the writer must make the writing appear random but still maintain his purpose.

The interior monologues of Christians should be different from the kind Catherine indulges in. Take a moment to think about what should characterize a Christian's interior monologue.

Your Turn

Choose a specific moment in which someone would be consciously thinking to himself. Think about who the person is. What is his main character trait? His goal? His attitude toward the situation he is in? Then write his interior monologue, using complete sentences.

Planning

✔ **Hone your listening skills.** Find a time to listen closely to the people around you. In the mall, at church, in a restaurant—listen to how people talk and how their thoughts flow naturally from one topic to the next. You may find it helpful to write portions of some of the conversations down in a journal so that you can refer to them later. (Be careful about recording anyone without prior consent to do so.)

✔ **Look for examples of interior monologue in your reading.** Once you begin looking for it, you will be surprised at how often you encounter examples of interior monologue in the newspaper, a magazine, or a book you are reading. Notice how and when the writer uses interior monologue. Decide what aspects of the monologue you find especially believable or amusing.

✔ **Decide on a character.** You may want to create a character or choose someone from history for whom you can fill in some fictional details. If you create a character, choose a name for him. Jamie Langston Turner, an author whose fictional characters always seem strikingly real, says, "Writing is such fun because you get to step into so many characters' lives and see what it's like to be all those different people." Make your character real to yourself before attempting to make him real to your audience.

✔ **Make a character web.** Write your character's name in the middle of a sheet of paper. Draw lines extending from the name as shown below. At the end of each line, write words and phrases that describe the character—from likes and dislikes to character qualities. Then circle the one trait that seems to best represent the character or embodies the dominant trait you want your fictional character to possess.

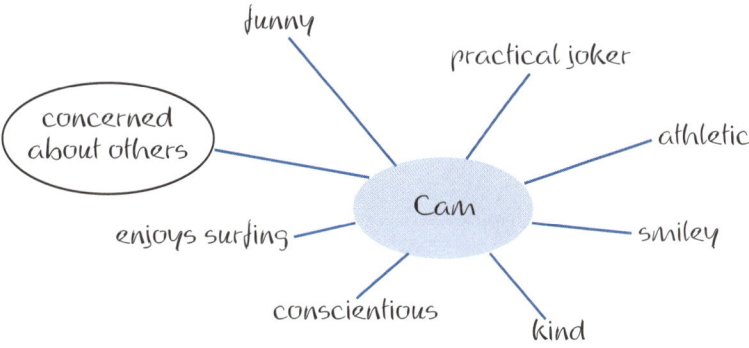

✔ **Decide on a goal for your character.** The discussion of interior monologue on page 84 indicates that good interior monologue appears to be random but in reality has a purpose or a goal. What will the goal of your character's written thoughts be? Will he answer for himself the question of where to attend college or which summer camp to work at? Write your character's goal in one sentence and keep it in mind as you complete your planning.

✔ **Construct a thought train.** At the left side of a sheet of paper, write the character's goal for himself. Draw a box around the sentence. Then draw a line extending to the right and make another box. Write a thought in the box that the character might have about getting to his goal. Continue the thought train. You can branch off on as many tracks as you need to.

- ✔ **Choose a track.** With a colored pen or pencil, trace one line of thought through the thought train. Next to each box you have chosen, write some details of action or description that might occur while the character is thinking.
- ✔ **Freewrite about the character you have chosen.** Set a time limit for yourself and write without stopping. This method may be especially helpful for the interior monologue since portraying an impression of free and continuous thought is the effect you want your writing to have.

Drafting

- ✔ **Follow the track.** Using the track you have highlighted and your freewriting, write an interior monologue, filling it out with details of action and description of each thought in the train.
- ✔ **Avoid overindulging yourself.** It can be tempting to allow your character to ramble on too much, making the character say everything you personally would like to say. Realize that a character can follow too many tracks of thought. Turner says of her own process that once "the words . . . start coming out in this new persona's voice, the ideas crowd in on each other, and before long I'm thinking, 'Okay, enough, you've got to stop now. This is getting too long.'" Use the same restraint with your character.

tip

Try to choose actions for the character that either complement what he is thinking or that are ironically opposite of it. For example, when Catherine is trying to discover whether someone has broken into her house, she stops to admire her hair in a mirror.

- ✔ **Remember the character's goal.** Although you want the character's goal to be clearly presented, be sure to include some elements that seem random or unplanned in order to maintain a sense of reality. Adding such elements may make your monologue longer, but it will keep the reader believing that the character is real.

For example, when a character hears a political advertisement on the radio, he begins to think of running for president himself. At the same time, however, an unopened envelope catches his eye and he absently reaches for it. It turns out to be a rejection letter from a law school. Even as he reads it, knowing that it has great bearing on his desire to be president someday, he still pursues his daydream of campaigning.

Revising

Sentence Energy
pp. 366–69

Quotation Marks
pp. 329–30

- ✔ **Read your monologue aloud.** Does it sound natural? Does it sound as though it is the record of a person's thinking? Do the details you have added to the monologue help or hinder this impression?
- ✔ **Use a balance of direct thoughts, indirect thoughts, speech, action, and description.** In the example about Catherine, the author sometimes lets us hear Catherine speak aloud, sometimes quotes her thoughts directly, sometimes summarizes her thoughts, and intersperses all of these techniques with action and description. How well did you balance these narrative modes in your monologue?

✔ **Add direct thoughts, indirect thoughts, speech, action, or description where needed.** Try not to have the same narrative mode dominate a section. You want the reader to notice the scene, not your method of creating it.

✔ **Allow a peer to evaluate the monologue.** Ask someone else to read the draft and tell you what he thinks of the character. Does his assessment match your intent? Ask him what questions came to his mind while he read. Listen carefully to his suggestions for making your monologue more interesting and believable.

✔ **Make changes to the monologue.** Compare your peer's comments about your monologue to your own observations about changes you want to make. Which changes are most important to make? Which ones will enhance the reader's enjoyment of the piece? Make changes for clarity and effect. Then proofread the monologue, checking for mistakes in grammar, usage, and spelling.

Publishing

✔ **Dramatize your monologue.** Make two copies of your monologue. Choose someone to act the part of your character. You will read the monologue as the other person pantomimes the scene. He will need to say aloud any lines the character actually speaks. Act out your scene for an audience.

✔ **Post your monologue on a website.** Allow others to share in your character's thoughts by posting the interior monologue either on a personal or class website. Encourage reader feedback to your piece.

✔ **Develop your monologue into a short story.** Use the character you have created to write a short story. Let the reader know whether your character accomplishes his goal.

✔ **Record your monologue.** Make a recording of all of the class monologues. Place the recording somewhere so that others can listen to the readings and then write their impressions of the monologues.

Some Ideas to Consider

History

- Write an interior monologue for a historical person at a crucial moment. For example, what might a soldier have been thinking as he prepared for the battle of Gettysburg? You might also imagine what Lincoln was thinking as he wrote his address to be delivered at Gettysburg after the battle.

Literature

- Write an interior monologue for a character from a classic novel.

GRAMMAR

PHRASES

Many English sentences contain groups of words that either add meaning to the subject, verb, or complement or replace a single-word subject or complement. These groups of words, both phrases and clauses, have a function in the sentence. A **phrase** is a group of related words that does not contain both a subject and a verb. Phrases can be divided into two types: **nonverbal phrases** and **verbal phrases.** Phrases may function as nouns, adjectives, or adverbs.

Nonverbal Phrases

Adjectives and Adverbs pp. 48–51

Prepositional Phrases

A **prepositional phrase** (the most frequently used of all the phrases) consists of a preposition, its object, and any modifiers of that object. The preposition shows a relationship between its object and another word in the sentence. Prepositional phrases function either as **adjectival prepositional phrases** that modify nouns or pronouns or as **adverbial prepositional phrases** that modify verbs, adjectives, or adverbs.

The elderly woman *with the tracts* arrived at the street corner.

This faithful woman stood *near the shipyard gate.*

She continued steadfast *in her purpose.*

To this woman, the task *before her* was one *of great importance.*

In some sentences an adjectival prepositional phrase will modify the object of a preceding prepositional phrase. In such sentences the second phrase is part of the first phrase because it is a modifier of the first.

She faithfully fulfilled her mission (*to the workers* (*of the shipyard*)).

(*On a cold winter night,*) she handed a salvation tract (*to a shipyard worker* (*from the local area*)).

Participial Phrase pp. 92–94

Absolute Phrases

An **absolute phrase** consists of a noun followed by a participle or participial phrase. The absolute phrase is independent (absolute) from the rest of the sentence. The phrase indicates a circumstance and loosely modifies the remainder of the sentence; the absolute phrase does not modify a specific word in the sentence.

When an adverb clause has a noun subject and expresses a circumstance, it can be reduced to an absolute phrase by the omission of the subordinating conjunction and replacement of the verb with the related participle.

ADVERB CLAUSE	*Because the woman was elderly,* the worker took the tract.
ABSOLUTE PHRASE	*The woman being elderly,* the worker took the tract.
ADVERB CLAUSE	*Because the woman was faithful in prayer,* the Holy Spirit began to work in the life of the shipyard worker.
ABSOLUTE PHRASE	*The woman being faithful in prayer,* the Holy Spirit began to work in the life of the shipyard worker.

Appositive Phrases

An **appositive** is a noun or pronoun that renames or identifies a preceding noun or pronoun. The appositive and its modifiers make up an **appositive phrase**. Most appositives are nouns; however, an appositive may be an intensive pronoun or a personal pronoun.

Dan, *the shipyard worker,* remembered the gospel tract in his pocket.

As he began to read the tract, Dan considered certain things: *God, life, and death.*

Dan *himself* saw his need of salvation.

Two workers, *Dan and he,* read their Bibles together.

Reflexive and Intensive Pronouns pp. 213–14

Although an appositive usually appears immediately after the word it is renaming, an appositive may appear later in the sentence. The sentence, however, could be written so that the appositive immediately follows the noun.

Eventually, all Dan's family members were saved: *Kathy, Matt, and Kara.*

Eventually, all Dan's family members—*Kathy, Matt, and Kara*—were saved.

Colon pp. 315–16

in SUMMARY

A **phrase** is a group of related words that does not contain both a subject and a verb.

A **prepositional phrase** consists of a preposition, its object, and any modifiers of that object. A preposition shows a relationship between its object and another word in the sentence.

Prepositional phrases are either **adjectival** or **adverbial**.

An **absolute phrase** is independent from the rest of the sentence. An absolute phrase consists of a noun followed by a participle or a participial phrase.

An **appositive** is a noun or pronoun that renames or identifies a preceding noun or pronoun.

An **appositive phrase** consists of an appositive and its modifiers.

4.1 PRACTICE *the skill*

Place parentheses around each prepositional phrase. Draw an arrow from each phrase to the word it modifies. Then label each phrase *Adj* (adjectival) or *Adv* (adverbial).

1. To the potential homeowner, the architecture of a house can be very important.

2. One style of house called Cape Cod has a steep roof, two or more dormer windows, and a door in the center of the front wall.

3. Other characteristics of Cape Cod houses include a chimney in the middle of the house, sometimes opening into several fireplaces in different rooms, and an exterior of wide clapboard siding.

4. There are dramatic differences between Cape Cod houses and Victorian Gothic houses.

5. Victorian Gothic houses have features like steep roofs, decorative windows, and chimneys that are grouped in a cluster.

6. The owner of a Victorian Gothic house could look down from his pinnacles and battlements, past oriel windows to a stately lawn.

7. The Victorian Gothic style was begun by Horace Walpole, a British writer of Gothic novels, who wanted his home to look like the castles in his writing.

8. In the United States today, ranch-style houses are quite common because of their simplicity and relaxed feeling.

9. During the 1950s, ranch houses were built throughout the country.

10. Ranch houses, with open and flexible interior space, usually have one story with a low-pitched roof and deep eaves.

4.2 PRACTICE *the skill*

Identify each italicized phrase as *prepositional*, *absolute*, or *appositive*.

_____ 1. Over the front door of a Georgian Colonial house sits a decorative crown, *an elaborate half-circle of wood or stone*.

_____ 2. Georgian Colonial, *a favorite style of the prosperous*, is the style of many imposing early dwellings.

_____ 3. The front door stands *between flattened columns*.

_____ 4. *The windows being most noticeable*, Georgian Colonial houses typically have rows of double-hung windows.

_____ 5. *On either end of a classical Georgian Colonial house* sits one or more chimneys.

_____ 6. One of three kinds of roofs covers a Georgian Colonial: *gabled, hipped, or gambrel style*.

_____ 7. *The roofs typically slanting down to the house with little overhang*, Georgian Colonial houses can easily be spotted.

_____ 8. Stratford, *Robert E. Lee's Virginia home*, exemplifies Georgian Colonial architecture.

_____ 9. The Old North Church *of Boston, Massachusetts*, is another example of the style.

_____ 10. *Inside the church* are arched and windowed balconies.

4.3 USE *the skill*

Use the given information to write a sentence that contains the kind of phrase indicated in parentheses.

1. Every homeowner should take steps to fireproof his home. (*prepositional*)

   _____

   _____

2. Gutters easily fill with debris. Potential debris includes leaves, pine needles, seeds, and trash. (*appositive*)

   _____

   _____

3. Gutters should be kept clear. The risk of a fire beginning on the roof decreases. (*absolute*)

   _____

   _____

4. A wildfire is very dangerous. Sparks can enter unscreened vents and set a house ablaze. *(prepositional)*

   _____
   _____

5. A chimney is safer with a cap. Sparks from the chimney will not start a fire in landscaping near the house. *(absolute)*

   _____
   _____

6. Faulty connections can spark a fire. Keep furnace and stove electrical plugs well repaired to reduce fire risks. *(prepositional)*

   _____
   _____

7. Overhanging tree limbs are a potential means of carrying fire to a house. Prune tree limbs so that they are at least ten feet from the house. *(appositive)*

   _____
   _____

8. Firewood is safest stored some distance from the house. A blaze in the woodpile will not spread to the house as easily. *(absolute)*

   _____
   _____

9. A messy yard full of tall grass and trailing vines is another fire hazard. Clean up and maintain such a lawn. *(appositive)*

   _____
   _____

10. An obscured or missing house number is problematic. Firefighters may have trouble finding a house. *(prepositional)*

    _____
    _____
    _____

Verbal Phrases

Parts of Speech
pp. 35–37,
42–45, 48–51

A **verbal** is a verb form used as another part of speech—a noun, an adjective, or an adverb. **Participles**, **gerunds**, and **infinitives** can function alone or as part of a phrase. A **verbal phrase** includes the verbal and any subjects, objects, or modifiers of the verbal. A verbal will not function as the simple predicate in a sentence.

Participles and Participial Phrases

Tense
pp. 178–79

A **participle** functions as an adjective. A **participial phrase** comprises a participle and any modifiers or complements of the participle. Basic participles use the present form of the verb and add a present- or past-tense ending (*-ing* or *-ed*, usually).

PARTICIPLE	The *approaching* basketball season will provide many opportunities to display school spirit.
	The *planned* schedule still needed some changes.
PARTICIPLE WITH MODIFIERS	The senior cheerleaders *chosen* **earlier in the school year** have prepared for the first pep rally.
PARTICIPLE WITH COMPLEMENTS (AND MODIFIERS)	*Repeating* the new **cheers** during the pep rally, the student body learned quickly.
	Having finished the **decorations** for the school gym, we were ready for the first game.

Present Participle

A **present participle** has an *-ing* ending attached to the first principal part of the verb. A present participle usually comes before the noun that it modifies and expresses action that is simultaneous with the main verb. A present participial phrase may appear before or after the word that it modifies.

A *cheering* crowd creates a feeling of anticipation.

The team *approaching the court first* was the opponent.

Settling into their offense, the Raiders handled the ball well.

A present participle may look like part of a progressive verb. However, a participle functions as an adjective, not as the predicate in a sentence.

PRESENT PARTICIPLE	*Dribbling* down the court, the player lost control of the ball.
PROGRESSIVE VERB	The player *was dribbling* the ball down the court.

ESL

If you have trouble distinguishing a progressive verb from a participle that follows a form of the linking verb *be (is, am, are, was, were)*, try changing the tense. Use *yesterday* and simple past tense, or use *tomorrow* and simple future tense. A progressive verb will lose its *-ing*, but a participle will not.

PROGRESSIVE VERB	The owner **is welcoming** guests to his restaurant. Yesterday the owner **welcomed** guests to his restaurant. Tomorrow the owner **will welcome** guests to his restaurant.
LINKING VERB + PARTICIPLE	That restaurant's décor is **welcoming**. Yesterday that restaurant's décor was **welcoming**. Tomorrow that restaurant's décor will be **welcoming**.

Also, you can sometimes add *very* before a participle: *It's* **very welcoming**. But *very* never modifies a progressive verb—or any other kind of verb. (Check with a native speaker of English if you are not sure whether a sentence sounds right.)

Past Participle

A **past participle** is the same as the third principal part of the verb. Past participles usually express a passive meaning. Past participles are formed from transitive verbs, and they modify the noun affected by the verb. On the other hand, when the third principal part of the verb is part of a simple predicate, a form of the helping verb *have* (*have, has, had*) will accompany the verb.

PAST PARTICIPLE	The *defeated* team soon began practices again.
	The team, *defeated because of inexperience,* soon began practices again.
PASSIVE MEANING	(*The team was defeated because of inexperience.*)
ACTIVE PREDICATE OF THE SENTENCE	The opposing team *has defeated* us every year.
PASSIVE PREDICATE OF THE SENTENCE	The team *had been defeated* by their inexperience but soon began practices again.

Perfect Participle

A **perfect participle** uses *having* with the third principal part of the verb. The perfect participle expresses an action that occurred or was completed before the action of the main verb.

Having practiced his free throws, the basketball player made all of his foul shots.

The coach, *having prepared* diligently during the week, substituted players freely.

Other Participles

Other less common participles, the **progressive passive participle** and the **perfect passive participle**, are easily recognized as participles because the first word of the phrase ends in *-ing*. Because these participles are passive, a form of *be* is present in the participial phrase. In the sentences below, the first revision uses a progressive passive participle, and the second revision uses a perfect passive participle, a form of *have* making it perfect. These kinds of participial phrases are helpful in sentence reduction.

LONGER	We are just completing a game, and it is our first victory of the season.
PROGRESSIVE PASSIVE PARTICIPLE	The game *being completed* will be our first victory of the season.
LONGER	The coach was called for an interview, but he did not reveal his game plan.
PERFECT PASSIVE PARTICIPLE	*Having been called* for an interview, the coach did not reveal his game plan.

in SUMMARY

A **verbal** is a verb form used as another part of speech.

A **verbal phrase** includes the verbal and any subjects, objects, or modifiers of the verbal.

A **present participle** has an *-ing* ending attached to the first principal part of the verb.

A **past participle** is the same as the third principal part of the verb.

A **perfect participle** uses *having* plus the third principal part of the verb.

Other participles, such as **progressive passive participle** and **perfect passive participle**, are helpful in sentence reduction.

4.4 PRACTICE *the skill*

Underline each participle or participial phrase. Draw an arrow from each participle to the word it modifies. Then identify the kind of participle as *present*, *past*, *perfect*, *perfect passive*, or *progressive passive*.

_____ 1. The persevering gardener carefully maintains his hedges.

_____ 2. Having planted the hedges in the ground, he prunes them to six or eight inches.

_____ 3. The pruned plants should develop a number of low branches, the foundation of the hedge.

_____ 4. Late in the season, the newly grown branches should be cut back about halfway.

_____ 5. Having been cut back, the hedge grows with new vigor.

_____ 6. A hedge with a shape of a descending wedge, widest at the bottom, thrives.

_____ 7. Being cut in a wedge-shape, the hedge receives sun and rain on all its branches.

_____ 8. Having flattened the top of a hedge, the gardener may have inadvertently weakened the hedge.

_____ 9. A rounded hedge has no ledge for heavy snow.

_____ 10. Having been carefully nurtured and shaped, a good hedge becomes an elegant screen, wall, or border.

4.5 USE *the skill*

To improve the conciseness of the following paragraph, rewrite the paragraph using eight participles or participial phrases. Underline the new participles or participial phrases.

One requirement for roses that bloom beautifully is regular care. After the gardener has planted a bush or shrub rose, he must prune it to only twelve to twenty-four inches in height. Thereafter, he must prune the rosebush every year in order to remove canes that have withered or died and to promote growth. A shrub rose that is pruned correctly should have the canes cut back by one-third of their height. Roses that climb require less care. Once a climbing rose has been trained to grow on its supports, the plant needs only moderate care. Once the gardener has identified any canes that have been damaged, he should cut the canes at least an inch below the damage. A rosebush that is well tended can produce lovely blooms for years.

Gerunds and Gerund Phrases

A **gerund** is a verb form used as a noun. Like nouns, gerunds can be subjects, direct objects, predicate nouns, objects of the preposition, appositives, and occasionally indirect objects.

    S   TrV   DO
Campaigning will improve a student's ability to interact with others.

    S (App.)   TrV   DO
His main goal, *winning,* should not affect his principles.

    S   TrV   IO   DO
The candidate gave *campaigning* his undivided attention.

The *-ing* ending is the indicator for a gerund. Distinguishing a present participle from a gerund depends on discernment of the function of the verbal in the sentence.

PRESENT PARTICIPLE	The *campaigning* students will have an opportunity to address the student body.
GERUND	*Campaigning* requires time and preparation.

A gerund and its modifiers and complements make up a **gerund phrase**. In a sentence, the gerund phrase functions as a single unit to perform a noun function.

       S   OP   LV   PA
The job of *preparing* materials for an election can be overwhelming.

     S   LV   PN
Choosing a campaign committee was a difficult task.

                 S LV   PN
The chairman's task was *determining* an effective plan.

                        S   TrV   DO
Early in the campaign, the chairman does his best *planning*.

Because gerunds are verb forms, gerunds can have subjects, complements, and modifiers. The "subject" of a gerund is actually a possessive adjective such as *his*, *my*, or *Tom's* that identifies the doer of the gerund's action.

    The candidate found that *adopting* a friendlier demeanor made people more likely to listen to him.

    The candidate found that **his** *adopting* a friendlier demeanor made people more likely to listen to him.

In the first sentence it is unclear whether the candidate or the people adopt a friendlier demeanor. Adding *his* as the subject of the gerund clarifies the meaning.

In addition, the use of a possessive as the "subject" of a gerund avoids confusion between a gerund and a participle that modifies a noun.

    The committee does not approve of that person planning the campaign for me.

    The committee does not approve of that **person's** *planning* the campaign for me.

Pronouns with Gerunds pp. 209–10

In the first sentence, the disapproval of the person is indicated. However, in the second sentence, the disapproval is of the planning.

A common error occurs when writers use an objective case pronoun as the "subject" of a gerund instead of a possessive case pronoun as the "subject." An understanding of sentence reduction will help to clarify this problem.

        S   TrV   DO
The students understood [that he campaigned vigorously for the position.]

        S   TrV   DO
The students understood his campaigning vigorously for the position.

It would be incorrect to write *The students understood him campaigning vigorously for the position.* The idea is not that the students understood *him* but that they understood his action.

ESL A gerund is the verb form that can serve as an object of a preposition.
Your goal **of** *running a race each month* is impressive.

Present Gerund

The **present gerund**, like the present participle, is identified by the *-ing* ending on the first principal part of the verb. A present gerund expresses action that occurs simultaneously with that of the main verb.

Running for an important office takes hours of preparation.

The candidate's goal should be *running an ethical campaign.*

When a gerund functions as a modifying noun, it looks very similar to a present participle. Based upon the context of the sentence, a modifying noun has a meaning different from that of a present participle.

PARTICIPLE | The candidate was supported by all his *writing* friends, some of whom wrote excellent letters to the newspaper.

GERUND | Gerald sat at his *writing* desk, working on a new brochure.

Modifying Nouns
p. 50

In the first sentence *writing* is a participle that tells what the friends do. In the second sentence *writing* is a gerund functioning as a modifying noun. The desk is not doing the writing; it is "a desk for writing."

Perfect Gerund

The **perfect gerund** uses *having* and the third principal part of the verb. A perfect gerund expresses action that occurred before the action of the main verb.

                S   LV   PN

The candidate's primary accomplishment was *having raised* an enormous amount of money for his campaign.

      S   TrV   IO   DO

His *having run* for office in the past gives him valuable experience.

Passive Gerund

Another kind of gerund is the **passive gerund**, which uses a form of *be* just before the third principal part of the verb. The first example sentence contains a **present passive gerund**. The second example sentence contains a **perfect passive gerund**. The action of the perfect passive gerund occurs before the action of the main verb.

      S   TrV   DO

Being coached in debate skills prepared the candidate for the student body debate.

                 S   TrV   DO

The slogan's *having been approved* by the faculty advisor created a feeling of anticipation.

in SUMMARY

A **gerund** is a verb form used as a noun.

The **gerund phrase** consists of a gerund and its modifiers and complements.

A **present gerund** uses the first principal part of the verb and the *-ing* ending.

A **perfect gerund** (*having* plus the third principal part of the verb) expresses action that occurred before the action of the main verb.

Passive gerunds express passive meanings. A **perfect passive gerund** expresses action that occurred before the action of the main verb.

4.6 PRACTICE *the skill*

Underline each gerund or gerund phrase. Identify its function as subject *(S)*, direct object *(DO)*, predicate noun *(PN)*, indirect object *(IO)*, object of the preposition *(OP)*, or appositive *(App)*.

1. Having moved to a foreign country requires missionaries to adapt to new accomodations.

2. Some missionaries must adjust to hot tropical temperatures without enjoying the luxury of air conditioning.

3. Their having built a home indicates the missionaries' commitment to their new culture.

4. Some missionary families give constructing their homes careful attention.

5. In warm climates a necessity is having numerous windows for cross-ventilation.

6. Carpet is often unavailable, so the family must choose between concrete's being poured and tile's being laid.

7. Some families eagerly anticipate having adapted to local wildlife.

8. Some missionaries choose sleeping under mosquito nets for protection from insects; others sleep in hammocks.

9. One luxury, having electricity, is limited for many missionaries unless they have generators.

10. Using grass mats on the floors and brightly colored tropical decorations on the walls may give the missionary home a local look.

4.7 USE the skill

Rewrite each sentence by replacing the italicized word or phrase with a gerund or a gerund phrase and making other changes as needed.

1. When I learned that color affects mood, I gave serious consideration *to a redecoration of the rooms of my house.*

2. Color can influence *a person to gain or lose energy or stress.*

3. *Walls that have been painted a warm color* cause a small room to seem smaller and more confining.

4. *To put cool colors on the walls of small rooms* makes them appear to expand.

5. *A room that is decorated in hues of red and orange* increases a person's appetite; therefore, these are good colors for a dining room.

6. *It had been painted deep purple*, the color of royalty, and that made my living room appear quite elegant.

7. I found that a good way to help me to relax at night was *to have my bedroom painted in blue tones.*

8. *The use of light yellow paint* helped me create a bright, cheerful kitchen.

9. *I painted the exterior of the house light brown* because I hoped to convey strength and practicality.

   _____

   _____

10. *The completion of my color scheme* allowed me to relax in a more comfortable environment than before.

    _____

    _____

Infinitives and Infinitive Phrases

Unlike participles and gerunds, which function as only one part of speech, the **infinitive** is a verbal that can function as a noun, as an adjective, or as an adverb. The infinitive consists of the word *to* plus a verb form.

Simple Infinitive

The **simple infinitive** is made up of the word *to* and the first principal part of a verb. The word *to* is considered the "sign" of the infinitive. The word *to* plus an uninflected verb is never a prepositional phrase.

INFINITIVE AS NOUN	*To answer* cheerfully is a desired characteristic.
INFINITIVE AS ADJECTIVE	Cheerfulness is a personal quality *to develop*.
INFINITIVE AS ADVERB	A cheerful disposition is important *to encourage* others.
PREPOSITIONAL PHRASE	A cheerful countenance draws people *to you*.

Prepositional Phrase pp. 53–54

> Do not confuse the *to* of the infinitive with the preposition *to*, especially when the preposition *to* is followed by a gerund as its object.
>
> **RIGHT** | For daily exercise, Jeannine prefers walking **to running**.
> **WRONG** | For daily exercise, Jeannine prefers walking ~~to run~~.

Infinitives may have "subjects," modifiers, and complements. The "subject" of an infinitive is in the objective case. An **infinitive phrase** includes the infinitive, its "subject" if applicable, and all of its complements and modifiers. The entire infinitive phrase can function as a noun, an adjective, or an adverb.

Pronouns with Infinitives p. 210

```
      S   LV    PN
My goal is to drink only two cups of coffee today.

           S  LV     PN
The coffee shop is the place to buy good coffee.

     S    TrV              DO
The clerk was leaving the counter to pour more coffee.

 S    TrV       DO
We wanted him to pour our coffee.
```

Perfect Infinitive

The auxiliary *have* can also be part of an infinitive. The **perfect infinitive** uses *to*, the auxiliary *have*, and the third principal part of a verb. The perfect infinitive expresses action that takes place before the action of the main verb of the sentence.

SIMPLE INFINITIVE	I am happy *to meet* you for lunch.
PERFECT INFINITIVE	When you called, I was happy *to have kept* my schedule free for the afternoon.

In the first example, the actions of being happy and meeting the person occur at the same time. The second example means "I am happy (now) because I kept my schedule free (earlier)." A sentence with *have* in both the main verb and the infinitive is usually wrong.

WRONG	I would have liked *to have met* you for coffee and pie.
RIGHT	I would have liked *to meet* you for coffee and pie.
	I would like *to have met* you for coffee and pie.

Passive Infinitive

Since transitive verbs can be passive, infinitives formed from transitive verbs can also be passive. A **passive infinitive** consists of *to*, the auxiliary *be*, and the third principal part of a verb. A passive infinitive shows that something is being acted upon.

SIMPLE	I want *to greet* you at the coffee shop.
PASSIVE	At the coffee shop, we want *to be greeted*.

A **perfect passive infinitive** adds the auxiliaries *have* (perfect) and *been* (passive) to the simple infinitive. The action of the perfect passive infinitive occurs before that of the main verb.

At the coffee shop, we were pleased *to have been greeted* by many.

Progressive Infinitive

A **progressive infinitive** indicates continuing action. The progressive infinitive consists of the word *to*, the auxiliary *be*, and a verb with an *-ing* ending.

My brother did not want *to be waiting* in line at the coffee shop.

His goal was *to be drinking* his coffee before the crowd arrived.

Elliptical *to* in Infinitives

An infinitive may appear without the sign of the infinitive (*to*). If the *to* in an infinitive sounds awkward, it can be omitted. Sometimes the *to* is included only in more formal English.

CORRECT	For hot coffee, the best thing to do is *wait until it cools.*
FORMAL	For hot coffee, the best thing to do is **to** *wait until it cools.*

Some verbs are more likely to be followed by a gerund (*enjoy, avoid, admit, finish, risk, consider, appreciate, understand,* and so forth). These verbs often refer to something that has already happened.

> Marvin finished **writing** a letter to his grandmother.

Some verbs are more likely to be followed by an infinitive (*want, wish, offer, hope, decide, ask, plan, wait,* and so forth). These verbs often refer to something only wished for or planned but not yet fulfilled.

> Marvin plans **to write** her a letter each week.

Some verbs can be used with either meaning.

> Marvin likes **writing** letters to his friends and relatives.
> He would like **to write** to a missionary family too.

in SUMMARY

An **infinitive** is a verbal that can function as a noun, an adjective, or an adverb.

A **simple infinitive** uses *to*, the sign of the infinitive, in addition to the first principal part of the verb.

An **infinitive phrase** consists of an infinitive, its "subject" if applicable, and any modifiers and complements of the infinitive.

A **perfect infinitive** consists of *to* plus the auxiliary *have* and the third principal part of the verb. The perfect infinitive expresses action that takes place before that of the main verb.

A **passive infinitive** consists of *to* plus the auxiliary *be* and the third principal part of the verb. The passive infinitive expresses action that is done to something.

A **perfect passive infinitive** consists of *to* followed by *have* and *been* and the third principal part of the verb.

A **progressive infinitive** indicates progressive action. A progressive infinitive consists of *to*, a form of *be*, and a verb with an *-ing* ending.

An **elliptical infinitive** is an infinitive in which the *to* is understood and not stated.

4.8 PRACTICE the skill

Underline each infinitive phrase. Then identify its function as noun (N), adjective (Adj), or adverb (Adv).

_____ 1. An opportunity to visit a traditional Japanese house should not be missed.

_____ 2. The floor of the house, like a very large chair, is intended to be used for sitting.

_____ 3. The owners of the house wanted the floor to be a pattern of tatami mats (straw and rush floor coverings).

_____ 4. The need to have portable furniture arises from the flexible nature of the house.

_____ 5. The best way of accommodating guests is to reconfigure the rooms.

_____ 6. Our friends were happy to have built a home in time-honored Japanese style.

_____ 7. At our visit Akiko and Ken had completed their traditional house; they had not wanted to be finishing the house during our stay.

_____ 8. Ken and Akiko did little with bamboo in building their house except create a fence surrounding the house and lands; much more bamboo is used inside the house.

_____ 9. We were thrilled to have seen the movable walls, *fusama* and *shoji*.

_____ 10. To have been invited to a traditional Japanese tea is an honor.

4.9 USE *the skill*

Combine each pair of sentences into one sentence by replacing one of the sentences with an infinitive phrase. Then identify the kind of infinitive in the new sentence as *simple, passive, perfect, perfect passive, progressive,* or *elliptical*.

_____ 1. Experts offered families tips for protection against burglars. The experts were pleased that the tips were helpful.

_____ 2. Many security systems are designed with special features. Some systems provide a link between emergency units and homes.

_____ 3. When away on vacation, use security lights with motion detectors. Security lights give the appearance that someone is home.

_____ 4. We were aware of something suspicious. We were fortunate when we noticed the stranger.

_____ 5. Burglars watched a house from surrounding shrubbery for several days. This was known.

_____
_____

_____ 6. This door isn't safe. It has only simple door locks rather than deadbolts.

_____
_____

_____ 7. Wide-angle peepholes should be installed on the exterior doors. We hope that we can start next month.

_____
_____

_____ 8. Lock all doors and windows even when at home. This is another precaution.

_____
_____

_____ 9. A homeowner could go to the pet store and get a dog. The dog might protect him.

_____
_____

_____ 10. Emergency responders like house numbers that are visible from the road. Looking for a number during an emergency is not what they want.

_____
_____

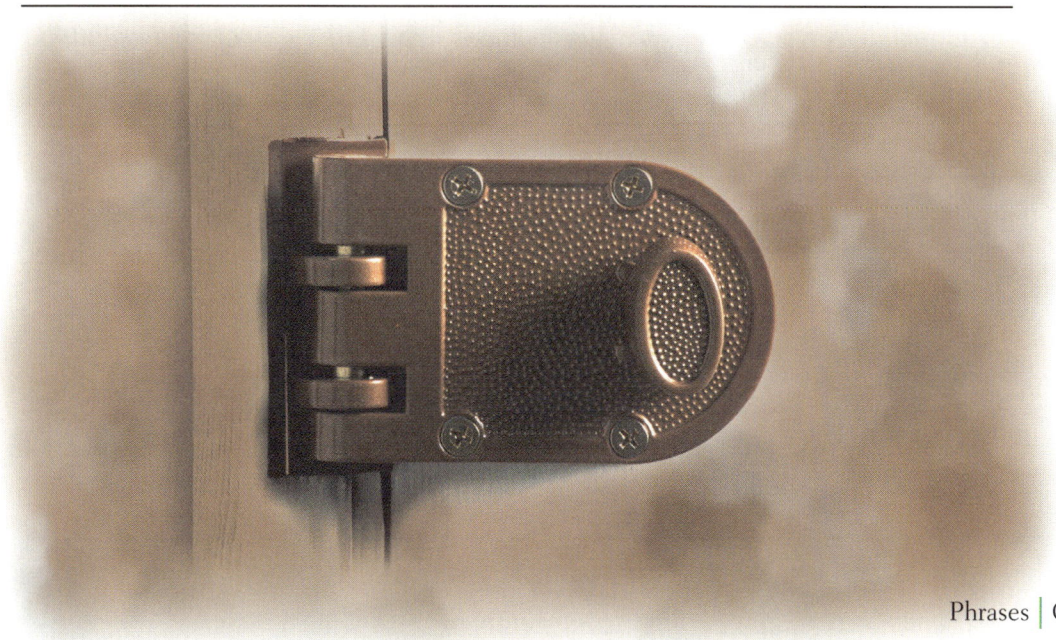

CUMULATIVE *review*

Label the sentence patterns in each of the sentences. In the first blank identify the italicized word or phrase as prepositional *(Prep)*, appositive *(App)*, absolute *(Abs)*, participial *(Part)*, gerund *(Ger)*, or infinitive *(Inf)*. Then identify the function of the word or phrase as noun *(N)*, adjective *(Adj)*, or adverb *(Adv)*. (Do not identify a function for an absolute phrase.)

_____ _____ 1. Ancient Egyptian houses *made from kiln-dried mud brick* had earthen floors and mud-plaster walls.

_____ _____ 2. *Pharaoh's daughter having rescued Moses from the bulrushes,* the royal household increased in size.

_____ _____ 3. For Moses' family, *having a limited amount of wood and living a nomadic existence* made owning furniture unlikely.

_____ _____ 4. One piece of furniture, *a stool of three or four legs with animal carvings,* existed in the homes of commoners and royalty.

_____ _____ 5. Common people like Moses' family chose *to paint the stools and furniture for a more expensive appearance.*

_____ _____ 6. The nobles, on the other hand, were able *to enjoy fine furniture and decorations.*

_____ _____ 7. People of wealth decorated their furniture by rubbing the furniture *with gold and silver leaf.*

_____ _____ 8. Some houses had *painted* walls and leather wall hangings.

_____ _____ 9. Differing from his previous common surroundings, Moses' daily experience included *seeing furniture with gold and silver leaf.*

_____ _____ 10. In spite of these luxurious surroundings, Moses was determined *not to forget the God of his fathers.*

FROM THE WRITTEN WORD

Formulating the Details

Narration does not often exist as an independent rhetorical strategy but frequently combines with another strategy such as description. A description may be of an idea, an object, or an event. Before Adam and Eve's sin, punishment was nonexistent. After their disobedience to God, however, three punishments were described: the snake's in Genesis 3:14, the woman's in Genesis 3:16, and the man's in Genesis 3:17–19.

Within the narrative warning of the coming Flood is a description of the ark that preserved Noah and his family. The narration regarding the young Moses being hid from the Egyptians includes a description of a smaller, protective ark. Later in Exodus, Moses stands before the people and speaks God's command to build yet another ark with an even greater purpose: to provide the place where God would commune with His people.

> And they shall make an ark of [acacia] wood: two cubits and a half shall be the length thereof, and a cubit and a half the breadth thereof, and a cubit and a half the height thereof. And thou shalt overlay it with pure gold, within and without shalt thou overlay it, and shalt make upon it a crown of gold round about. (Exod. 25:10–11)

Joshua, Israel's new leader after the death of Moses, describes his personal experiences leading Israel. At Jericho he describes victory based on obedience, but at Ai he describes defeat because of one man's disobedience. In Joshua 10:12–13 Joshua describes a momentous occurrence in the lives of the Israelites. Not only does God fight for Israel by causing great stones to fall upon the enemy, but God also allows Joshua to record a miraculous answer to prayer.

> And he [Joshua] said in the sight of Israel, Sun, stand thou still upon Gibeon; and thou, Moon, in the valley of Ajalon. And the sun stood still, and the moon stayed, until the people had avenged themselves upon their enemies. (Josh. 10:12–13)

Personal Response

Read Psalm 121. Reflect upon a time when this or another psalm was of particular encouragement to you. Write a personal narrative that illustrates Psalm 121.

Persuasive Essay | 110
Clauses | 116
Think About It | 141

PERSUASIVE ESSAY Writing
CLAUSES Grammar

5

A successful persuasive essay presents facts logically and influences the reader to take specific action. Have you ever felt so strongly about a current issue that you have even thought about writing a letter to your local newspaper? Or have you and your friends entered into a lively discussion about some particular idea? In either of these situations, you are trying to persuade someone to accept your position. Notice how Charlotte K. Frank's article "Signs of the Times: Littering the Verbal Landscape" presents specific examples to support her strong outcry against "littering" and urges her readers to take action to correct the problem.

Signs of the Times: Littering the Verbal Landscape *by Charlotte K. Frank*

Why can't kids spell today? While there are no doubt lots of reasons, one may have to do with signs I've been seeing lately on the shops and in the streets of New York.

One large sign on a fence around an empty lot in the Bronx, for example, reads: "Will *Built* to Suit."

Not far from the United Nations, above an art and framing shop, massive block letters advertise: "Jackie Kennedy: An Exhibition of *Photograghs.*"

The sign above a convenience store in Westchester County notes that the establishment sells *"Stationary."* And the awning of a store near Times Square that sells musical instruments announces the availability of *"Harmonica's, Metronome's, Flute's, Trumpet's, Violin's."*

New York is not, of course, alone. I saw this warning posted on a boat docked in Puerto Rico: "Keep *water tight* door *close* at all times."

If I *rote* this *peace* the *weigh* many *sighns* are written, *u wood* understand why many kids can't spell or send grammatically correct letters.

Such mistakes may be worth a laugh—but it's a laugh at the expense of our children. The reason: The signs around us are among the tools that model for children how to use words and spell them—skills they'll need later to get good jobs, support themselves, and become intelligent citizens.

Signs are a time-honored teaching tool. In a kindergarten classroom, simple signs introduce children to the alphabet, the sounds of letters, and the words that identify the objects around them. Can you imagine the reaction of the student whose teacher marks "photogragh" wrong on a spelling test and who then sees the same misspelling on a large sign on the corner store?

Thinking Biblically

Why learn to spell well? Charlotte Frank points ultimately to two reasons in her essay: spelling is a skill needed to make money and to become an intelligent citizen. These are certainly legitimate reasons for learning to spell, but Christians seek deeper, more lasting purposes in life. For example, good spelling is an essential skill for writing anything persuasive. As Frank contends in her essay, people will ignore ideas—no matter how good they may be—if the writer cannot spell. Since Christians have the most important message in the world, they ought to be "ready always to give an answer" to anyone who asks the reason for the hope in them (1 Pet. 3:15). Some Christians are called to stand and debate—persuasively—with a hostile culture, just as Paul did (Acts 18:4). Some are called to persuade not so much by argument as by offering a compelling and beautiful vision of the way things ought to be. Either of these tasks becomes increasingly difficult for a person who cannot spell.

Businesses with such linguistically challenged signs also do themselves a disservice. When I need notepaper and pass a store that sells "stationary," I unconsciously ask myself, as a former teacher, what quality of notepaper will I find there? I pass it by. Jacqueline Kennedy was a woman dedicated to the quality of furnishings in the White House and protecting the landmark status of buildings in New York City. When I see a display of her "photogrgahs," I find myself questioning the care and authenticity that went into that exhibit and wonder how Jackie would have reacted. I pass it by. I have no plans to "built" a building on that empty lot—but if I did, I wonder how well I could communicate my ideas with its owner. I would pass it by.

To help ensure properly spelled signs, wouldn't it be nice, the First Amendment notwithstanding, if we could impose a fine on the sign painter or the storeowner who litters the verbal landscape just as others litter the sidewalks? Isn't the damaging of our country's most precious property, the developing minds of our children, a crime? We have a rating system for software and movies to protect our children from inappropriate content. How about demanding a standard of quality for the signs they see in their world?

Legislation and rulemaking aside, there may be a simpler way to get the job done. Each of us can become a one-person "Literacy Squad." When we see a misspelled sign, we can simply walk into that store and, factually and politely, point out the mistake as well as the possibility of the store's losing customers. Some shopkeepers will welcome the information; others may respond with some version of "mind your own business." But I suggest that helping our children learn how to spell properly, to use words correctly, to communicate effectively, and to grow up to be intelligent citizens and neighbors *is* part of our business.

Providing an environment that encourages children to spell, punctuate, and use words and sentences correctly is critical for an educated and literate society. This will help reinforce and extend what they learn in school. Let's leave no sign unscrutinized.

© McGraw-Hill Companies, Inc.

PERSUASIVE ESSAY

Then Agrippa said unto Paul, Almost thou persuadest me to be a Christian.
Acts 26:28

A persuasive essay asserts that one idea is more legitimate than another idea, motivates the reader to adopt a certain point of view, and urges the reader to take a particular action. Although efforts to persuade are apparent in many areas of our lives, they are quite evident in the political realm. Consider reporters who described President George W. Bush's plans as "divisive" or his speech as "bellicose." What were the reporters trying to do?

Another example of persuasive writing is a gospel tract. The tract presents organized facts in the form of a personal testimony or a series of Bible verses. In either case the purpose is to persuade the reader to acknowledge his sin and accept Christ as his personal Savior. In Acts 26 Paul gives his personal testimony to win Agrippa. In fact, Paul speaks directly to Agrippa: "King Agrippa, believest thou the prophets? I know that thou believest" (Acts 26:27). Agrippa had knowledge of these facts, but he failed to act upon that knowledge.

Charlotte K. Frank presents a two-fold discussion of the sign problem. Not only are children affected by the inaccuracies of the signs, but also the businesses compromise their integrity. Frank goes beyond informing the reader of the problem. She admonishes the reader to action: "Each of us can become a one-person 'Literacy Squad.'" She combines factual information and emotional appeal with the purpose of doing something about the situation.

Plan and write a three-paragraph persuasive essay on a topic of your choice.

Planning

✓ **Choose a topic.** At this point you are ready to choose a topic for your essay. What current issues do you feel strongly about? Is there a product you believe lives up to its claims? Are there social changes that need to be adopted? Be sure to choose a topic that is controversial. You should be able to state a "pro" and a "con" position about the topic and, keeping Philippians 4:8 in mind, be able to take either position for your essay. For this writing assignment, however, you will be either "pro" or "con," not both.

- Consider some obvious sources that are available to you.
- Consider ideas and issues about which you feel strongly.
- Consult the list of ideas you have compiled in your journal or on your computer.
- Read newspaper or magazine articles on controversial issues.
- Brainstorm with a friend.

As you consider the persuasive essay, keep in mind that Charlotte Frank has been involved in education all of her life. She earned a PhD in education, served on the New York City Board of Education, and became vice president of McGraw-Hill Education. Her life-long goal has been excellence in education. Knowing this background, you find it easy to understand her choice of a topic.

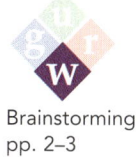
Brainstorming
pp. 2–3

You, too, have had experiences that have influenced your life, and you have interests that cause you to feel strongly about certain subjects. You may have been involved in a youth group that participated in a short-term summer mission trip. As a result of your participation on that mission team, your attitude toward being a pastor or youth pastor or a Christian teacher may have changed. Because of the change in your life, you may now feel strongly about the opportunities that a mission trip provides. Or perhaps you know someone with a particular hobby. As you have interacted with that person, you may have seen the enjoyment and education derived from that hobby. You might choose to persuade another person to adopt the same hobby.

✔ **Narrow your topic.** As you consider the three-paragraph assignment, you will need to limit the scope of your topic. For example, three paragraphs would not be sufficient to persuade someone concerning the impact of modern education or the decision for school vouchers.

Broad Idea	Limited Idea
football	compensation for NFL players
education	history class
shopping	Internet shopping (eBay)
collectibles	Byers Carolers

✔ **Consider the audience.** Since the purpose of your writing is to persuade, your audience should have views different from your own. Be careful, though, that the audience is not made too hostile by your confrontation. You must maintain a rational approach in order to persuade your audience. As you consider your audience in relation to your topic, ask yourself these questions.

- How much does my audience know about my topic?
- Is my audience opinionated or apathetic?
- Do I agree on any point with my audience?

The closing paragraphs of Frank's article reveal her audience. "Each of us can become a one-person 'Literacy Squad.'" She emphasizes that helping our children "*is* part of our business."

✔ **Gather information.** Gather information to support your position. Charlotte Frank needed only to observe what was all around her. Depending on the topic, you may find that your surroundings are a source of information. However, it may be necessary for you to go beyond your own knowledge and experience. For current information read magazine articles, newspaper reports, and editorials. You might consider interviewing a person who is an authority on your topic. In the library, consult books that might be helpful to you. Remember that statistics, first-hand observations, and expert testimony must come from credible sources in order to give support to your writing. An interesting example or anecdote is useful in the introduction to gain the reader's attention.

Drafting

✔ **Determine your position and state the thesis clearly.** The thesis is a one-sentence proposition or statement of your main idea and is the guiding sentence for your essay. Remember to be thoughtful and rational as you determine your position and as you choose the language of your essay. Although a subject may have logical arguments for or against it, you must determine your position and hold to it. Do not begin to write the essay without first developing the thesis statement.

You must remember that your primary purpose is to persuade the reader that your thesis is valid. You may have other purposes in your essay, but unless you achieve your primary purpose, all others will fall by the wayside. You must commit yourself to your thesis. Believe that you are right and then prove what you have proposed.

Limited Idea	**Thesis Statement**
compensation for NFL players	Compensation for NFL players is excessive.
history class	Mrs. Franz's teaching reveals her competence and understanding in World History.
Internet Shopping (eBay)	Internet shopping will not replace mall shopping.
Byers Carolers	Purchasing a Byers Caroler is an investment.

What do you think is the thesis of Frank's article? What idea does she want to prove? Why is she writing this essay?

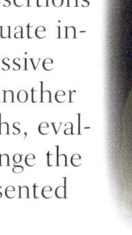

✔ **Organize information.** If you are making several assertions about your topic, be sure that you have secured adequate information about each point. Avoid presenting an excessive amount of information about one idea and slighting another idea. If your essay contains multiple middle paragraphs, evaluate the material you have about each point and arrange the middle paragraphs so that your strongest point is presented immediately prior to the concluding paragraph.

In the article by Frank, notice how she moves from the importance of signs as a teaching tool for the kindergarten child to the necessity of accuracy in spelling for the older child. Then she moves to the importance of correct signs for businesses. Ultimately she shows how important correctness is in many areas of life.

Organization pp. 14–17

✔ **Develop a successful introductory paragraph.** The introductory paragraph should gain the reader's attention. Perhaps you could use a true story or an anecdote to get the reader thinking about your topic. Storytelling has long been recognized as one of the best ways to get a message across to an audience. In addition to using a story or anecdote, you might present a fact or statistic to gain your reader's attention.

For example, Frank begins her essay with the question "Why can't kids spell today?" Then she uses various examples to show the importance of correctness in signs: "Will *Built* to Suit," "*Harmonica's, Metronome's, Flute's, Trumpet's, Violin's*," and "Keep *water tight* door *close* at all times." After her various examples, she moves to the thesis of her essay.

The introductory paragraph should close with a well-constructed thesis statement that gives the main idea of the essay. In her essay Frank uses more than one paragraph to gain the reader's attention. Read the last sentence of paragraph seven. Here you will see her purpose for writing.

✔ **Develop supporting middle paragraphs.** Whether you write a single middle paragraph or several, begin the paragraph with a topic sentence that gives direction to the paragraph. Organize your supporting information in such a way that you present your strongest ideas last.

✔ **Develop a strong conclusion.** The concluding paragraph begins with a restatement of the thesis of the essay. Based upon the information that you have presented in the middle paragraph, you are now ready to urge your reader to take some kind of action in relation to your topic.

In the closing paragraph, Charlotte Frank restates her thesis or main purpose for writing: "Providing an environment that encourages children to spell, punctuate, and use words and sentences correctly is critical for an educated and literate society." She admonishes her readers to "leave no sign unscrutinized."

Persuasive Essay | Chapter 5

Paragraph Development p. 11

Document Sources p. 268

Biased Language pp. 390–91

✓ **Give concrete examples.** You will increase the credibility of your position by including examples that support your position. Examples are interesting as well as necessary. In Charlotte Frank's article, the examples help support her position. How much clearer it is to show an example of multiple apostrophe errors than to list the rules about the apostrophe.

Remember that you must document any source that you quote, paraphrase, or summarize in your paper.

✓ **Use persuasive language effectively.** Many words have both a denotative and a connotative meaning. Denotative meanings are their literal definitions, and connotative meanings are their emotional associations. Although both types of word usage may be present in a piece of writing, you must remember not to rely heavily on connotative language but to present sound evidence to persuade your reader.

Consider the following two words: *disappointment* and *dud*. Both of these words have similar definitions. Yet your emotional responses to these words are probably very different. Referring to someone as a *disappointment* conveys the idea of his not meeting certain expectations but does not conjure strong emotional feeling. On the other hand, referring to someone as a *dud* implies strong condemnation and elicits a far different response. Connotative language can be very important because your reader's personal feelings can influence his response to your writing.

The Christian writer must avoid giving unnecessary offense. One of the most common types of offense is the use of a stereotype. A **stereotype** is an oversimplified generalization of a person or an event—usually based on ignorance, malice, or carelessness. Stereotypes continue because people do not take the time to gather all the information needed for a fair judgment about people or situations. Many generalizations that are based completely on age, cultural or ethnic background, gender, race, or physical characteristics have no place in the Christian's spoken or written communication. The Scriptures warn us that "a brother offended is harder to be won than a strong city: and their contentions are like the bars of a castle" (Prov. 18:19). Do not allow your stereotypical references to hamper your effectiveness in presenting the gospel.

For the examples and the entire paper, be sure to write in active voice.

✓ **Determine the action that the reader should take.** What is your purpose in writing this essay? Do you want the reader simply to read your essay with no motivation to change? Or do you want the reader to take some action? Charlotte Frank is clear in her purpose: The reader must "become a one-person 'Literacy Squad.'" Although the prospect of legislation on the matter of inaccurate signs is highly unlikely, each person can wage his own war against inaccuracies.

In the concluding paragraph of her essay, Frank begins by restating her thesis idea: "Providing an environment . . . is critical for an educated and literate society." She emphasizes again the action that she wants her readers to follow: "Let's leave no sign unscrutinized."

Revising

✓ **Allow yourself time to read your essay carefully.** As you read your essay, ask yourself whether you have presented a clear purpose for your writing and whether you have accomplished that purpose. Does the introductory paragraph compel the reader to go on? Does the middle paragraph present well-organized, accurate information that would persuade the reader to agree with you? Is the conclusion clear about what you want the reader to do?

✔ **Evaluate your style.** At this stage of revision, search for opportunities to use precise words and fresh vocabulary that convey your thoughts clearly. Avoiding clichés and overused words will give life and variety to your writing. In addition to these considerations, read for smoothness and conciseness.

✔ **Revise for correctness.** As you wrote your essay, you were probably concentrating on content rather than on correctness. Now you have the opportunity to carefully consider sentence structure and usage. Be sure to check for correct spelling, punctuation, and capitalization.

Publishing

✔ **Choose a title.** Now that you have polished your writing, you need to choose an appropriate title for your essay. The title should be specific and could suggest the approach of your essay.

✔ **Make a neat copy.** Type or print a final copy to submit to your teacher. The copy should be error free and should meet the standards established by your teacher.

✔ **Adapt the information for a speech.** If you are taking a speech class, you may be able to use the information in your essay for a persuasive speech. If the topic is a current issue, perhaps you could give the speech at a town meeting.

✔ **Consider writing a tract.** If your persuasive essay is based on a Christian topic, you might consider working it into a tract for publication.

✔ **Post your writing on your class website.** If your class has a website, you might choose to post your writing there. Be sure that the copy is free of errors.

✔ **Include the writing in your writing folder.** Depending on the topic that you have chosen, you might also be able to use the information you researched for a future assignment.

Some Ideas to Consider

History
- Should the United States have a more restrictive policy concerning immigration?
- Should acceptance into a college or university be based on a quota system?

Social Studies
- Should motorcyclists be required by law to wear helmets?
- Should your state require bilingual public education programs?

Mathematics
- Should a high school math program include two years of algebra?
- Should the use of a calculator be accepted in basic math courses?

Health
- Should a high school student use a weight-loss substance?

GRAMMAR

CLAUSES

Subjects and Predicates pp. 70–71

Kinds of Sentences p. 69

Subordination pp. 364–65

Every sentence consists of at least one clause. A **clause** is a group of related words that contains both a subject and a predicate. An **independent clause** can stand alone as a sentence. A **dependent clause** cannot stand alone; it functions within a sentence as a modifier or in place of a noun. Each dependent clause includes a subordinating word that makes it depend on the independent clause to complete its meaning. Independent clauses are sometimes called main clauses, and dependent clauses are sometimes called subordinate clauses.

INDEPENDENT CLAUSES	The decade of the 1970s was a time of political and social turmoil.
	However, technological advances and noteworthy athletic accomplishments also characterize the 1970s.
DEPENDENT CLAUSES	One significant development in a military conflict that had been raging in Southeast Asia for decades was the entry of U.S. troops into Cambodia in April 1970 during the Vietnam War.
	After Vietnamese troops regained control of their country from France in 1954, the country was split into noncommunist South Vietnam and communist North Vietnam.
	Historians still debate what the role of the United States should have been in Southeast Asia.

Identifying Kinds of Dependent Clauses

There are three kinds of dependent clauses: adjective clauses, adverb clauses, and noun clauses. A dependent clause is named for its function in the sentence. Every dependent clause begins with some kind of subordinating word. These subordinating words signal that the clause is dependent, unable to stand alone as a sentence.

ESL When identifying dependent clauses, look for subject and predicate pairs introduced by words such as relative pronouns (*who, which, that*) and subordinating conjunctions (such as *if, since, because*).

Adjectives pp. 48–50

Adjective Clauses

An **adjective clause** is a dependent clause that acts like an adjective in a sentence. In other words, it modifies a noun or a pronoun in another clause. An adjective clause may modify a word in the independent clause or a word in another dependent clause. Two different kinds of words can introduce adjective clauses.

Relative Pronouns

Most adjective clauses begin with a **relative pronoun**. A relative pronoun communicates several pieces of information.

Relative Pronouns p. 39

- It signals that the clause is dependent.
- It *relates* the adjective clause to the word it modifies in another clause.
- It functions as a *pronoun* to replace its antecedent. (The antecedent of the relative pronoun is the noun or pronoun that the adjective clause modifies in the other clause.)
- If nonpossessive, it functions as a subject or an object within the adjective clause. *Whose* can function as a possessive determiner within the adjective clause.

who   whom   whose   which   that

One athlete *who enjoyed success in the 1970s* was the tennis player Arthur Ashe.

In 1975 Ashe won the men's singles title at Wimbledon, *which is considered the most prestigious tennis tournament.*

A blood transfusion during heart surgery in 1983 may have infected Ashe with HIV, a diagnosis *that he and his wife announced in 1992.*

Since his death in 1993, people have remembered Arthur Ashe as an athlete *whose charity work matched his athletic accomplishments.*

> **ESL**
> Although most relative pronouns look like interrogative pronouns, there is no subject-verb inversion in clauses introduced by relative pronouns. The relative pronoun comes at the beginning of a clause and functions as the subject or is followed by the subject and verb in normal order.

In some sentences, the adjective clause does not begin with a relative pronoun but with a preposition instead. In these sentences, the relative pronoun *whom* functions as the object of the preposition within the adjective clause. In less formal English, the relative pronoun *that* can replace *whom*, and the preposition appears elsewhere in the adjective clause.

FORMAL   Where is the man *to whom we gave our tickets?*

INFORMAL   Where is the man *that we gave our tickets to?*

Clauses | Chapter 5 | **117**

Reducing Adjective Clauses pp. 374–75

The relative pronoun *that* is sometimes omitted (simply "understood") when it functions as a direct object or an object of the preposition in the adjective clause.

                           (OP) (S) (TrV)   (DO)
Where is the man *[that]* we gave our tickets to?

                       (DO) (S)   (TrV)
This is the tournament *[that]* we watched on television last year.

To make your writing and speaking clear to your audience, carefully choose the correct relative pronoun. When referring to persons, use *who, whom, whose,* or *that.* When referring to things and most animals, use *which* or *that.*

In 1970 the U.S. government created the Environmental Protection Agency, *which* oversees policies on air, land, and water quality.

The inspiration for the modern environmentalism movement may have been Rachel Carson, *whose* book *Silent Spring* discusses the effects of pesticides.

As a marine biologist, Rachel Carson had studied the creatures *that* live in the ocean near her home.

Commas p. 308

Whether you are referring to persons, things, or animals, use *that* only for restrictive clauses. A restrictive adjective clause adds information necessary to identify or specify the antecedent and is not set off by a comma. (*Who, whom, whose,* and *which* can be used in either restrictive or nonrestrictive clauses, but many writers prefer to use *which* only in nonrestrictive clauses.)

       Restrictive | *Silent Spring* is a controversial book *that* mixes scientific fact with Carson's opinion about the issues.

  Nonrestrictive | The public debate sparked by Carson's book, *which* became a bestseller, continues today.

 **ESL**   Never use the relative pronoun *that* after a comma. Instead, use *who, whom,* or *which* as appropriate.

Relative Adverbs

Relative Adverbs p. 51

Some adjective clauses begin with a **relative adverb.** A relative adverb is often a better choice than a relative pronoun when the adjective clause modifies a noun of time, place, or reason in the main clause. Like a relative pronoun, a relative adverb accomplishes several things.

- It signals that the clause is dependent.
- It *relates* the adjective clause to the word that the adjective clause modifies in another clause.
- It functions as an *adverb* to modify the verb in the adjective clause itself.

    when   where   why

                            (S)   (TrV)   (DO)

The year *when* the United States reestablished communication with China after two decades of official silence was 1972.

In February President Nixon and his wife, Pat, traveled to

                (S) (InV)

China, *where* they met with the leaders of China's communist government.

> An adjective clause beginning with **when** modifies a **"time"** noun, such as *day* or *era*. An adjective clause beginning with **where** modifies a **"place"** noun, such as *California* or *house*. An adjective clause beginning with **why** modifies a **"cause"** noun, usually *reason* or *cause*.

in SUMMARY

A **clause** is a group of related words that contains both a subject and a predicate. An **independent clause** can stand alone as a sentence. A **dependent clause** cannot stand alone; it contains a word that makes it dependent on another clause.

An **adjective clause** is a dependent clause that functions like an adjective in a sentence. It modifies a noun or a pronoun in another clause.

A **relative pronoun** relates an adjective clause to the noun or pronoun that the clause modifies; it functions as a subject, an object, or a possessive determiner within the adjective clause.

A **relative adverb** relates an adjective clause to the noun or pronoun that the clause modifies; it modifies the verb in the adjective clause.

5.1 PRACTICE *the skill*

Place parentheses around each adjective clause. Draw an arrow from each adjective clause to the word it modifies. Underline each relative pronoun once and each relative adverb twice.

1. The history of advertising is a subject that has fascinated many people.

2. Many Americans, for whom advertisements are a way of life, may not know the rich and diverse history of advertising.

3. From the beginning, advertising has been a useful tool for people who needed to introduce a product, a concept, or a candidate.

4. The successful advertiser whose goal is to promote political candidates, new products and services, or new ideas and concepts uses the strategies for other purposes as well.

5. Encouraging audiences to take certain actions was the reason why advertising became an art form in itself.

6. Successful advertising is the means by which man sells his products or ideas.

7. One of the first forms of advertising began with people who were on the street shouting out promotions of their wares.

8. Eighteenth- and nineteenth-century advertisements, which were both political and nonpolitical, promoted tea, clothing, and political parties.

9. Then came the twentieth century, when advertising took on a new meaning.

10. One of the most successful advertising campaigns in history began in Atlanta, Georgia, where the Coca-Cola Company began.

5.2 USE *the skill*

Combine each set of sentences by changing one sentence into an adjective clause, using an appropriate relative pronoun or relative adverb.

1. Public relations personnel prepare an audience for a message. The message focuses on promises to be fulfilled.

   _____

   _____

2. The use of public relations programs was not common until the twentieth century. During World War II, however, public relations programs became a powerful tool for the Allies.

3. Public relations is divided into many categories. These include reputation management and public and international affairs.

4. One avenue of public relations focuses on the public's view of a company or an individual. Another focuses on a nation's view of another nation.

5. The popularity and effectiveness of public relations strategies required independent public relations companies. Many companies exist for that reason.

6. Corporations and businesses as well as governments have public relations departments. International relations is a division of public relations.

7. Government officials attempt to establish amiable international relations. These officials pursue amiable international relations partly to help avoid war.

8. Perhaps the hardest public relations job is restoring a company's reputation. At times people have developed negative opinions about a company.

9. Now the public relations department is a key part of any organization. It strives to create a good image and to encourage investment.

10. Public relations skills are a valuable asset. People with these skills are a precious commodity to many companies.

Adverbs
pp. 50–51

Commas
p. 304

Conjunctions
pp. 54–55

Reducing
Adverb Clauses
pp. 375–76

Writer's Toolbox

Adverb Clauses

An **adverb clause** is a dependent clause that acts like an adverb in a sentence. Adverb clauses usually modify verbs, but sometimes an adverb clause will modify an entire clause. Adverb clauses can also modify adjectives or other adverbs.

Subordinating Conjunctions

An adverb clause begins with a subordinating conjunction. Like other conjunctions, a **subordinating conjunction** joins two sentence elements, in this case clauses. However, a subordinating conjunction is part of one of the clauses, and it makes its own clause dependent on the other clause. (A subordinating conjunction is only an introducer, having no other function within its clause.) The idea expressed in the dependent clause should be less important than (subordinate to) the idea in the main clause.

Subordinating conjunctions convey a variety of meanings; thus, adverb clauses convey a variety of meanings. Many of these are the same meanings that adverbs themselves convey. A skillful writer chooses the subordinating conjunction that will clearly express the logical relationship between the two clauses. (In the list below, each word in parentheses is a modifier and not a part of the subordinating conjunction.)

TIME	when, while, as, before, after, since, now that, once, until, till, whenever
PLACE	where, wherever
CAUSE	because, since, as, inasmuch as
CONDITION	if, on condition that, provided that, unless
CONTRAST	whereas, while
MANNER	as, as if, as though, however
PURPOSE	so that, so, that, in order that, lest
CONCESSION	although, even though, though, even if
COMPARISON AND DEGREE	than, (as . . .) as, (so . . .) as
RESULT	so that, (so . . .) that, (such . . .) that

Margaret Thatcher became Europe's first woman prime minister *after* she gained a momentous 1979 victory for the Conservative Party.

Björn Borg, Swedish tennis legend of the 1970s, still preferred wooden rackets in the 1990s, *as though* the modern types were second-rate.

Even though mechanical difficulties kept her from finishing the 1977 race, Janet Guthrie became the first woman to compete in the Indianapolis 500.

ESL · A few of the subordinating conjunctions on this list can also be prepositions, followed only by objects. These are *after, as, before, since, till,* and *until.*

SUBORDINATING CONJUNCTION | Eat supper *before* you go to church.
PREPOSITION | Eat supper *before* six o'clock tonight.

When using *whereas, while, although, though,* or *even though* in a dependent clause to contrast or concede something, do not use *but* in the independent clause.

INCORRECT | Even though I do not like milk, ~~but~~ I do like chocolate milk.
CORRECT | Even though I do not like milk, I do like chocolate milk.

When using *because* or *since* in a dependent clause to describe a reason or a cause, do not use *so* in the independent clause.

INCORRECT | Since I have a test tomorrow, ~~so~~ I must study tonight.
CORRECT | Since I have a test tomorrow, I must study tonight.

An **elliptical adverb clause,** which has the same function as a full adverb clause, begins with a subordinating conjunction but omits one or more other words that can be clearly understood from the context. The words omitted from an elliptical adverb clause often include the subject and perhaps the auxiliary or the full verb.

While [she was] dismounting from the uneven bars, gymnast Olga Korbut shocked the judges at the 1972 Olympics by completing a backward somersault.

At the time, the backward somersault was considered more dangerous *than* other moves [were dangerous].

Although [it was] later banned from Olympic competition, the Korbut Flip has a memorable place in Olympic history.

Whether the subject of the elliptical adverb clause is stated or omitted, it must be the same as the subject of the independent clause (or be a noun or a pronoun standing for the subject). If the subjects of the two clauses are different, the result will be an error called a dangling modifier.

Dangling Modifiers p. 251

Indefinite Relative Pronouns

Occasionally, an **indefinite relative pronoun** ending with *-ever* will introduce an adverb clause. An indefinite relative pronoun does not have an antecedent; it refers to something indefinite or unknown in the dependent clause. Although the indefinite relative pronoun fills a noun function in the adverb clause, the clause as a whole still functions adverbially to modify the independent clause as a whole.

  (S) (InV)
Whatever happens in the world of fashion, you will undoubtedly still see yesterday's fashions recycled as those of today.

 (PN) (S) (LV)
Whoever he is, his appearance certainly reminds me of President Nixon's.

Noun Clause, not Adverb Clause p. 386

Relative Pronouns p. 39

in SUMMARY

An **adverb clause** is a dependent clause that functions like an adverb in a sentence.

A **subordinating conjunction** joins a dependent clause to an independent clause and expresses the relationship between the two clauses.

An **elliptical adverb clause** is a clause that keeps the introductory subordinating conjunction but omits certain other words that are clearly understood from the context.

An **indefinite relative pronoun** ending with *-ever* can introduce an adverb clause.

5.3 PRACTICE *the skill*

Place parentheses around each adverb clause. Draw an arrow from each adverb clause or elliptical adverb clause to the word it modifies. (Do not draw an arrow from an indefinite relative pronoun to the entire main clause.) Underline each subordinating conjunction once and each indefinite relative pronoun twice.

1. A Christian must be well established in his personal convictions before he chooses to consider a public relations position.

2. Whatever happens, he must live by biblical commands and standards.

3. Establishing trust is the basis for a successful public relations career even though one's counterparts may ignore this principle.

4. If you do not adopt the command of James 5:12 to "let your yea be yea; and your nay, nay," you will likely succumb to the manipulation of the world.

5. Despite the temporal cost, God's blessing upon your life is more important than the world's.

6. Maintaining honesty and trustworthiness should be paramount in the Christian's life when he assumes a position in the area of public relations.

7. Paul's admonition of "lie not one to another" (Colossians 3:9), although given to the early church, should be our standard of practice today as well.

8. Success in the public relations area will not materialize unless a Christian adopts the command of Ephesians 5:6: "Let no man deceive you with vain words."

9. You must be cautious with your words and promises since you are obligated to fulfill your promises.

10. As you reflect upon the field of public relations, remember that some Christians have been destroyed because of their departure from biblical standards.

5.4 USE *the skill*

Expand each sentence by adding an adverb clause, using an appropriate subordinating conjunction or indefinite relative pronoun. Try to vary the location of the adverb clauses and the meanings that they convey.

1. Often thought of as limited to press conferences alone, public relations management actually includes a variety of strategies.

2. According to some studies, media relations may include news releases, news conferences, and personal letters.

3. Special events such as fundraisers, trade shows, or award ceremonies are additional opportunities to improve public relations.

4. Newsletters, whether long or short, can keep clients apprised of new company policies and personnel changes.

5. Information sheets of one or two pages, another public relations tool, are directed at motivating the reader to make a donation or to purchase a product.

6. Tip sheets with bulleted lists of information about a newly released product are sent to customers.

7. Companies respond to news items about their products through a letter to the editor, another public relations strategy.

8. Sponsoring a local ball team, musical group, or community event is an obvious attempt to improve public relations. However, many companies overlook this opportunity.

9. Consistent—but not always large—contributions to local charities will foster good public relations.

10. A thank-you note to a customer will often encourage repeat business; many companies, however, fail to write such notes.

Noun Clauses

Nouns
pp. 35–51

A **noun clause** is a dependent clause that functions as a noun in a sentence. Noun clauses appear as subjects, predicate nouns, objects, and appositives in sentences. Three kinds of words can introduce noun clauses.

Subordinating Conjunctions

Most noun clauses begin with the subordinating conjunction *that*; some other noun clauses begin with the subordinating conjunction *whether*, which indicates a choice. The subordinating conjunction introduces the noun clause, but it does not have any other function within the noun clause.

---

tip

Do not confuse the subordinating conjunction *that* with the relative pronoun *that*. The relative pronoun stands for a noun and has a function in the adjective clause it introduces.

     S   LV PN   (S)
A common assumption once held was *that* King Tut's treasure
(LV) (PA)
was unparalleled among the riches of the ancient world.

126 Chapter 5 | Clauses

      S   (S)   (TrV)   (DO)   LV
That a tomb in China's Shanxi province contained great wealth was
   PA
unknown.

                                    S   TrV   DO   (S)   (TrV)
In 1974 some Chinese farmers wondered *whether* they could dig
   (DO)   S   TrV   DO
a better well, but their attempt revealed the burial grounds of Emperor

Qin Shi Huang instead.

The subordinating conjunction *that* is sometimes omitted when the noun clause functions as the direct object of the sentence.

                                                                 S
Upon unearthing emperor Qin Shi Huang's terra cotta army, archaeologists
TrV DO   (S)   (LV)   (PN)
said *[that]* the former emperor's obsession had been protection.

In designing the thousands of lifelike individualized figurines, Chinese
    S   TrV   DO   (S)   (TrV)   (DO)
artisans hoped *[that]* superior height would indicate superior rank.

When a noun clause functions as the subject of the sentence, a writer can re-arrange the sentence, putting the subject last. The word *it* then functions as an **expletive**, a subject substitute that acts as a "placeholder" for the noun clause. When an expletive appears, the reader does not have to read and remember the entire noun clause before he finds out what is being said about it.

       S   (S)   (TrV)   (DO)
Whether other archaeological sites surrounded this ancient Chinese tomb
  LV   PN
became a matter of interest.

  LV   PN   S   (S)
It became a matter of interest *whether* other archaeological sites
  (TrV)   (DO)
surrounded this ancient Chinese tomb.

S-*be*-Advl
p. 76

---

tip

The subordinating conjunction *if* sometimes substitutes for *whether* in informal speech and writing. In formal English, use *whether*.

Indefinite Relative Pronouns

Another kind of word that can introduce a noun clause is an **indefinite relative pronoun.** Unlike a regular relative pronoun, an indefinite relative pronoun does not have an antecedent in the independent clause. It refers to something indefinite or unknown in the noun clause that it introduces.

   S   (S)   (TrV)   (DO)   TrV   DO
Whoever arranged the terra cotta figures put the emperor's clay soldiers in battle formation.

Relative Pronouns
p. 39

                       S   LV PN (S) (TrV) (DO) (OC)
The 1974 discovery of the terra cotta warriors is *what* made people aware

of Chinese culture during the Qin Dynasty.

                        S   TrV-P   OP (S) (be) (Advl)
The ancient burial site had been vandalized by *whoever* was there

immediately following the emperor's committal.

---

tip — The case of a relative pronoun depends only on its use within its own clause.

Indefinite Relative Pronouns

who	whoever
whom	whomever
whose	whosever
which	whichever
what	whatever

Kinds of Adverbs
pp. 50–51

Indefinite Relative Adverbs

An **indefinite relative adverb** is another kind of word that can introduce a noun clause. An indefinite relative adverb refers to something unknown and functions as an adverb to modify the verb in the noun clause itself.

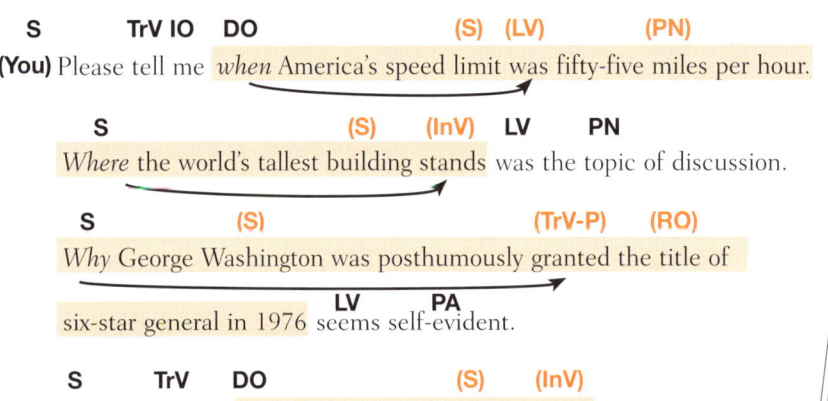

      S   TrV IO DO   (S)   (LV)   (PN)
(You) Please tell me *when* America's speed limit was fifty-five miles per hour.

       S   (S)   (InV) LV   PN
Where the world's tallest building stands was the topic of discussion.

      S   (S)   (TrV-P)   (RO)
Why George Washington was posthumously granted the title of
                            LV   PA
six-star general in 1976 seems self-evident.

   S   TrV   DO   (S)   (InV)
Agnes explained *how* supermarket bar codes work.

in SUMMARY

A **noun clause** is a dependent clause that functions like a noun in the sentence.

The **subordinating conjunctions** *that* and *whether* can introduce noun clauses.

An **indefinite relative pronoun** or an **indefinite relative adverb** can also introduce a noun clause.

5.5 PRACTICE *the skill*

Place parentheses around each noun clause. Identify the function of each noun clause as subject *(S)*, predicate noun *(PN)*, direct object *(DO)*, indirect object *(IO)*, object of the preposition *(OP)*, or appositive *(App)*. Underline each subordinating conjunction once and each indefinite relative pronoun twice. Circle any indefinite relative adverb.

_____ 1. It is debatable whether the success of the Coca-Cola Company comes from the taste of its product or from the talents of its advertising staff.

_____ 2. Did you know that from 1886 to 1993 the bottling company used thirty-one slogans to promote Coca-Cola?

_____ 3. Dr. John S. Pemberton's invention, what became Coca-Cola, was marketed as a tonic for brain and nerve problems.

_____ 4. Whatever an advertiser spends should be less than the product's earnings; however, the syrup's marketers spent $73.00 on advertising in 1886 when gross sales were only $50.00.

_____ 5. The mixture of Coca-Cola syrup and soda water was what a patron needed to relieve his headache.

_____ 6. In 1886 Jacob's Pharmacy in Atlanta sold whoever paid five cents a glass of fizzy fountain drink called Coca-Cola.

_____ 7. Coca-Cola became a marketed item, and soon the company paid dividends to whoever had become an investor.

_____ 8. Beginning in 1942, advertisers liked how the "Sprite Boy" promoted the new name, Coke.

_____ 9. That a Coca-Cola advertisement appeared on the cover of *Time* magazine became an advertising boost.

_____ 10. Innovative techniques and strategies reveal why advertising is important to the success of this industry.

5.6 USE *the skill*

Combine each group of sentences by using a noun clause with an appropriate subordinating conjunction, indefinite relative pronoun, or indefinite relative adverb.

1. The history class learned about the New York City mayoral race of 1886. Theodore Roosevelt, Abram Hewett, and Henry George campaigned for the office.

2. Twenty-eight-year-old Roosevelt had just returned to New York City. Interestingly, he was planning to be married shortly after the election.

3. Abram Hewett was a popular sixty-four-year-old millionaire and philanthropist. He alone could save New York City from socialism and communism, he claimed.

4. Redheaded Henry George was forty-seven years old. The supporters of the Central Labor Union considered George a favorite candidate in the mayoral election.

5. The campaign gained prominence. Active in the election in many ways were labor parties and the nation's most powerful political machine, the Tammany Hall organization.

6. The Tammany Hall organization had become strong in New York City by achieving its goal. That goal was to get votes from the newly arrived immigrants.

7. The opportunities Tammany offered reached all groups of immigrants. Becoming a naturalized citizen was made easy for them.

8. On one occasion 40,000 certificates for potential citizens were available in a saloon on Center Street. The certificate read "Naturalize the bearer."

9. By 1870, 44 percent of New York City's population was foreign born. The Tammany Hall political machine sought out the foreigners.

_____

_____

10. Abram Hewett won the election. George accused Tammany Hall of illegal registrations.

_____

_____

5.7 REVIEW the skill

Place parentheses around each dependent clause. Identify each dependent clause as an adjective clause (Adj), an adverb clause (Adv), or a noun clause (N). If it is a noun clause, also identify its noun function. If it is an adjective or adverb clause, underline the word that it modifies.

_____ _____ 1. In the latter part of the nineteenth century, Thomas Nast, who is most famous for his wood engravings, drew cartoons about many major events and political issues.

_____ _____ 2. Because the United States was a booming country with increased industrialization and immigration, political corruption was everywhere.

_____ _____ 3. One major problem was that politicians "rigged" elections and bought votes of uninformed immigrants.

_____ _____ 4. One series of cartoons depicted the corrupt leaders who controlled New York's Tammany Hall.

_____ _____ 5. Whomever Nast chose for his cartoon drawings could not escape the attention of the New Yorkers.

_____ _____ 6. Although many of the newly arrived immigrants could not read English, they were able to interpret the cartoon pictures.

_____ _____ 7. Nast directed a series of cartoons against Boss Tweed, who ruled Tammany Hall for years.

_____ _____ 8. During the time when Tweed ruled Tammany Hall, Tweed and his fellow criminals channeled hundreds of millions of dollars from the city to themselves.

_____ _____ 9. Nast continued his cartoons against Tweed and eventually saw that Tweed served a sentence in jail.

_____ _____ 10. Thomas Nast was already a strong influence on politics before he created the symbols for both the Democratic and Republican parties.

Using Independent and Dependent Clauses

Knowing how to use the various kinds of clauses is an important skill. Effective writers combine different kinds of clauses in different ways to convey different meanings. Analyzing the number and kinds of clauses that a sentence contains is one way to categorize sentences. (Another is to categorize sentences by their purpose, as we did in Chapter 3.)

A **simple sentence** consists of only one independent clause. There are no dependent clauses.

> China joined the United Nations in 1971.
>
> The architecture of both the Eiffel Tower and the Centre Pompidou instigated national controversy.

Conjunctions
pp. 54–55

A **compound sentence** contains two or more independent clauses but no dependent clauses. The method a writer uses to join the independent clauses often indicates the relationship between the clauses.

- A coordinating conjunction (usually preceded by a comma) can indicate similarity and association (*and, both—and, nor, neither—nor*), contrast (*but, yet*), choice (*or, either—or*), cause or reaction (*for*), or result or consequence (*so*).

    > The six-story Centre Pompidou in Paris was startlingly revolutionary, *for* all of its pipes were brightly colored and displayed on the structure's exterior.
    >
    > Some feared that the avant-garde architecture would be disliked, *but* the Centre Pompidou became overwhelmingly popular.

Commas and Semicolons
pp. 302, 315

- A semicolon indicates that the second clause reinforces the first clause. A conjunctive adverb sometimes appears in the second clause (often set off by a comma or a pair of commas) to clarify the exact relationship between the two independent clauses.

    > The Nike athletic shoe logo bears mythological import; the "swoosh" was designed to resemble the wing of Nike, a Greek goddess of victory.
    >
    > Track coach Bill Bowerman began experimenting with his wife's waffle iron; consequently, Nike's "waffle trainer" entered the shoe market in 1974.

- A colon (which is used only rarely) indicates that the second clause explains the first clause or develops the idea further.

    > In 1972 President Richard Nixon made a historic visit to China: prior to his visit, America and China had spent two decades in open opposition.
    >
    > The media initially failed to report Secretary of State Henry Kissinger's 1971 visit to China: no word of his secret mission escaped until after the secretary's return.

Coordination and Subordination
pp. 363–65

A **complex sentence** contains only one independent clause and at least one dependent clause. The dependent clause can appear before, within, or after the independent clause.

> Because supermarkets needed a more efficient checkout system, Bernard Silver and Joseph Woodland began developing the bar code system.

Sentence Expansion and Reduction
pp. 371–78

> Joseph Woodland tried to develop a method in which ultraviolet lights would scan ink patterns.
>
> The ink that Woodland designed proved too expensive and too unreliable for mass automated use.

A **compound-complex sentence** contains two or more independent clauses and at least one dependent clause.

In 1973 George J. Laurer, who worked for IBM, patented the familiar black-lined bar code, but his successors popularized this symbol that now appears on most commercially sold retail products.

Marsh's supermarket, which is located in Troy, Ohio, became the first business to use the bar code; here in June of 1974 a clerk scanned the first purchase bearing this code, a packet of Wrigley's gum.

in SUMMARY

A **simple sentence** consists of only one independent clause.

A **compound sentence** contains two or more independent clauses.

A **complex sentence** contains one independent clause and at least one dependent clause.

A **compound-complex sentence** includes two or more independent clauses and at least one dependent clause.

5.8 PRACTICE the skill

Identify each sentence as simple (S), compound (Cd), complex (Cx), or compound-complex (Cd-Cx).

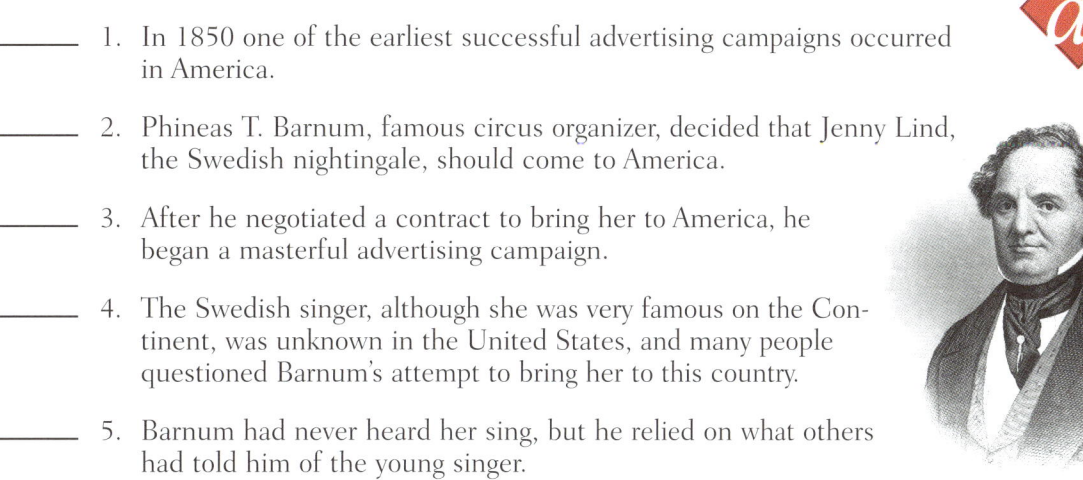

_____ 1. In 1850 one of the earliest successful advertising campaigns occurred in America.

_____ 2. Phineas T. Barnum, famous circus organizer, decided that Jenny Lind, the Swedish nightingale, should come to America.

_____ 3. After he negotiated a contract to bring her to America, he began a masterful advertising campaign.

_____ 4. The Swedish singer, although she was very famous on the Continent, was unknown in the United States, and many people questioned Barnum's attempt to bring her to this country.

_____ 5. Barnum had never heard her sing, but he relied on what others had told him of the young singer.

_____ 6. Barnum used newspaper ads, handbills, and broadsides, large sheets of paper printed on one side, to advertise the coming of the famous singer.

_____ 7. When she arrived in New York harbor, 30,000 New Yorkers met her at the dock to welcome her to America.

_____ 8. On the wharf was a bower of decorated trees, and two arches welcomed Jenny Lind to New York and America.

_____ 9. Many people thought that the city of New York had provided these decorations, but the cost of the trees and arches was probably an advertising charge in Barnum's accounting books.

_____ 10. Barnum's successful advertising made Jenny Lind famous in New York, and his advertising spread her fame throughout the country.

5.9 REVIEW *the skill*

Rewrite each sentence or set of sentences to create the kind of sentence indicated in parentheses.

1. Advertising is nothing new; it can be traced to ancient times. *(complex)*

2. Some of the earliest advertisements have been found in Rome. Other early advertisements have been found in Pompeii. *(simple)*

3. Archeologists have discovered some ancient methods of advertising. One of the first known methods of advertising was an outdoor display. The display might once have been a sign painted on the side of a building. *(compound-complex)*

4. Archeologists have found a sign advertisement. One Roman excavation revealed a sign for property for rent. *(complex)*

5. Another excavated sign was found on a wall in Pompeii. The advertisement called travelers' attention to a building in another town. *(compound)*

6. During medieval times merchants employed another form of advertising. Town criers walked the streets and shouted the value and praise of a merchant's products. *(complex)*

7. Printed advertising was not available prior to 1445. Gutenberg's movable-type printing press provided a means for printed advertising. *(simple)*

   _____

   _____

   _____

   _____

8. Fliers became a popular form of advertising. Sometimes fliers appeared on the walls as posters. *(compound)*

   _____

   _____

   _____

9. Fliers often included the symbols of guild members. Fliers also included the symbols of the tradesmen. *(simple)*

   _____

   _____

   _____

10. Other forms of advertising followed. In the 1800s in the United States, manufacturers published mail-order catalogs. Catalogs reached many people. *(compound-complex)*

    _____

    _____

    _____

    _____

Avoiding Sentence Errors

Knowing the difference between dependent clauses and independent clauses—and knowing how to combine them correctly—will help you avoid serious sentence errors. The following information will help you develop your ability to find and correct some common problems.

Fragment

A **fragment** is a group of words wrongly punctuated as if it were a complete sentence. A fragment is usually considered a serious error. There are three basic kinds of fragments.

Missing Elements

Every sentence must have both a subject and a predicate. An imperative sentence, which has an understood subject, is the only exception. If a group of words punctuated as a sentence is missing either a subject or a verb, it is a fragment. Correct this kind of fragment by supplying the missing element or by joining the fragment to an adjacent sentence.

INCORRECT	Childproof safety lids introduced in 1970.
	Opened a subway in its capital city in this same year.
CORRECT	Childproof safety lids were introduced in 1970.
	Mexico opened a subway in its capital city in this same year.

ESL Fragments introduced by multiple-word prepositions are difficult to identify. When you use a multiple-word preposition, make sure that the phrase it introduces is attached to an independent clause.

INCORRECT	In spite of her desire for convenience.
CORRECT	In spite of her desire for convenience, her children's safety came first.

Subordinating Words

A sentence must be (or at least contain) an independent clause. A dependent clause standing alone is a fragment. Any group of words that includes both a subject and a predicate but also contains a subordinating word is a dependent clause and cannot stand alone as a sentence.

INCORRECT	Since the automotive industry introduced the catalytic converter in 1975. Pollution rates have dropped significantly.
CORRECT	Pollution rates have dropped significantly since the automotive industry introduced the catalytic converter in 1975.

Wrong Punctuation

Semicolons p. 315

Incorrect use of a semicolon can also produce a fragment. A semicolon can appear only between two grammatically equal groups of words, usually between two independent clauses. When a semicolon appears between an independent clause and a dependent clause, the result is a fragment. The most common way to correct a semicolon fragment is to remove the semicolon, replacing it with a comma if necessary.

INCORRECT	Personal grooming became a bit easier in 1975; when the first disposable razor appeared on the market.
CORRECT	Personal grooming became a bit easier in 1975 when the first disposable razor appeared on the market.

Permissible Fragments

Although fragments are common and acceptable in conversation, they are usually considered errors in writing. However, an effective writer will sometimes choose to use a short fragment to express informality or for special effect, such as emphasis or irony.

INFORMALITY	The 1970s brought the first successful crossbreeding of cattle and buffalo. Beefalo burgers, anyone?
EMPHASIS	In November of 1971 the *Mariner 9* spacecraft failed to transmit highly detailed pictures of Mars back to earth. Only furious red dust storms.
IRONY	Scientists discovered an ocean floor garden at the Galápagos Rift in the late 1970s. Plants thriving without photosynthesis!

Don't overuse intentional fragments. An occasional fragment can be effective, but too many fragments become tiresome, drawing attention to themselves and distracting the reader from your message.

If you include an intentional fragment in a writing assignment for class, mark it in some way so that your teacher doesn't mistake it for an error.

Comma Splice and Fused Sentence

Just as it is incorrect to punctuate a fragment as though it were a complete sentence, it is also incorrect to punctuate two sentences as though they were only one. A **comma splice** is a serious error that occurs when two independent clauses are joined by a comma without a coordinating conjunction. A **fused sentence** is a serious error that occurs when two independent clauses are joined with no punctuation at all. Correct these errors by using the strategy that best expresses the relationship between the two clauses: add a period or a semicolon between the two clauses, combine the two with a comma and a coordinating conjunction, or change one of the independent clauses into a dependent clause.

Conjunctions pp. 54–55

COMMA SPLICE	In 1976 Americans enthusiastic about CB radios discovered that First Lady Ford shared their interest, she often broadcast in the CB world under the name "First Mama."
CORRECT	In 1976 Americans enthusiastic about CB radios discovered that First Lady Ford shared their interest; she often broadcast in the CB world under the name "First Mama."
CORRECT	In 1976 Americans enthusiastic about CB radios discovered that First Lady Ford shared their interest. She often broadcast in the CB world under the name "First Mama."
FUSED SENTENCE	Congress approved the construction of the Trans-Alaska Pipeline System (TAPS) in 1973 oil production began in June of 1977.
CORRECT	Congress approved the construction of the Trans-Alaska Pipeline System (TAPS) in 1973, and oil production began in June of 1977.
CORRECT	After Congress approved the construction of the Trans-Alaska Pipeline System (TAPS) in 1973, oil production began in June of 1977.

tip

Be careful not to correct a fused sentence by inserting only a comma; the resulting comma splice would be no improvement.

in SUMMARY

A **fragment** is a group of words wrongly punctuated as if it were a complete sentence.

A **comma splice** is two independent clauses wrongly joined by a comma only.

A **fused sentence** is two independent clauses wrongly joined without any punctuation.

5.10 PRACTICE the skill

Identify each group of words as a sentence (S), a fragment (F), a comma splice (CS), or a fused sentence (FS).

_____ 1. Successful evangelistic campaigns in the early 1900s had prayer as their base.

_____ 2. Choosing the evangelist for the campaign was most important, the people wanted a man who could "preach the stars down."

_____ 3. Men such as Bob Jones Sr., Billy Sunday, and others who preached successful campaigns.

_____ 4. Local church leaders met together to plan the advertising for the campaign these leaders sought God's blessing on the preaching.

_____ 5. An advertising committee would oversee the design of signs and fliers that would advertise the dates and times of the preaching services.

_____ 6. Newspapers from local communities and from distant ones that often sent journalists to the meetings.

_____ 7. Journalists would then write an article in the paper telling of the evangelistic meetings this in itself served as a form of advertising for the campaign.

_____ 8. Another form of advertising was word of mouth, people who had been saved in the meetings would tell others and invite them to the meetings.

_____ 9. That these preaching campaigns were successful and effective without loud speakers, radio, or television.

_____ 10. God honored the prayers of His people who sought revival in their communities.

5.11 REVIEW the skill

Identify each group of words as a sentence (S), a fragment (F), a comma splice (CS), or a fused sentence (FS). If the item is a sentence error, rewrite it as a correct sentence.

_____ 1. The campaign slogan "Tippecanoe and Tyler Too" the rallying cry for the presidential campaign of 1840.

_____

_____

_____ 2. From 1801 to 1812 William Henry Harrison served as governor of the Indiana Territory.

_____

_____

_____ 3. During that time the Indian tribes rallied behind their leader, Tecumseh, to fight against the white settlers the Indian tribes wanted to protect their hunting lands.

_____

_____

_____

_____ 4. On November 7, 1811, the Indians surprised Harrison's army at Tippecanoe, the Americans suffered many casualties.

_____

_____

_____

_____ 5. Harrison and his army managing to drive the Indians away and later destroying a nearby Indian town.

_____

_____

_____ 6. Harrison was both praised and condemned for what happened at Tippecanoe.

_____

_____

_____ 7. In 1835 Harrison, who was then unaffiliated with any political party, campaigned for the presidency, he lost the election.

_____

_____

_____ 8. The Log Cabin Campaign of 1840 having placed Harrison against the incumbent President Van Buren.

_____

_____

_____ 9. Harrison's running mate for the vice-presidency was John Tyler hence "Tippecanoe and Tyler Too" became their campaign slogan.

_____

_____

_____ 10. As a result of a very rigorous campaign, William Henry Harrison became weak and contracted pneumonia, he died after one month in office.

_____

_____

5.12 CUMULATIVE *review*

Rewrite the following paragraph, correcting the five sentence errors. Then underline each verbal or verbal phrase and place parentheses around each dependent clause in your answer. (Be prepared to identify the types of phrases and clauses and to label the sentence patterns if your teacher asks for that information.)

By the 1880s the United States had entered a new era for advertisements. By this time manufacturers had improved their operations, increased their capabilities, and made more products available. In addition, consumer costs having been decreased. Advertisements were further changed by the telegraph and railroad service that now connected the country, it was possible to have nationwide advertisements and nationwide distribution of goods. Within twenty years ad firms marketing patent medicines, food, soap, cosmetics, and automobiles. Some of the first brand names promoted by nationwide advertisements were Ivory, Colgate, Wrigley, and Coca-Cola. Then in the 1920s radio became a chief means of presenting a product to the public its popularity, however, was eclipsed by the advent of television commercials in 1950. Manufacturers knew that to advertise their products on television would be essential. Because advertisers use so many means of communication today, consumers can hardly escape their messages, some people would welcome a return to a simpler world.

THINK ABOUT IT

Authorial Intention

A critical thinker is a person who draws reasonable conclusions from a body of information and then uses those conclusions to make sound judgments about life. But before he can reach these reasonable conclusions from something that he hears or reads, he must analyze it thoroughly.

Sometimes an author's purpose and message are obvious. A book entitled *How to Build a Shed* probably has as its purpose to teach the reader how to build a shed. Sometimes, though, the author's purpose and message are not quite so easy to identify. Most people assume that a novelist's purpose is to entertain his readers. After all, if the novel isn't "a good read," no one will want to buy it. But some novelists want to inform their readers as they entertain them. A historical novel, for example, gives the reader insight into a particular time period. A mystery novel may introduce its readers to the work habits of police detectives. Some novelists go even further, attempting to persuade their readers to adopt a particular belief about their topic. For instance, in *Hard Times,* Charles Dickens condemns utilitarianism.

To analyze what you read, follow these steps.

- Read the passage carefully and completely. You must examine all of the evidence before you can draw a valid conclusion.
- Identify the author's message by pinpointing the most prominent idea that the author emphasizes. Look for key words or phrases that the author repeats.
- Evaluate the writer's attitude as revealed in his writings. Note any emotionally charged language that indicates the author's opinion about the subject, his message, and his audience. Notice how he portrays the characters he creates (in fiction) or the experts that he cites (in nonfiction). Who is presented in a positive light? Who appears in a negative light?
- Does the writer present both sides of an issue? Does he seem especially sympathetic to those on one side of the issue? If he presents just one side, is it presented favorably or unfavorably?
- If possible, investigate the writer's background. What else has he written? Whom does he work for? What experience does he have in this field? Where did he receive his training? The answers to these questions can reveal whether the author is qualified to discuss his topic and whether his opinion may be biased.

One warning: Be careful not to judge any writer too harshly or to approve anyone too readily. Although your observations and evaluations are reliable up to a point, all human reasoning is imperfect. Remember that "man looketh on the outward appearance, but the Lord looketh on the heart" (1 Sam. 16:7).

Thinking It Through

Find a newspaper editorial (not just a letter to the editor but rather an opinion piece written as an article) and analyze it by using the steps described above.

Dramatic Scene	144
Agreement	148
From the Written Word	171

DRAMATIC SCENE Writing
AGREEMENT Usage

6

God's Word teaches that the words a person speaks reveal much about his character. (See Matt. 12:34 and Luke 6:45.) The following excerpt is from This Same Jesus, a play about a glazier who has allowed events to make him bitter. Dan is the pastor of the church in which Adonis (ad-uh-NEES) is repairing the stained-glass windows. As you read the scene, look for hints about Adonis's and Dan's characters revealed through their dialogue. How does Burke show you other details, such as plot, through the conversation? Later, you will write a dramatic scene in which the characters are developed primarily through dialogue.

This Same Jesus *by David Burke*

DAN Adonis, the windows look better than they have since we moved here. Why don't you come see them tomorrow with the morning sun streaming through?

ADONIS Looks like the storm's finally passed.

DAN We may even get a little sun before the day's over.

ADONIS Hey, I want you to know I appreciate all the talk today. It's been real interesting.

DAN For me too.

(ADONIS *is finishing the bill.*)

ADONIS Second Avenue Baptist Church?

DAN That's right.

ADONIS Hey, you don't have to wait for me. I got this stuff to clean up. I'll leave the invoice and you can send me a check in the mail. Okay?

DAN Okay. . . . Are we finished talking?

ADONIS Well, I don't think I'm gonna' change your mind about anything.

DAN You asked a lot of good questions. Can I ask you one?

ADONIS Yeah, sure.

DAN When you mentioned your wife earlier, you said she used to talk to you about God?

ADONIS You seem like a nice guy, Dan, but I don't think you want me to unload the whole story of my life on you here.

DAN Only if you want to.

ADONIS You know you and your little girl—you two remind me a lot of my wife here today. Charmaine was a genuine, Bible-believing Christian woman.

DAN Sounds like quite a testimony.

Thinking Biblically

Dramatic writing can address biblical themes without specifically stating them or becoming overtly didactic. Thornton Wilder's *Our Town* provides a good example. The play explores life and death in the small New Hampshire town of Grover's Corners. Though Wilder himself was not a believer, a Christian who knows Scripture cannot watch the play without thinking of Ecclesiastes and the brevity of life (James 4:14). Drama is a powerful tool for inspiration, edification, even rebuke. It is powerful precisely because (and when) it is not preachy.

ADONIS Matter of fact, she's the reason I'm here. This was her church back when it was Methodist. That's why I called to see if I could come fix the windows. She looked out these same windows every week. Used to be in church every time the doors were open. Always volunteered her time with Meals on Wheels—you know to get food to shut-ins?

DAN Is that right?

ADONIS Week in and week out when I bring fresh flowers out here, I see your windows. Her grave's at the far end of the cemetery. Near the big oak.

DAN I'm sorry, Adonis. I had no idea.

ADONIS Almost four years ago.

DAN I am so sorry.

ADONIS Cancer. Like so many. Hadn't been out of the house the last months of her life except in a wheelchair. Even the ladies at Meals on Wheels had stopped coming to see her. Folks from her church came to see her at first. But I guess it got discouraging to see one of their own like that. Or maybe they didn't like to hang around me. I don't know. But I . . . well, I took care of Charmaine. Fed her. Cleaned her. Washed her hair—long brown hair just as fine as when she was a teenager. Clipped her nails. Read to her when she couldn't go to sleep. Sat up with her when she wanted to watch TV. Turned off the TV when she got tired of that. Use to turn off the lights and just talk to her—plain old talk about anything and nothing—windows I was making. Restorations in churches. Long into the night . . .

DAN Adonis, God can fill the void in your heart.

ADONIS I wish He could.

Dramatic Scene

Set a watch, O Lord, before my mouth; keep the door of my lips.
Psalm 141:3

    A play or a dramatic scene is different from most prose in two main ways: (1) it is usually meant to be presented orally, and (2) the elements of character, plot, and setting depend almost entirely on **dialogue**. Dialogue, however much it may sound like ordinary speech, is carefully crafted. If you were to overhear a conversation, it might contain the same information that would be in a dramatic scene, but it would also contain much that the scene would not.

    Good dialogue sifts out the distractions of everyday life but leaves the core issues; excellent dialogue presents the issues in such a way that the scene still feels as though you are overhearing an everyday conversation.

    The trick to good craftsmanship is not to let it show. Dramatic scenes seem contrived when you can see how the dialogue is being steered toward a topic or an end—they do not convince you that the characters are real people with real concerns. The careful craftsman keeps his audience so engaged in the conversation that the audience arrives at the destination without having bothered to watch the road.

Your Turn

Think of an issue that is important to you. Have you had conversations about it? What is your viewpoint on the issue? Imagine holding a conversation with people who disagree with you. Turn that conversation into a crafted dramatic scene.

Planning

✔ **Talk with a peer about an issue important to you.** Take notes on your peer's response to the issue. Does he question your reasoning? Does he challenge your opinions? Does he agree too readily? What seems to be the focus of your conversation?

✔ **Narrow your focus.** Looking at your notes, find the crux of your issue. For example, if you are talking about finding God's will for your life and your conversation seems to turn again and again to what your friends think you should do, perhaps your issue is not finding God's will but rather putting God's will before your friends' approval. You might want to write a scene about someone who struggles with trying too hard to please people.

✔ **Write the problem in one sentence.** In a dramatic scene, the problem, or **conflict**, is the struggle between persons (or forces). If you have narrowed your topic and defined it well enough, you should be able to express the problem in one sentence. All of the following are types of conflict:

>   man vs. man
>   man vs. himself
>   man vs. society
>   man vs. nature
>   man vs. God or the gods

The conflict in the scene described probably would be one of man against himself (what he knows to be right) and man against God (what God has commanded). The problem might be stated this way: *Trying to please people can cause an individual to violate his own conscience and to weaken his fellowship with God.*

✔ **Decide on a resolution for the problem.** Now that you've stated your problem clearly, consider how your main character will resolve the problem. Will she decide to please her friends or to please God? If she chooses to please God, will she continue to spend time with those friends who don't support her desire? Will she explain her decision to them and try to persuade her friends to change their attitudes? Or will she separate from those friends who might weaken her resolve to obey God? Before you begin writing, have a plan for solving the conflict of your scene.

✔ **Show—don't just tell about—the problem.** You are not writing an essay about the problem. You are presenting a scene that looks much like a moment in real time and characters that seem like real people. The audience should be able to draw the right conclusions about your subject without being told. In the excerpt from *This Same Jesus*, Burke shows us that Adonis is searching for something (seen by his desire to visit the church that his wife attended) and that he is kind and compassionate (apparent through the way he cared for his wife and takes flowers to her grave weekly).

✔ **Choose a setting and main characters.** Do you want the scene to be contemporary or set in another time? How does the place contribute to the effect or meaning of the scene? Remember that this scene is to be staged—settings too exotic will be difficult to represent. How many characters do you need? Usually only two or three characters are needed for a single scene. Getting too many in a scene makes the scene hard to control. Your main character will be your **protagonist**, a character who usually changes in some way. Opposite the protagonist is the **antagonist**, who generally attempts to thwart the actions of the main character. The antagonist may or may not be a **villain**, or an evil character. In Burke's play, Adonis is the protagonist. By the end of his dealings with Dan, the play's antagonist, Adonis changes from an embittered man to one who is willing to choose Christ.

✔ **Think about stage business.** Stage business is the movements, gestures, and other physical actions actors use on stage. The best stage business subtly reinforces the meanings of the characters' lines. For example, in the scene before the one you read here, Dan and Adonis are talking. Adonis is tapping on a pane of old glass to see how hard it will be to remove from the leading. Dan is witnessing to Adonis with a series of examples of God's sovereignty—in effect, tapping "the old glass" of Adonis's thinking.

✔ **Find a real person to imitate.** When you write dialogue, think of someone you know. Make your character sound like that person. This technique will help your characters sound not only real but also different from each other. Visualize the action and think through the dialogue before you write the rough draft.

✔ **Map out your scene.** Use your conflict and resolution, setting, characters, stage business, and any bits of dialogue you have thought about to construct a scene map. Put the first three items (conflict and resolution, setting, and characters) at the top of a page and then make a chart for the beginning, middle, and end of your scene, filling in stage business and dialogue for each part.

tip

Mention only essential stage business. Giving too many stage directions limits the director's and actors' interpretation.

Drafting

✔ **Set aside a block of time.** It's best to try to write out the scene all in one sitting. There will be time to refine it later. But you will want to keep the momentum and the tone going in this first effort. Drama depends heavily on the "sweep" (pacing) of the action.

✔ **Draft the scene.** You have all the parts of your scene. Now you must drop your characters into your setting and write what they say about the conflict and then move the dialogue toward the resolution. It is generally best to begin at the beginning chronologically; however, some writers begin at the end or somewhere in the middle and then go back to the chronological beginning. As you write, remember that you will rework the scene later, so now you can focus on just getting down on paper what the characters say. Include the following points:

- Establish your setting. Look at the beginning of your scene map. What do you want to have the audience know within the first few lines? How can the dialogue reveal this information? *This Same Jesus* opens with Pastor Dan standing and practicing a sermon about God's allowing bad things to happen. As he "preaches," the audience learns that Dan and his family have encountered heartache and yet have found "Peace for the Storm Inside" (the announced title of the message).

- Ask yourself what actions need to be included. Again, do not prescribe too much of the action but include information that is necessary for the success of the scene. Burke's play has Adonis entering midway through Dan's sermon and clearing his throat to get the pastor's attention. Write stage directions into the opening of your scene. Often these instructions will be entrances of one or more main characters.

tip Avoid burying information essential to move the scene along in the directions outlining stage business.

- Decide on the scene's high point. How can you make the lines of the rising action increasingly energized? Can you feel tension building in the scene? In *This Same Jesus* we begin to feel that Dan is going to confront Adonis about his need for a Savior when Dan says, "Are we finished talking?" and later asks whether he may ask the glazier a question. Burke artfully brings us to the major dramatic question of the play.

tip As you write, you may find that a line of dialogue or stage business stymies you. Do not get bogged down. Go on with the scene and come back to the sticking point later.

✔ **Check your scene map again.** Where do you want the scene to end? What do you want the audience to carry away from their experience? Because we do not have the ending of Burke's play, we are left wondering what happens to Adonis. Avoid leaving your readers wondering about the outcome of your scene.

Revising

✔ **Read over your scene.** Does the scene sufficiently demonstrate the problem you identified? Does the scene move toward a resolution? Is it convincing? Are the lines natural? Do they follow each other logically and smoothly? Does the scene produce the effect you wanted? Revise to eliminate any problems that you identify.

✔ **Read the scene aloud.** Are the lines easy to articulate? Does each character have a reason (motivation) for the words he says in each line? Are there any awkward combinations of words? (What actor would want to say "All I could remember later was weeping and sleeping"?)

✔ **Ask someone else (or several people) to read the scene aloud.** Watch for places where your readers hesitate or misinterpret lines. Ask the readers how they feel about the lines and how easily they think they could project them to an audience. Are there any changes they would make for clarity or ease of speaking?

✔ **Refine your scene.** Make changes for clarity and effect. Then proofread your scene for correctness and consistency in format and for errors in spelling, grammar, usage, and mechanics.

Publishing

✔ **Stage the scene.** Choose your cast members and direct your scene. Rehearse a few times before presenting it to an audience. Get any equipment you will need. (For example, if a line calls for someone to sit down, you will need a chair.)

✔ **Adapt the scene for radio.** Because you will not have the advantage of visual **spectacle**, give the audience auditory clues about the action they cannot see.

✔ **Produce a book of scenes.** Collect the scenes you and your peers have written into a book of scenes. Sell the books as a fundraiser.

Some Ideas to Consider

History
- Read *A Man for All Seasons* and compare the play to historical accounts of the same time period.

Literature
- Compare two plays on a similar topic. Discuss how each reveals and handles the conflict.

Speech and Drama
- Time your scene (using actors and allowing for stage business). Then edit it to make it fit an exact time slot as if it were a commercial or a radio drama limited to a certain number of minutes.

AGREEMENT

Achieving the goal of clear communication requires an understanding of and an attention to the rules of agreement. Too often, mistakes in agreement draw our attention away from the communication to the mistake itself. How often have you read a composition littered with pronoun-antecedent agreement errors or heard a speaker err in subject-verb agreement? Written and oral communication, especially that of the gospel message and of biblical principles, should be clear and without error. Mistakes in the areas of agreement can compromise the integrity and effectiveness of our communication.

Subject-Verb Agreement

Subjects and Predicates

Correct **subject-verb agreement** combines a singular subject with a singular verb and a plural subject with a plural verb. Each verb must agree with its subject in person and in number.

Plural Forms of Nouns
pp. 35–37

	S TrV DO
SINGULAR	*Plimoth Plantation provides* an example of our country's earliest horticulture.
	S LV PN
	Horticulture is a part of our national history.
	S TrV DO
	Plimoth Plantation does reflect seventeenth-century life.
	S TrV DO
PLURAL	The *landscapes* of Plimoth Plantation *provide* an insight into the lives of the people.
	S LV PN
	The *gardens will be* a source of learning for years to come.
	S TrV DO
	Garden *re-creations do reveal* a part of the settlers' lives.

Present Tense pp. 178–79

Present-tense verbs change form with third-person nouns and pronouns. Except for *was/were*, most past and future tenses stay the same whether singular or plural. As a main verb and as an auxiliary, the irregular verb *be* changes in person and tense. Other auxiliaries, such as *have* and *do*, also change form.

The table below shows the basic forms of *be*. The future tense is always *will be*.

Forms of Be

	Present		Past	
	Singular	Plural	Singular	Plural
First Person	I am	we are	I was	we were
Second Person	you are	you are	you were	you were
Third Person	he is	they are	he was	they were

ESL

If a complete verb contains one or more auxiliaries, then the first auxiliary agrees with the subject. Only the first auxiliary shows agreement; auxiliaries that appear later in the complete verb do not change form. However, the only auxiliaries that change form to agree with a singular or plural subject are *be*, *have*, and *do*. Other auxiliaries do not have different singular and plural forms.

	Singular	Plural
be	I **am looking** for my brother and sister.	My brother and sister **are washing** the car.
have	My father **has been planning** to wash the car for a week.	My parents **have been driving** the same car for several years.
do	My father **does** not **want** to trade in the car for an SUV.	My parents **do** not **want** to trade in the car for an SUV.
will (and all modal auxiliaries)	An SUV **will be** difficult to park.	Eventually, my parents **will buy** a new car of some kind.

Agreement | Chapter 6

Subject Identification

Being able to identify the subject of the sentence correctly will help you avoid using a verb that does not agree with the subject. Certain sentence constructions can make subject identification difficult.

Intervening Phrases

Prepositional Phrases p. 88

Words that come between the subject and the verb can draw your attention away from the true subject of the sentence. The most common **intervening phrases** are the **prepositional phrase**, the **appositive phrase**, and the **negative phrase**. When analyzing a sentence that contains one of these intervening phrases, first isolate the phrase from the rest of the sentence; then identify the verb and the subject. The true subject of the sentence should agree with the verb.

Appositive Phrases p. 89

PREPOSITIONAL PHRASE	**Gardening** *for the early settlers* **was** a difficult task.
	Gardening **tasks** *in certain areas of modern America* **present** problems.
APPOSITIVE PHRASE	The settlers' **allies** *in the gardening process, the Native American Indians,* **were** willing to help with the work.
	Today, American **farmers**, *men with modern machinery for expansive acreage,* still **have** difficult tasks.
NEGATIVE PHRASE	American **settlers**, *not the Indian population,* **were** discouraged during the winter.
	Hard **work**, *not just modern machines,* **produces** a successful crop.

Gerunds and infinitives are always treated as singular.

GERUND	**Gardening was** difficult.
	Growing vegetables **was** an important task.
INFINITIVE	**To grow** vegetables **is** rewarding.

Predicate Nouns of a Different Number

S-LV-PN p. 75

A subject and its predicate noun are usually both singular or both plural. In some sentences, however, the predicate noun will differ in number from the subject. When choosing the correct verb for a sentence, remember that the verb agrees with the subject, the word that precedes the verb, and not with the predicate noun.

        S   **LV**   **PN**
The settlers' *gardens were* an area divided into specific parts.

    S   **LV**   **PN**
One *part* of the gardens *was* medicinal plants.

Inverted Order

Inverted Order p. 71

In most sentences the subject precedes the verb. Occasionally, however, the order of the sentence is **inverted,** placing the subject after the verb. As with any sentence analysis, be sure to identify the verb first and then the true subject of the sentence: The verb must agree with the true subject.

Interrogative Sentences p. 69

Many sentences can show inverted order, but certain sentences indicate that inversion has taken place. In many interrogative sentences, the subject will follow the verb or come between the first auxiliary and the main verb. Another type of inverted sentence begins with *here* or the expletive *there*.

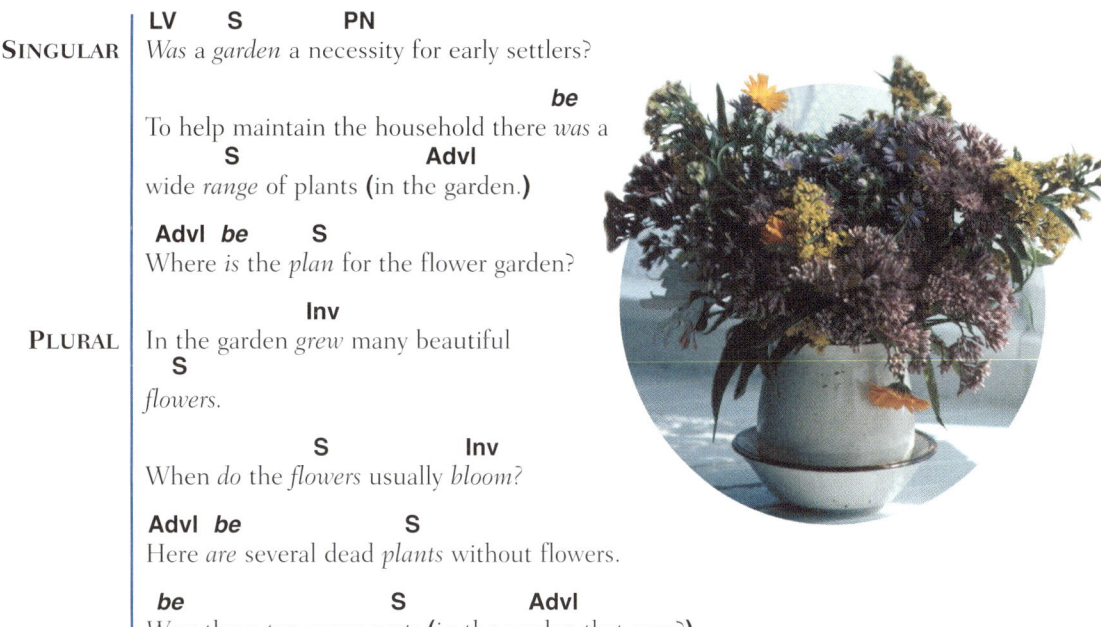

SINGULAR	LV S PN *Was* a *garden* a necessity for early settlers? be To help maintain the household there *was* a S Advl wide *range* of plants **(**in the garden.**)** Advl be S Where *is* the *plan* for the flower garden?
PLURAL	Inv In the garden *grew* many beautiful S *flowers*. S Inv When *do* the *flowers* usually *bloom*? Advl be S Here *are* several dead *plants* without flowers. be S Advl *Were* there too many *pests* **(**in the garden that year?**)**

in SUMMARY

Subjects and verbs must **agree** in number and in person.

When determining agreement between a subject and a verb, ignore any **intervening phrases.**

In a sentence with a **predicate noun,** the verb agrees with the subject, not the predicate noun.

In some sentences the order of the subject and verb is **inverted.** Identify the true subject and make the verb agree with it.

6.1 PRACTICE *the skill*

Underline the simple subject(s) in each sentence. Then underline the correct verb from the choices in parentheses.

1. John Dryden, one of the seventeenth century's greatest playwrights and authors, *(is, are)* still read today.

2. Dryden's many contributions to literature *(is, are)* one reason for his popularity.

3. According to some critics, Dryden, not his contemporaries, *(deserves, deserve)* the highest accolades.

4. In the Dryden canon *(exists, exist)* multiple plays, poems, satires, and essays.

5. An adaptation of Shakespeare's *Antony and Cleopatra (is, are)* among his plays.

Agreement | Chapter 6

6. Certain common practices in the Restoration era, such as introducing a drastic innovation into an old play, *(outrages, outrage)* some modern readers.

7. Dramatic criticism, one of many areas of literature, *(owes, owe)* much to John Dryden.

8. Analyzing plays and drama through inductive methods *(was, were)* among his contributions to dramatic criticism.

9. In the modern era, opinions on seventeenth-century writing *(has, have)* varied.

10. Even so, his plays and literary criticism *(receives, receive)* acclaim today.

6.2 REVIEW *the skill*

Write the letter of the sentence that shows correct subject-verb agreement.

_____ 1. A. One famous medieval collection, the York Corpus Christi Cycle of plays, dates from before 1394.
B. One famous medieval collection, the York Corpus Christi Cycle of plays, date from before 1394.

_____ 2. A. Researchers, not even the best scholar, does not know exactly when the Cycle began.
B. Researchers, not even the best scholar, do not know exactly when the Cycle began.

_____ 3. A. The sources of the Corpus Christi Cycle are not an area of uncertainty: most details come from the Bible or from tradition.
B. The sources of the Corpus Christi Cycle is not an area of uncertainty: most details come from the Bible or from tradition.

_____ 4. A. Another realm of dispute are the causes for the season of the Cycle's performance.
B. Another realm of dispute is the causes for the season of the Cycle's performance.

_____ 5. A. Performance of such plays was reserved for the Easter season.
B. Performance of such plays were reserved for the Easter season.

_____ 6. A. Why is the plays performed in England on Corpus Christi, which is in late May, rather than at Easter?
B. Why are the plays performed in England on Corpus Christi, which is in late May, rather than at Easter?

_____ 7. A. The plays of Corpus Christi portrays scenes from the entire Bible.
B. The plays of Corpus Christi portray scenes from the entire Bible.

_____ 8. A. Wagons, one for each play, serve as stages and roll from one town to another for performances.
   B. Wagons, one for each play, serves as stages and rolls from one town to another for performances.

_____ 9. A. There is still performances of these plays in York, England.
   B. There are still performances of these plays in York, England.

_____ 10. A. Of all the Cycle's plays, there remain only forty-eight today.
   B. Of all the Cycle's plays, there remains only forty-eight today.

Problem Nouns and Pronouns

Subject-verb agreement is usually easy once you have identified the true subject of the sentence. Some subjects, however, require especially careful analysis.

Nouns of Plural Form

Some nouns have only one form—plural. These nouns may be used just one way; some of them are always singular and others are always plural.

ALWAYS SINGULAR | *Molasses* **is** a tasty topping for pancakes.
ALWAYS PLURAL | The *proceeds* from the bake sale **go** toward the school project.

Some of the nouns that are plural in form can be used with *pair of* to indicate how many items are meant. In these sentences the subject is *pair*.

A *pair* of glasses **was found** under the bench in the park.

Two *pairs* of pants **are** necessary for the weekend trip.

The following chart lists some plural-form nouns and categorizes them by their correct usage—as singular or plural. For other words, check the dictionary.

Singular	Plural
billiards	clothes
checkers	(eye)glasses, goggles, contacts [lenses]
measles	pants, slacks (etc.)
molasses	pliers
news	proceeds
Niagara Falls	riches
the United States	shears, scissors
	soapsuds, suds
	thanks
	tights
	tweezers

The names of many teams and organizations exist in the plural form as well. These names require a plural verb.

The *Atlanta Braves* **play** their home games at Turner Field.

The *Rough Riders* **were** led by Theodore Roosevelt.

Words ending in *-ics* may be singular or plural, depending on the meaning of the sentence. When the word indicates a field of study, use a singular verb. When the word refers to a characteristic, an activity, or a product, use a plural verb. A dictionary may help you distinguish the singular and plural meanings of words like these.

> **Singular** | *Statistics* **is** a difficult course in his college major.
>
> **Plural** | The new campaign *statistics* **were** overwhelmingly in his favor.

Collective Nouns

Collective Nouns
p. 37

A **collective noun** refers to a group as a unit rather than to the individual people or things in the group. A singular collective noun often requires a singular verb, and a plural collective noun always requires a plural verb. A singular collective noun may require a plural verb if the meaning of the sentence emphasizes the individuals in the group rather than the group as a unit.

> **Singular Use** | The landscape *committee* **is leaving** the assembly room.
>
> The soccer *team* **has won** all of its games this season.
>
> **Plural Use** | The landscape *committee* **are arguing** about the decision to plant trees.
>
> The soccer *team* **have taken** their positions on the playing field.

In the singular sentences, the group is functioning as a unit. In the plural sentences, the members of the group are acting individually.

 Americans often reword a sentence to avoid using a collective noun such as *team* with a plural verb.

> The political party **members vote** for their own candidate.

The British, on the other hand, treat many more words as collective nouns (including singular-sounding names of teams and corporations), and they freely treat these nouns as plural.

> The **political party are nominating** the candidates that they think can win.

Americans would use *is* in this sentence.

> The **political party is nominating** the candidates that it thinks can win.

 Some nouns always take plural verbs:
1. Some collective nouns derived from adjectives that refer to groups of people
   The **elderly are** sometimes neglected by their families.
2. The noun *people* (to indicate singular, use *person*)
   People want to be remembered, and an elderly **person is** no exception.
3. The noun *police* (to indicate one member of the police force, use *police officer*)
   Inner-city **police experience** many dangers.
   An inner-city **police officer is** constantly alert.

Titles, Quotations, and Amounts as Singular

The **title** of an individual work of art, music, or literature is always singular, even though words in the title may be plural.

BJU Living Gallery presentation of *The Three Crosses* by Rembrandt, The Metropolitan Museum of Art, New York. Photo by Unusual Films.

      S   LV   PN
The Three Crosses is a Baroque-style etching.

      S   TrV   DO
"Trust and Obey" reflects God's promises to us.

      S   LV PN
Anne of Green Gables is a favorite of many readers.

A **quoted word or phrase** is a single item and needs a singular verb.

   S LV PN
Yours is what you meant to write, not *your's*.

                  S   InV
"You can't teach an old dog new tricks" does not apply to my grandfather.

Amounts are considered singular and need a singular verb even when the items that make up the amounts are plural. The principle applies to measured amounts, amounts of money, and periods of time.

      S   LV PA
Two cups of coffee is sufficient for the morning.

      S   LV   PN
Ten dollars was a reasonable price for the book.

      S   TrV   DO
Three weeks provides plenty of time for rest and relaxation.

in SUMMARY

Certain nouns have only one form, which appears to be plural. Some of these nouns are always used with singular verbs, and some of these nouns are always used with plural verbs.

A **collective noun** refers to a group. Usually, a singular collective noun needs a singular verb. A sentence that emphasizes the individual members of the group, however, needs a plural verb.

Titles, **quoted words or phrases**, and **amounts** are considered singular and need singular verbs.

6.3 PRACTICE *the skill*

Underline the simple subject(s) of each verb in parentheses. Then underline the correct verb from the choices in parentheses. You may use a dictionary.

1. "All the world's a stage" *(was, were)* the motto of the Globe Theatre, where Shakespeare acted and wrote.

2. The Lord Chamberlain's Men, Shakespeare's company, *(was, were)* occupants of a different playhouse, The Theatre, but by 1598 the lease had lapsed.

3. The troupe *(was, were)* not the owner of the land occupied by The Theatre, and the property owner did not renew the lease.

4. The tactics adopted by the troupe *(was, were)* to dismantle the theater and move it overnight to new property.

5. The news *(was, were)* a shock to the owner, but he could not stop the actors.

6. The poor *(was, were)* delighted by the cheaper admission costs in the yard, which offered standing room for "groundlings."

7. Two hundred pounds *(is, are)* the estimated annual income Shakespeare made from his share in the Globe.

8. *The Merry Wives of Windsor (was, were)* performed in the new theater.

9. Acoustics *(was, were)* not a science in Elizabethan times.

10. In fact, the acoustics of the Globe Theatre *(was, were)* likely quite poor.

6.4 REVIEW *the skill*

Rewrite each sentence to correct any errors in subject-verb agreement. If the sentence is already correct, write C.

1. *The Romancers* were written by Edmond Rostand.

   _____
   _____

2. Riches are not an issue in the play; rather the conflict concerns love.

   _____
   _____

3. A pair of young lovers are the focal point of the play.

   _____
   _____

4. Many years are the length of the feud between the fathers of Sylvette and Percinet.

   _____
   _____
   _____

5. Actually, the ethics of the fathers is dubious, because the feud is a pretense to make their children fall in love.

   _____
   _____
   _____

6. A band of robbers is hired to pretend to kidnap Sylvette.

   _____
   _____

7. Ninety pistoles are the sum the fathers promise to pay the robbers.

   _____
   _____

8. Percinet's ineffectual athletics seems to frighten the phony brigands.

   _____
   _____

9. The band hide themselves while the fathers declare that the children can marry.

   _____
   _____

10. "Hatreds always end in marriages" are the statement of Percinet's father.

    _____
    _____

Indefinite Pronouns

Most **indefinite pronouns** do not usually cause problems. Singular indefinite pronouns need singular verbs, and plural indefinite pronouns need plural verbs.

ALWAYS SINGULAR	*Everyone* **is** going to the soccer game.
	No one **wants** to be late.
ALWAYS PLURAL	*Several* **are** injured and cannot play for this game.
	Many **have planned** to stay for the reception afterwards.

Indefinite Pronouns pp. 38–39

Always Singular				
another	each	everything	neither	one
anybody	either	less	nobody	somebody
anyone	everybody	little	no one	someone
anything	everyone	much	nothing	something

Always Plural				
both	few	fewer	many	several

Some indefinite pronouns, however, can be either singular or plural. These indefinite pronouns may be understood as singular or plural, depending on what modifies them. These words have a singular meaning when they are modified by an *of* phrase that has a singular object. These same words have a plural meaning when they are modified by an *of* phrase that has a plural object. In some sentences the *of* phrase can be understood.

SINGULAR | Some of my homework is not completed for tomorrow.
| I could not find my assignments, so some is not here.

PLURAL | Some of the assignments were finished on time.
| I wanted to finish all my assignments, but some were too difficult.

The word *none* follows this rule with one exception. Although *none* is singular when followed by an *of* phrase with a singular object, *none* may be singular or plural when followed by an *of* phrase with a plural object.

None of the turkey dinner *is* left for tomorrow.

None of these recipes *is* a secret.

None of the desserts *are* left from the meal.

In very formal writing, *none* may be singular even in the third example sentence.

Singular or Plural		
all	more	none
any	most	some

Measure Words

Measure words, such as *half*, *part*, and *percent*, follow the same guidelines as indefinite pronouns. These words take a singular verb when they are modified by an *of* phrase that has a singular object, but they take a plural verb when they are modified by an *of* phrase that has a plural object.

SINGULAR | Half of the team is in the locker room right now.

PLURAL | Half of the required hours for graduation are taken in the first two years.

The word *number* follows special rules of agreement. *The number of* (like *the number*) is always singular, but *a number of* (meaning "several") is always plural.

SINGULAR	Because all five of us in our family can now drive, **the *number*** of *cars* in our driveway *has increased* to five.
PLURAL	**A *number*** of *neighbors say* teasingly that my family can start its own used-car business.

Relative Pronouns

A **relative pronoun** (*who, whom, whose, which,* or *that*) does not change form to indicate singular and plural, but we treat a relative pronoun as though it has the same number as its antecedent.

Relative Pronouns p. 39

          S   InV
He is the player who plays in the goal box.

                              S   InV
The members of the team who have played all year are eligible for the trip.

Before you decide on a singular or a plural verb, consider the meaning of the dependent clause to help you determine the antecedent of the relative pronoun.

Antecedents of Pronouns p. 37

                            S   TrV-P
Here is the roster of players that has been submitted to the school newspaper.

                        S   TrV   DO
The list of players who have completed their schoolwork is posted on the bulletin board.

Certain constructions need special attention. A sentence that contains "the only one of the" or "one of the" before a noun and relative pronoun is sometimes a problem. In most cases, use a singular verb after a relative pronoun that follows "the only one of the" and use a plural verb after a relative pronoun that follows "one of the."

                                    S   TrV   DO
James is the only one of the players who has a perfect score in class.

In this sentence the antecedent of *who* is *one*. Although there were many players in class, James was the only one to achieve a perfect score; the other players did not.

                                  S   InV
Charles is one of the players who are practicing diligently for the game.

In this sentence the antecedent of *who* is *players*; a plural verb is necessary. Many players practiced for the game; Charles was a part of that group.

in SUMMARY

Some **indefinite pronouns** used as subjects are always singular; some are always plural; and some can be either singular or plural.

Certain words may be determined as singular or plural depending on what modifies those words. To determine whether to use a singular or a plural verb, consider the object of the following *of* prepositional phrase.

Measure words—half, part, percent—take singular or plural verbs according to the same guidelines as indefinite pronouns.

A **relative pronoun** that is the subject of a dependent clause is treated as having the same number as its antecedent.

6.5 PRACTICE *the skill*

Underline the subject(s) of each verb in parentheses. Then underline the correct verb from the choices in parentheses.

1. There are three types of stages that (*is, are*) in common use.
2. Some (*prefers, prefer*) to use an arena stage for added immediacy.
3. On an arena stage, one hundred percent of the acting area (*is, are*) surrounded by the audience.
4. Many (*chooses, choose*) the thrust stage, which (*extends, extend*) out into the seating area like a peninsula.
5. Theaters come in a variety of configurations, but most (*has, have*) a traditional proscenium stage.
6. Some people think half of the effect (*is, are*) lost if the wrong type of stage is used.
7. The arena stage is the only one of these stage types that (*has, have*) no regular wings.
8. None of these three types (*is, are*) lacking a lip, or edge.
9. The new Globe Theatre, which (*was, were*) opened in 1997, has a thrust stage.
10. Everyone (*forms, form*) his own opinion of his favorite type of stage.

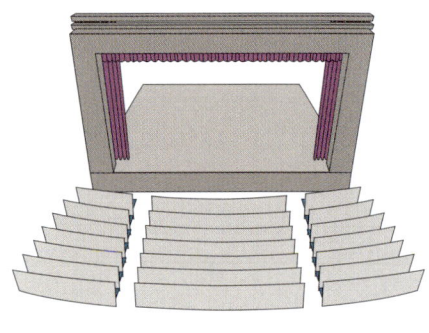

6.6 REVIEW *the skill*

Underline each incorrect verb. Then write the correct verb in the blank. If the sentence is already correct, write C.

_____ 1. One of the forms of drama are the Italian *commedia dell'arte*.

_____ 2. Some of the major characters is Harlequin, Columbine, and Pierrot.

_____ 3. Harlequin, who wear a costume decorated with black-and-white or colored diamond shapes, is sometimes a clown and sometimes the protagonist.

_____ 4. No one among the actors memorizes the script in advance; the show is improvised around a basic plot.

_____ 5. Part of the drama usually involves the tricking of Pantaloon, a bumbling and foolish character.

_____ 6. Harlequin is one of the clowns, or *zanni*, who plagues Pantaloon.

_____ 7. The English word *zany*, which means "clownish or bizarre," comes from the Italian word *zanni*.

_____ 8. Everyone in *commedia dell'arte* are a stock character, a character with little individuality.

_____ 9. The number of characters in a given performance vary.

_____ 10. Half of Americans has probably never seen an example of *commedia dell'arte*.

Compound Subjects

Determining the correct verb for a compound subject depends upon the conjunction used to join the parts of the subject.

Compound Subjects p. 71

Compound Subjects Joined with And

Compound subjects joined by *and* or *both—and* are usually plural. The sentence requires a plural verb.

> **PLURAL** | Overseeding **and** adequate fertilization were necessary for success.
>
> **PLURAL** | **Both** utilitarian plants **and** flowers decorate our gardens today.

Conjunctions pp. 54–55

However, two words joined by *and* may refer to the same person or thing or to a single idea. In that case, the subject is considered a singular unit, and the verb is singular to agree with it.

> **SINGULAR** | Today apple pie **and** ice cream is an American tradition.
>
> **PLURAL** | **Both** apple pie **and** ice cream taste best when homemade.

In the first sentence, the subject looks plural, but the verb is singular. The subject parts refer to one combined thing, a dessert, and so a singular verb is needed. In the second sentence, the subjects refer to two different things, pie and ice cream; therefore, the verb is plural. Usually, though, *and* joins separate things and requires a plural verb.

Compound Subjects Joined with Or

For compound subjects joined with *or* (also *either—or, neither—nor*), the subject nearer to the verb (or to the first auxiliary in a complete verb) determines the form of the verb. Remember that *or* indicates a choice.

> Mr. Quinn or *Mr. and Mrs. Adams are* proctoring the test.
>
> *Are you* or your brother ready for the history test?
>
> Neither James nor his *friends are staying* after school to study.
>
> *Is* James or his *friends* coming to study tonight?

Shifts in Person p. 216

Agreement | Chapter 6 **161**

in SUMMARY

Compound subjects joined by *and* or *both—and* are usually plural.

If a compound subject joined by *and* refers to the same idea, person, or entity, the verb should be singular.

For compound subjects joined by *or, either—or,* or *neither—nor,* the verb agrees in number with the subject nearer to the verb or the first auxiliary.

6.7 PRACTICE *the skill*

Underline each incorrect verb. Then write the correct verb in the blank. If the sentence is already correct, write C.

1. Plays and poems about lovers has often been written.
2. In one medieval ballad, a king and a maid fall in love.
3. Both *Romeo and Juliet* and *Antony and Cleopatra* ends with the death of the lovers.
4. Either Tybalt or the Capulets threatens Romeo's life.
5. The Capulets' pride and joy commit suicide at the end.
6. Neither Mercutio nor the Capulets were willing to stop the fighting.
7. Both the young lovers and the rogue, Autolycus, has double identities in *The Winter's Tale*.
8. Are Goethe's Faust or Gretchen aware of the evil of Mephistopheles?
9. In "The Eve of St. Agnes," neither the beadsman nor the revelers knows of the lovers' escape.
10. Either young lovers or romance in general is a very popular topic for poems and plays.

6.8 REVIEW the skill

Correct the ten errors in subject-verb agreement by crossing out each incorrect verb and writing a correct verb above it.

One of the developments of Renaissance drama was the comedy of humours. The main instigator and user of this genre were Ben Jonson, a contemporary of Shakespeare, who also used elements of it. The basis of the comedy of humours come from the Greek idea of four humours, or liquids, corresponding to four personality types. An imbalance of humours cause personality differences. Both blood (sanguine) and yellow bile (choleric) is humours. Either too much blood or too much yellow bile produce excess warmth of personality. Falstaff and Autolycus is examples of the sanguine humour, and Hotspur and Tybalt typifies the choleric humour. Another humour is black bile (melancholic). Either Hamlet or Richard II are a good example of melancholy. The last of the four humours is phlegm (phlegmatic). In *A Midsummer Night's Dream*, neither the lovers nor Titania are phlegmatic, but both Flute and Starveling is. As the comedy of humours developed, its characters became dramatic stereotypes, instantly recognizable for their qualities.

Pronoun-Antecedent Agreement

Another important area of correct usage is that of pronoun-antecedent agreement. Just as a subject and a verb must agree, so must a pronoun agree with its antecedent, the word or phrase to which the pronoun refers.

Personal Pronouns pp. 37–38

Nouns as Antecedents

A noun or a noun phrase is the usual antecedent of a pronoun. If the antecedent is singular, the pronoun must be singular; if the antecedent is plural, the pronoun must be plural.

SINGULAR	The *storm* has destroyed many houses in *its* path.
PLURAL	As a result of the rain, the *rivers* have overrun *their* banks.

Antecedents of Pronouns p. 37

Pronouns can also show gender as well as number. The pronoun, therefore, must also agree in gender with its antecedent—masculine, feminine, or neuter.

MASCULINE	*Robert* rescued *his* outdoor animals from the coming storm.
FEMININE	*Dr. Rachel Roth*, the meteorologist, made *her* prediction for the storm's path.
NEUTER	The *storm* made *its* way up the coast in only a few hours.

Shifts in Number p. 216

Agreement | Chapter 6 **163**

If a singular antecedent does not indicate a specific gender, use a singular masculine pronoun. Do not use a plural personal pronoun if the antecedent is singular.

RIGHT	The *homeowner who* lost *his* house in the storm was able to salvage a few belongings.
WRONG	The *homeowner who* lost *their* house in the storm was able to salvage a few belongings.

tip

To avoid a gender choice, try making the sentence plural.
Each student read his story aloud.
All the students read their stories aloud.

ESL Some native speakers, in conversation, may insert a pronoun immediately after the antecedent. However, unless you are trying to achieve a colloquial effect, do not use this extra pronoun in your writing.

WITH THE EXTRA PRONOUN	Aiden, ~~he~~ fixed my car.
WITHOUT THE EXTRA PRONOUN	Aiden fixed my car.

It is incorrect to use both a personal pronoun *(he, her)* and a relative pronoun *(who, whom, whose, which, that)* in the same clause to refer to the same antecedent.

INCORRECT	My cat is the one that ~~she~~ clawed up the carpet.
CORRECT	My cat is the one that clawed up the carpet.

Compound Antecedents

Compound Subjects p. 71

Conjunctions pp. 54–55

Compound antecedents are determined to be singular or plural in the same way that compound subjects are. Use a plural pronoun when the antecedents are joined by *and* or *both—and*. When the antecedents are joined by *or, either—or,* or *neither—nor,* use a pronoun that agrees with the nearer antecedent.

PLURAL	As a result of the storm's destruction, the *parents and their children* went to *their* relatives' house.
SINGULAR	Either the twin *boys* or *their* older *brother* will lay out *his* sleeping bag upstairs.
PLURAL	*Neither Dad nor the children* could close *their* eyes while the wind blew violently.

ESL Although *either—or* indicates a choice, *neither—nor* is different. The meaning of *neither—nor* is the same as *both—and* plus the negative idea of *not*.

Neither my good deeds **nor** my Christian family can get me into heaven.

This sentence means that the speaker's good deeds cannot get him into heaven *and* the speaker's Christian family cannot get him into heaven.

Or works the same way when *not* is present: It makes *not* apply to all the items named.

Salvation is **not** in what I can do **or** in what my family can do; it is in what Jesus has done for me.

In this sentence salvation does not result from what the speaker can do *and* it does not result from what the speaker's family can do.

Correcting a sentence with a pronoun-antecedent agreement problem may create an awkward sentence. To avoid the awkwardness, reword the sentence. A plural pronoun is not acceptable for a singular antecedent.

AWKWARD | *Either Susan or Sam* will take *his* turn bailing water.

WRONG | *Either Susan or Sam* will take *their* turn bailing water.

BETTER | *Either Susan* will take *her* turn bailing water, or *Sam* will take *his*.

in SUMMARY

A pronoun must agree with its antecedent in gender and number.

If the singular antecedent does not specify gender when referring to a person, use a singular masculine pronoun.

If a **compound antecedent** is joined by *and* or *both—and*, the pronoun should be plural. If the compound antecedent is joined by *or, nor, either—or,* or *neither—nor*, the pronoun should agree with the antecedent nearer to it.

6.9 PRACTICE the skill

Underline the correct pronoun from the choices in parentheses.

1. Does Hamlet have difficulty making up (*his, its*) mind?

2. A reader of the play forms (*his, their*) own opinion.

3. Either Horatio or the guards could have offered Hamlet (*his, their*) advice.

4. Both Hamlet and his mother, Gertrude, mourn the death of (*his, their*) relative.

5. Reynaldo, a servant of Polonius, receives (*his, their*) instructions to spy on Laertes.

6. Neither the players nor Rosencrantz understands (*his, their*) friend's distress.

7. A player recites (*his, their*) speech about the Trojan War.

8. Both Laertes and Claudius scheme against Hamlet in (*his, their*) own ways.

9. Rosencrantz and Guildenstern go to (*his, their*) deaths unknowingly.

10. An ambassador with (*his, their*) entourage brings news of their deaths.

6.10 REVIEW *the skill*

Write an appropriate pronoun to complete each sentence.

_____ 1. In *A Midsummer Night's Dream,* each character has **?** own struggles.

_____ 2. Both Demetrius and Helena are in love with people who do not love **?**.

_____ 3. Lysander and Hermia abandon **?** homes and flee into the woods.

_____ 4. Neither Oberon nor Titania has **?** priorities straight.

_____ 5. A player is concerned about memorizing **?** lines.

_____ 6. A second player thinks that **?** should be the one to roar like a lion.

_____ 7. Either Puck or the fairies are able to use **?** skills to befuddle the travelers.

_____ 8. Quince and the other players are nervous about performing **?** play.

_____ 9. Both Helena and Hermia are distressed about **?** situation.

_____ 10. The reader will find that all **?** questions are answered at the end.

Collective Nouns as Antecedents

Collective nouns can be singular or plural. A collective noun that emphasizes the group as a unit needs a singular verb and any pronoun referring to it is likewise singular. If the collective noun refers to the individuals of the group, the noun needs a plural verb and any pronoun referring to it is plural. Analyze the sentence for its meaning.

SINGULAR USE	The rescue *unit* does *its* best to rescue an endangered family pet.
	The *team* worked through the night to achieve *its* goal of rescuing the trapped dog.
PLURAL USE	The rescue *unit* perform *their* jobs with speed and precision.
	The *team* encouraged each other in *their* pursuit of the trapped pet.

In the singular examples, the noun functions as a unit and is referred to by a singular pronoun. The plural examples emphasize the members of the group, and so the collective nouns require plural pronouns. In a sentence with a collective noun, the verb is often a clue, as with the *unit* examples. A past tense verb does not indicate singular or plural, as in the *team* examples.

See note about collective noun use in England and America on page 154.

Indefinite Pronouns as Antecedents

Indefinite pronouns can function as antecedents for other pronouns that follow. The later pronoun must agree in number with the indefinite pronoun that precedes it. A prepositional phrase may indicate the true number of the indefinite pronoun.

Indefinite Pronouns pp. 38–39

Singular	*Everybody* put *his* full effort into listening for sounds of life from the dog.
	Part of the rescue was successful when *it* revealed a dusty paw.
Plural	*Most* were eager to show *their* relief when the paw appeared.
	All of the children showed *their* excitement when the freed puppy ran toward them.

Indefinite pronouns do not show gender. The context of the sentence, however, may indicate the correct gender. When the gender is not clear, use the masculine singular pronoun.

Masculine	*Each* of the men on the team took *his* time packing away the rescue gear.
	Did *anyone* leave *his* gear behind the truck?
Feminine	*Neither* of the girls was willing to give up *her* opportunity to play with the puppy.
Neuter	*Another* of the rescue units was ready to give *its* help.

When the gender of a singular indefinite pronoun is not clear, you may also choose to use both masculine and feminine pronouns to refer to it. The sentence, however, may appear awkward. To avoid an awkward sentence, reword the sentence without the personal pronouns. Standard English does not permit a plural personal pronoun to refer to a singular indefinite pronoun.

Awkward	*Everybody* packed *his* or *her* suitcase for the long evacuation trip.
Reworded	*Everybody* packed a suitcase for the long evacuation trip.
Wrong	*Everybody* packed *their* suitcase for the long evacuation trip.

Agreement with nouns modified by indefinite determiners is similar to agreement with indefinite pronouns. A singular noun modified by an indefinite determiner is always singular.

Determiners pp. 48–49

Indefinite Pronoun	The police encouraged *everyone* to bring *his* sleeping bag.
Indefinite Determiner	The police encouraged *every evacuee* to bring *his* sleeping bag.

For a list of indefinite pronouns, see the chart on page 38.

in SUMMARY

Collective nouns may be singular or plural. When the group is regarded as a unit, it is singular and needs a singular verb. Any pronoun referring to it must be singular. When the collective noun emphasizes the individuals of the group, it is plural and needs a plural verb. Any pronoun referring to it must be plural.

A pronoun should **agree in number and gender** with an indefinite pronoun that acts as its antecedent.

A **singular indefinite pronoun** does not show gender. Do not refer to a singular indefinite pronoun with a plural personal pronoun. Choose one of these options instead: use a singular masculine pronoun; use both a singular masculine pronoun and a singular feminine pronoun; or reword the sentence to make it plural or to avoid personal pronouns.

A singular noun modified by an **indefinite determiner** is always singular.

6.11 PRACTICE the skill

Write the letter of the sentence that shows correct pronoun-antecedent agreement.

_____ 1. A. All of the plays require appropriate settings to present them well.
B. All of the plays require appropriate settings to present it well.

_____ 2. A. The team of designers does their best.
B. The team of designers does its best.

_____ 3. A. The designers divide the work; each tackles their own part.
B. The designers divide the work; each tackles his part.

_____ 4. A. Everyone must be able to perform their task.
B. Everyone must be able to perform his or her task.

_____ 5. A. Someone will perform his task of planning the set.
B. Someone will perform their task of planning the set.

_____ 6. A. No one, including the lighting designer and the costume designer, can shirk their responsibilities.
B. No one, including the lighting designer and the costume designer, can shirk his responsibilities.

_____ 7. A. One arc light is causing a designer some trouble as he tries to fix it.
B. One arc light is causing a designer some trouble as they try to fix it.

_____ 8. A. Another arc light is doing their job magnificently.
B. Another arc light is doing its job magnificently.

_____ 9. A. Most of the pieces are finally in their places.
B. Most of the pieces are finally in its place.

_____ 10. A. The group congratulates itself on its effort.
B. The group congratulate themselves on their efforts.

6.12 REVIEW the skill

Underline each incorrect pronoun. Then write the correct pronoun in the blank. If the sentence is already correct, write C in the blank.

_____ 1. In the 1590s the company of the Lord Chamberlain was famous for their actors, as was the company known as the Admiral's Men.

_____ 2. Each troupe had their own star: Richard Burbage for the Lord Chamberlain's Men and Edward Alleyn for the Admiral's Men.

_____ 3. Was either of these actors greater than their rival?

_____ 4. Anyone could enrich their day by watching Alleyn in *Dr. Faustus* or *Tamburlaine*.

_____ 5. Most said their favorite of Burbage's roles was Richard III.

_____ 6. Neither of the men focused their career on comic roles.

_____ 7. Burbage's troupe worked in its various roles to bring success to the Globe Theatre.

_____ 8. During their lifetimes, few have seen the portraits that the talented Burbage painted.

_____ 9. Every student of theater can see that Alleyn was esteemed as a great actor if he reads Ben Jonson's tribute to him.

_____ 10. All in Dulwich were happy when Alleyn retired to its town and built a college and a hospital.

Edward Alleyn

Richard Burbage

Agreement | Chapter 6

CUMULATIVE *review*

Rewrite the following paragraph, correcting the ten errors from these categories: fragments, comma splices, fused sentences, subject-verb agreement, and pronoun-antecedent agreement.

    The Passion play of Oberammergau, Germany, is renowned worldwide. The Passion play depicts scenes from the Bible it focuses on the life of Christ. The play, which is performed every ten years, was first performed in 1634. Nearly half of Oberammergau's five thousand inhabitants takes part, everyone participates eagerly in their hometown's tradition. During the Crucifixion scene there is four hundred actors on stage. However, in the past many have expressed concerns. That the plays are anti-Semitic. Now the director of the plays is attempting to alleviate such concerns by their updated script. Several major changes include the following: Jewish characters are now simply citizens instead of moneygrubbers. Both Hebrew and Greek names are used to show the various layers of Jewish society. Certain negative characters are altered to portray Jews more positively, and some disappears entirely. The crowd before Pilate divides into two parts, those for Jesus and those against Jesus, while Jesus Himself is called "Rabbi" in order to emphasize His Jewish heritage. One of the most significant changes is the deletion of a controversial sentence: "The blood be upon us" have been removed from the text. The goal of the play's director and other reformers are to remove the anti-Jewish stigma and to balance change with tradition.

FROM THE WRITTEN WORD

Presenting an Argument

Elijah the prophet and Ahab, the king of Israel, were contemporaries with opposite perspectives and convictions. In spite of his human weaknesses, Elijah determined to serve God. On the other hand, Ahab, influenced by his ungodly heritage and his wicked wife, Jezebel, allowed pagan temples and idols in the land. More than once Elijah feared for his life as he appeared before Ahab. Despite his antagonistic audience, Elijah was able to articulate clearly before Ahab.

What about you when you are confronted by those who disagree with you? How successful are you in expressing logical ideas on the spur of the moment? Are you able to focus on an idea and reason clearly?

In 1 Kings 18 Elijah makes use of one of the most important rhetorical strategies available to a writer or speaker. Successful argumentation depends on the writer's or speaker's ability to formulate logical ideas and organize them effectively. Elijah makes a proposition and sets about to prove that proposition.

> And he answered, I have not troubled Israel; but thou, and thy father's house, in that ye have forsaken the commandments of the Lord, and thou hast followed Baalim. And Elijah came unto all the people, and said, How long halt ye between two opinions? If the Lord be God, follow him: but if Baal, then follow him. And the people answered him not a word.
> (1 Kings 18:18, 21)

Elijah declares his argument: Ahab has provided the wrong leadership for Israel. With this idea in mind, what then are Elijah's proof statements? Ahab has forsaken the law of God; Ahab has followed false gods.

One problem that often appears in argumentation is the use of universal statements. As you argue, avoid statements including *only*, *all*, or *every*. How many times have you argued that everyone was doing a certain thing or that you were the only one who could not participate in an activity? First Kings 19:14 records Elijah's complaint that "I, even I only, am left." Careful reading of 1 Kings 19:18 reveals that seven thousand who had not bowed to idols remained in Israel.

Personal Response

Read Romans 12:2. Imagine yourself in a discussion with another student about some current trend or issue of the day. Remember that an argument could be approached from either the pro or con side. Basing your argument on Romans 12:2, write a paragraph stating your position and the reasons for your position.

Extemporaneous Essay	174
Verb Use	177
Think About It	196

EXTEMPORANEOUS ESSAY Writing
VERB USE Usage

7

Think for a moment about your friends. How long have you known your closest friend? How have your friendships changed from the time you were young until now? Have you ever lost contact with a friend who moved away? When asked to write an essay about friendship, one student recounted how her relationship with one of her childhood friends has changed over the years. Read her essay and compare her experience to your own.

A Record of Our Journeys by Ilana Sibley

As I read the latest message from my friend Nicole, I realized how much our friendship has changed—and yet endured—over the years. We met in kindergarten, where we learned to tie our shoes and write our names. From kindergarten through junior high school, Nicole and I saw each other almost every day. We shared experiences—going to classes, playing softball. We shared discoveries—a new poem, a truth about God. And we shared heartaches—a broken arm, an argument with a classmate.

One summer we spent a month together in Mexico on a youth mission team. Those four weeks of praying, failing, learning, and rejoicing brought us even closer. When the trip was over, we returned—but Nicole went to her new home in another state. At first I missed Mexico and I missed Nicole. Then her first message arrived. She described her new house, her new school, her new church. Although she was sad about leaving her hometown, she enjoyed the adventure of exploring a new city.

Soon the messages flew between us. We shared news about friends, phrases in Spanish, and snatches of poetry. But the letters changed as our high school years passed. Now we discuss college plans, career goals, God's plan for the future. We are learning what really matters in life. What has lasted is the simple faith in God's Word that our parents and our teachers have modeled for us.

"My grandmother has been diagnosed with cancer," my latest message from Nicole reads. "It's so hard for me to be away from her. Please pray for her." I wondered how to answer. I had no advice or poem to meet her need. I turned instead to the Psalms, the only poetry with any real power to comfort.

Through our correspondence, Nicole and I have kept a record of our journeys—of our thinking, of our changing, of our growing in Christ. We have learned this: Even more important than the friendships that we make are the friendships that we keep. They have years to develop and grow, as do the two participants.

Extemporaneous Essay

A friend loveth at all times, and a brother is born for adversity.
Proverbs 17:17

By this point in your academic life, you have probably encountered an essay test at least once. An essay test measures your knowledge about the subject and your ability to communicate that knowledge clearly in writing. An extemporaneous essay, on the other hand, focuses solely on your ability to express yourself on a given topic. Good essays, whether on a test or extemporaneous, demonstrate your ability to think, to organize your thoughts, and to express those thoughts clearly under time constraints. Even if you are never asked to write an extemporaneous essay outside class, you will be asked to think "on your feet." Memos, business letters, employee evaluations, proposals for new products, applications for funding—all of these are realistic writing projects that must be completed within a prescribed time limit and in addition to the regular workload. Learning to communicate under pressure is a skill that will serve you well in every aspect of life.

Write an extemporaneous essay on a topic your instructor assigns. Your teacher will give you guidelines regarding the length and time limit. Be prepared to identify the purpose, audience, and specific topic that you choose.

Planning

- ✔ **Analyze the assignment.** Be sure that you know exactly what is expected of you. Some assignments will specify what kind of essay you are to write as well as who your intended audience is. This assignment, however, leaves most of the decisions up to the writer.

- ✔ **Generate some ideas about the assigned topic.** Create a brainstorming list or a clustering diagram with all the general ideas and specific details that occur to you. Then examine the results. What groupings appear? Do any themes stand out? Use these notes as you plan your essay. Look at Sibley's original notes to see how she generated ideas on the topic of friendship.

> "A man that hath friends must show himself friendly."
> "Jesus, What a Friend for Sinners"
> Is having friends important?
> Nicole
>   messages
>   meeting in kindergarten
>   still friends even though she moved away
> How to make new friends
>   meeting Jenny at her piano recital
>   Dad and his college roommate
>   Mom's friendship with her coworkers
> Abraham—a friend of God
> David and Jonathan

- ✓ **Decide on the parameters for your essay.** Now that you have noted some possibilities, you should settle on the specifics. You need to specify a purpose for your essay, identify your intended audience, and choose your specific topic. For example, Sibley chose to discuss her friend and the messages they have shared. But she could just as easily have chosen to persuade teens of the importance of making new friends, to inform children about the influence that one friend can have on another, or to inspire adults to study the friendship between David and Jonathan in the Bible.

- ✓ **Create a thesis statement and supporting statements.** Use the ideas you generated earlier to identify the main point that you want to make. State that point as your thesis statement, identifying both your topic and the main thing you intend to say about that topic. Then sketch out the key points you plan to make in support of your thesis. Remember to include such details as facts, examples, and illustrations. Notice that Sibley specifically mentions softball, poetry, and a mission trip to Mexico among the events that she and her friend shared.

- ✓ **Organize a rough outline.** Choose an appropriate organizational strategy and then number your points in the order in which they will appear. Note which details you will use to support your main points. Sibley uses chronological order for her essay, recounting the history of her friendship and the changes that their correspondence has recorded.

- ✓ **Sketch out a conclusion.** Before you begin to draft your essay, you should know how you want it to end. Your concluding statements are the last thing your readers will see—and probably the first thing they will remember. The conclusion should restate your thesis statement and then show the importance of your point. Examine the sample essay to discover how Sibley uses this strategy.

Drafting

- ✓ **Write with revision in mind.** You probably will not have time to rewrite your entire essay before you turn it in. If you write on every other line, you will be able to add words in the spaces between when you revise. Writing on only one side of the paper allows you to make any needed longer revisions on the back.

- ✓ **Maintain a consistent tone.** Keep your audience and your purpose in mind as you write. A personal essay can benefit from an informal tone, but an informational essay usually requires some degree of formality. Both word choice and sentence structure contribute to the tone of a piece of writing. In general, reserve first-person and second-person references for essays that are informal or personal in nature.

- ✓ **Begin with your thesis statement.** Unless the assignment specifically requires you to write an introduction, your thesis statement should suffice. There is usually little time and no need for a formal introduction to an extemporaneous essay.

- ✓ **State each point clearly and provide adequate support.** Because your time is limited, you should begin with your strongest point, leaving less important points for later in the essay. (If you run out of time, your best arguments will be included already.) Depending on the nature of your essay, your first main point will begin a new paragraph or appear immediately after your thesis statement. Support that point with sentences that include the details you identified during the planning stage. Continue stating your points and providing support in subsequent paragraphs. Use transitional words to link ideas together as you move from point to point.

- **Write steadily.** Do not waste precious time by agonizing over word choice or sentence structure. For example, if you cannot think of a particular word you want to use, simply leave a blank space and continue writing. When you have completed your point, go back to insert the best word that comes to mind.

- **Avoid irrelevant information.** Keep your thesis statement in mind as you draft. Padding your essay with unnecessary details or useless points will take time that would be better spent polishing your key points.

- **Draw your essay to a close.** Do not use all your time to draft the body of your essay; save some of your time for your conclusion and for revising. Start with the statement that you sketched in the planning stage. Then reword that statement as necessary to incorporate any changes you made to your essay as you drafted it. An effective conclusion may be as simple as a restatement of your thesis or as complex as a short conclusion paragraph that goes beyond your thesis to show its importance. Ilana Sibley begins her conclusion by restating the connection between letters and her changing yet enduring friendship with Nicole. Sibley then emphasizes the value of maintaining such a friendship over the years: As the friends grow and change, they develop a deeper relationship than newly met friends are able to share.

Revising

Thinking Biblically

The more Bible education you have, the more likely it is that others are going to ask (and expect!) you to share devotional thoughts—sometimes on short notice. Even when you don't have the time to plan a lesson carefully, you may want to write out your thoughts; so the skill of writing extemporaneous essays is important. While you probably will not read your manuscript verbatim, the effort of crafting a few words "fitly spoken" (Prov. 25:11) adds power and memorability to what you say. The apostle Paul did not rely on powerful turns of phrase to make his points; he trusted in the powerful Spirit of God (1 Cor. 2:1-5). But he still very clearly crafted his words.

- **Reserve enough time to read over your essay at least once.** As you read, look for statements that lack adequate support or passages that seem unclear or awkward. You will not have time to rewrite your entire essay, but you should make any minor improvements that are necessary.

- **Delete anything that detracts from your focus.** If any off-topic details slipped in to harm the unity or coherence of your essay, cross them out neatly. Notice what Sibley deleted from her first draft in order to keep the focus on what she shared with her friend.

    > As I read the latest message from my friend Nicole, I realized how much our friendship has changed—and yet endured—over the years. We met in kindergarten, where we learned to tie our shoes and write our names. ~~Our teacher paired us up when she assigned classroom buddies during recess one day.~~ From then on, Nicole and I saw each other every day. ~~In fact, we sometimes spent more time with each other than we spent with our families.~~ We shared experiences—going to classes, playing softball. We shared discoveries—a new poem, a truth about God. And we shared heartaches—a broken arm, an argument with a classmate.

- **Add any necessary support or clarification.** Use the space between the lines for additions of only a few words. If you need to insert a longer passage, mark the place with an asterisk and write the new passage at the end of the essay or on the back of your paper. Compare a sentence from Sibley's original draft to the same sentence from her revision to see how even minor changes can clarify the meaning of a passage.

ORIGINAL	From then on, Nicole and I saw each other every day.
REVISION	From kindergarten through junior high school, Nicole and I saw each other almost every day.

✔ **Edit for grammar and mechanics.** Examine your original essay and any new information that you have added during revision. Look for errors in grammar, usage, word choice, spelling, punctuation, and capitalization. Cross out any mistake neatly and write any necessary correction in the margin or in the spaces between the lines.

Publishing

✔ **Read your essay aloud to an appropriate audience.** For example, consider performing a humorous essay as entertainment at a public gathering.

✔ **Adapt your essay as an article for the school newspaper.** Interview experts on your topic or interested peers and incorporate their comments into an article based on your essay.

✔ **Expand your essay into a lesson with additional support.** An informational essay on an academic topic could become a lesson for younger students. An inspirational essay on a biblical topic may make an excellent lesson for a Sunday school class, a Bible club, or a church youth group.

Some Ideas to Consider

History
- Discuss a notable figure from history. (Since the essay is extemporaneous, any historical topic you pick should be one you already know well and will not have to research.)

Science
- Identify the technological innovation of the past decade (or century) that has affected your life the most.

Bible
- Write an essay about family relationships.

VERB USE

Notice the verbs used by the apostle John to describe the actions of Christ against those who made the temple a place of business. "And when he had made a scourge of small cords, he drove them all out of the temple, and the sheep, and the oxen; and poured out the changers' money, and overthrew the tables" (John 2:15).

Because a verb is considered the backbone or support of a sentence, choosing strong verbs and using those verbs correctly help convey your message clearly. In this passage there is no question as to the Lord's actions and the result of His actions. In the process of choosing and using verbs correctly, the speaker and the writer must understand the varied possibilities of form, function, and type.

Verbs
pp. 42–45

Appendix
Adding Suffixes
pp. 429–30

Principal Parts

English verbs have three **principal parts**. Using these principal (or main) parts, you are able to make any form of those verbs. The principal parts are the present, the past, and the past participle forms.

tip
Use a good dictionary to find the three principal parts of verbs that are unfamiliar to you.

Verbs that form their second and third principal parts by adding *-d* or *-ed* to the first principal part are **regular verbs**. Most verbs are regular verbs.

oppose	opposed	opposed
play	played	played
hurry	hurried	hurried
occur	occurred	occurred

Some verbs that are otherwise regular substitute a *t* for the *d* of the first principal part instead of adding a suffix.

build	built	built
bend	bent	bent

Irregular verbs form their second and third principal parts in different ways. Some irregular verbs have a different form for each principal part. These differences may appear as vowel changes, ending changes, or a combination of the two.

drink	drank	drunk
know	knew	known
shake	shook	shaken
freeze	froze	frozen

Other irregular verbs have two of their principal parts the same.

swing	swung	swung
run	ran	run
lead	led	led

Sometimes all three principal parts of the verb are identical.

cost	cost	cost
burst	burst	burst

tip
As you write, look for opportunities to replace *be* verbs with strong action verbs.

Tenses

Tenses are verb forms that suggest the time of an action or of a state or situation. There are three simple tenses as well as perfect and progressive tenses.

Simple Tenses

The three simple tenses are present, past, and future. **Present tense** can indicate a state or a situation that exists in the present. For an action verb, it expresses

178 Chapter 7 | Verb Use

habitual action (what normally happens). The present tense uses the first principal part of the verb.

> Numbers of people *enjoy* fishing every year.
> My brother *has* an interest in fishing.
> Alec usually *fishes* on Lake Erie.
> Either he or his wife *cleans* and *fillets* the fish.

The first principal part of nearly every verb is used almost unchanged throughout the present tense, simply adding *s* or *es* to agree with third-person singular subjects (see p. 149). However, three verbs are irregular. As you know, **be** uses **is**, **am**, and **are** instead of a principal part (p. 149). Two other verbs have irregular forms for third-person singular in the present: **have** ("he **has**") and **do** ("he **does**," which is irregular only in pronunciation).

Past tense indicates a state or an action that took place in the past. Past tense verbs use the second principal part of the verb.

> We *watched* our friends fishing from the shore.
> Several of our friends *scheduled* a time to fish.

Future tense indicates a state or an action that will take place in the future. The future tense uses the auxiliary *will* (or *shall*) and the first principal part of the verb.

> We *will ask* our friends about their experience.
> Next year, I *will take* the opportunity to fish.

Auxiliaries p. 44

Perfect Tenses

The **perfect tenses** indicate a state of being or an action that is completed. In this sense, *perfect* means "complete." Perfect tenses are formed by using forms of the auxiliary verb *have* and the third principal part of the verb.

The **present perfect tense** indicates a state of being or an action that is completed during the present time or that began in the past and has continued until the present time. Present perfect verbs use the auxiliary *have* or *has*.

> My brother *has read* many articles about parasailing.
> Both of my brothers *have planned* to parasail next summer.
> Watching them plan this experience *has been* fun.

The present perfect is often used for actions that took place at an indefinite time in the past, especially the recent past. However, if the time of the action is specified, the simple past tense must be used.

PRESENT PERFECT | Yes, I *have read* that article.
SIMPLE PAST | In fact, I *read* it this morning.

The **past perfect tense** indicates a state of being or an action that was completed before a certain time in the past. Past perfect verbs use the auxiliary *had*.

> My friends did not realize that my brothers *had waited* several years to "fly."
> Both John and Charles *had* eagerly *anticipated* the experience.

The **future perfect tense** indicates that a state will exist or that an action will be completed before a certain time in the future. Future perfect verbs use the auxiliaries *will have* (or *shall have*).

> They *will have taken* their first ride before Dad arrives at the ocean.
> By this evening Dad *will have watched* them parasail several times.

Perfect Participles, Perfect Gerunds, Perfect Infinitives pp. 94, 98, 102

ESL One unusual thing about English is the expression of future time in dependent clauses that begin either with **if** or with a time word such as **when**, **while**, **as**, **before**, and **after**. Instead of future tense, these dependent clauses use the simple present tense to express future time.

After I **finish** my homework, I'll clean my room.
If I **clean** my room today, I won't have to clean it tomorrow.

When the verb in the independent clause is in the future perfect tense, the *if* clause or time clause can use either present tense or present perfect to express future time.

When I **have finished** (or: When I **finish**) high school, my sister will have finished four years of college.

Progressive Tenses

Present Participles pp. 92–93

Progressive tenses show continuing action. They use a form of the auxiliary verb *be* and add *-ing* to the first principal part of the main verb. The form of *be* reflects the simple or perfect tense of the verb.

Tense	Meaning	Form of *be*	Example
Present Progressive	Present continuing action	am, is, are	I **am learning** a new sport right now.
Past Progressive	Past continuing action	was, were	I **was learning** to parasail when I read about the accident.
Future Progressive	Continuing action in the future	will be	I **will be learning** new safety techniques this week before I parasail next week.
Present Perfect Progressive	Continuing action performed during the present time period	has been, have been	I **have been learning** water safety measures for the past month.
Past Perfect Progressive	Continuing action completed before a certain time in the past	had been	Until this summer, I **had been learning** from a book, not from experience.
Future Perfect Progressive	Continuing action that will be completed before a certain time in the future	will have been (shall have been)	By noon, we **will have been watching** the parasailers for two hours.

in SUMMARY

The three **principal parts** of verbs are the present, past, and past participle.

A **regular verb** forms its second and third principal parts by adding *-d* or *-ed* to the first principal part. **Irregular verbs** form their second and third principal parts in various ways.

Simple tenses are present, past, and future.

Present tense indicates a state that exists in the present or an action that takes place habitually.

Past tense indicates a state or action that occurred in the past.
Future tense indicates a state or action that will occur in the future.
Perfect tenses indicate a state or action that is completed.
Progressive tenses indicate an action that is continuing.

7.1 PRACTICE *the skill*

Underline the complete verb in each independent clause. Then identify its tense.

_____ 1. As technology improves, new forms of communication are continually developing.

_____ 2. The electromagnet allows an electrical current to pass through wires that surround a piece of metal and make it magnetic.

_____ 3. In 2025, electromagnets will have existed for two hundred years.

_____ 4. Many years ago Samuel Morse realized the potential for this device and invented the telegraph.

_____ 5. The telegraph consists of a wire through which an electromagnetic current passes and a receptor at the other end that clicks when the current arrives.

_____ 6. The first message sent by telegraph in America announced the nomination of Henry Clay as a presidential candidate in 1844.

_____ 7. In May of that year, the telegraph line opened when the first official message was transmitted.

_____ 8. Samuel Morse had allowed the daughter of a friend to choose the text of the message—Numbers 23:23.

_____ 9. "What hath God wrought!"

_____ 10. By 1877, when the telephone was developed, the telegraph had been sending messages worldwide for thirty-three years.

7.2 REVIEW *the skill*

Write the verb in parentheses in an appropriate tense. Try to use a variety of tenses and be prepared to identify the tense you choose.

_____ 1. Not everyone (*know*) the story of the pony express, which began on April 30, 1860, and (*develop*) into one of the greatest legends of the American West.

_____ 2. Despite the many risks and dangers in the year and a half of its existence, the pony express (*lose*) only one rider and only one mail delivery.

_____ 3. Before the pony express, the trip overland across the United States (*take*) twenty days, but the pony express riders (*make*) the trip in ten days or less.

_____ 4. On the trail, riders (*face*) many risks, including snowstorms and hostile Indians.

_____ 5. One rider, Warren Upson, (*hurry*) through the Sierras when a fierce ice storm forced him to walk his horse many miles.

_____ 6. The shortest trip (*take*) seven days and seventeen hours. The riders (*carry*) the inaugural address of the new president, Abraham Lincoln.

_____ 7. "Pony Bob" Haslam (*carry*) Lincoln's speech when he was attacked by Indians; despite wounds, he survived and delivered his message.

_____ 8. Initially the pony express (*charge*) five dollars per half ounce of mail, but when financial troubles hit, they lowered the price to one dollar per half ounce—a loss for the company.

_____ 9. By the time of its financial failure, the pony express (*provide*) the people of the United States with a series of stories that were the very essence of American culture.

_____ 10. Americans (*remember*) the pony express through the years because of the way it typified perseverance and bravery.

182 Chapter 7 | Verb Use

7.3 USE the skill

Rewrite the following paragraphs, correcting the five verb errors.

Although Samuel F. B. Morse originated the telegraph in America, he did not invent the first working telegraph system. The British inventors William Fothergill Cooke and Charles Wheatstone are making the first usable telegraph system by 1837. In Britain, however, the popularity and usefulness of the telegraph was slow in coming. At first, train stations uses the telegraph to inform other stations of arriving trains.

By 1845 the telegraph had gave essential help in catching two criminals. The men boarded a train from Paddington, London, to Slough. Although the police in London were unable to catch the criminals, they sent a telegram to the police in Slough. When the criminals gotten off the train, the police wait. The publicity created by the spectacular capture and by the telegraph-aided capture of a murderer the next year sent the popularity of the telegram skyrocketing.

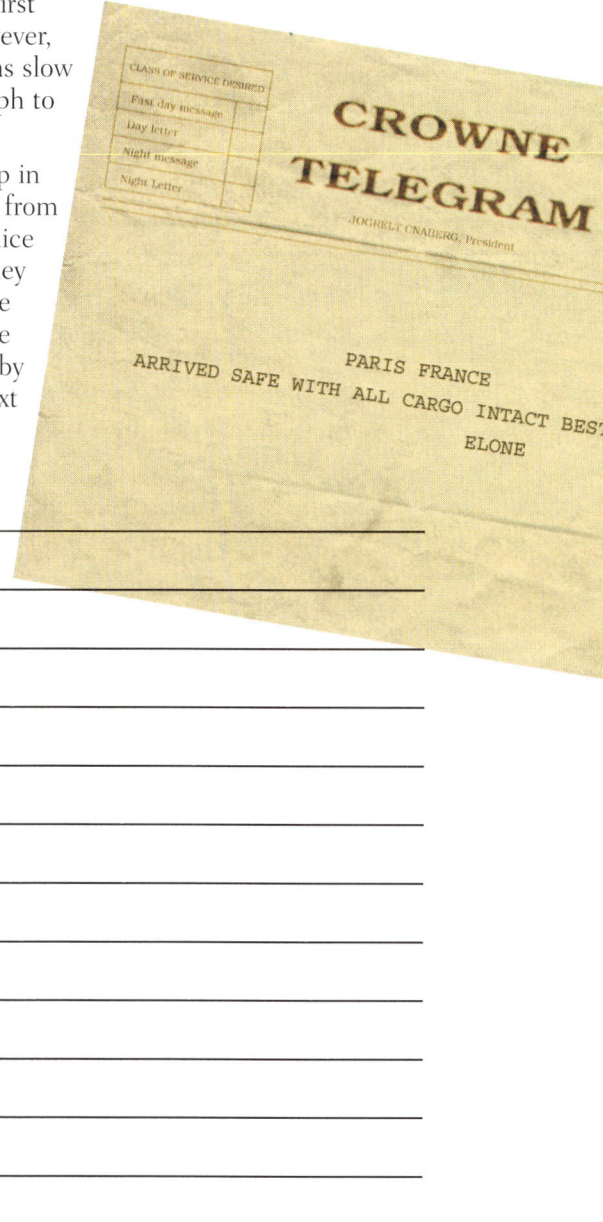

Consistency and Sequence of Tenses

Using verb tenses correctly enables your reader to have a clear understanding of what you are writing. Have you ever read a lengthy sentence or passage that left you wondering about the sequence of events? Perhaps the problem was inconsistent or inaccurate verb tenses.

Several guidelines govern the use of verb tenses in particular situations. Use present tense to tell about the events in someone's story or another literary work. This "literary present" indicates that the events of the story are considered to exist in the eternal present. In a present-tense passage, use the present perfect for earlier events.

PRESENT	Detective James *takes* his place at the weekly round-table discussion.
PRESENT PERFECT	After Detective James *has studied* a case for a while, he *gathers* new information for the investigation.
LITERARY PRESENT	Hamlet *kills* Polonius mistakenly, thinking that it *is* Claudius behind the arras.

Use the past tense (and past perfect) to tell a story that is not a work of fiction.

NORMAL PAST	Detective Stein *discovered* the truth.
PAST PERFECT	Before the last incident, however, Detective Stein *had marred* his investigative record.

The present tense may be used in conversation to relay past events and to make the events more vivid. The past tense is expected in written communication.

ORAL	Then the assistant *walks* into the room and *throws* the tattered papers on the lawyer's desk.
WRITTEN	Then the assistant *walked* into the room and *threw* the tattered papers on the lawyer's desk.

Whether you are speaking or writing, be consistent in the tenses that you use. Avoid mixing the tenses unnecessarily.

MIXED (INCORRECT)	When the villain *returned*, he *whispers* furtively to his accomplice.

Accurate tense sequence is particularly important within a sentence. Written English often uses the past perfect for an action that precedes another action in the past. Do not use the plain past when the past perfect is needed.

IMPRECISE	When the villain *revealed* his identity, he *fled* to a remote villa.
REWORDED	When the villain *had revealed* his identity, he *fled* to a remote villa.

If two things took place or were true at the same time in the past, use the past to express both of them. If, however, one of them is a **universal truth**—something still true today—use the present tense for the universal truth.

God *directed* Moses to the Red Sea and *parted* the Sea for the children of Israel.

The Bible *states* that all men *are* sinners.

Knowing when to shift tenses can be difficult. Here are some common reasons for shifting tenses.

From present tense to past tense or present perfect:
- To provide background information

    Our substitute teacher **is** Miss Johnson. She **studied** (or **has studied**) French for seven years and **lived** in France for two years.

From present tense to past tense:
- To support a claim with an example from the past

    Sometimes, adverse circumstances **alter** a person's plans for the future. The composer Robert Schumann **wanted** to become a piano virtuoso. However, when his right hand **became** crippled, he **turned** instead to composing brilliant music.

- To compare a present situation with a past one

    The choir **sings** well this year. Last year they **sang** poorly.

From past tense to present tense:
- To express a comment, opinion, or evaluation

    The Schultes recently **redecorated** their living room. The result **is** lovely.

in SUMMARY

To relate the events in a **literary work**, use the present tense for the main action of the story and the present perfect tense for earlier events.

To relate the events in a **true story**, use the past tense and the past perfect tense, as appropriate. (Although you may use the present tense in ordinary conversation, you should always use the past tense in writing.)

Use the past perfect tense to relate **two past actions** if one of the actions occurred prior to the other.

To state a **universal truth**, use the present tense.

7.4 PRACTICE *the skill*

Underline each verb in incorrect tense. Write the verb in corrected tense in the blank.

_____ 1. The man in the telegraph office told Mother, "The number of words in a telegram had determined its cost."

_____ 2. Conserving words becomes a necessity for any telegram. Through the years people omitted short words such as articles.

_____ 3. Even auxiliaries such as *do, does, are,* and *is* are absent from a telegram. The result was a savings of several dollars.

_____ 4. Through years past, politicians and generals will use telegrams to report news about campaigns or battles.

_____ 5. Queen Victoria had been the first British monarch to send telegrams; she even used them to congratulate the subjects who reached their one hundredth birthdays.

_____ 6. After receiving telegrams quite frequently during the early years of the telegraph, British police will have their own address: Handcuffs, London.

_____ 7. Through a collection of telegrams from Victorian England, we understood the history of the battle of Mafeking, South Africa.

_____ 8. In June 1826 Robert Stephenson, father of the British railroad, sends the first British telegram: "Bravo."

_____ 9. Telegrams even became part of fiction: they played important roles in many Sherlock Holmes stories.

_____ 10. In Mackinlay Kantor's story "The Grave Grass Quivers," a telegram provided confirmation of the murderer's identity.

7.5 USE *the skill*

Write a sentence (or sentences) in response to each prompt. Use the correct tense or sequence of tenses.

1. Recount a sequence of two or more actions from a short story or novel.

   _____
   _____

2. Describe at least two things that you and your family did last week.

   _____
   _____

3. Pretend to tell someone about a sequence of events that you are observing right now. (Use conversational style.)

   _____
   _____

4. Now write about the same sequence of events as though you observed it yesterday. (Use standard written style).

5. Write a statement of a scientific universal truth.

6. Report an event from history. Describe both the cause and the effect.

7. State a universal truth from Scripture.

8. Describe two events that happened at the same time.

9. Retell a short episode from a famous folktale or other fictional story.

10. Describe a sequence of at least two actions from the life of the prophet Elisha.

Passive Gerund, Passive Infinitive pp. 98, 102

Active or Passive pp. 361–62

Voice

Another characteristic that verbs possess is voice. The relationship of the subject and the verb determines voice. If the subject *is* something or is doing something, the verb and the sentence are in **active voice**. If the subject is being acted upon by the verb, the verb and the sentence are in **passive voice**. Passive verbs use a form of the auxiliary *be* before the main verb. Only transitive verbs can be made passive.

ACTIVE VOICE	Claudio is a black Labrador retriever.
	Slipper, a small dog, hid under the couch.
	Berkley ate the bowl of dog food.
PASSIVE VOICE	The bowl of dog food was eaten by Berkley.
	Slipper was found by Claudio.

Tense	Active Voice	Passive Voice
Present	Jordan **owns** a book on World War II.	A book on World War II **is owned** by Jordan.
Past	Jordan **owned** a book on World War II.	A book on World War II **was owned** by Jordan.
Future	Jordan **will own** a book on World War II.	A book on World War II **will be owned** by Jordan.
Present Perfect	Jordan **has owned** a book on World War II.	A book on World War II **has been owned** by Jordan.
Past Perfect	Jordan **had owned** a book on World War II.	A book on World War II **had been owned** by Jordan.
Future Perfect	Jordan **will have owned** a book on World War II.	A book on World War II **will have been owned** by Jordan.

Using Active and Passive Sentences

Active voice is more direct and emphasizes the doer of the action. In addition, active sentences are usually shorter. Therefore, active sentences are usually more effective and desirable than passive sentences.

Sometimes, however, passive sentences are useful. For example, a passive verb is necessary in a sentence when the doer is unimportant or unknown. In other sentences, using a passive verb creates a flowing sentence or paragraph that has the same subject for several verbs in a row. A passive verb may also allow you to move certain ideas from the subject position to the end of the sentence for emphasis.

GOOD USE OF PASSIVES	The office doors were locked at five o'clock.
	The money was donated to the mission fund.
ACCEPTABLE	When *Dad* asked *John* to work on the family farm, *John* accepted the job. Though *Dad* expected John to work extra hours, *John* knew he would learn valuable lessons.
BETTER (CONSISTENT SUBJECTS)	When *John* was asked to work on the family farm, *he* accepted the job. Though *he* was expected to work extra hours, *he* knew he would learn valuable lessons for life.
AWKWARDLY LONG SUBJECT	*Missionaries, senior and associate pastors, choir directors, and Sunday school superintendents* planned the schedule.
BETTER	*The schedule* was planned by missionaries, senior and associate pastors, choir directors, and Sunday school superintendents.

Revising Active and Passive Sentences

In order to change an active voice sentence into a passive sentence, you will need to follow several steps. First, change the transitive verb into the past participle form, if it is not already in that form. Second, add a form of the auxiliary *be* before the main verb. Then, make the direct object (or receiver of action) the subject of the sentence. (Make sure the auxiliary agrees with the subject once all the steps are complete.) The subject (or the doer) of the original sentence may be omitted or may be made the object of the preposition *by* in the passive sentence.

	S TrV-A DO
ACTIVE	Joshua *took* the dog for a walk.

	S TrV-P
PASSIVE	The dog *was taken* for a walk.

	S TrV-P OP
	The dog *was taken* for a walk (by Joshua).

To change a passive voice sentence into an active voice sentence, do the steps in reverse. If there is a *by* phrase in the sentence, make its object the subject of the new sentence. Otherwise, supply a subject (doer) for the active sentence. Make the subject of the passive sentence the direct object of the active sentence. Omit the *be* auxiliary and change the form of the verb to active.

	S TrV-P
PASSIVE	A theme for the banquet was chosen by the senior class.

	S TrV-A DO
ACTIVE	The senior class chose a theme for the banquet.

When the passive sentence does not state the doer, decide who or what the doer is. You may use an indefinite word for the subject.

	S TrV-P
PASSIVE	The books were returned to the library.

	S TrV-A DO
ACTIVE	Somebody returned the books to the library.

In each of the active-voice examples above, the sentence pattern S-TrV-DO appears. Two other sentence patterns, however, use transitive verbs. The sentence pattern S-TrV-IO-DO can be made passive in two ways. When the indirect object becomes the subject, the direct object becomes a **retained object** in the passive voice.

S-TrV-DO
p. 76

	S TrV-A IO DO
ACTIVE	My brother gave Seth two new books.

	S TrV-P RO OP
PASSIVE	Seth was given two new books (by my brother).

S-TrV-IO-DO
p. 76

When the direct object becomes the subject, the indirect object may become a retained object or the object in a prepositional phrase.

	S TrV-A IO DO
ACTIVE	The company gave Julie a new sales position.

	S TrV-P RO
PASSIVE	A new sales position was given Julie (by the OP company).

	S TrV-P OP
	A new sales position was given (to Julie) OP (by the company).

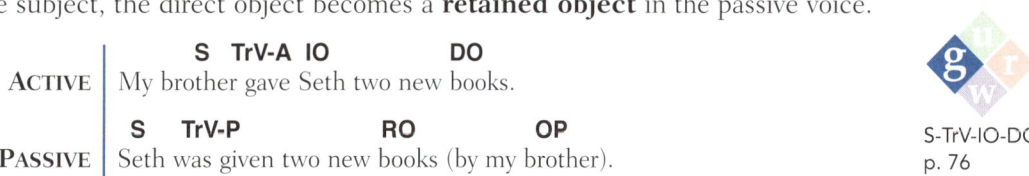

The sentence pattern S-TrV-DO-OC can also be made passive. In a passive voice sentence, the objective complement, which renames or describes the direct object, becomes a **subjective complement** that renames or describes the subject.

	S TrV-A DO OC
ACTIVE	The company made Julie a supervisor.

	S TrV-P SC OP
PASSIVE	Julie was made a supervisor (by the company).

S-TrV-DO-OC
p. 76

ESL Most English textbooks for native speakers present only the usual passive forms with *be,* as seen above. However, in spoken English you may also notice a special passive using *get* instead of *be* as the auxiliary.

ACTIVE	The ball **smashed** through the glass window.
NORMAL PASSIVE	The glass window **was smashed** by the ball.
GET-PASSIVE	The glass window **got smashed** by the ball.

As in this example, *get*-passives usually express unfavorable occurrences. Because they tend to be informal, you should usually use the normal *be*-passive in your writing for school or business.

in SUMMARY

A sentence is in the **active voice** when the subject *is* something or is doing something. A sentence is in the **passive voice** when something is being done to the subject.

A **passive verb** includes a form of the auxiliary *be* and the past participle form of a transitive verb.

Although active sentences are clearer and more economical than passive sentences, **passive sentences** are sometimes useful.

7.6 PRACTICE *the skill*

Underline the verb in each independent clause once. Then identify its voice as *active* or *passive*. If the verb is passive, underline any retained objects or subjective complements twice.

_____ 1. Many New Testament epistles, or letters, addressed to both churches and individuals, were written by Paul.

_____ 2. Paul focused his epistles on the person and work of Christ.

_____ 3. Paul, who was probably in prison in Rome, wrote a letter to the believers in Philippi, a city in western Macedonia.

_____ 4. The believers in Philippi were given an encouraging letter about God's promises and care.

_____ 5. Paul's kindness to the members of the church at Philippi was expressed through his epistle.

_____ 6. Having faced hardship and imprisonment from hostile people in Philippi, Paul sought to encourage the beloved brethren.

_____ 7. Paul was shown kindnesses so that he was not in want.

_____ 8. The believers at Philippi were made strong as they grew in sound doctrine.

_____ 9. Paul's letter to the Philippians focuses on Christ's presence within each believer.

_____ 10. Spiritual growth is revealed in believers who do all things through Christ.

USE *the skill*

Underline each passive-voice verb. Then rewrite the paragraph in active voice.

Missionary letters, also known as prayer letters, have a multifaceted purpose. First, the reader is informed about the work that is being done on the mission field. Perhaps the missionary was directed by God to be a pastor, a church planter, or a Bible translator. Those who read his letter are informed about his progress on the field. Perhaps the missionary has had the opportunity to lead someone to the Lord, or a major portion of translation was completed. Maybe a children's ministry has been started. Next, the reader is informed about the missionary family. The background for a ladies' ministry may be included in the prayer letter as well as important milestones in the children's lives. Last, the needs that the missionary and his family may have on the field will be placed before the reader. Of utmost importance is the need for the reader to pray diligently for the missionary. Spiritual, financial, or physical needs are presented for special prayer. Through missionary letters Christians learn to pray more effectively for missionaries as they serve the Lord.

Mood

Kinds of Sentences p. 69

Mood identifies the speaker's attitude toward what he is saying. English verbs have three moods: indicative, imperative, and subjunctive.

The **indicative mood** is the most frequently used mood. The indicative mood makes a factual statement.

> The weather in June is usually quite warm.
>
> I enjoy visiting the local ice-cream shop.

Understood Subjects p. 70

The **imperative mood** expresses a direct command. The subject *you* is usually understood (omitted), and the verb is in the simple present-tense form.

> Close the kitchen door behind you, please.
>
> Avoid eating too many snacks before meal time.

The **subjunctive mood** expresses the idea that a thing is untrue but desired. It may express a wish, a necessity, or an obligation.

> I wish that I *were* buying the new car today.
>
> The prince's mother insisted that he *act* his age.

ESL Notice that these subjunctive sentences have a *that* clause, and it is the verb in the *that* clause that is subjunctive. The base form of *be + past participle* (passive) is also possible.

> The legislature recommends that the districts *be* redrawn.

Forms of the Subjunctive

The forms of subjunctive mood verbs may be familiar, but their time references differ from those of verbs in the indicative mood. Use the simple past form of the verb to make a statement about something in the present or future. If the verb is *be*, use *were* (not *was*).

PRESENT | If he *came* late to class, the professor would surely notice.
| If the job *were* completed, we could go home.

FUTURE | If we *arrived* at the restaurant by five o'clock on Friday, we would not have to stand in line.
| If he *were* to leave early Saturday morning, he would arrive in Arizona on Sunday.

Use the past perfect to make a statement about something in the past. Use the simple present without *s* to make a "timeless" statement (of necessity).

PAST | After seeing your slides, I wish that I *had detoured* by way of the Grand Canyon.
| If Enrique *had been* with you, he would have pointed out the famous landmarks.

TIMELESS | The teacher insisted that we *be* in our seats before the bell rings.
| For the job interview, it is necessary that he *come*.

In conversation you will sometimes hear English speakers use *was* instead of *were* as the present subjunctive of *be*. In written or formal use, however, *was* is considered nonstandard for conditions contrary to fact.

Uses of the Subjunctive

Use the subjunctive mood to express a **condition contrary to fact**. In these sentences the clause begins with *if* (condition clause) and tells of something known to be untrue (contrary to fact). If you are unsure of the truth of the statement, use the indicative mood.

SUBJUNCTIVE (UNTRUE)	If I *were* you, I would study diligently for the test.
	If she *had studied* diligently, she would have earned a higher grade
INDICATIVE (UNKNOWN)	If he *studied* diligently, he probably did well.
	If my sister *comes*, then I will leave early.

Use the subjunctive mood to express a **doubtful future condition**. You could also use the auxiliary *would* in addition to an indicative form of the verb. Using the indicative only, however, eliminates the idea of uncertainty.

SUBJUNCTIVE	If they *were* to leave by seven this evening, they would arrive at the opera on time.
WOULD + INDICATIVE	If they *would leave* by seven this evening, they would arrive at the opera on time.
INDICATIVE	If they *leave* by seven this evening, they will arrive at the opera on time.

Use the subjunctive mood in a clause after an **expression of obligation or recommendation**. The idea of obligation disappears without the subjunctive.

SUBJUNCTIVE (OBLIGATION)	The chairman made the motion that the meeting *be* adjourned.
	The chairman insisted that the committee *be* ready for the presentation.
INDICATIVE (STATEMENT)	The chairman insisted that the committee *is* ready for the presentation.

Use the subjunctive for certain **set expressions**. Notice that some of these express desire.

God be with you.	Thy will be done.
Long live the king.	Suffice it to say, . . .
Be that as it may, . . .	Come what may, . . .

in SUMMARY

The **indicative mood** states a fact or makes a simple statement about something.

The **imperative mood** gives direct commands.

The **subjunctive mood** expresses conditions contrary to fact, doubtful future conditions, and obligation or recommendation; it is also used after expressions of necessity.

7.8 PRACTICE the skill

Identify the mood of each italicized verb as *indicative*, *imperative*, or *subjunctive*.

_____ 1. Letters from soldiers who served at the front line *reveal* many previously undisclosed stories about the D-day activities of 1944.

_____ 2. My story *focuses* on a commanding officer's bodyguard, a fine young man barely out of his teens.

_____ 3. After I spent a long day at the frontline gathering statements for my report, my commanding officer insisted that I *be* in his tent immediately.

_____ 4. If it *had been* possible, I would have wished to avoid this visit.

_____ 5. The commanding officer *asked* me to speak to a soldier who had just learned that his sister and brother had been killed in the South Pacific.

_____ 6. "*Give* him comfort, but *tell* him that another brother is critically wounded here in France," he admonished.

_____ 7. For this kind of confrontation, it was necessary that I *be* well prepared.

_____ 8. "John, *encourage* this young soldier and *help* him return to his duty," my commanding officer said.

_____ 9. After the young soldier heard the news, he wished that he *were* home to comfort his mother.

_____ 10. We *have met* the enemy daily; we perform our duties with emptiness and fatigue.

7.9 USE the skill

Write a sentence in the mood indicated in parentheses.

1. Describe a cost-effective advantage of digital communication. (*indicative*)

   _____

   _____

2. Warn the user to write messages that cannot be misinterpreted. (*imperative*)

   _____

   _____

3. Your friend is ready to send a message regarding a job problem, but he does not want his boss to misinterpret what he says. What would you advise your friend to do before he sends the message? (*subjunctive*)

   _____

   _____

4. Tell your friend that he must be cautious in his message because of the rapid transmission of the messages. (*imperative*)

5. If you decide to send a digital message, what might be some advantages? (*subjunctive*)

6. Write a sentence about the role of courtesy phrases such as the words *please* and *thank you* in digital communications. (*indicative*)

7. Warn a writer that he should avoid including his credit card number in his message. (*imperative*)

8. Write a sentence describing the positive value for the corporate traveler of wireless availability in hotels. (*indicative*)

9. Your friend sent a message with this idea: "That was a ridiculous statement. How could anyone be so silly!" What is your advice to your friend? (*subjunctive*)

10. Write a sentence about the positive value of digital communication. (*indicative*)

7.10 CUMULATIVE *review*

Rewrite the following paragraph, correcting the ten errors or inconsistencies from these categories: agreement, principal parts, tense, voice, and mood. (Assume that all sentences in this paragraph should have active voice.)

Christina Rossetti, accomplished poet and writer, wrote more than 2,100 letters during her lifetime. Through her letters interesting facets of her life are learned by the reader. Rossetti began her letter writing before she reached the age of twenty. Although two-thirds of her letters remain unpublished, many letters to her friends and family is available for reading. If a person was to study the life of Christina Rossetti, they would find that her brother encouraged her in her early writing. In these writings she will be enthusiastic about life and eager for success. During her early forties, however, the tone of her letters had been changed by her. She experienced many personal losses; her writing was affected by these losses. Amid problems with her health and family relationships, Rossetti continued to write. I recommend that a person takes a close look at Rossetti's Christian life. In both her letters and her words, she had spoke of the love of Christ to friends and family. Letter writing was approached by Christina Rossetti as a means of communication when other means failed.

THINK ABOUT IT

Subjectivity and Objectivity; Fact and Opinion

Before a critical thinker can draw reasonable conclusions and make sound judgments, he must evaluate the information available to him. The soundest decisions are usually those based on objective, factual evidence rather than on feeling or opinion. A critical thinker, then, must be able to differentiate between subjective and objective viewpoints and between opinion and fact.

What does it mean to be "objective" or "subjective"? As an example, the winner of a race is determined by an objective measurement: whoever crosses the finish line first wins the contest. The criterion is specific and measurable. The winner of a gymnastics meet, however, is determined by a combination of objective and subjective means. Some criteria are measurable: Did the gymnast finish the routine within the allotted time limit? Did he or she stay within the bounds? Did the gymnast fall or slip? Other criteria are less specific and require the judge to render an opinion. How well did the gymnast execute each skill? Was the routine balanced with a variety of difficult skills?

Similar to objectivity and subjectivity are fact and opinion. A fact is something that can be proved to be true or untrue. An opinion, however, is a belief that has not yet been proved (or cannot be proved) by observation, measurement, or other objective means. Most opinions are based on facts—or at least what someone believes to be a fact. But opinions are not facts themselves.

Use these strategies as you evaluate sources.

- First, evaluate the topic itself. Is it something that can be judged objectively? Or is subjectivity inherent to any discussion of this topic? For instance, the facts of a person's life are objective: the dates when King George III of Great Britain and Ireland was born and died, whom he married, where he lived, who succeeded him after his death. But an evaluation of a person's life must be subjective, for it depends upon one's point of view. Was George III a good king or a bad king? Were his actions regarding the American colonies proper or unjust? Was he or his son responsible for their volatile relationship?
- Search for key words or phrases that indicate opinion. "I think that" or "I feel" or even "This seems" is clearly opinion. But sometimes opinions are harder to spot. Any statement that expresses a value judgment is probably an opinion. Words such as *good, bad, wise, foolish, effective, useless,* and *beautiful* may signal a value judgment. The exception, of course, is a value statement based on a biblical criterion or expressed by God Himself in Scripture.
- When you find a value statement, look for factual support to back it up. A statement of opinion is not necessarily incorrect. If the speaker or writer offers facts and other objective evidence to support the opinion, examine the evidence for truth and validity. Only then should you decide whether to accept or reject the opinion.

Critical thinking allows for both facts and opinions; the key is to be able to distinguish between the two. Basing a decision solely on someone else's opinion is dangerous. Your decision is more likely to be sound if you base it on fact. However, it is sometimes acceptable or even unavoidable to make a decision based on opinion. As long as you recognize that your decision is based on opinion, you will be ready to adjust your plans if that opinion is later proved wrong.

Thinking It Through

Compare a letter to the editor and a newspaper article on the same topic. If possible, examine an encyclopedia article on that topic as well. Evaluate each source for objective and subjective arguments and distinguish the facts from the opinions.

Video Report | 200
Pronoun Use | 203
From the Written Word | 219

VIDEO REPORT Writing
PRONOUN USE Usage

8

Certain types of journalists depend not only on the stories they write but also on the photographs, illustrations, or video clips they incorporate into their reports. Think of the last news story you viewed—probably the text is linked inextricably in your mind with the images you saw. The combination of words and images is extremely powerful. In this chapter's writing assignment, you will combine text with video to present a news story to your high school, youth group, or family.

Invest in Teens

VIDEO	AUDIO
TEEN SLIDING DOWN WATERSLIDE INTO LAKE; TEENS ROASTING HOT DOGS OVER CAMPFIRE; TEEN READING GOD'S WORD WITH MOUNTAINS IN BACKGROUND	music cue—"How Great Thou Art" or "This Is My Father's World"
TEENS PILING ONTO BUS WITH SUITCASES VISIBLE	It's time again for the teens of Mt. Bethel Church to begin planning for summer camp.
TEEN COUNTING MONEY OUT OF WALLET OR CHECKING THE BALANCE IN CHECKBOOK	But before they go, each must raise the $275 needed to attend Camp Sunrise.
TEEN RAKING LEAVES; TEEN SWEEPING PORCH; TEENS SELLING REFRESHMENTS AT SOFTBALL GAME	In the past, teens have gotten money in a variety of ways. Voice: "I collect aluminum cans all year. ~~I even go up and down the highway near my house looking for old cans and stuff that I can recycle.~~ That way, I'm doing something to help better my community *and* raising money for camp."
TEEN THROWING NEWSPAPERS EARLY IN A.M.	Some have even taken on extra work to raise the needed funds for the week of camp.
PASTOR BECKER AND OTHER STAFF MEMBERS IN STAFF CONFERENCE	This year, the church pastoral staff has proposed a new plan
YOUTH WORKERS TALKING WITH TEENS	to alleviate some of the financial strain on teens and their families. The new program is called
INVEST LOGO	Invest.

CONTINUED

VIDEO	AUDIO
TEEN READING BIBLE	Each week teens involved in Invest will give time and energy to reading and memorizing God's Word
TEENS WITNESSING OR WORKING IN THE COMMUNITY	and to witnessing and service projects within the community.
PARENT AND TEEN LISTENING TO ANOTHER TEEN QUOTE SCRIPTURE	Parents and other interested persons will then be asked to reinvest in the teens of the church
ADULT AND TEEN PRAYING TOGETHER	by helping with memorization and partnering with specific teens.
PASTOR BECKER HANDING OUT AWARD CERTIFICATES AND CHECKS	Pastor Becker: "A portion of the church's offerings will be invested in teens who complete the semester-long Invest Program. ~~There are several levels to the program.~~ Teens can earn the registration fee as well as the entire camp sum. ~~Some will obviously earn more than others.~~"
INVEST LOGO	Further information is available in brochures to be handed out following the meeting.

VIDEO REPORT

I have heard of thee by the hearing of the ear: but now mine eye seeth thee.
Job 42:5

Documentaries or news reports like this one about a church's plan to help fund its teens' camp fees can explain many facts briefly and memorably. One's ability to observe closely and to view a topic or event through another's eyes is called upon as he decides both what his audience would *like* to see and what they *should* see about the topic.

Write and produce a two- to three-minute audiovisual report of either an event or a topic of importance to your church, family, or school. You may choose to create your report using video or presentation software. Do your best to capture for your audience the essence of the event or story.

Planning

✔ **Choose an event or topic to feature.** Remember that you have only two or three minutes; therefore, your topic must be something that can be adequately covered in the given time frame. Keep in mind that you must be able to record in person the event you choose, so an event like the Super Bowl or Tour de France is probably out of the question.

 An idea for a video report might be to show how to cook a popular food from your country.

✔ **Jot down the main points of your story line.** For the "Invest in Teens" story, the author decided that the main points were the need, what teens have done in the past to raise money, and how the new plan could help. Listing the main points will help you to focus the details of your report on what is important.

tip — Think about the past (what led up to the event), present (the event), and future (how the event will affect people) when making a video report.

✔ **Consider your report.** Think about the main points you want to get across. Will your report proceed chronologically? Or will you need to give your audience some background information in order for them to understand your topic? Will it be possible to get sound bites (short statements edited from longer recordings) or video clips from past events?

✔ **Brainstorm for ideas.** Allow peers to assist you in thinking of ideas or facts that your report should include. Write these under the main points you decided upon earlier. Look for holes in the chronology or for places your audience might become confused and decide how to correct these problems.

✔ **Decide on an angle for the report.** Will you shoot your footage as an onlooker or as a participant? The "Invest in Teens" story appeared as though written by an impartial observer merely reporting the facts, but many news stories (especially so-called "undercover" stories) use the camera as a first-person eyewitness to or a participant in an event.

✔ **Choose a frame of reference for your report.** Decide whether you want to establish yourself as a "reporter" (as in a newscast) or whether you want to film your story more like a documentary. In a typical newscast, the reporter usually appears both at the beginning of the report and at the end—usually on location at the site of the event being recorded. If your equipment has editing capabilities, these segments can be shot at any time and edited into the report.

✔ **Practice with your equipment.** Before you go on location, acquaint yourself with the devices you will be using. What special effects can the equipment achieve? What are its limitations? Prepare yourself with extra supplies and make sure that the batteries are charged and the equipment is working correctly. Consider shooting a practice video before the event.

Thinking Biblically

Opera has been called the greatest art form because it combines grand stage drama and impressive music. By that measure, however, movies could be considered much more powerful. Certainly, for many, they are much more entertaining. This popularity of film is largely due to its power as an art form. Movies lift the audience out of their places, push them past the orchestra pit, and put them right into the action. Christians who seek to use this tool for God's glory must consider some current criticism. Christian films have been criticized for being overtly didactic to the point of jeopardizing plot and characterization for the sake of message. A Christian film maker must ask the question, how can I make my film entertaining without sacrificing Christian values? Can a thoroughly Christian movie balance artistry and message, entertainment and Christian worldview? One thing is certain: if such a film can be created, it will start with good writing.

Drafting

✔ **Script your report.** With some news stories you will need to write the script before you shoot. Decide what you want to say, and write text to tell your story. Use a format like the one on pages 199–200 for your script and for video ideas. If you will be using sound clips or footage that you already have, write a script that incorporates these smoothly. News stories generally use a more factual, declarative style than other types of writing. You will want to state your ideas directly and logically so that your audience will understand what you mean. The ideas about sentence logic in Chapter 14, pages 383–88, may help you as you script your report.

tip — News scriptwriters sometimes use all capital letters for one column in the script. This can help differentiate between the two columns at a glance.

✔ **Make informed choices.** Use the following chart to make important choices about lighting, framing, and so on, for your report.

Recording Considerations

Camera Movement	Will you hold the camera steady, or will you move it? How will either affect your message?
Editing	Will you use a **montage**, a technique that places a variety of images in close succession? Or will you record steadily through an event?
Framing	What will you include/exclude in your shot? Is there anything that you desire attention taken away from? What will your framing say about your viewpoint—is it neutral or biased?
Lighting	Can you control the lighting of your shot? If so, what will you emphasize or conceal with lighting? What kind of atmosphere will you create?
Music/Sound	What kind of mood do the sounds of your report establish?
Narration	Will you have one narrator or several? What kind of voice is appropriate for your story? Is there any type of voice that would be inappropriate?

✔ **Shoot your report.** Once you have your script, begin shooting footage to tell your story in pictures. Remember to use a variety of close-up and long shots. Avoid placing the camera in one locale and shooting everything from a single vantage point.

✔ **Select sound effects.** Especially if your footage has no sound of its own, include some sounds you either record yourself or locate on a CD or online. (Avoid copyright infringement; some sound effects sources allow you to use the sounds however you wish.) For example, the writer of the "Invest in Teens" report could have added water sounds or sounds of leaves being raked or newspapers hitting the floor to his list of audio effects.

Revising

✔ **Review your report.** Look at your script and your footage again. If possible, get opinions from others, especially eyewitnesses to the event you are covering. Look for places that your story is weak or inaccurate. Make sure that all sound effects and music cues add to, not detract from, the story.

✔ **Rethink the visuals.** Are any of your visuals merely "talking head" visuals? Think of ways that are unusual or interesting to illustrate your report. For example, the "Invest in Teens" report could show a close-up of leaves before pulling back to a shot of the person raking.

✔ **Edit your report.** If the equipment allows for editing, cut and paste your piece after you identify places that need tightening or moving. Add or delete sound cues accordingly. Note that in the "Invest in Teens" script some words have been crossed out. Use this option to help you remember the context of the parts you are keeping should you desire to reconstruct part of the speech later.

> **tip**
> Beware of too much cutting and pasting, especially with someone else's words. You might end up misrepresenting a person or an issue.

✔ **Check the spelling of text that appears in the report.** Nothing is more distracting to a viewer than a glaring spelling or punctuation error in giant print on the screen. Read carefully any text—title, quotations, and so on—for mechanical errors.

Publishing

✔ **Arrange for a school-wide viewing.** Allow your principal to preview your report and ask about a showing for the whole school—especially if the event you covered has significance for the students.

✔ **Host a premier night.** Show several of the video reports from your class at a video night. Invite special guests who were involved in the recordings to attend and to answer questions afterwards.

✔ **Compare and contrast reports.** After viewing reports on the same topic, use the guidelines for comparison/contrast writing discussed in Chapter 3 to discuss (or write about) similarities and differences among the reports. Comment on how the point of view changes from report to report.

✔ **Post your report.** If your report is a digital file, post it on a website—yours or your class's.

Some Ideas to Consider

History
- Produce a history of an event in your community, school, or family.

Government
- Cover election night after a local political race.

Art
- Document a visit to a local arts festival.

PRONOUN USE

Pronoun Case

Pronouns show one or more of four characteristics: person, number, gender, and case. Personal pronouns, the most common, show all four characteristics. Case is probably the characteristic that gives writers the most difficulty. An understanding of the three cases—subjective, objective, and possessive—is important for clear, correct writing.

Pronouns
pp. 37–40

General Principles

Use **subjective case** pronouns—*I, we, you, it, he, she,* and *they*—for subjects and predicate nouns.

> *We* watched a debate between the two gubernatorial candidates.
>
> Tyler and *she* could not stay for the entire debate.
>
> It was *I* who answered the campaign phone.

Informal speech often uses the objective case for a predicate noun. In formal written or spoken English, only the subjective case is acceptable for predicate nouns.

Use the **objective case** pronouns—*me, us, you, it, him, her,* and *them*—for direct objects, indirect objects, and objects of prepositions.

> Local reporters called *me* for an interview.
>
> Did they give John and *you* a list of questions before the interview?
>
> Campaign organizers forwarded the list of volunteers to *me*.
>
> As a result of hard work and positive campaigning by *you* and *them*, our candidate won by a large majority.

Gerund Phrases
p. 97

Use the **possessive case** to show ownership and other close relationships. Possessive case pronouns can have two forms. The more common forms—*my, our, your, its, his, her,* and *their*—modify nouns.

> *Your* idea to campaign on specific issues was a successful one.
>
> Why did the press dislike *his* approach to the campaign?

ESL The form that shows ownership (possessive) can show a number of other relationships. Here are some of the relationships expressed by possessives.

OWNERSHIP	That is *their* dog. (They own it.)
DOER OF ACTION	*Her* sharp words were inappropriate. (She spoke sharp words.)
PRODUCER	I like *his* colorful paintings. (He produced the paintings.)
OBJECT OF ACTION	Praise is *her* reward. (People rewarded her.)
FAMILY RELATIONSHIP	He will live with *his* cousins this summer.
REPRESENTATION	I like *your* graduation photo. (It represents you.)
OTHERS	What is *your* address?
	Mr. and Mrs. Hedican watch *their* health.

Pronouns
pp. 37–40

Use the **independent possessive** form of a pronoun—*mine, ours, yours, its, his, hers,* and *theirs*—to stand alone as a subject, predicate noun, or object.

SUBJECT	*His* was the best campaign advice to follow.
PREDICATE NOUN	The feeling of skepticism was *mine*.
DIRECT OBJECT	I thought our plan for education was good, but the newly elected governor chose *theirs* instead.

Chapter 8 | Pronoun Use

Most possessive modifiers make the noun definite in meaning—that is, the noun refers to a specific person or thing. *Her pencil* is a specific pencil, and *my cousin* is a specific person. However, a special construction with independent possessives enables us to express possession and yet keep the noun indefinite.

> I borrowed **a pencil of hers** yesterday (some pencil that she owns).
> Jennifer taught piano lessons to **a cousin of mine** (an unspecified one of my cousins).

As you see, this is the construction for possession of indefinite nouns:

a/an + noun + *of* + independent possessive

in SUMMARY

Use **subjective case pronouns** for subjects and predicate nouns. In formal English usage, the objective case is not used for a predicate noun.

Use **objective case pronouns** for direct objects, indirect objects, and objects of prepositions.

Use **possessive case pronouns** to show ownership and other close relationships.

Use the **independent possessive** form of a pronoun to stand alone as a subject, a predicate noun, or an object.

8.1 PRACTICE *the skill*

Underline each personal pronoun and identify it as subjective *(S)*, objective *(O)*, possessive *(P)* or independent possessive *(IP)*.

_____ 1. Have you ever considered volunteering to help a camp ministry?

_____ 2. Uncle Del's favorite ministry is working at the rescue mission; mine is serving at Camp Calvary.

_____ 3. Camp Calvary's staff needed some help to get the camp ready for its busy summer.

_____ 4. The Lord gave me a burden to help by doing any job, no matter how small.

_____ 5. Kevin and I swept the miniature golf course free of fallen leaves.

_____ 6. The waterslide looked more inviting after several of us cleaned it.

_____ 7. One teen with artistic ability painted our camp theme onto a mural.

_____ 8. For supper the experience of having a lakeside barbecue was ours.

_____ 9. The camp director, Pastor Reece, thanked us for helping and then shared the history of the camp.

_____ 10. After the staff had worked all day at the camp, our thoughts turned to the privilege of Christian ministry.

8.2 REVIEW *the skill*

Write an appropriate personal pronoun in the blank. Then identify the pronoun as subjective (S), objective (O), possessive (P), or independent possessive (IP).

_____ _____ 1. _?_ are probably familiar with the National Park Service that manages areas designated to the Department of the Interior.

_____ _____ 2. The National Park Service began _?_ duties in August of 1916.

_____ _____ 3. Since 1916 _?_ has determined areas to be national parks based on historical or scientific importance.

_____ _____ 4. Other areas have become national parks because of _?_ recreational importance.

_____ _____ 5. What is your favorite park? Glacier National Park is _?_.

_____ _____ 6. In some parks, flowers are abundant; a visitor can see _?_ during several months of the year.

_____ _____ 7. The purpose of the park service is to conserve wildlife, scenery, and natural objects; _?_ success has been outstanding.

_____ _____ 8. Large numbers of visitors have made the park system successful; many of _?_ visit year after year.

_____ _____ 9. Park employees have varied responsibilities; _?_ oversee the more than 83 million acres that make up the park system.

_____ _____ 10. Many of the 375 national parks are open throughout the year; some of _?_ close in the winter because of weather.

Appositives

Pronouns in subject and object positions may be renamed by appositives. The appositive noun does not affect the case of the pronoun.

                S   InV

At the senior class retreat, we *seniors* listened closely to the evangelist's challenge.

  S   TrV   DO

He challenged us *teenagers* about living for Christ.

Pronouns may function as appositives. The case of an appositive pronoun should match the case of the word that it renames.

            S   TrV

The senior class officers—Jim, Sharon, and *I*—appreciated the evangelist's

  DO

concern for our class.

        S   TrV   DO

His enthusiasm for the gospel encouraged several soccer players—Robert, Stephen, and *him*.

Adverb Clauses
p. 122

S-V Agreement
pp. 148–61

Comparisons Using *Than* or *As*

The subordinating conjunctions *than* and *as* introduce dependent clauses of comparison. Often the second part of the comparison is "understood." In order to choose the correct pronoun case after *than* or *as*, determine how the pronoun would function in the full understood clause.

My closest friend was more eager to work at camp than *I*. (than *I* was [eager to work at camp])

But I am now as happy about working there as *he*. (as *he* is [happy about working there])

In some sentences the meaning of the sentence will determine the pronoun that you use.

The youth sponsor encourages the new converts as much as *I*. (as much as *I* [encourage the new converts])

The youth sponsor encourages the new converts as much as *me*. (as much as [he encourages] *me*)

English speakers often say the *be* verb or the auxiliary after the subject pronoun of the implied comparison, as in the first two examples above.

My closest friend was more eager to work at camp than **I was**.

Following this practice can help you choose the correct pronoun form.

in SUMMARY

The **appositive noun** does not affect the case of the pronoun it renames.

The case of an appositive pronoun is determined by the case of the noun it renames.

Determine the case of a pronoun after *than* or *as* by determining how the pronoun would function in the full understood clause.

8.3 PRACTICE *the skill*

Underline the correct pronoun from the choices in parentheses.

1. (*We, Us*) campers still rely upon an invention of the late 1800s.

2. During our last camping trip, the flashlight prevented us—Rob, Isaiah, and (*I, me*)—from getting lost when darkness settled more quickly than we had anticipated.

3. During the long hike back to the campsite, Rob entertained (*we, us*), his audience, with the history of the flashlight.

4. Although inventor David Misell thought he had developed a mere bicycle lamp, his employer, Conrad Hubert, had a better idea than (*he, him*).

5. Hubert remodeled his employee's patented bicycle lamp into the long torchlike beam so valuable to (*we, us*) today.

6. Isaiah interrupted Rob's lesson to tell how they—his family and (*he, him*)—like to take late night bike rides using modern bike lights.

7. Hubert donated many of his prototype flashlights to New York City policemen because he wanted to make others as interested in his invention as (*he, him*).

8. Although Hubert failed at selling his earlier inventions (illuminated tie racks and flowerpots), his persistence inspired (*we, us*) boys to pursue our dreams.

9. Because we knew that the first flashlights could not produce a continuous beam of light, *(we, us)* hikers figured out how the flashlight got its name.

10. After Rob gave us—Isaiah and *(I, me)*—a demonstration of the original flashlight, we all were much more thankful for our modern ones.

8.4 USE *the skill*

Rewrite any sentence that contains an error in pronoun usage. If the sentence is already correct, write C in the blank.

1. My entire family—Mom, Dad, my two sisters, and me—visited Yellowstone National Park.

   _____
   _____
   _____

2. Extending into Idaho, Montana, and Wyoming, the park provided we five a vast expanse for camping and exploration.

   _____
   _____
   _____
   _____

3. My sisters did not like the park as much as me.

   _____
   _____
   _____
   _____

4. Yellowstone, the oldest park in the system, has many activities for we students.

   _____
   _____
   _____
   _____

5. My sister Julie, who usually has a much shorter attention span than I, enjoyed watching the Old Faithful geyser for forty-five minutes.

   _____
   _____
   _____

Lower Yellowstone Falls

6. Several cranes in a nearby pond gave my sister and me an entertaining afternoon.

7. My sisters laughed at us when Dad and me imitated the bugle call of an elk.

8. One exciting sight for my sisters and I was the grizzly and black bears that we saw in the distance.

9. My sisters needed a storage pole at their backpacking campsite as much as I.

10. Boating and hiking were other activities enjoyed by the family—Mom, Dad, my two sisters, and I.

"Subjects" and Objects of Verbals

Pronouns with Gerunds

A noun or pronoun that precedes a gerund and acts as its "subject," or doer, is in the possessive case. The "subject" of the gerund is the doer of the gerund's verb meaning. A common error places an objective case pronoun rather than a possessive case pronoun before a gerund.

Gerund Phrases
p. 97

         S   TrV   DO
The *students'* leaving the service early discouraged Pastor Allen.

    S   TrV   DO
We students noticed *their* leaving during the invitation.

In these sentences, the students' action of leaving is the focus, not the students themselves. The possessive form before the gerund is correct.

The "subject" of a gerund is different from a noun or pronoun that is followed and modified by a participial phrase.

                          S   LV   PN
Pastor Allen's *preaching* was a challenge to many teens.

                 S TrV DO
Did you see him preaching to the teens?

The first example shows a possessive acting as the "subject" of a gerund. The main idea of the sentence is *what he was doing*—preaching the gospel. The last example shows a pronoun functioning as the direct object and being modified by a participial phrase. The sentence asks if you saw *him*, not what he was doing.

A pronoun that follows a gerund and acts as its object is in the objective case.

      S   LV   PN   S   LV   PN
Christ was the focus of the sermon; *trusting* **Him** is the only way to salvation.

               S   InV   (OP)
The evangelist had prepared by *praying* earnestly for the students before

(OP)
teaching **them** this lesson from Scripture.

Pronouns with Infinitives

Infinitive Phrases
pp. 101–2

A pronoun that precedes an infinitive and acts as its "subject," or doer, is in the objective case.

        S   TrV   DO
Pastor Allen wants **us** *to withstand* the temptations of the world.

      S   TrV   DO
He urges **us** *to read* our Bibles daily.

In both examples the entire infinitive phrase functions as the direct object of the sentence. The objective case pronoun identifies the persons performing the action of the infinitive.

A pronoun that follows an infinitive and acts as its object is in the objective case.

          S   InV
We will go *to see* **him** for encouragement from God's Word.

              S   TrV   DO
Pastor Allen would like *to give* **them** some encouragement.

A pronoun that follows a linking-verb infinitive must be in the same case as the earlier word that it is renaming. The pronoun *he* in the following sentence renames the subject of the main verb. The case, then, is subjective in formal usage.

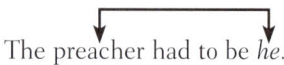
The preacher had to be *he*.

The same pronoun case should be used for both the subject and object of a linking-verb infinitive. Since the subject of the infinitive is in the objective case, the pronoun that renames it must also be in the objective case.

The teens thought *him* to be *me*.

Everyone believed the leader to be *him*.

Who and Whom

The pronouns *who* and *whom* follow the same principles as personal pronouns do. The subjective case pronouns *who* and *whoever* function as subjects or predicate nouns. Use the objective case pronouns *whom* and *whomever* as objects. When the pronoun appears in a dependent clause, the case of the pronoun is determined by its function within the clause, not by the function of the dependent clause.

Pronouns
pp. 37–38

      S   LV   PN
Who is the new president of the youth group?

    S LV   PN   DO   S   TrV
He is the one *whom* we met at camp last week.

Clauses
pp. 126–28

  S   InV   (OP)   S   TrV   DO
Sam voted for *whoever* would do the best job.

    (OP)   S TrV   DO
For *whom* did you cast your vote?

    S   TrV   DO DO   S   TrV
My friends will support *whomever* the youth group elected.

In sentences with parenthetical expressions such as *do you think, I believe,* or *did they say,* ignore the parenthetical expression when you determine the function and case of *who/whom*.

     DO   S   TrV
Whom do you think he will choose as his assistant? (*He will choose whom?*)

  S LV   PN   S   LV   PN
He is the one *who* I believe is the better choice. (*who is the better choice*)

   S   LV   PA
Who did they say is most capable to lead the group? (*Who is most capable?*)

ESL

As you may have noticed, in colloquial English (informal conversation) there is a strong tendency to use *who* at the beginning of all questions, regardless of its function. In written and formal use, however, you should follow the rules stated here in the text.

INFORMAL | Who did you meet?
FORMAL | Whom did you meet?

---

in SUMMARY

Use a possessive case pronoun as the **"subject" of a gerund**. Use an objective case pronoun as the **object of a gerund**.

Use an objective case pronoun as the **"subject" or object of an infinitive**.

A pronoun that follows a linking verb infinitive must be in the same case as the earlier word that it is renaming.

Use **who** and **whoever** for subjects and predicate nouns.

Use **whom** and **whomever** for direct objects, indirect objects, and objects of prepositions.

When *who* or *whom* appears in a dependent clause, the case of the pronoun is determined by its function within the clause, not by the function of the dependent clause.

Ignore parenthetical expressions when you determine the function and case of *who* and *whom*.

8.5 PRACTICE the skill

Underline the correct pronoun from the choices in parentheses.

1. A teen (*who, whom*) attends a Christian camp often makes life-changing decisions.
2. Parents may pray for the teen, (*who, whom*) they hope will serve the Lord.
3. (*Him, His*) being set apart from the distractions of home, school, and friends helps him to focus on spiritual issues.
4. Spiritual messages challenge (*whoever, whomever*) the Holy Spirit convicts.
5. Giving (*they, them*) a chance to focus on Christ is the purpose of setting aside time for campers to read the Bible and pray.
6. As a result of Christ-honoring preaching, many teens purpose to serve (*He, Him*).
7. God directs (*whoever, whomever*) is willing to be a missionary, a preacher, a teacher, or a Christian lay worker.
8. (*They, Their*) serving God requires eliminating habits that would hamper their testimonies.
9. Many teens are helped by those to (*who, whom*) they go for counsel and prayer.
10. After a teen's week at a Christian camp, (*him, his*) following through on a decision to yield his life to Christ is most important.

8.6 REVIEW the skill

Underline each pronoun that represents a case error in "subjects" or objects of verbals or in *who* and *whom*. Write the correction in the blank. If the sentence is already correct, write C in the blank.

_____ 1. Recreational vehicles vary in purpose and design in order to meet the needs of whomever wants one of them.

_____ 2. After talking with some families, a salesperson often expects they to choose a conversion van.

_____ 3. Us considering a camper is a big step for our family.

_____ 4. Whoever buys a motor home can choose from a variety of designs.

_____ 5. A boat may be a good choice for the person whom enjoys activities on the water.

_____ 6. Who should the choice of a nonmotorized or motorized boat be given to?

_____ 7. Dad, viewing the variety of boat choices—speedboats, ski boats, sailboats, and cruising boats—realized that him choosing a boat was going to be difficult.

_____ 8. Noticing him near the boats was the salesperson's cue to approach us.

_____ 9. The salesperson told him to buy the most expensive boat because it is, of course, the best.

_____ 10. Who do you think Dad listened to, the salesperson or his own reason?

Pronoun Courtesy Order

Correct courtesy order is necessary when you join a personal pronoun with another personal pronoun or a noun. Be sure to observe these two rules. In a compound construction, mention yourself last.

> **SAY** | Senator James wants *Thomas and me* to make campaign calls tonight.
> **NOT** | Senator James wants *me and Thomas* to make campaign calls tonight.

Second, mention your hearer before anyone, unless the emphasis of the sentence is otherwise.

> **SAY** | *You, Thomas, and I* should help the senator win the election.
> **NOT** | *Thomas, you, and I* should help the senator win the election.

Reflexive and Intensive Pronouns

Reflexive and intensive pronouns are personal pronouns that have *-self* or *-selves* as a suffix. A **reflexive pronoun** is used as an object—direct object, indirect object, or object of the preposition—only when it refers to the same person or thing as the subject of the clause. It can never be used as a subject. An **intensive pronoun** is used only as an appositive to emphasize a noun or another pronoun in the sentence. Do not use a reflexive or intensive pronoun in place of a regular personal pronoun.

> **WRONG** | The candidate assured the workers of his commitment to *themselves*.
> **RIGHT** | The candidate assured the workers of his commitment to *them*.
> **RIGHT** | The campaign workers should applaud *themselves* for their efforts.

Pronouns
p. 40

Appositive Pronouns p. 40

WRONG	Sylvia and *myself* listened to the speech carefully.
RIGHT	Sylvia and *I* listened to the speech carefully.
RIGHT	The candidate *himself* will be visiting our area again tomorrow.

Only certain personal pronouns can have *-self* or *-selves* as a suffix. Words such as *ourself, themself, theirself, theirselves,* and *hisself* are incorrect and should be replaced with the correct forms: *ourselves, themselves, himself.*

| WRONG | Senator James made all the campaign arrangements *hisself*. |
| RIGHT | Senator James made all the campaign arrangements *himself*. |

in SUMMARY

In a compound construction, mention your **hearer first** and **yourself last**.

Use a **reflexive pronoun** as an object only when it refers to the same person or thing as the subject of the clause.

Use an **intensive pronoun** as an appositive to emphasize a noun or another pronoun already in the sentence.

8.7 PRACTICE *the skill*

Underline the correct pronoun or pronoun group from the choices in parentheses.

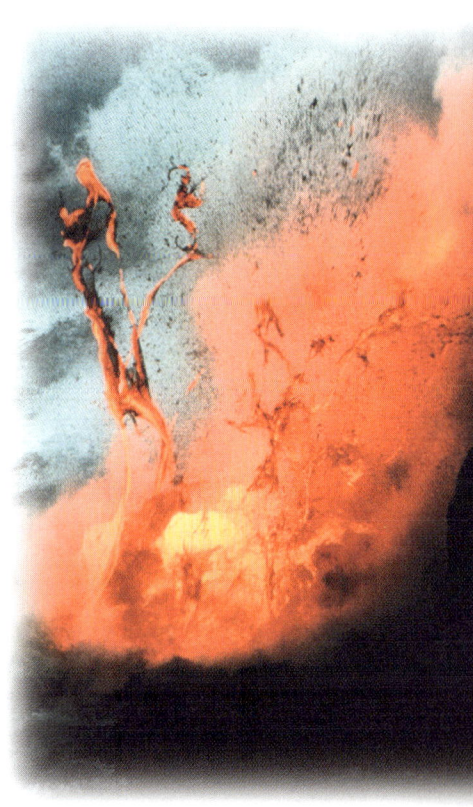

1. While my family was visiting Hawaii, my parents gave (*me and my brother, my brother and me*) the opportunity to visit the Hawaii National Volcano Park.

2. We packed a lunch for (*ourselves, ourself*) and drove to the park, located near Hilo on the big island of Hawaii.

3. The park ranger showed (*ourselves, us*) this place with unusual foliage and land formations that became a national park in 1916.

4. My mother and (*I, me*) enjoyed seeing Mauna Loa, the earth's most massive volcano.

5. In addition to seeing Mauna Loa, my family and (*myself, I*) saw Kilauea, the earth's most active volcano.

6. My family learned for (*theirselves, themselves*) how scientists have gained insight into the formation of the Hawaiian Islands.

7. Since more than half of the park is wilderness area, my brother allowed (*himself, hisself*) several hours to hike some of the trails.

8. A unique opportunity for any visitors is to see for (*themselves, theirself*) that Kilauea still erupts.

9. Between (*me and you, you and me*), hearing that Kilauea is active scared me.

10. Our entire family enjoyed our vacation, even the volcanoes (*theirselves, themselves*).

8.8 REVIEW *the skill*

Underline the part of the sentence that contains an error in courtesy order or in the use of reflexive or intensive pronouns. Write the correction in the blank. If the sentence is already correct, write C in the blank.

_____ 1. Another park for me and you to visit is Mount Saint Helens National Park in Washington.

_____ 2. On May 18, 1980, the eruption that had begun about one mile beneath the earth's surface showed itself and lasted for nine long hours.

_____ 3. A group of students constructed an elaborate model of Mount Saint Helens based on what themselves had learned about the volcano that had been dormant since 1857.

_____ 4. A scientist told myself that the eruption caused the north face of the mountain to collapse.

_____ 5. One student learned by hisself that almost 150 square miles of forest were destroyed or left dead but standing.

_____ 6. Thousands of game animals such as deer, elk, and bears had no chance to save themselves.

_____ 7. The visiting scientist explained to me and my friend that the volcano destroyed more than twelve million fish-hatchery salmon.

_____ 8. The eruption itself produced so much debris that the level of Spirit Lake rose sixty meters.

_____ 9. We learned that mudflows themselves deposited more than ninety-five million cubic yards of sediment in the Cowlitz and Columbia Rivers.

_____ 10. The scientist and you discussed the implications of the Mount Saint Helens incident on the Creation/evolution debate.

Pronoun Shift

Clear writing keeps the reader focused on the writer's intended purpose. Since a shift in the person or number of a pronoun confuses the reader, a careful writer will be consistent in the use of pronouns.

S-V Agreement
pp. 163–65

Shifts in Person

A shift in person often occurs when a writer refers to unnamed people. In these examples, notice the shift from one person to another and the possible corrections.

SHIFT	If a *camper* remembers to bring the camp stove, *you* will be able to cook on the camping trip. *(third person to second person)*
CORRECTION	If a *camper* remembers to bring the camp stove, *he* will be able to cook on the camping trip.
	If *you* remember to bring the camp stove, *you* will be able to cook on the camping trip.
SHIFT	*Anyone* can forget that *you* need more than a camp stove. *(third person to second person)*
CORRECTION	*Anyone* can forget that *he* needs more than a camp stove.

In the last example, the corrected sentence also changes the verb form to match the person of the pronoun.

Shifts in Number

A shift in number occurs when a writer mixes singular and plural in the same general statement. Although most general statements can be either singular or plural, a problem occurs when the two are mixed.

SHIFT	Campers need their sleeping bag for warmth.
CORRECTION	Campers need their sleeping bags for warmth.
	A camper needs his sleeping bag for warmth.
SHIFT	Anyone can forget their sleeping bag.
CORRECTIONS	Anyone can forget his sleeping bag.
	Campers can forget their sleeping bags.

In each example the shift in number can be corrected by making the sentence singular or plural throughout, depending on which meaning is appropriate.

in SUMMARY

When using pronouns to refer to unnamed people in general statements, avoid shifts in person and number.

8.9 PRACTICE *the skill*

Underline the correct pronoun from the choices in parentheses.

1. As a student reads the Old Testament, *(you, he)* might study Exodus 14, which records the Israelites' encamping between Migdol and the Red Sea.

2. If students could have seen Pharaoh, *(they, he)* would have seen a man who looked upon this encampment as the opportunity to destroy the Israelites.

3. When you read Exodus 11–12 carefully, *(one, you)* will see that Israel had escaped the final plague in Egypt, but the Egyptians had not.

4. We know that *(we, you)* Christians, like the Israelites, have God's promises.

5. Anyone who reads *(their, his)* Bible can see that God's promise was to destroy the Egyptians.

6. In spite of God's promise, Israel feared when *(you, they)* saw the Egyptians.

7. The angel of the Lord went behind the encamped Israelites to protect *(it, them)*.

8. If you read Moses' account carefully, *(they, you)* will know that the pillar of cloud stood between the camp of Israel and the camp of the Egyptians.

9. Sometimes God asks Christians to encamp in a seemingly dangerous place, but His presence is always with *(you, them)*.

10. God may not always protect the Christian as He did Israel, but He promises to be with *(him, them)* always.

8.10 REVIEW *the skill*

Write the letter of the correct sentence in the blank.

_____ 1. A. Dad is considering our request for a rafting trip as they survey a vacation place for this year.
B. Dad is considering our request for a rafting trip as he surveys a vacation place for this year.

_____ 2. A. Not only does he want a cabin on a lake, but you also want a reputable rafting business nearby.
B. Not only does he want a cabin on a lake, but he also wants a reputable rafting business nearby.

_____ 3. A. When one plans a whitewater rafting adventure, he must choose the raft carefully.
B. When one plans a whitewater rafting adventure, they must choose the raft carefully.

_____ 4. A. Anyone who chooses a good raft makes their choice based on durability, performance, and safety.
B. Anyone who chooses a good raft makes his choice based on durability, performance, and safety.

_____ 5. A. If a person chooses fiberglass paddles, he will have paddles that handle the currents well.
B. If a person chooses fiberglass paddles, you will have paddles that handle the currents well.

_____ 6. A. For the rafter, gloves keep their hands safe and give them a sure grip.
B. For the rafter, gloves keep his hands safe and give him a sure grip.

_____ 7. A. Remind the rafters to have their life jackets fastened securely.
B. Remind the rafters to have your life jackets fastened securely.

_____ 8. A. The rafter must choose a good helmet to protect his head.
      B. The rafter must choose a good helmet to protect your head.

_____ 9. A. The novice rafter can choose rubber booties and a wet suit as their optional equipment.
      B. The novice rafter can choose rubber booties and a wet suit as his optional equipment.

_____ 10. A. You must consider a rafting trip for your next vacation.
       B. You must consider a rafting trip for one's next vacation.

8.11 CUMULATIVE *review*

Rewrite the following paragraph, correcting the ten errors from the following categories: agreement, verb use, pronoun case, courtesy order, reflexive and intensive pronoun use, and pronoun shift.

Camping along the Blue Ridge Parkway might be the ideal vacation for whomever enjoys the great outdoors. A tent camper's delight is his pitching his tent in a campground along this scenic highway. The Blue Ridge Parkway begin in Shenandoah National Park in Virginia and ends in the Great Smokies. If a person has the time, you can drive the entire distance of 355 miles. The traveler should take their time to see Grandfather Mountain. Just between me and you, the Lincove Viaduct, perhaps the most complicated segmented bridge ever built, is a breathtaking sight. During the spring, flowering plants such as the rhododendron, mountain laurel, and azalea provided a spectacular view for the visitor. Wildflowers also bloom profusely from spring through autumn. The ranger at Grandfather Mountain had given my brother and me a flower guide. I enjoyed seeing the wildflowers more than him. In part of the parkway area, travelers theirselves can pan for precious stones such as garnet, topaz, and sapphire. One might even find a gold nugget. A camper can enrich their mind at educational stops such as gem museums and the Moses H. Cone Memorial.

_____

_____

_____

_____

_____

_____

_____

FROM THE WRITTEN WORD

Recognizing the Differences

Think about the following: Abram and Lot, Jacob and Esau, light and darkness, good and evil, belief and unbelief. What comes to your mind? You probably think of these as being contrasting elements. Comparison (showing similarities) or contrast (showing differences) is a writing strategy evidenced throughout the Scriptures.

Consider Genesis 4:2–5, 8.

> And Abel was a keeper of sheep, but Cain was a tiller of the ground. And in process of time it came to pass, that Cain brought of the fruit of the ground an offering unto the Lord. And Abel, he also brought of the firstlings of his flock and of the fat thereof. And the Lord had respect unto Abel and to his offering: But unto Cain and to his offering he had not respect. And Cain was very wroth, and his countenance fell. . . . And Cain talked with Abel his brother: and it came to pass, when they were in the field, that Cain rose up against Abel his brother, and slew him.

When using the contrast writing strategy, you might need to make some concessions. For example, before you focus on the differences between Cain and Abel, you must recognize that they were alike. They had had the same parents and had grown up in the same home. They had observed the giving of animals for the covering of sin. With these concessions made, what do you observe about Cain and Abel?

Notice how the Scriptures show differences between Cain and Abel. Cain was a farmer and brought an offering to God that represented the work of his hands. God did not accept his offering. As a result, Cain was angry, jealous, and proud. Not only did he murder his brother, but he denied the murder and failed to seek forgiveness. Abel, on the other hand, was a shepherd and brought an offering that God accepted, an offering that satisfied God's plan. Abel was sincere, humble, and righteous. The point of contrast was not their occupations or their personalities, for God blesses both farmers and shepherds, and He blesses people of different personalities. The contrast grew out of the ways that these brothers approached redemption.

Personal Response

Read 1 Samuel 1:1–20 and Judges 13:2–24. Write a short paragraph comparing or contrasting the fathers of Samuel and Samson, Elkanah and Manoah, or the two mothers, Hannah and the unidentified mother of Samson.

College Application Essay	222
Pronoun Reference	225
Think About It	237

COLLEGE APPLICATION ESSAY Writing
PRONOUN REFERENCE Usage

9

A prospective college student must present himself in a way that gives the college officials confidence in his ideas and his ability to communicate them. Notice in the essay below how the writer positions himself as a candidate for acceptance in a missionary aviation major.

New Heights *by Dan Berber*

In the past, whenever I thought of my future, I envisioned myself piloting commercial jets across our country and around the world. I wanted an exciting career, and I believed that that profession would provide adventure and fulfillment. It was that same desire for excitement and adventure that prompted me to join others in my church on a mission trip to Kenya. Our trip was indeed exciting, but it was also life changing. I came home with a new sense of purpose and responsibility and a new definition of fulfillment.

In Kenya I saw little children lying helpless on grass mats, their stomachs distended from hunger; they will probably not live to be two years old. I saw adults willing to stand for hours under a blazing sun just to hear the Bible read in their own language. I knew for the first time how selfish I have been. I realized how much I have been given and how little I have given back. My thoughts of becoming a commercial pilot turned to thoughts of getting the gospel to people who have never heard God's Word. As a result I started to pray about being a missionary.

Looking through the catalog of your college, I saw the missionary aviation major. Everything I had been thinking suddenly came together.

I would like to enter the missionary aviation program. If accepted, I believe I would do well. I excel in math and mechanics and have a longstanding but refocused interest in flying. The Bible classes combined with the aviation classes would prepare me for the unique work of a missionary pilot.

Should the Lord lead me there, I would like to go back to Kenya someday to take the gospel to its people. And I would like to be the one flying the plane.

COLLEGE APPLICATION ESSAY

> For Ezra had prepared his heart to seek the law of the Lord, and to do it, and to teach in Israel statutes and judgments.
> *Ezra 7:10*

Some colleges to which you apply will require that you write an essay during the application process. Most application essays should reveal something about the applicant: goals, desires, interests, strengths, and so on. When you write an essay as an application to college, you should give an accurate picture of yourself—not boastful but not overly modest either. Too much boldness about yourself will not make a good impression, but not being able to objectively assess your God-given abilities will also make your application less persuasive. Strive for a balance of what you can do and what you need to learn.

Choose a field of study and perhaps a college. Write an application essay, telling why you have made these choices and why you are a good candidate for the program.

Planning

- ✓ **Look through college catalogs.** Read about the programs that interest you. Imagine yourself taking some of the classes. Or investigate colleges online.

- ✓ **Prayerfully consider God's plan for you.** God has promised to lead His children. He often uses parents and other godly counselors, so enlist their help as you research colleges and majors. You will invest a great deal of time and money in the college you select, so your decision is important.

- ✓ **Narrow your field of interest.** Notice which programs you return to and those you pass over quickly. Which studies intrigue you the most? Which ones are you best suited for? Berber recognizes his strengths (math and mechanics). He is also looking ahead at how his strengths could be used for God. Can you think of ministries or careers that would follow the degree you are considering?

- ✓ **Choose a field of study.** For this assignment, settle on one major. If you already know where you want to go to college and what you want to study, this assignment might be used as part of your application. If you are still deciding, this assignment can help you focus your interests and practice for a later application.

- ✓ **Make a word web.** Draw a circle and label it with the major you have chosen. Draw other circles around the outside of the first circle and connect them to the inner circle with lines. In each outer circle, write reasons, examples, and experiences that could be used as support for your choice of that particular field of study.

Dan Berber's word web looked like this:

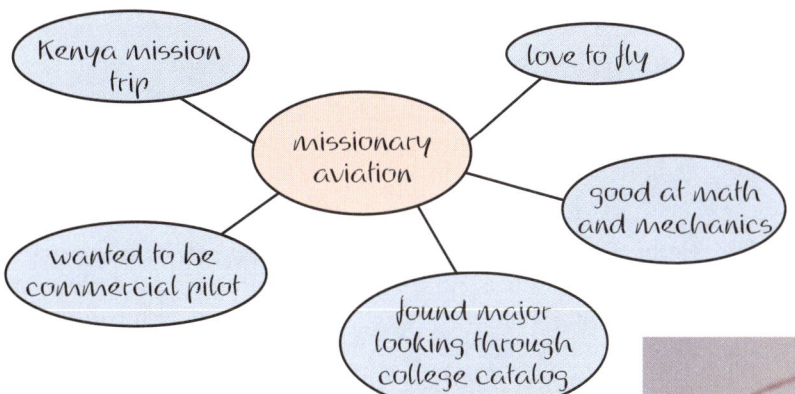

- ✓ **Develop an outline.** Decide how you will open the essay, how you will arrange the material in your word web, and how you will end the essay.

  For example, Dan may have written something like this:

  Opening: Change in goal to be a pilot
      I. Experiences in Kenya
      II. Desire to be a missionary
      III. Interest in missionary aviation
  Ending: Ultimate goal

tip Try to end the essay with something that will encourage the reader to take a personal interest in you.

- ✓ **Think of your audience.** Remember that you are writing to someone who will decide whether you can enter the college. The essay should have a human-interest appeal. For example, do you think you would like Dan Berber? Why? He seems sincere and kind. Suppose he had written his essay as though to his friends? He might have sounded flippant to a college admissions official. Or suppose he had tried to sound more formal. He might have sounded stilted and impersonal, as well as stuffy and conceited.

Drafting

- ✓ **Write an introductory paragraph.** Remember the purposes of an introduction: to catch the reader's interest, to introduce the topic, and to draw attention to the main idea of the essay. Keep your opening interesting by using an appropriate quotation, a compelling question, or a memorable story. Look at two possibilities for Berber's introductory paragraph below. Which one catches your interest better?

  ### Example 1
  Last summer I went on a mission trip to Kenya with my church. When I set out, I was expecting a summer of adventure and new experiences. I came home, however, with a new sense of purpose and responsibility.

  ### Example 2
  In the past, whenever I thought of my future, I envisioned myself piloting commercial jets across our country and around the world. I wanted an exciting career, and I believed that that profession would provide adventure and fulfillment. It was that same desire for excitement and adventure that

Thinking Biblically

What role should a biblical worldview and Christian ideas play in a college application essay? In an application to a Christian college, a Christian's faith should obviously play a prominent role. But it should also be present in an application to a local state university if God leads a student there. Choosing to discuss controversial issues such as homosexuality and abortion in a college application is hardly exercising biblical wisdom (Prov. 25:15). But acting as if faith has nothing to do with a Christian's desire to go to college would also be wrong. A believer could state that his search for knowledge is based on the foundation of the fear of the Lord (Prov. 1:7). The applicant could also mention that his pursuit of engineering or nursing has Christian purposes—not just making money, but loving and serving others through his work.

prompted me to join others in my church on a mission trip to Kenya. Our trip was indeed exciting, but it was also life changing. I came home with a new sense of purpose and responsibility and a new definition of fulfillment.

Notice how the second paragraph makes the opening more interesting and focuses the reader on the main point: his new goal.

✓ **Draft your essay.** Be direct and succinct. Using your outline, write your essay in one sitting. Reserve your most convincing statement for your conclusion. What effect do you think Dan Berber's last sentence would have on the reader?

✓ **Be specific.** Berber's details about the people he saw will help the reader to envision what Berber saw in Kenya. An image of "children lying helpless" will affect the reader much as it did the writer. Berber struck a good balance between being specific and avoiding sensationalism. Had he continued to describe each detail of the conditions he witnessed, Berber might have alienated his audience.

✓ **Keep your goal in mind as you write.** Everything in your essay should advance your goal of being admitted to the college. In this case, less is probably more. If Berber had written three more paragraphs about his time in Kenya, his essay would not have been as focused and effective. Stay close to the topic at hand. Had Berber discussed his passion for spicy foods or his love of soccer, his essay would have been far less effective.

Revising

✓ **Read your essay aloud.** Pretend you are speaking to the admissions officer. Does the essay represent you well? Does it sound like your voice? Does it seem sincere? Are there any sentences that distract or confuse?

✓ **Look for ways to improve your presentation.** Look again at your opening. Does it make the reader want to read on? Dan Berber's opening has an element of suspense: he says he used to think one way, implying he has changed his position. The reader may be interested to see how. Does the essay flow well, uncluttered by unnecessary details? Does it gain power as it goes, ending with the strongest appeal?

✓ **Ask a peer to read the essay.** After he reads it, ask him whether he has any questions. Does he think the essay presents the true you? Get his opinion on your opening and closing. Ask for suggestions on improving the piece.

✓ **Make changes to the essay.** Compare your peer's response to your own ideas. Recast sentences or add material (or omit some) to strengthen your writing and improve your chances of being remembered well. Examine the first and second drafts of Berber's second paragraph. Notice the changes made by reworking the sentences and adding or omitting detail.

> **First Draft**
> I saw little children who were sick and who were hungry and who probably would not live to be two years old. Some of them had hardly any clothing or toys. I also saw people stand for hours in the heat to listen to someone read the Bible in their language.

> **Second Draft**
> In Kenya I saw little children lying helpless on grass mats, their stomachs distended from hunger; they will probably not live to be two years old. I saw adults willing to stand for hours under a blazing sun just to hear the Bible read in their own language. I knew for the first time how selfish I have been. I realized how much I have been given and how little I have given back. My thoughts of becoming a commercial pilot turned to thoughts of getting the gospel to people who have never heard God's Word. As a result I started to pray about being a missionary.

✔ **Proofread your paper.** Be sure that the spelling, mechanics, and grammar are impeccable. An error in any of these elements could seriously hinder your goal of being seen as college material.

Publishing

✔ **Print a perfect copy.** Be sure you have followed any guidelines you were given. Following instructions is an important skill that can set you apart.

tip
Avoid odd or hard-to-read fonts for an application essay. A plain serif font is a safe choice.

✔ **Submit your essay to the school counselor or principal.** It would be good to see how these people respond, especially if you are planning to submit it to a college.

✔ **Conduct a mock interview.** Ask another student to play a college admissions officer. Present the material in your essay to him during a mock interview.

✔ **If appropriate, select a title.** Some college admissions policies may require you to title your essay. If so, write one that is interesting and specific. For this type of essay, a short title is probably best. Berber's title, "New Heights," is taken from his essay and applies to the subject of flying as well as to his aspirations to attend college.

✔ **Mail your essay to a college.** If you are planning to apply to a college that asks for an essay, use your revised essay when you apply.

Some Ideas to Consider

History
- Write a college application essay for Abigail Adams or some other famous person. Try to write as that person might have.

Literature
- Write an application for an English or writing major. Tell what pieces of literature have inspired you to study in this field.

All subjects
- Write an application for any major. Tell what qualities you bring to the study and what you plan to do with the degree.

PRONOUN REFERENCE

Although a few pronouns do not have antecedents (indefinite pronouns, mainly), most pronouns are understood as replacements for other words. The relationship between a pronoun and its antecedent (the noun or other pronoun that it replaces) must be clear if the reader is to understand the sentence. This relationship is often called **pronoun reference**, indicating that the pronoun refers to its antecedent. Follow the principles in this chapter to achieve correct pronoun reference.

Pronouns p. 37

Pronoun-Antecedent Agreement pp. 163–65

Clear Reference

A pronoun must refer clearly to only one antecedent. If two nearby nouns could be possible antecedents, the sentence will be ambiguous.

Ambiguous	**Mary** told her **sister** that **she** could do anything.
Clear	**Mary** told her **sister**, "**You** can do anything."
	Mary told her **sister**, "**I** can do anything."
Ambiguous	Both **Daniel** and **Ben** were running for class president; **he** was the first to congratulate **his** rival when **he** won the election.
Clear	Both **Daniel** and **Ben** were running for class president; **Ben** was the first to congratulate **his** rival when **Daniel** won the election.

A pronoun should follow its antecedent closely enough to make the relationship between the two words clear. If the antecedent is too remote, the reader may have trouble following the passage and identifying the word to which the pronoun refers.

Remote	In the book *The Plague and I*, **Betty MacDonald** recounts **her** experiences as a tuberculosis patient in the 1930s. At that time TB patients were usually confined to sanatoriums where they endured rigorous treatment programs to enforce rest and healthful habits. The discovery of effective antibiotics in the 1940s drastically changed the standard treatment procedures. Acknowledging the difficult conditions, **she** nevertheless tells **her** story with wit and energy.
Clear	In the book *The Plague and I*, **Betty MacDonald** recounts **her** experiences as a tuberculosis patient in the 1930s. At that time TB patients were usually confined to sanatoriums where they endured rigorous treatment programs to enforce rest and healthful habits. The discovery of effective antibiotics in the 1940s drastically changed the standard treatment procedures. Acknowledging the difficult conditions, **MacDonald** nevertheless tells **her** story with wit and energy.

in SUMMARY

Avoid **ambiguous reference** by having a single noun nearby that is the obvious antecedent of the pronoun.

Avoid **remote reference** by not having the antecedent too far away from the pronoun.

9.1 PRACTICE *the skill*

Identify the following sentences as clear (C) or unclear (U). If the meaning is unclear, underline the unclear pronoun.

_____ 1. Andrea met a number of new friends and teachers during her first weeks in college. They were important to her as she adjusted to college life.

_____ 2. During the wait to register for classes, her roommates made her feel welcome. Their being with her made it seem less difficult.

_____ 3. Jason moved into the residence hall with the idea of having the bottom bunk. It was the last one on Library Drive.

_____ 4. Jason bought his chemistry textbook from his roommate. He found it at the bottom of a stack of books.

_____ 5. Another roommate, Nathaniel, invited Jason to play a game of tennis. He looked everywhere in his room but could not find his racket.

_____ 6. With a heavy sigh, Andrea asked Susan and Laurie about the homework assignment. They were unable to give Andrea any advice.

_____ 7. Walking between classes, Julia accidentally dropped her books in front of her friends. They scattered recklessly on the ground.

_____ 8. Sitting at the computer, Joe asked his roommate some advice about the assignment. He was unable to understand the directions.

_____ 9. Bryan, my premed roommate, rushed out of the room with his hair uncombed. He was more concerned about the first-hour biology exam.

_____ 10. While the professor talked about transcendental functions, Cheri drew pictures in the margins of her notes. They were quite interesting.

9.2 REVIEW *the skill*

Rewrite each sentence to correct any unclear pronoun reference. If the sentence is already correct, write *C* in the blank.

1. Oxford University, the oldest English-speaking university in the world, continues to excel today. It equips its graduates to perform well in many fields.

2. Oxford grew slowly at first, but after Henry II banned English students from attending the University of Paris, it developed quickly.

3. The university's tradition of international scholarship began in 1190. It began with an overseas student from Friesland.

4. The first chancellor of Oxford was a scholar known as Oxonie. According to historical records this individual had been serving it faithfully since 1201.

   _____

   _____

5. In the thirteenth century, riots between students and townspeople erupted. At this point Oxford leaders established halls for them.

   _____

   _____

   _____

6. Oxford students lived in dormitory-like halls. Many of them remain notable to this day.

   _____

   _____

   _____

7. Early halls of residence focused on particular fields of study. They were under the supervision of masters.

   _____

   _____

   _____

8. A modern example of this system exists at Wycliffe Hall, with most of its students preparing for ministry as clergy in the Church of England.

   _____

   _____

9. Though academically outstanding, it is a very dark place spiritually.

   _____

   _____

10. As one of the best-known colleges in the world, Oxford offers a wide variety of study topics, with some of the most qualified professors in the world teaching them.

    _____

    _____

Reference to a Noun, Not an Implied Noun

A pronoun must refer to a noun that is actually stated, not to an idea only implied by the sentence. To correct a sentence with implied reference, either provide an antecedent for the pronoun or replace the unclear pronoun with a specific noun.

IMPLIED	Even though the coach has added morning practices, **they** haven't yet broken **their** season-long losing streak.
STATED	Even though the coach has added morning practices for the **players**, **they** haven't yet broken **their** season-long losing streak.
	Even though the coach has added morning practices, the **team** hasn't yet broken **its** season-long losing streak.
IMPLIED	When I got to the desk, **he** told me that I had waited in the wrong line.
STATED	When I got to the desk, the ticket agent told me that I had waited in the wrong line.

Reference to a Noun That Is Not a Modifier

A pronoun should refer to a noun that has a regular noun function, such as a subject or an object. A possessive noun or any other noun that modifies another word is a poor antecedent.

Modifying Nouns p. 50

WEAK	Our neighbor's **barn** roof flew off during the storm, but **it** remained standing with no damage to the walls or contents.
BETTER	Our neighbor's barn roof flew off during the storm, but the **barn** remained standing with no damage to the walls or contents.
WEAK	The **museum's** new exhibits brought **it** public acclaim.
BETTER	The new exhibits at the **museum** brought **it** public acclaim.

Occasionally, the pronoun may precede the antecedent in the sentence.

CLEAR	**Its** new exhibits brought the **museum** public acclaim.

in SUMMARY

Avoid reference to an implied noun by ensuring that an actual noun is the antecedent of the pronoun.

Avoid reference to a noun that is a modifier.

9.3 PRACTICE *the skill*

Try to match each pronoun (except *you* and *I*) to its antecedent. If a pronoun refers to an implied noun or if its antecedent is a modifier, underline that pronoun and supply an appropriate noun or noun phrase. If the sentence is already correct, write C in the blank.

_____ 1. If you visit a college or university, they will probably let you tour one of the residence halls.

_____ 2. My sister Elise visited one college residence hall twice, but she never got to stay overnight in it until her freshman year of college.

_____ 3. When my sister and I drove on campus, they directed us to the registration building.

_____ 4. Elise's roommate Juanita offered to help carry her luggage when she moved in.

_____ 5. After getting settled into her room, Elise bought a miniature ladder for her bunk bed so that it would be easily accessible.

_____ 6. Juanita patiently explained each document in Elise's registration packet while she listened.

_____ 7. The supervisor was expecting maximum occupancy in each room, but she had just one roommate as far as I could tell.

_____ 8. The new roommates designed a memo board, where they could be posted to inform them of messages while they were out.

_____ 9. When Elise asked about wireless access, she said it was available.

_____ 10. As far as I could tell, Elise is adjusting well to her first college experiences, and it will continue to nurture and train her well for life.

9.4 REVIEW *the skill*

Rewrite each sentence to correct any unclear pronoun reference. If the sentence is already correct, write C in the blank.

1. In America in the early nineteenth century, the opportunity for a woman to become a doctor was nonexistent because they were not accepted in the colleges.

_____

_____

2. Elizabeth Blackwell knew that women could become teachers, so she received training to be a teacher.

3. After Blackwell finished her training, she realized the pressing need for them to become doctors.

4. Although she tried to meet this need, many medical schools turned down Blackwell's applications because they were not well received.

5. In 1849 Elizabeth Blackwell became America's first woman doctor after she graduated from Geneva Medical College in New York.

6. Blackwell had gained acceptance as a medical student only because they thought her application was a joke.

7. England's acceptance of Dr. Blackwell became obvious when they admitted her name to the British Medical Register.

8. The Female Medical College of Pennsylvania opened in 1850; it was the first medical school in the world to train only women.

9. The college's name has changed several times; it was first renamed the Woman's Medical College of Pennsylvania in 1867.

10. Since 1969 the school's doors have been open to men, but it maintains a strong commitment to women.

Definite Reference of Personal Pronouns

A personal pronoun should refer to a definite individual or group. In formal and academic writing the pronouns *they, it,* and *you* should not be used in an indefinite sense.

Indefinite *They*

Unlike an indefinite pronoun (*anyone, everybody,* etc.), the personal pronoun *they* requires an antecedent. Do not use *they* for indefinite reference.

INDEFINITE	Contrary to the popular image, **they** say that Viking helmets never had horns.
CLEAR	Contrary to the popular image, **historians** say that Viking helmets never had horns.
INDEFINITE	At the café, **they** don't serve breakfast after ten o'clock.
CLEAR	The **café** doesn't serve breakfast after ten o'clock.

Indefinite *It*

Do not use the personal pronoun *it* for indefinite reference in expressions such as *it says.* Replace *it* with the source of information.

INDEFINITE	**It** said in the paper that we can expect snow next week.
CLEAR	The **weather forecast** in the paper reported that we can expect snow next week.
INDEFINITE	In Galatians 6:2 **it** says that we should bear each other's burdens.
CLEAR	In Galatians 6:2 **Paul** says that we should bear each other's burdens.
	Galatians 6:2 says that we should bear each other's burdens.

Certain set expressions use the pronoun *it* in an indefinite sense. These idiomatic expressions are perfectly acceptable even in standard English.

TIME	What time is **it**?
	It is half past eight.
DISTANCE	**It** is only two blocks from our house to the grocery store.
WEATHER	Is **it** still raining?
ENVIRONMENT	Is **it** louder than usual in here today?

Indefinite *You*

Except in casual conversation, avoid using the personal pronoun *you* to refer to people in general. Use a more specific noun or an appropriate indefinite pronoun.

INDEFINITE	In most communities, **you** need a special license to drive a bus.
CLEAR	In most communities, a **bus driver** needs a special license.
	In most communities, **anyone** who drives a bus needs a special license.
	Most communities require a **bus driver** to have a special license.

Although informal writing allows the indefinite *you* in certain idioms, such as folksy proverbs, these expressions are usually out of place in formal discourse.

INFORMAL	You are what you eat.
FORMAL	The eating habits of a **person** affect **his** health.

Not all uses of the personal pronoun *you* are indefinite. In informal situations, a writer may use *you* when it refers definitely to the reader. When the writer can logically include both himself and the reader in a statement, *we* is acceptable. For very formal situations, however, use the pronoun *one* instead.

INFORMAL	**You** should always remember to thank those who have helped **you** achieve success.
	We should always remember to thank those who have helped **us** achieve success.
FORMAL	A **person** should always remember to thank those who have helped **him** to achieve success.
	One should always remember to thank those who have helped **him** to achieve success.

Although *you* is appropriate in imperative sentences (such as a set of instructions), some teachers prefer that students avoid all uses of *you* and the imperative mood in academic writing such as research papers and reports.

INFORMAL	Be sure to plug in the machine before **you** turn it on.
FORMAL OR ACADEMIC	The **operator** should connect the machine to a power supply before **he** turns it on.

Reference to a Noun, Not a Broad Idea

A pronoun must refer to a specific noun, not to a broad idea stated in a preceding sentence or clause. This rule applies most strongly to *which*. In careful writing it also applies to the demonstratives *this* and *that*.

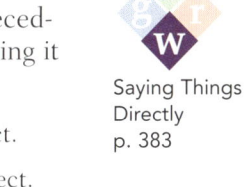

Saying Things Directly
p. 383

BROAD REFERENCE	Jason thought a chameleon is an amphibian, **which** is incorrect.
	Jason thought a chameleon is an amphibian, but **this** is incorrect.
CLEAR	**Jason** thought a chameleon is an amphibian, but **he** is incorrect.
	Jason's belief that a chameleon is an amphibian is incorrect.
BROAD REFERENCE	Kangaroos are able to thrive and multiply under even very harsh conditions. **That** creates problems for Australian sheep herders.
CLEAR	The ability of kangaroos to thrive and multiply under even very harsh conditions creates problems for Australian sheep herders.
	Australian sheep herders have problems with **kangaroos**, **which** are able to thrive and multiply under even very harsh conditions.

in SUMMARY

Do not use the personal pronoun **they** in an indefinite sense to refer to people in general.

Replace the indefinite **it** in phrases such as "it says" with a definite source of information.

Reserve the indefinite **you** that refers to people in general for conversation and informal writing.

Avoid **broad reference** by making the antecedent of the pronoun a noun, not the general idea of the preceding clause.

9.5 PRACTICE the skill

Identify each sentence as clear (C) or unclear (U). If it is unclear, underline the pronoun causing the indefinite or broad reference. Avoid informal English.

_____ 1. When looking for a suitable college to attend, someone who is a Christian should consider the opportunities that a Christian college offers.

_____ 2. In Christian colleges they offer the opportunity for students to grow academically as well as spiritually.

_____ 3. They will put an emphasis on how the hand of God has worked in history, science, or whatever courses of study you choose.

_____ 4. One can also make godly friends, and that lasts a lifetime.

_____ 5. In secular schools, however, you will encounter the ideals and philosophies of the world with little to no biblical guidance.

_____ 6. It says in this secular college catalog that freshman orientation includes diversity training in religions and alternative lifestyles.

_____ 7. In many Christian colleges, freshman students receive training in how they can effectively share God's Word with diverse peoples.

_____ 8. Faculty members at many Christian institutions help their students with academic and spiritual needs, and it really makes a difference.

_____ 9. One should seriously consider a Christian college or university before making the final decision about where to receive his higher education.

_____ 10. In making such a life-shaping decision, Christians find assurance in God's Word. In Proverbs 3:5–6 it says, "Trust in the Lord with all thine heart; and lean not unto thine own understanding. In all thy ways acknowledge Him, and He shall direct thy paths."

9.6 REVIEW the skill

Rewrite each sentence to correct any unclear or informal pronoun reference. If the sentence is already correct, write C in the blank.

1. Although many older universities in the United States were begun as theological institutions, you can find little gospel truth in them today.

   _____

   _____

2. When it began, Harvard turned out many Puritan ministers, which greatly furthered the gospel.

   _____

   _____

3. In many secular universities they promote worldly philosophy and ideology.

4. One of the downfalls of religious schools is the election of liberal administrative officers. It weakens the school's underpinnings.

5. One verse explains the amazing transformation in these institutions of higher learning: in Jude 4 it says, "Certain men crept in unawares."

6. If one examines the history of secular universities, he will realize that a single man in an important position can destroy the Christian stand of an institution.

7. If only one person questions the validity of the Scriptures upon which the school stands, it can ruin the whole institution.

8. Strong belief and great faith are necessary for you as well as for an academic institution to remain faithful to Christ and His gospel.

9. It shows throughout academic history that faithfulness cannot be retained through the power of man alone.

10. They must be bathed in the prayers of saints and upheld by the arms of God.

CUMULATIVE *review*

Rewrite the following paragraph, correcting the ten errors from these categories: verb tense, subject-verb agreement, pronoun-antecedent agreement, pronoun use, and pronoun reference.

The oldest educational facility still in use in the United States, the Sir Christopher Wren Building at the College of William and Mary, possessed a fascinating history. To begin, no one can say for certain that they know Wren actually designed the building. Only one extant letter refers to him "modeling" the building. However, what you can know for certain about the building proved equally intriguing. Used as the temporary seat of government until the completion of the colonial capitol at Williamsburg, the Wren Building later provided classroom space for three especially notable pupils: Thomas Jefferson, James Monroe, and John Tyler. George Washington hisself even made use of it on numerous occasions when he served as chancellor of the college in 1784. During both the Battle of Yorktown and the American Civil War, the site has served as a makeshift military hospital. Its long history did not continue uninterrupted, though: three times flames engulfed the building and brought terrific damage to its structure. Nevertheless, after they restored the Wren Building to its original grandeur, the facility, complete with both of its original wings, now stands open to whomever desires to tour the building or even to attend college classes there.

THINK ABOUT IT

Truth and Validity

A critical thinker must examine the evidence to evaluate the validity of a speaker's or writer's claims.

Every argument should meet the dual criteria of truth and validity. Truth, of course, depends on the accuracy of the statements themselves. Knowing the difference between fact and opinion will help you to decide whether a statement is true, false, or evaluative (an opinion that cannot be proved or has not yet been proved). If the statements are false, you will probably reject the argument. If the statements are evaluative, you will need to decide whether the opinions on which the argument rests are reasonable opinions.

Validity refers to the form of an argument. If the form of the argument is reasonable, the argument is valid, regardless of its truth or falsity. Study the following examples. Can you explain why they are labeled as they are?

UNTRUE AND INVALID	If a student studies for the test, he will pass it.
	Rick did not study for the test.
	Rick will not pass the test.
	(But Rick already knew the material well enough that he didn't need to study for the test.)
UNTRUE BUT VALID	All normal dogs have four feet.
	My cat is a normal dog.
	My cat has four feet.
	(But my cat is a cat, not a dog.)
TRUE AND VALID	All people are sinners.
	Marcia is a person.
	Marcia is a sinner.

Only the last argument is completely sound. It is easy to reject arguments based on false premises. But what about validity? If the premises are true, does it matter whether the form of the argument might be invalid? Consider another example.

POSSIBLY TRUE BUT INVALID	Atheists oppose prayer in schools.
	My senator opposes prayer in schools.
	My senator is an atheist.

Perhaps this last statement is true; the senator under discussion may be an atheist. But perhaps the senator is not an atheist. Some politicians oppose prayer in school because they believe that prayer in schools is unconstitutional. A person is not an atheist simply because he or she shares one particular characteristic with atheists (unless, of course, it is the defining characteristic: rejecting all belief in God). The invalidity of the argument could lead to serious problems if a person were to make decisions about the senator based on these statements. Critical thinkers examine both the truth and the validity of the evidence before they accept any argument.

Thinking Biblically

Establishing facts is not as simple as it seems. The evidence a person collects during research needs to be evaluated first. Though such evaluations are made every day, most people do not realize that they are evaluating because their assessments take place at the level of assumptions about the world—at the level of worldview. For example, if an evolutionist encounters a trilobite fossil, he will not see it as evidence for a worldwide flood unless he changes his beliefs (his assumptions) about the earth's origins. Likewise, a creation scientist interprets the same evidence in light of his own beliefs about things he has never witnessed personally (Heb. 11:3). Assumption-based thinking affects more than just scientific evaluations; all evaluations are shaped by worldview. Ultimately, for a statement to be both true and valid, it has to do more than appear to match the facts. It has to be founded on the right assumptions. "The fear of the Lord is the beginning of knowledge" (Prov. 1:7).

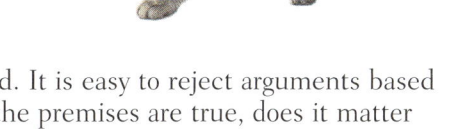

Thinking It Through

Evaluate current popular arguments, testing them for truth and validity. To find possible topics, examine the editorial pages of a newspaper, listen to a news broadcast, or visit the website of a news organization.

Sonnet	240
Adjective and Adverb Use	243
From the Written Word	257

SONNET Writing
ADJECTIVE AND ADVERB USE Usage

10

The language of poetry is intensely expressive and emotive. Often a poem uses language that is metaphorical; that is, the words have a meaning other than what is at the surface. In this Shakespearean sonnet, the speaker seems to be addressing the weather. But with only a little imagination, we can see that he is really talking to his love, who hurt him and then felt bad about it. Do you think he forgave her?

Sonnet 34 *by William Shakespeare*

Why didst thou promise such a beauteous day,
And make me travel forth without my cloak,
To let base clouds o'ertake me in my way,
Hiding thy brav'ry in their rotten smoke?
'Tis not enough that through the cloud thou break,
To dry the rain on my storm-beaten face,
For no man well of such a salve can speak
That heals the wound, and cures not the disgrace:
Nor can thy shame give physic to my grief,
Though thou repent, yet have I still the loss,
Th' offender's sorrow lends but weak relief
To him that bears the strong offense's cross.
Ah, but those tears are pearl which thy love sheds,
And they are rich, and ransom all ill deeds.

SONNET

That which was written was upright, even words of truth.
Ecclesiastes 12:10

As you may have learned in studying literature, a **sonnet** is a fourteen-line poem in iambic pentameter that has one of two main rhyme schemes. The English sonnet rhymes *abab cdcd efef gg;* the Italian sonnet usually rhymes *abba abba cde cde* or *abba abba cdcdcd.*

English sonnets usually make a shift of thought in the last two lines (the **couplet**), and Italian sonnets in the last six (the **sestet**). The speaker in Sonnet 34 implies in the first twelve lines that there is no remedy for his broken heart. But in the closing couplet, he reveals that her tears have mended his wounded feelings.

Most sonnets are serious, but occasionally one is written in jest. For example, Shakespeare wrote a sonnet declaring that his love is no great beauty—and it is a sonnet that seems refreshingly realistic amid the many flowery sonnets of exuberant praise.

Writing a sonnet requires both imagination and discipline. Imagination must find the subject and the approach; discipline must follow the form and choose the precise expression. Together, they should produce a poem that is at once orderly and comprehensible.

Think of something that is very important to you right now. Or think of something that amuses you. Compose a sonnet—English or Italian—about your idea.

Planning

✔ **Get an idea.** Some poets get ideas from their observations, some from their reading (the Bible and sermons inspire many Christian poets), and some from conversations or comments or pictures. Wherever your ideas come from, they must compel you to write. It is no good to try to write a poem on a topic you care little about or something you think you should care about but really do not. It will read stiffly—if it gets read at all.

Even humorous poems must spring from a desire to communicate something. In the Shakespearean sonnet in which the speaker states that his ladylove is not especially beautiful, the point is serious (true love is not based on looks), but the presentation is amusing. The formal tone of the sonnet increases the humor, because the form is more elevated than the topic.

✔ **Talk to a friend.** Explain your idea to someone else. Ask him what he thinks. As you talk to him, you will be refining your own thoughts. Perhaps Shakespeare talked to his friends about how someone had hurt his feelings before he wrote Sonnet 34. Maybe his friends told him that his situation sounded like a nice day that had turned suddenly rainy. Or maybe Shakespeare just happened to be thinking about this topic on such a day. Talking to a friend about your topic will give you another perspective—and perhaps some more ideas.

- ✓ **Make a brief outline.** Think of your sonnet in two parts: Part One sets up the situation and the speaker's feelings about it, and Part Two (the couplet or the sestet) reveals a new insight and resolves the tension. Here, for example, is how Sonnet 34 might be outlined:

    Part One
    - A. Quatrain 1—Ask the sun why he allowed bad weather.
    - B. Quatrain 2—Complain that the sun is not curing the real problem.
    - C. Quatrain 3—Assert that nothing will set this offense right.

    Part Two Couplet—Admit that tears from the offender are enough to make up for the hurt.

Drafting

- ✓ **Follow the outline.** Using the outline you have written, prepare a rough draft of Part One or Part Two. Some people like to write the ending first, finding that it helps them write Part One toward it. Others like to write from beginning to end, letting Part Two arise as a culmination of the previous work.

- ✓ **Use iambic pentameter.** All spoken English has a rhythm or pattern of stress with weak and strong syllables. Regular recurrence of these stresses is known as **meter**. An **iamb** is a weak stress followed by a strong stress. The sonnet form, which uses iambic pentameter, dictates that the writer compose lines that contain five ("penta") weak-strong stress units, or **feet**.

    ‿ / ‿ / ‿ / ‿ / ‿ /
    If ever two were one, then surely we.

    ‿ / ‿ / ‿ / ‿ / ‿ /
    If ever man were loved by wife, then thee;

    ‿ / ‿ / ‿ / ‿ / ‿ /
    If ever wife was happy in a man,

    ‿ / ‿ / ‿ / ‿ / ‿ /
    Compare with me, ye women, if you can.

    (from "To My Dear and Loving Husband" by Anne Bradstreet)

tip Simple—even one-syllable—words carry emotion and meaning better and are easier to work with than complicated ones.

- ✓ **Remember rhyme scheme.** As you write, be aware of the end words of your lines. Note the choices Bradstreet makes in the excerpt above: *we, thee; man, can.* Choose simple words to end lines; your rhyming will be less forced, more likely to blend into the flow of the ideas naturally. If a line ends with *petition*, it will be difficult to find a pleasing and natural partner for it: *remission, suspicion,* or *fission*, perhaps. But lines ending with *bright, way, song,* or *meet*, for example, will be less troublesome. However, you would not want to choose words only for their ease of making a rhyme. It is never a good idea to let the form overpower the message.

tip If you use an unusual word as a rhyming word, use it first and later rhyme it with a better-known word. Then the rhyme will not seem forced.

- ✓ **Keep in mind your goals for the sonnet.** As you write, always remember the final effect you want the poem to have. Think through each line: does it support the big idea? Do the sounds and images contribute to the whole or draw attention away from it? Does it read naturally?

Thinking Biblically

Do you have a Christian view of adverbs and sonnets? Or is the Christian view of these things the same as the Hindu view, the atheist view, or the Muslim view? Every English speaker on earth uses adverbs and sonnets (well, at least adverbs) in essentially the same way. *Quickly* means the same thing in New York as it does in York. Does that mean that adverbs—and sonnets and essays and interjections and any other literary genre or feature of language—are exempt from God's demand to do all to His glory (1 Cor. 10:31)? No. The key is to view adverbs and sonnets as tools, ready for various purposes. The question is, then, are you using adverbs and sonnets for Christian purposes—to show love to a neighbor, to bring glory to God through the beauty of language? The believer should have a Christian view of everything in the world, even adverbs. The Christian should glorify God in whatever he does and with whatever tool he uses—on purpose!

You must be setting up for the shift in thought and tension, even as you seem to be going in a different direction. For example, in Sonnet 34, the speaker gives you clues that he will not hold a grudge forever. His tone is not angry, but rather incredulous. He asks almost pleading questions. If he had meant never to mend the relationship, would he have not used direct statements, leaving her no room to answer or approach him? Notice in stanza one that he says that base clouds hide the sun's bravery. He seems more upset about the situation (the clouds coming in) than he is with the person (the sun).

Revising

✓ **Read your sonnet aloud.** Does it read smoothly? Does it produce the effect you want? Does it resolve the tension realistically?

✓ **Check the rhyme scheme.** Do you have three quatrains and a couplet? Or an octet and a sestet? Do the end-words fall naturally in the sentences? Do any rhyming words seem to stick out, to be there just for the sake of the rhyme?

✓ **See whether your message is clear.** Even if the rhyme and rhythm are perfect, the poem can still fail. If what you meant to convey is obscured by how you conveyed it, the reader will leave empty-handed. What did you want him to carry away with him?

✓ **Allow a peer to evaluate the sonnet.** Ask someone else to read the sonnet and tell you what he thinks of it. Does he see the shift in the couplet? Does it convince him? Listen carefully to his comments for making your sonnet more readable and meaningful.

✓ **Make changes to the sonnet.** Compare your peer's comments about your poem to your own observations about changes you want to make. Which changes are most important to make? Which ones will enhance the reader's enjoyment of it? Make changes for clarity and effect. Then proofread the sonnet, checking for mistakes in grammar, usage, and spelling.

Publishing

✓ **Hold a poetry reading.** Choose a comfortable place where a small group can meet. Take turns reading the sonnets aloud.

✓ **Make a chapbook.** Collect sonnets by theme or tone (humorous or serious). Make copies and gather them into a book. Give the book a title.

✓ **Make an audio recording.** Find a good reader and ask him to record his reading of the sonnets from your chapbook.

Some Ideas to Consider

Math
- Write a sonnet in another iambic line—like iambic heptameter. How does your new iambic line change the sound and effect of the "sonnet"?

History
- Discover other sonneteers. Do not overlook the twenty-first century.

Literature
- Read Robert Frost's "The Silken Tent." It is one long sentence in perfect sonnet form.

Adjective and Adverb Use

As you know, adjectives and adverbs modify other words in sentences. In general, adjectives modify nouns or pronouns; adverbs modify verbs, adjectives, and other adverbs.

ADJECTIVES | He maketh me to lie down in *green* pastures; he leadeth me beside *the still* waters. (Ps. 23:2)

ADVERBS | *Then* they *willingly* received him into the ship. (John 6:21)

Sometimes, however, adverbs can modify nouns. These adverbs usually specify time or place and come after the noun.

The leaf cleanup *yesterday* was the best that I have ever seen.

After a hard day at work, the crew will meet in the office *below*.

On occasion another part of speech may function as an adverb. In meanings of time, place, or manner, nouns (or nouns and their modifiers) can modify verbs. These words that meet the noun test but modify verbs are called **adverbial nouns**.

The grounds crew worked *all week* to rake the leaves from the premises.

This Friday they will go *home* early.

The crew has never planned *that way* before.

Adjectives and Adverbs
pp. 48–51

S-LV-PN, S-LV-PA
pp. 75–76

Showing Comparison with Modifiers

Most adjectives and adverbs show one of three degrees: positive, comparative, or superlative. The **positive degree** describes one person, thing, or action; no comparison is made. The **comparative degree** compares two people, things, or actions. The **superlative degree** compares three or more people, things, or actions.

POSITIVE | The gum tree is *big*.
COMPARATIVE | The gum tree is *bigger* than the maple tree.
SUPERLATIVE | The gum tree is the *biggest* tree in the yard.

Adverb Clauses of Comparison
pp. 122–23

Because the superlative degree indicates an extreme, the definite article *the* usually goes with it.

My friend is *the tallest boy* in our school.
His cousin is *the tallest* in their family.

Regular Comparison of Adjectives and Adverbs

Regular adjectives and adverbs form the comparative and superlative degrees in one of two ways. One-syllable adjectives and most two-syllable adjectives, particularly those ending in *-y, -ly,* and *-le,* form the comparative and superlative degrees by adding *-er* and *-est.* Two-syllable adverbs and most three-syllable adjectives form the comparative and superlative degrees with *more* and *most.* Adverbs made from adjectives by the addition of *-ly* use *more* and *most.*

Positive	Reginald is *tall*.
	Playing the center position on the basketball team is *easy* for him.
	His playing center is *important* to his team.
	He approached the championship game *cautiously*.
Comparative	Reginald is *taller* than his brother Charles.
	Playing the center position on the basketball team is *easier* for him than playing the guard position.
	His playing center is *more important* than his playing forward.
	He approached the championship game *more cautiously* than his brother did.
Superlative	Reginald is the *tallest* of the five brothers.
	Of all positions on the basketball team, the center position is the *easiest* for him to play.
	His position as center is the *most important* of the different positions that he plays.
	Of all the players on the team, he approached the championship game the *most cautiously*.

Absolute Comparative and Superlative of Adjectives

Comparative and superlative degrees of adjectives used without specific comparison to other things are in an **"absolute"** sense. Often, this absolute sense is indicated by certain expressions that have become idioms in English.

Absolute Comparative	Tickets to the basketball game will be provided to the children of *lower-income* families. (*In this context* lower *does not mean "less than low"; it is a general term for "below average."*)
Absolute Superlative	"We had a great time! We had *the best* seats, and the game was exciting." (*The intended meaning is "very good seats."*)

Irregular Comparison of Adjectives and Adverbs

Some adjectives and adverbs are irregular in the formation of the comparative and superlative degrees. When you have a question, consult a dictionary.

Adjectives			Adverbs		
bad	worse	worst	badly	worse	worst
good	better	best	well	better	best
	little	less		least	

in SUMMARY

Adverbial nouns are nouns that modify verbs.

Adjectives and adverbs have three degrees of comparison: **positive**, **comparative**, and **superlative**.

One-syllable adjectives and most two-syllable adjectives, particularly those ending in -y, -ly, and -le, form the comparative and superlative degrees by adding -er and -est. Others use *more* and *most*.

Comparative and superlative degrees of adjectives used without specific comparison to other things are in an **"absolute" sense**.

Some adjectives and adverbs are irregular in the formation of the comparative and superlative degrees.

10.1 PRACTICE *the skill*

Underline each adjective, including the correct choice from the adjectives in parentheses. Double underline each adverb that modifies a noun.

1. The biblical account of Mephibosheth in 2 Samuel 9 illustrates the *(blessed, more blessed)* position of a believer in Christ.

2. After a long war between the houses of Saul and David, the Lord granted David a *(decisive, more decisive)* victory that raised doubts about whether any descendants of Saul remained.

3. Nevertheless, David, because of his past covenant with Jonathan, ordered his men to seek for *(clearer, more clear)* information that would lead to even one descendant.

4. One of the *(most loyal, loyalest)* servants told David about one remaining son.

5. Mephibosheth, the sole surviving descendant, must have wondered whether matters could be *(worse, worst)* for a lame man who had lost all of his kindred.

6. Entering the palace, Mephibosheth bowed before the king, called himself a servant of the *(low, lowest)* degree, and waited for his likely sentence of death.

7. David urged Mephibosheth not to fear, for David wished to honor his covenant with Jonathan and to bless this *(helpless, more helpless)* former enemy.

8. One of the *(great, greatest)* blessings that Mephibosheth received was that he would dine upon the best food and would receive the land of his ancestors.

9. The procedure of conquering kings in the period then was to remove *(seditious, more seditious)* enemies rather than to allow them to renew their plans.

10. Mephibosheth remained in Jerusalem, where he was welcomed in the *(regal, more regal)* court of the king.

10.2 REVIEW *the skill*

Underline each adverb, including the correct choice from the adverbs in parentheses. Double underline each noun that modifies a verb.

1. An approach that one (*especially, more especially*) notices today is "Do not get mad, get even!"

2. From a worldly perspective, Abraham Lincoln could have (*justifiably, more justifiably*) trounced an old enemy named Edwin Stanton.

3. Prior to Lincoln's election as president of the United States, a group of big-city lawyers abused Lincoln openly and (*hatefully, more hatefully*); Lincoln returned home to Springfield, Illinois, a crestfallen man.

4. Of these lawyers, Edwin Stanton was the one who spoke (*more caustically, most caustically*) of Lincoln.

5. During the presidential election Stanton had even (*maliciously, most maliciously*) spread reports of Lincoln's lowly background, unbecoming appearance, and supposed stupidity around Washington, D.C.

6. However, upon becoming president, Lincoln treated his former enemies amazingly well; instead of treating them the way in which he had been treated, he offered key leadership positions to various lawyers who had treated him (*snobbishly, most snobbishly*).

7. Lincoln's appointment of Edwin Stanton as the secretary of war must have surprised many, for people do not (*often, most often*) respond as Lincoln did.

8. Looking beyond his own personal grievances, Lincoln wanted what was best for the struggling nation: he (*wisely, more wisely*) appointed a man who possessed quite remarkable ability and experience in matters of national import.

9. Interestingly, Stanton became one of Lincoln's closest allies; as time passed, Stanton witnessed Lincoln's amazing leadership ability and (*greatly, most greatly*) regretted his past criticisms of the president.

10. Upon Lincoln's untimely death, Stanton (*clearly, more clearly*) proved his genuine constancy to the memory of his fallen leader; Stanton grieved with Lincoln's family and reportedly uttered the following eulogy: "Now he belongs to the ages."

Problems with Modifiers

Modifiers That Cannot Be Compared

Certain adjectives cannot be compared. If something is unique, it is the only one of its category; therefore, it cannot be described as more unique or most unique. Other such adjectives that cannot be compared are *perfect, dead,* and *eternal.* Many adverbs, especially qualifiers, cannot have degrees of comparison. Examples of adverbs that cannot be compared include *not, daily, almost, here, very, now, somewhat, really,* and *too.*

Wrong | Stefanie's science fair project was the most unique.
Right | Stefanie's science fair project was unique.
Right | Stefanie's science fair project was the most unusual.

Double Comparisons

Do not use both *-er* and *more* to form the comparative degree or both *-est* and *most* to form the superlative degree.

Wrong | She was the *most kindest* student in Mrs. Jenkins's chemistry class.
Right | She was the *kindest* student in Mrs. Jenkins's chemistry class.

Double Negatives

Use only one negative word to give a sentence a negative meaning. When the adverb *not* is used along with another negative word, the **double negative error** occurs. Keep in mind that *no, nothing, no one, never, scarcely, hardly,* and similar words are negative.

Wrong | After a long Christmas vacation, some of the students *did not* have *no* interest in a new class project.
Right | After a long Christmas vacation, some of the students had *no* interest in a new class project.
Right | After a long Christmas vacation, some of the students *did not* have *any* interest in a new class project.

Adverbs
pp. 50–51

ESL

When a sentence with the word *some* is made negative, *some* is replaced by *any*.

Janine opened **some** windows in the house.
Janine did **not** open **any** window in the house.
She said **something**.
She did **not** say **anything**.

---

in SUMMARY

For modifiers that cannot be compared, do not use *-er/-est* or *more/most*.

Do not use both *-er* and *more* to form the comparative degree or both *-est* and *most* to form the superlative degree.

Use only one negative word to give the sentence a negative meaning.

10.3 PRACTICE the skill

Underline each incorrect adjective or adverb and write the correction in the blank. If the sentence is already correct, write C in the blank.

_____ 1. Joseph's forgiving spirit challenges us to follow his uniquest example.

_____ 2. In spite of his brothers' cruelty toward him, Joseph considered the circumstances to be a part of God's most perfect plan.

_____ 3. Although Joseph was sold into slavery, was brought into Egypt, and faced almost certain death, he was protected and received a high position in the Egyptian royal court.

_____ 4. God enabled Joseph to interpret the king's dream; therefore, Joseph was considered the wisest man in the land.

_____ 5. As a result of Joseph's wise leadership, Egypt was not in want during the years of famine; Joseph's brothers, however, did not have no stockpile of corn.

_____ 6. Joseph's brothers and almost all the people of the land came to Egypt to buy corn from Joseph.

_____ 7. Joseph's forgiveness of his brothers found its basis in Joseph's very perfect faith in God's providence.

_____ 8. After Joseph revealed his identity to his brothers and was reunited with his father, Joseph had the most unique opportunity to provide for his family.

_____ 9. Although Joseph's brothers thought evil against him, God meant it for a good result.

_____ 10. The example of Joseph's forgiveness of his brothers prepares us for the most eternal example of forgiveness, Jesus Christ's forgiveness.

REVIEW *the skill*

Rewrite each sentence, making the modifier clear or correct. If the sentence is already correct, write C in the blank.

1. History records some most unique examples of presidential pardons given to those who may or may not have deserved the pardon.

2. Dr. Samuel Mudd was accused of, convicted of, and sent to prison for helping John Wilkes Booth in his most horriblest deed, the assassination of Abraham Lincoln.

3. Dr. Mudd said that he did not have no part in the assassination, but in 1865 a military commission convicted Mudd of aiding Booth because Mudd had treated Booth's broken leg.

4. Dr. Mudd claimed that he did not have no idea that Lincoln had been assassinated and that he did not recognize Booth.

5. Mudd's claim that he did not know Booth was not the most smartest declaration since witnesses could testify that these men had met previously.

6. Testimony indicated that Mudd and Booth had met in Washington in March of 1865 and even more earlier, in November of 1864.

7. The commission did not give in to no pleas; Dr. Mudd was convicted of conspiracy and of harboring Booth.

8. A most remarkable decision was rendered; Dr. Mudd escaped the death penalty by one vote and was imprisoned at Fort Jefferson in south Florida.

9. At Fort Jefferson soldiers may not have thought that no illness would befall them, but an outbreak of yellow fever took the lives of many, including the resident physician.

10. Dr. Mudd used his skill as a physician to help. As a result of his outstanding medical help, he received a pardon, but his conviction was not ever overturned.

Adjectives and Adverbs pp. 48–51

Placement of Modifiers

Prepositional Phrases p. 88

Misplaced Modifiers

A word, phrase, or clause modifier that appears to modify the wrong word in a sentence is a **misplaced modifier**. In order to avoid an ambiguous or illogical sentence, move the modifier close to the word that it modifies.

Participial Phrases pp. 92–94

MISPLACED WORD	Charles *almost* studied everything on the study sheet.
CLEAR	Charles studied *almost* everything on the study sheet.
MISPLACED PHRASE	Charles threw the basketball from the middle of the court *with a mighty effort.*
CLEAR	*With a mighty effort,* Charles threw the basketball from the middle of the court.
MISPLACED CLAUSE	The basketball team was ready for the scrimmage game *that appeared on the court.*
CLEAR	The basketball team *that appeared on the court* was ready for the scrimmage game.

Adjective Clauses pp. 116–19

250 Chapter 10 | Adjective and Adverb Use

The following words are likely to cause confusion if they are not placed correctly in a sentence.

almost	just
especially	merely
even	nearly
exactly	only
hardly	simply

MISPLACED Charles and Mia *nearly* practiced their scene from the play for an hour.

Charles had *only* memorized half of his lines.

CLEAR Charles and Mia practiced their scene from the play for *nearly* an hour.

Charles had memorized *only* half of his lines.

> Sentences like "Charles had only memorized half his lines" are often heard in conversation, where oral emphasis on *half* provides clarity. In writing, however, a word like *only* should be next to the specific word it modifies. **ESL**

Two-Way Modifiers

A **two-way modifier** is one that comes between two sentence elements, either of which it could modify. As a result, the reader cannot determine which of the two it modifies. In order to clarify the sentence, move the modifier or reword the sentence so that its meaning is clear.

AMBIGUOUS Drama students who rehearse *diligently* learn their lines.

CLEAR Drama students who *diligently* rehearse learn their lines.

Drama students who rehearse learn their lines *diligently*.

Modifiers That Split Infinitives

A modifier that comes between the sign of the infinitive, *to,* and the verb form produces a **split infinitive**. Although split infinitives are not ungrammatical, they may be awkward. Correcting a split infinitive often improves the sentence.

Infinitive Phrases pp. 101–2

AWKWARD Miguel began *to* with keen interest *practice* the piano.

BETTER With keen interest, Miguel began *to practice* the piano.

It is, however, better to split an infinitive with a one-word modifier than to create an awkward sentence.

ACCEPTABLE To *really* play the piano, he must be prepared to work hard.

AWKWARD *Really* to play the piano, he must be prepared to work hard.

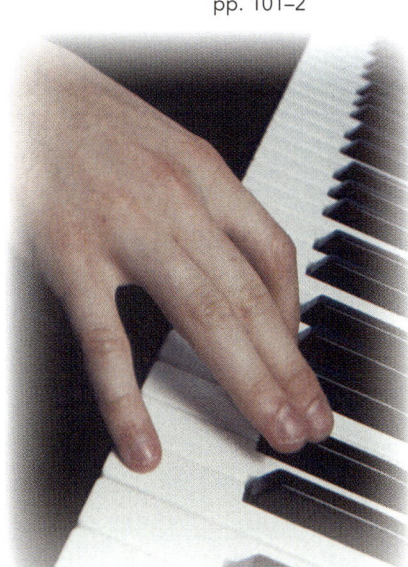

Adjective and Adverb Use | Chapter 10 **251**

Participial Phrases pp. 92–94

Elliptical Adverb Clauses p. 123

Dangling Modifiers

A **dangling modifier** is a modifier with no logical word to modify. The modifier is not grammatically connected to any word in the sentence. A dangling modifier cannot be corrected by merely moving it to a different place in the sentence; you will need to reword the sentence. Although most dangling modifiers appear at the beginning of the sentence, some appear at the end of the sentence.

DANGLING MODIFIER	Playing the concerto beautifully, the piano lid fell with a bang.
CORRECTED	While he was playing the concerto beautifully, the piano lid fell with a bang.
DANGLING MODIFIER	Music should be chosen carefully when planning a recital.
CORRECTED	He should choose the music carefully when planning a recital.
	Music should be chosen carefully when one is planning a recital.

In these examples of dangling modifiers, the implied subjects of *playing* and *planning* are not the same as the stated subjects in the independent clauses.

in SUMMARY

Place each modifier reasonably close to the word it modifies.

Avoid placing a modifier between two elements that it could modify.

In most cases, do not place a modifier between the sign of the infinitive, *to*, and the verb form.

Reword the sentence to correct a **dangling modifier**.

10.5 PRACTICE *the skill*

Write the letter of the correct or better sentence in the blank.

_____ 1. A. Providing an outstanding example of how a man's bitterness can destroy himself and others, *The Count of Monte Cristo* was written by Alexander Dumas.

B. Providing an outstanding example of how a man's bitterness can destroy himself and others, Alexander Dumas wrote *The Count of Monte Cristo*.

_____ 2. A. In the story, a character known as Edmond Dantés, a Frenchman, is betrayed by one of his closest friends and is sent to a notorious prison called Château d'If.

B. In the story, a character known as Edmond Dantés, a Frenchman, is sent to a notorious prison called Château d'If, betrayed by one of his closest friends.

_____ 3. A. He determines that he will eventually exact a bitter revenge on those who have betrayed him, dwelling on his bitterness.

B. Dwelling on his bitterness, he determines that he will eventually exact a bitter revenge on those who have betrayed him.

Chapter 10 | Adjective and Adverb Use

_____ 4. A. In prison Dantés learns the location of a great treasure.
       B. Dantés learns the location of a great treasure in prison.

_____ 5. A. Dantés escapes, locates the treasure, and elevates himself to a noble position following much hard work and planning.
       B. Following much hard work and planning, Dantés escapes, locates the treasure, and elevates himself to a noble position.

_____ 6. A. Once back in society, he assumes a new identity, "befriends" his old enemies, and proceeds to relentlessly destroy them.
       B. Once back in society, he assumes a new identity, "befriends" his old enemies, and proceeds to destroy them relentlessly.

_____ 7. A. While Edmond Dantés quietly looks on, two of his chief enemies have tragic losses.
       B. While quietly looking on, two of his chief enemies have tragic losses.

_____ 8. A. In the end, however, he almost ruins every one of his enemies, his fiancée, and himself.
       B. In the end, however, he ruins almost every one of his enemies, his fiancée, and himself.

_____ 9. A. Danté did not have to purposefully exact revenge upon his foes: his life would have been much happier had he not.
       B. Dantés did not have to exact revenge purposefully upon his foes: his life would have been much happier had he not.

_____ 10. A. Creating destruction and havoc, *The Count of Monte Cristo* portrays an especially poignant example of a bitter spirit.
        B. *The Count of Monte Cristo* portrays an especially poignant example of a bitter spirit's creating destruction and havoc.

10.6 REVIEW *the skill*

Underline each misplaced modifier once and each dangling modifier twice. Then rewrite each sentence, making the modifiers clear or correct. If the sentence is already correct, write C in the blank.

1. When reading William Shakespeare's *The Tempest*, Prospero emerges at the end of the play as a gracious and forgiving character.

2. He who rules the island powerfully changes his demeanor at the end.

3. One character who is to finally be set free is Ariel, Prospero's servant.

4. Prospero often believes that Ariel is not being a willing servant and threatens to imprison Ariel in a tree.

5. Having granted Ariel his freedom, Prospero returns home with the other travelers.

6. Prospero's forgiveness gives everyone the chance to immediately begin a new life.

7. Ariel began to with great fervency fulfill all the duties Prospero required.

8. In the epilogue the character who threatened others repeatedly asks forgiveness from the audience.

9. Prospero carefully approaches his audience to ask forgiveness.

10. Receiving the audience's approval and applause, forgiveness is complete.

10.7 CUMULATIVE *review*

Rewrite the following paragraph, correcting the ten errors from these categories: pronoun-antecedent agreement, pronoun case, comparison, double negatives, and modifier placement.

Jesus' words "Father, forgive them" are beautifully paralleled by the words spoken by Stephen in Acts 7:60. As Stephen was being stoned to death, he too cried out, "Lord, lay not this sin to their charge." How could anyone request forgiveness for those whom were in the act of taking his life? Moreover, in both cases Christ and Stephen had been unjustly accused, condemned, and subjected to sham trials. Then while suffering horrific deaths, their enemies looked on and jeered. Still, Jesus Christ's words and Stephen's dying words demonstrated his concern for the more eternal souls of men. They did not have nothing revengeful to say to their enemies. By comparison, how often are we quick to take offense, to simmer with anger, and to even harbor bitterness toward those who have hurt us? We would do more better to daily remember the dying examples of Christ and his faithful follower Stephen. Forgiving our enemies faithfully fulfills God's command to His children.

FROM THE WRITTEN WORD

Analyzing the Cause

Perhaps you have discussed with a friend why a particular college basketball team did not make the NCAA Final Four, or perhaps you have debated whether the three-point shot line for basketball should be moved. Or maybe you have discussed why the girls' soccer team lost in overtime last week. As you talk about these ideas, you are commenting on the causes for these particular results. Analyzing a subject to identify its causes or effects is another rhetorical strategy.

The Scriptures abound with this rhetorical strategy. Why did God send the Flood? The cause is evident: man was wicked.

> And God saw that the wickedness of man was great in the earth, and that every imagination of the thoughts of his heart was only evil continually. And the Lord said, I will destroy man whom I have created from the face of the earth; . . . for it repenteth me that I have made them. (Gen. 6:5, 7)

You might think about what caused Job's testing or Israel's captivity or Ruth's allegiance to her mother-in-law.

Consider Numbers 20:2–12. Moses, the leader of Israel, heard perhaps the most disappointing declaration of his lifetime. Although Moses had led Israel through many hardships and trials, Moses was not to bring the Israelites into the land of promise. The evident cause was Moses' disobedience. But what other causes do you read about in this passage? The people had complained to Moses and Aaron because there was no water. They had even questioned why Moses had brought them to such a place. Perhaps their harsh complaints caused Moses to doubt God's leading. Standing before this multitude, Moses may have lost his temper, or he might have thought that speaking would not be enough to cause water to come from the rock. Moses' failure to recognize God's power and presence must also have contributed to his disobedience.

Personal Response

Read Judges 8:1–4. As Gideon and his three hundred were returning from battle with the Midianites, the men of Ephraim complained to Gideon. Gideon may have had cause to answer the men of Ephraim with harsh words. Do you think that he did have a cause to? What was the effect of his answer and his manner in answering them?

Now read Proverbs 15:1–2. From your personal experience, write a paragraph that illustrates cause and effect in either a positive or a negative way.

Research Report | 262
Capitalization | 270
Think About It | 289

RESEARCH REPORT Writing
CAPITALIZATION Usage
11

Learning about something that interests you can be both enjoyable and educational. After reading about an unfamiliar topic in an article or coming across a new idea in a novel, have you ever taken the next step and looked up information on that topic or idea? If you have, you took a step into the research process. You probably found your "research" to be enjoyable and rewarding. Researching various sources, gathering information, and formulating this information into an outline and report can be an exciting and rewarding experience.

In "Piltdown Chicken," scientist Stephen Caesar refutes the supposed evidence of a "link" between dinosaurs and birds. After a brief introduction regarding the finding, he moves to his main idea: "The fossil was a fraud." Notice that Caesar focuses on his main idea and incorporates a number of varied sources into his writing.

Piltdown Chicken *by Stephen Caesar*

In November 1999, *National Geographic* published photographs of what it claimed was incontrovertible proof that birds evolved from dinosaurs. In an article titled "Feathers for T. Rex?" the magazine announced, "New Birdlike Fossils Are Missing Links in Dinosaur Evolution" (Sloan 99). The article featured a photograph, taken under ultraviolet light, of a creature "[w]ith arms of a primitive bird and the tail of a dinosaur" (Ibid. 100). The fossil, named *Archaeoraptor*, was discovered in Liaoning Province, China, and was trumpeted as "a true missing link in the complex chain that connects dinosaurs to birds" (Ibid.). The photo was accompanied by a quotation in large letters by Stephen Czerkas, who led the study of the fossil: "IT'S A MISSING LINK between terrestrial dinosaurs and birds that could actually fly" (Ibid. [emphasis original]). Czerkas also commented, "This fossil is perhaps the best evidence since *Archaeopteryx* that birds did, in fact, evolve from certain types of carnivorous dinosaurs" (Ibid. 101).

Eventually, the word got out—like so many other "proofs" of Darwinism, the fossil was a fraud. In the "Letters to the Editor" section of the March 2000 issue of *National Geographic*, Xu Xing of the Institute of Vertebrate Paleontology and Paleoanthropology (Chinese Academy of Sciences) wrote: "I have concluded that *Archaeoraptor* is a composite. . . . Though I do not want to believe it,

Archaeoraptor appears to be composed of a dromaeosaur [a small, carnivorous dinosaur] tail and a bird body." *National Geographic*'s embarrassment was immense. In its October 2000 issue, it published an article by investigative reporter Lewis Simons, who uncovered the truth behind the hoax. His lengthy investigation, which took him all the way to China, revealed

> a tale of misguided secrecy and misplaced confidence, of rampant egos clashing, self-aggrandizement, wishful thinking, naive assumptions, human error, stubbornness, manipulation, backbiting, lying, corruption, and, most of all, abysmal communication (Simons 128).

Simons learned that a Chinese farmer, eager to sell a fossil to foreigners who would pay top dollar, had dug two fossils out of his land and glued the parts together with homemade paste. He attached the tail from one fossil to the body of the other and then proceeded to add on the legs and feet (Ibid. 128–129). "The result," reported Simons, "was the 'missing link'—the body of a primitive bird with teeth and the tail of a landbound little dinosaur, or dromaeosaur" (Ibid. 129).

The doctored item was bought by a Chinese fossil dealer who "acknowledged that he often sold 'composites'" (Ibid.). The bogus fossil eventually found its way to Stephen Czerkas (quoted above), who, along with his wife, is a dinosaur enthusiast with no scientific qualifications. Upon obtaining the fossil, the Czerkases contacted leading paleontologist Philip J. Currie of the Royal Tyrrell Museum of Paleontology in Alberta. The Canadian scientist didn't spend a lot of time investigating the find; Simons wrote that "Currie was so distracted by other commitments around the world that he gave the *Archaeoraptor* project short shrift" (Ibid. 130).

As it turned out, Currie did have reservations about the fossil but neglected to inform the National Geographic Society's Christopher Sloan, the driving force behind the November 1999 article. Simons referred to this as a "most damaging lapse of responsibility" on Currie's part (Ibid.). Later, Currie and the Czerkases had the fossil examined at the University of Texas High-Resolution X-ray CT Facility in Austin. Professor Timothy Rose, who ran the examination, noticed something wrong and said "there was a chance that it was a fraud" (Ibid.). In response, Currie sent Kevin Aulenback, a fossil technician at the Tyrrell Museum, to investigate the fossil. Aulenback concluded that the fossil "is a composite specimen" (Ibid. 131).

Stephen Czerkas, meanwhile, along with Currie and other scientists, tried to submit a scholarly paper on the "missing link" to the prestigious scientific journals *Nature* and *Science*; both rejected the article due to lack of evidence (Ibid. 131–132). Simons, describing the original draft of the *Nature* submission, wrote:

> On its fifth page the paper stated that the dromaeosaur-like tail on a birdlike creature suggested a previously unknown element in the evolution of birds from landbound dinosaurs. In short, this was what Czerkas would tell National Geographic was "a missing link" (Ibid. 131).

Despite the rejections, the November 1999 issue of *National Geographic* went ahead and published the highly doubtful fossil. Simons referred to the media frenzy that surrounded this alleged proof of evolution as "[a] dog-and-pony show for reporters" (Ibid. 132).

The following month, Xu Xing (who first went public with the fraud) e-mailed Christopher Sloan (the author of the *National Geographic* article) stating, "I am 100% sure . . . we have to admit that *Archaeoraptor* is a faked specimen" (Ibid. 132). Simons describes the less-than-honest way that Xu, who had collaborated in the blunder, tried to cover his tracks: "*National Geographic* published a cleaned-up version of Xu's letter in its March issue [quoted above], at his request changing 'faked' to 'composite'" (Ibid.).

Once the jig was up, those responsible began confessing their foolishness. Czerkas admitted that he and his wife had made "an idiot, bone-stupid mistake." Currie said it was "the greatest mistake of my life." Sloan said, "I was dragging in a monster" (Ibid.). William L. Allen, Editor-in-Chief of *National Geographic*, asked, "How did we get in this mess?" (Ibid. 128). Simons hints at the reason why so many experts fell for the hoax: "To some prominent paleontologists who saw it . . . the little skeleton was a long-sought key to a mystery of evolution" (Ibid.). In other words, they *wanted* to see evidence for dino-to-bird evolution, so that is precisely what they saw. Interestingly, the original article from November 1999 practically admitted as much (without, of course, even realizing it). The article stated that the anatomical features of the *Archaeoraptor* are "exactly what scientists would expect to find in dinosaurs experimenting with flight" (Sloan 101). This is an absolutely golden example of the way in which evolutionists "see" evidence for evolution when there is none—all based on pre-determined assumptions rather than scientific facts.

Criticism of the hoax has been harsh. In its October 2000 issue, *Discover* magazine featured an article titled "Twenty of the Greatest Blunders in Science in the Last Twenty Years." One of the Top 20 was "Piltdown Chicken," a sarcastic term for *National Geographic*'s evolutionary fraud. The term derives from Piltdown Man, the greatest hoax in the history of the theory of human evolution, in which a human skull had been artificially melded with an ape jaw and "discovered" in England in 1912 (Newman 80). For half a century it was used as "proof" of human evolution. The epithet "Piltdown Chicken" was actually coined several months earlier by *U. S. News & World Report*. In February 2000 it reported:

> Imaginations certainly took flight over Archaeoraptor liaoningensis, a bird-like fossil with a meat-eater's tail that was spirited out of northeastern China, "discovered" at a Tucson, Ariz., gem-and-mineral show last year, and displayed at the National Geographic Society in Washington, D.C. Some 110,000 visitors saw the exhibit, which closed January 17; millions more read about the find in November's National Geographic. Now, paleontologists are eating crow (Lord 53).

Storris Olson, curator of birds at the Smithsonian Institution's National Museum of Natural History, had warned the editors at the National Geographic Society about the possible fraudulence of the fossil back in November 1999, when the article was first published. "The public is being completely bamboozled," he said when the scandal broke (Ibid.). Just as earlier paleontologists had embraced Piltdown Man because they were dying for evidence of human evolution, more recent scientists embarrassed themselves by gullibly embracing *Archaeoraptor*—a gullibility stemming from their own overwhelming desire to prove a theory that is incorrect from the start. Yes, Dr. Olson, the public is indeed being bamboozled.

References

Lord, Mary. "The Piltdown Chicken." *U.S. News & World Report*, 14 February 2000.

Newman, Judith. (2000). "Twenty of the Greatest Blunders in Science in the Last Twenty Years." *Discover* 21, no. 10.

Simons, Lewis M. (2000). "Archaeoraptor Fossil Trail." *National Geographic* 198, no. 4.

Sloan, Christopher P. (1999). "Feathers for T. Rex?" *National Geographic* 196, no. 5.

WRITING RESEARCH REPORT

> But let your communication be, Yea, yea; Nay, nay.
> *Matthew 5:37*

The idea for a research report often begins with a question or two. For example, who was Ernest Shackleton and what did he do? What nations supply the United States with oil? Are the locations of these nations important? What were the Dayton Peace Accords? Who was T. Edward McCully? Questions such as these will lead you to an encyclopedia, library sources, periodicals, or Internet sites. You might also have the opportunity to interview someone who has had a first-person experience relating to your topic. Keep in mind that research of any kind answers questions such as *who? what? where? when?* and *why?*

Your teacher may provide you some general topics that can be springboards to more specific ideas. Take time to think about related ideas and issues as you consider your research report.

Choose a topic and write a two-page printed research report. Since your report will be no more than two pages, you must limit your topic to one that you can treat successfully in a short report. Your report should have a thesis statement that is verifiable and declarative. In addition, you will write a paragraph of introduction, three paragraphs of support, and a paragraph of conclusion. Within your research report, you will want to include factual evidence you have gathered that will support the claim that you make about your topic. Included with your report will be a list of the works cited.

Planning

✔ **Choose a topic.** Now is the time to consult your list of ideas in your journal or notebook or on your computer. If none of these spark your interest, consider reading articles about current events, looking for thought-provoking ideas. If you are still at a loss for ideas, take time to ask yourself a few questions. What am I interested in? Is there a topic that I would like to learn more about? As you consider a topic, determine your audience and keep in mind your desire to communicate evidence that you have discovered.

After reading an article about polar exploration that mentions Ernest Shackleton, you might ask these questions.

- Who was Ernest Shackleton?
- From what country did he come?
- When did he live?
- Where did he explore?
- Why was he important in the history of exploration?
- What was the name of his ship?
- Was he successful in his exploration?
- Did he have some unique experiences?

You will probably find that your research is more interesting if you pursue an idea with which you are not familiar. As you consider a topic, remember that you must develop a thesis statement that is verifiable. Your teacher may also ask that you develop a thesis that is controversial.

✔ **Find sources for your report.** Your first consideration for a source is an encyclopedia, either an online copy or a hard copy. This general information will inform you about your topic and will help you focus on more specific ideas. Since the encyclopedia information is only a broad overview, you will not include it in your report. However, the encyclopedia may suggest additional readings that will help you. Once you have some general knowledge about your topic, search the library catalog for more detailed sources. In addition to books and periodicals, be sure to research newspaper, radio, and television transcripts and interviews with authorities on the topic. Your sources of information will be either primary or secondary. Firsthand information such as historical documents, letters, speeches, and journals of the time are considered **primary sources.** Other sources of information from scholars who have studied a subject are **secondary sources.** Secondary sources include most encyclopedia articles and books. You may, on occasion, find a primary source within a secondary source. Information from a primary source is preferred to information from a secondary source.

Library Skills
pp. 399–401

tip

For research writing on the collegiate level, your college instructor may require you to search out several different types of sources. Try branching out some now.

It is important for you to evaluate the trustworthiness of the sources that you consider for your research. In "Piltdown Chicken," notice the quotation from Lewis Simons, a primary source who investigated the hoax. He did not make unfounded accusations; rather he traveled to China and researched firsthand. As you continue in the article, notice the reference to Stephen Czerkas, also a primary source. The reference to Czerkas is far from complimentary and states that he "is a dinosaur enthusiast with no scientific qualifications." Although he is a primary source, his conclusion is faulty and invalid.

✔ **Narrow your topic.** Once you have general knowledge of your subject, you are ready to focus on a specific aspect of that subject. After reading a biographical sketch of Ernest Shackleton, you might focus on his ship the HMS *Endurance,* on the view of a fellow sailor taken from his diary, on an idea taken from an interview with Shackleton's granddaughter, or on Shackleton's strong character in the face of adversity. Consider these suggestions for narrowing your topic.

- Ask yourself questions about what you have read.
- Talk with a friend about your topic. As a result of your conversation, you should be able to determine what really interests you.
- Focus your reading on a specific idea that you would like to know more about.

✔ **Determine whether your topic is narrow enough.** Since this is a two-page report, you must decide whether you can manage your topic within this page limit. If you find that you cannot, keep narrowing.

✔ **Determine the audience to whom you will be writing your research report.** It is important to identify your audience so that you can shape your report to reach that audience.

Thinking Biblically

Since no one can know everything, a research report you write will include ideas from other people and sources. Consequently, trusting the right sources—and not the wrong ones—is extremely important. In some cases, books are more reliable than the Internet. Since online publishing is easy and inexpensive (sometimes free), many people publish their ideas on the Internet. Some of these people may not be credible or may publish content that has not been properly researched or substantiated. For instance, college students have been known to use papers written by seventh graders because the papers turned up in a search engine list. Because books cost more to produce and have a longer shelf life than Internet content, publishers have at least some incentive to insure that they are accurate and therefore salable. But printing something in ink still does not make it true. And the Internet, because it changes rapidly, can have the benefit of being more up-to-date. Knowing which authority to trust takes education, but it also takes wisdom. The worldview a Christian gets from knowing and loving the Bible helps him know whom to trust. Ultimately, the only trustworthy authority on questions of importance is God Himself. The Bible, then, is our ultimate source.

✔ **Take notes from your research.** As you compile information for your report, keep in mind your purpose for writing and write down only information that you will use for your report. Record your research information accurately on your computer or on paper. You will have two kinds of notes: source notes and content notes.

- Source notes include the title (book, article, periodical, electronic database), author/editor, and publication information (publisher, city of publication, date of publication or date on which you accessed a website). You will use these source notes to compile a works-cited list to accompany your paper.
- Content notes record the exact words from the source or summarize in brief phrases the information from the source. Be sure to include page numbers from the source.

Consider this example of paraphrasing.

Original
In 1914 Ernest Shackleton, commander of the HMS *Endurance,* attempted the first transcontinental crossing of Antarctica. After the expedition ship became frozen in ice and sank, Shackleton focused on earning the complete trust of his men, maintaining the morale of his men, and negotiating the safe return of all twenty-seven men.

Brief Notes
- an accomplished seaman
- commander of HMS *Endurance*
- began first transcontinental crossing of Antarctica
- lost ship
- determined to lead and save his men

Paraphrase
Ernest Shackleton saved his crew of twenty-seven men after the HMS *Endurance* sank. Although his mission to cross Antarctica failed, his men remained in high spirits and learned to trust him.

tip
Correct paraphrasing reworks the wording, syntax, and order of the ideas. Writing down just the facts in your own words helps you to paraphrase thoroughly.

✔ **Quote your sources accurately.** Many of your content notes will be a summary or paraphrase of the material that you have read. You may, on occasion, wish to use a brief quotation to emphasize the authority of your source. A quotation is a precise word-for-word copying of the original. When you write a quotation, you must copy the exact words and punctuation of the source. If there is an error of punctuation or a misspelled word in the source, you must copy the mistake and indicate the mistake by inserting [sic] after the error.

Original
Almost overpowered by the natural elements, Shackleton remained stationery as he determined a course to save his men.

Quotation
"Almost overpowered by the natural elements, Shackleton remained stationery [sic] as he determined a course to save his men."

264 Chapter 11 | Research Report

✔ **Formulate your thesis.** The thesis statement is the guiding or controlling statement for your research report. Remember that the thesis of your report is a statement (not a question), is verifiable, and may be controversial.

Brackets
pp. 335–36

QUESTION	Who knows about the history of the Iditarod?
STATEMENT	A near tragedy and seemingly insurmountable odds marked the original Iditarod.
UNVERIFIABLE	Many people enjoy hearing about the Iditarod.
VERIFIABLE	Staging the Iditarod requires millions of dollars and hundreds of volunteers each year.
NONCONTROVERSIAL	The Iditarod is a grueling race.
CONTROVERSIAL	Iditarod dogs face inhumane physical conditions.
ANNOUNCEMENT	I want to give you some information about the Iditarod.
STATEMENT	The Iditarod, a complex and multifaceted race, requires careful planning and training.

tip
Avoid hasty generalizations ("All newscasters are liberals"). Instead, be willing to qualify your statement with *most* or *some*.

✔ **Outline your paper.** You are ready to develop an outline that will help you organize your ideas. Your outline is the skeleton for your report; your paragraphs will be the substance of your report. Look at the information you have gathered. Group your related ideas and identify the main idea in each group. The main idea of each group may be the topic sentence for one of the middle paragraphs of your report. Remember that your outline is your guide and that your sentences may change as you write your report.

tip
Topic sentences support the thesis statement. A good topic sentence can often be expressed logically as a dependent clause if attached to the thesis statement with the subordinating conjunction *because*.

Drafting

✔ **Write the rough draft.** Set aside a block of time to write, perhaps an hour, and write your report in one sitting. With your outline and content notes in front of you, strive for clear thinking as you write. Keep in mind that this is a rough draft and will probably not be free of error. Be prepared to use a variety of methods of organization for the middle paragraphs. You may wish to use one or several examples to support a statement about the thesis. You may wish to include statistics or research results. Your goal should be a clear, logical arrangement of complete sentences. Here is how a rough draft copy of a paragraph might look.

> Shackleton's interest in each member of his crew developed a sense of strong loyalty. In dealing with his crew, Shackleton treated everyone eqully. He did not have any favorites. When the men had to desert the *Endurance*, Shackleton announced that they were allowed to take only two pounds of personal things such as books, money, and mementos. Shackleton set the example by throwing away "a handful of gold coins and his gold watch" (Interview with Granddaughter) and his Bible from Queen Alexandra. (Interview with Granddaughter) The Bible was retrieved by a sialor. Another example of his equal treatment of his men was that he would take each sailor's duty at some time during the voyage. One night Sir Ernest rescued a man who had fallen between two ice _____. (*Diary of a Survivor*) Ernest Shackleton was interested in every man.

> **tip**
> Avoid propaganda devices in your writing.

✓ **Insert quotations.** When you are writing your research report, carefully consider the use of quotations. Remember that quotations should come from reliable sources and should not be overused. If you choose to insert a quotation into your text, be sure to introduce the quotation in such a way that it becomes an integral part of your report. Quoting just a phrase is a helpful technique that enables you to work the quotation into your own sentence. Concerning the description of the creature in "Piltdown Chicken," Caesar writes, "The article featured a photograph, taken under ultraviolet light, of a creature '[w]ith arms of a primitive bird and the tail of a dinosaur.'" Notice how smoothly he incorporates this quotation and others throughout his article.

✓ **Do not plagiarize.** You have a responsibility to handle your sources carefully and correctly. Accurate documentation of words and ideas, whether quoted or paraphrased, insures the credibility of your writing. Whether your inaccurate documentation is intentional or unintentional, you are responsible. Remember—if you plagiarize, you are stealing someone else's work.

> **tip**
> If a fact is common knowledge—something mentioned by nearly everyone who writes on the subject—you need not cite your source.

Revising

✓ **Reread your report.** If at all possible, allow yourself a day or two after writing your research report before you reread your work. As you reread, ask yourself the following questions.

- Is the thesis a focused, declarative idea? Do the topic sentences support the thesis statement?
- Is the material well organized and presented clearly? Do the supporting ideas in the paragraphs flow smoothly from one thought to another?
- Are there any grammatical or mechanical mistakes? Are there any misspelled words?
- Have I quoted sources accurately or paraphrased correctly?

✓ **Mark any point of revision.** Do not take time to correct the mistakes or make changes to the draft at this time. You are reading for continuity and clarity.

✓ **Make changes to the draft.** After you have read your report and marked the corrections and points of consideration, you are ready to make changes. You may wish to incorporate the techniques of reduction and expansion to improve your sentence structure. Try a variety of reduction and expansion techniques in your writing.

Sentence Expansion and Reduction pp. 371–78

> **tip**
> Joining sentences on an equal basis indicates that the ideas are equal; joining sentences on an unequal basis indicates that some ideas are more important than others.

Now you are ready to determine the most effective arrangement of your middle paragraphs. One helpful strategy is to sandwich the weakest of the arguments between two stronger arguments. Your topic, however, may necessitate a logical or a chronological arrangement. An additional and important strategy is to place the strongest of the arguments just before the conclusion of your paper. By doing so, you leave the reader thinking about the best of your ideas.

> **tip**
> On the collegiate level your instructor may refer to the *Nestorian* structure of an argument paper (placing the weakest of the arguments between the two stronger ones).

In "Piltdown Chicken" Caesar follows a chronological arrangement as he presents the refutations for the "fossil." He relays Simons' experience of learning of the Chinese farmer who "glued" it together and the dealer who sold the "composite." Then Caesar moves to Czerkas's published article in *National Geographic*.

✓ **Read your report again.** Now is your opportunity to look very carefully at your writing. Have you used logical transitions between sentences and paragraphs? In addition, do you recognize an overuse of a particular word in your writing? Have you chosen your words carefully?

Here is how a revision of the paragraph on Shackleton might look.

Shackleton's interest in each personal member of his crew created a bond of unwavering strong loyalty. In dealing with his crew, Shackleton had no favorites and treated everyone equally. He did not have any favorites. When Shackleton realized the men had to desert the *Endurance* was doomed, he planned for survival. Shackleton announced that they were each man was allowed to take only two pounds of personal things such as books, money, and mementos. Shackleton set the example by throwing away "a handful of gold coins and his gold watch" a Bible from Queen Alexandra and (A. Shackleton, p 4). (Interview with granddaughter) and his Bible from Queen Alexandra. (Interview with Granddaughter) The Bible was retrieved by a sailor. Another sailor, but the other possessions were lost. example of his Shackleton's equal treatment of his men was that he would take each perform any job. sailor's duty at some time during the voyage. One During an encampment on ice night, Sir Ernest rescued a man who had fallen between two ice parts of a floe (Orde-Lees). (Diary of a Survivor) Not only did Shackleton save the man, but he saved the Ernest Shackleton was interested in every man man's sleeping bag as well.

Research Report | Chapter 11 **267**

✔ **Enter your source notes in correct form.** At this point, you are ready to check the accuracy of your parenthetical citations. Parenthetical citations give the source information inside parentheses within the text. These parenthetical notes should be placed at the end of the sentence or at a natural pause within the sentence. The citation should come before any punctuation needed for the sentence.

> The truth of God is eternal and unchanging; truth does not develop, and we do not invent it (Sidwell 71).

The citation above identifies Sidwell as the author of the work from which the statement about the truth of God came; it also specifies that the statement appears on page 71 of that source. The reader can find complete bibliographic information for that source on the works-cited list at the end of the paper.

The entry in the works-cited listing would appear as follows.

> Sidwell, Mark. *The Dividing Line: Understanding and Applying Biblical Separation.* Greenville: Bob Jones UP, 1998. Print.

Parenthetical citations should identify specific sources clearly. When you use two or more works by the same author, add the title, shortened or complete, after the author's name and a comma between author and work.

> Our model for Christianity is to be found in the Bible, not in the history of any nation (Sidwell, *The Dividing Line* 72).

If you include the author's name or the work within the text of your report, you may omit this information from the parenthetical note.

> In his book *The Dividing Line,* Sidwell discusses the influence of Harold Ockenga in the new evangelical movement (114–18).

✔ **Compile a works-cited list.** This page is an alphabetical list of the works that you have cited at least once in your report. Use hanging indentation format: the first line begins at the left margin and the following lines are indented one-half inch or five spaces. Use the author's complete name as it appears on the title page, putting the last name first. If there is more than one author, list the first author putting last name first and succeeding authors putting first name and then last name. If the author is unknown, alphabetize by title and ignore beginning articles.

If you are citing more than one work by the same author, alphabetize by the title of the work and use three hyphens to replace the author's name in all entries after the first.

> Sidwell, Mark. *The Dividing Line: Understanding and Applying Biblical Separation.* Greenville: Bob Jones UP, 1998. Print.
>
> ---. *Free Indeed: Heroes of Black Christian History.* Greenville: Bob Jones UP, 2001. Print.

✔ **Proofread your paper.** After you have incorporated all of your additions and corrections, make a new copy for the final proofreading. As you proofread, be aware of sentence structure errors (fragments, fused sentences, comma splices), usage problems (subject/verb agreement, pronoun/antecedent agreement, pronoun case), and punctuation, capitalization, and spelling errors. A good spell-check program cannot read for context and does not fully replace your ability to catch errors. Your writing should be as clear and appealing to your audience as possible, and the presentation of your report should be without offense.

Publishing

✔ **Choose a title for your work.** Follow your teacher's instruction for placement of your title on the page or for preparing a separate title page. The title should suggest the topic of the report.

Too General	Polar Exploration
Good Possibilities	A Story of Polar Survival
	One Man's Determination

✔ **Print a neat copy.** You are ready to submit your final copy to your teacher. This copy should be neat and error free. Be sure to include all necessary ancillary pages, such as the title page, outline, and works-cited page.

✔ **Illustrate your report with appropriate photographs.** Remember that many professional photographs are copyrighted; you must be sure not to violate copyright laws. You might take your own photographs with a standard or digital camera.

✔ **Present your report orally for a class.** If you have written on a current-event topic, you may have opportunity to present your report in a history or government class.

✔ **Submit your report to the school paper or the local library.** You may wish to continue your research and develop your report further for submission to the school paper or the local library.

Some Ideas to Consider

Family and Consumer Science
- Research the effectiveness of vitamin supplements.
- Research a certain diet plan.

History
- Write about the leadership value of a specific general from the Civil War or World War II.

Social Studies
- Write about the impact of a mother's working outside the home.
- Research the impact of imports on the garment industry or the auto industry.

Physical Education
- Research the importance of aerobic exercise for senior citizens.

CAPITALIZATION

Common and Proper Nouns pp. 35–36

Languages of the world differ in the use of capitalization. Hebrew does not capitalize to indicate the beginning of a sentence; German capitalizes all nouns; Arabic words are written in reverse order without capitalization. English, of course, capitalizes for various purposes. English capitalization helps readers to identify the beginning of a sentence and to identify proper nouns and titles. Because there has been a recent movement to capitalize fewer words than have been traditionally capitalized, a writer should consult a recent dictionary if he is unsure about the capitalization of a word.

Proper Adjectives p. 50

Personal Names, Religions, Nationalities, & Proper Adjectives

Personal names and initials	Jordan W. Johnson R. W. B. Lewis
Titles used with a name	Prime Minister Cameron General MacArthur Dr. Lydia E. Blackstone Lydia E. Blackstone, DDS
Do not capitalize titles used in place of a person's name.	The general gave an inspiring charge to his soldiers.
Family words used as proper nouns	Aunt Karen Grandma Allen
If the word is modified by an adjective, do not capitalize it.	We are planning a surprise party for Grandpa. Her great-grandmother lives in a small town in New Jersey.
Terms used as descriptive substitutes for proper nouns	Father of our Country (George Washington) the Butcher of Baghdad (Saddam Hussein)
Personifications	Die not, poor Death; nor yet canst thou kill me. (John Donne, "Death, Be Not Proud")
Names of religions	Taoism Baha'i
Nouns and personal pronouns referring to the one true God	After Christ saw their sadness, He called for Lazarus to come forth.
Do not capitalize common nouns or pronouns that refer to pagan gods.	The worship of Diana, goddess of the Ephesians, caused conflict during Paul's missionary journey.
The words *Holy Bible* or *Bible* and parts of the Bible as well as the sacred writings of other religions	New Testament Philippians Koran
Nationalities and languages	Turkish, British, Canadian English, Hmong

CONTINUED

Ethnic groups	Caucasian, Asian Kurds, Croats
Proper adjectives	Italian marble, Swiss watch
Do not capitalize a word modified by a proper adjective unless the two together form a proper name.	British literature includes works written in the British Isles as well as works written elsewhere by British citizens.
Some words that were once considered proper adjectives are no longer capitalized when they form part of a compound noun. Check a dictionary if you are unsure of the capitalization of these words.	The Jankowskis have recently installed venetian blinds on every window in their house. Has your family ever owned a car with a diesel engine?

A proper adjective referring to a certain nationality and language can also be used as a noun (in singular form, always modified by *the*) to refer to persons from that country or area. Words of this type usually end in *ish* or *ese*, such as *Danish, Irish, Spanish, Japanese, Portuguese,* and *Vietnamese. French* can also be used this way.

The Faroese speak a language that developed from Old Norse, whereas *the Finnish* speak a Finno-Ugric language.

Many other proper adjectives referring to nationalities can be used as nouns in singular or plural form, according to the meaning of one or more than one person from that country or area. These are mostly words ending in *an*, such as *African(s), Armenian(s), Belgian(s), Laotian(s), Mexican(s),* and *Russian(s).*

Asians among the foreign-exchange students included *a Cambodian,* two *Koreans,* and *a Thai.*

11.1 PRACTICE *the skill*

Underline each word with a capitalization error.

1. One of the greatest scientific hoaxes of all time was perpetrated in the British isles: Piltdown Man.

2. In 1912, charles dawson, an amateur geologist, discovered bones supposedly belonging to a prehistoric british man, as well as other ancient fossils.

3. Dawson recruited several experts to help in the search for and authentication of the bones, including arthur smith woodward and sir arthur keith.

4. The bones were accepted as genuine by many british scientists.

5. The americans and the french, however, tended to be more skeptical.

6. Many were eager to claim Piltdown Man as the ancestor of their Grandfathers.

7. According to some people, Piltdown Man dealt a blow to christianity and the bible. However, as early as 1914 some expressed doubt about Piltdown Man.

8. Captain st. barre and major marriott claimed to have seen dawson in 1913 staining bones to cause them to appear older.

9. The claims of the captain and the Major were not made public for many years, but Dr. j. s. Weiner investigated the structure and makeup of the Piltdown Man.

10. In 1953, forty-one years after dawson announced his find, new scientific tests confirmed that Piltdown Man was a fake: a blend of a medieval human skull and an orangutan jaw.

11.2 REVIEW *the skill*

Rewrite each sentence so that it contains no capitalization errors. If the sentence is already correct, write C in the blank.

1. After forty-one years of deception, the truth finally triumphed in the matter of the Piltdown Man.

2. Scientists also concluded that an elephant tooth found at the same site was likely from Tunisia, and a hippopotamus tooth may have been maltese or sicilian.

3. Who created the hoax about the grandfather of the human race?

4. Since the revelation of 1953, accusations of fraud have come from germans, americans, british, french, spanish, and others.

5. Amateurs and professionals promoted many theories, accusing everyone from dawson, woodward, and keith to sir arthur conan doyle, Author of the sherlock holmes stories.

6. Another helper of dawson was a frenchman who had recently been in the african and mediterranean regions.

7. A few people suspect sir arthur conan doyle—the author and amateur paleontologist—of planting the fabricated fossils, but the evidence is not strong.

8. One reason so many scientists accepted the discoveries without testing them may have been national pride: Piltdown Man was the first such "discovery" on british soil.

9. Also, Piltdown Man matched scientists' preconceptions of ancient humans.

10. Ultimately, some of the blame falls on human refusal to accept God and his word.

Sir Arthur Conan Doyle

Place Names, Transportation, & Astronomy Terms

Countries	Uzbekistan
Continents	Asia
Cities	Evansville
States	Indiana
Sections of a country or the world	Outer Banks, Grand Strand, Amazonia The South is sometimes called the Bible Belt.
Do not capitalize direction words when they refer to compass directions.	We live in the northwest corner of the state. Bill drove south on Interstate 85.
Geographic features and recreational areas	Niagara Falls Grand Canyon National Park
Streets and roads	Pinnacle Drive Sunshine Parkway
Bodies of water	Bay of Fundy, Lake Louise, Caribbean Sea, Pacific Ocean
Do not capitalize a geographical noun unless it is part of a proper noun.	Across the bay several large houses stood tall.
Aircraft	*Spirit of St. Louis*
Spacecraft	*Voyager, Curiosity*
Ships	*H. L. Hunley*
Trains	*Crescent Limited*
Planets, stars, other heavenly bodies	Jupiter, Saturn, Betelgeuse, Orion
Capitalize the word earth *when used as a proper name for our planet, especially when listed with the names of other heavenly bodies that must be capitalized.*	Mercury, Venus, or Mars can be the closest planet to Earth, depending on their locations in their respective orbits.
Do not capitalize earth *when it is preceded by* the.	Water covers approximately seventy percent of the earth.
Capitalize sun *and* moon *only when listed with heavenly bodies that must be capitalized.*	The sun and moon help regulate the ecosystem of the earth. The planet closest to the Sun is Mercury.

Lake Louise

274 Chapter 11 | Capitalization

PRACTICE *the skill*

Underline each word with a capitalization error.

1. Not everyone knows that Edgar Allan Poe, the master of the short story, also enjoyed creating literary hoaxes, including one about a type of early Aircraft.

2. Known as Poe's Great Balloon Hoax, the story was published in the *New York Sun* and told of a balloon flight across the atlantic ocean from europe to north america.

3. The tale claims that balloonists set out from london, england, for paris, France, but were caught in a gale and blown South to charleston, south carolina.

4. The balloon, built in an elliptical shape, bore the name *victoria*.

5. While crossing the ocean, the balloonists passed over many ships, including one called the *atalanta*.

6. Poe claimed the balloon landed at Fort Moultrie in Charleston harbor. Interestingly, Poe himself was once stationed at Fort Moultrie.

7. Another of Poe's newspaper hoaxes told of the first European to cross the rocky mountains, one Julius Rodman, in 1792.

8. According to the story, Rodman and his men crossed the missouri river and then headed North.

9. A third canard concerned the life of Hans Pfaall, a human who flees to the moon in a Balloon in order to escape his creditors.

10. Pfaall keeps a diary in which he records his observations of the earth; the diary is later brought to rotterdam by a native of the moon.

11.4 REVIEW *the skill*

Rewrite each sentence so that it contains no capitalization errors. If the sentence is already correct, write C in the blank.

1. One notable hoax said to have occurred on manhattan island in 1824 may itself have been a hoax.

2. A common meeting place in new york was Centre Market at the intersection of baxter, centre, and grand streets.

3. At Centre Market, a retired ship's carpenter named Lozier supposedly convinced the people of the island that manhattan was in danger of tipping over into the atlantic ocean.

4. According to the story, Lozier claimed that the weight of buildings in the battery area of the city had unbalanced the Island.

5. His daring plan for saving the island involved sawing it in half at kingsbridge.

Chapter 11 | Capitalization

6. Lozier said he had arranged for fifteen hundred boats to tow the half-island into New York Harbor.

7. Once out in the Bay, the half-island would be turned around and reattached.

8. As part of this great feat, long island would have to be towed out of the way to make room for the turning of manhattan.

9. More than three hundred men signed up to help. Lozier told half of the men to meet at the corner of broadway and bowery; the other half, on spring street. But Lozier never showed up.

10. Retold as fact for decades, there is no proof that the practical joke about saving Manhattan ever really happened.

Businesses & Organizations, Cultural & Historical Terms

Businesses and their abbreviations	**M**adawaska **H**ardscapes **G**eneral **E**lectric (**GE**)
Do not capitalize the common noun for a business.	Before we finished our yard work, we visited several landscape supply companies.
Brand names of commercial products	**H**ershey's **K**isses **F**ord **T**hunderbird
Do not capitalize the product name unless it is part of the brand name.	**T**imex watch

CONTINUED

Capitalization | Chapter 11 **277**

Businesses & Organizations, Cultural & Historical Terms

Government departments	Department of the Interior Federal Aviation Administration (FAA)
Political parties	Tory Party, Democratic Party
Organizations	United Service Organization Young Republicans
Members of most organizations	a Republican
Do not capitalize the common name of a club or team.	The soccer team practices on Monday afternoons.
Schools	Ironside Middle School Wharton School of Business
Buildings	Metropolitan Auditorium Gaviidae Common
Structures	Hadrian's Wall
Monuments	Washington Monument
Months	January, December
Days	Tuesday, Wednesday
Holidays	Christmas, Mother's Day
Do not capitalize the names of the seasons unless personified.	The first day of summer is usually quite warm.
The abbreviations BC and AD *Notice that BC ("before Christ") is correctly placed after the year and that AD (anno Domini, "in the year of the Lord") is correctly placed before the year.*	Between 2700 and 2500 BC the great pyramids of Egypt were constructed. In AD 1066 William of Normandy became the first Norman king of England.
The abbreviations a.m./p.m., A.M./P.M. *These abbreviations may be either lowercased or capitalized but should be used consistently.*	10:00 A.M., 5:00 P.M. 10:00 a.m., 5:00 p.m.
Historical events and periods	Battle of the Bulge Age of Reason
Documents	Treaty of Versailles
Awards	Nobel Peace Prize
Special events	St. Paul Winter Carnival

ESL To decide whether a name for a business is a proper noun or a common noun, consider whether you could write a check payable to that name. If you could, then you should capitalize the name.

11.5 PRACTICE *the skill*

Underline each word with a capitalization error. If the sentence is correct, write C in the blank.

_____ 1. Lying near Fossil Butte national monument in Wyoming and extending into Utah and Colorado, the Green River Formation fascinates scientists, both creationist and evolutionist.

_____ 2. On wednesday, october 30, 2002, at the annual meeting of the geological society of America, geologists from Loma Linda university presented a paper on the Green River Formation.

_____ 3. Evolutionary scientists believe that the Green River Formation gives valuable evidence about the eocene period and the earth's age. They say the number of varves, finely laminated sediment layers, in the formation date it to millions of years bc.

_____ 4. Trapped in the varves are spectacular fish fossils, some with skin remaining. Their presence is a problem to evolutionists, for if the varves had been laid down at a "normal" rate, two per year, the fish would have decayed before they could have fossilized.

_____ 5. The Chicago natural history museum performed an experiment showing that fish can decay within a week, even in settings with little oxygen.

_____ 6. In addition, events can change the varve deposit rate; in AD 1960 Hurricane Donna left six inches of varvelike mud in a short time.

_____ 7. Finally, the number of layers is not constant across the formation, varying by over four hundred layers. Scholars from the university of Wisconsin and the Lamont-Doherty earth observatory have studied the formation's age.

_____ 8. The Green River Formation is also a source of oil; in may 2012 a spokesperson for the government accountability office (gao) testified before congress about oil shale deposits in the formation.

_____ 9. Do any geologists hope to receive the day medal for research at Green River?

_____ 10. "Green River blues," a magazine article, is an intriguing look at the formation from a creationist perspective.

REVIEW *the skill*

Rewrite each sentence so that it contains no capitalization errors. If the sentence is already correct, write *C* in the blank.

1. The story of Darwin's deathbed recantation is the basis of an invalid argument for Creation. There is no proof that Darwin, who died in april 1882 during the victorian era, ever made such a statement.

2. Darwin's daughter, Henrietta, stated that the woman who claimed to have heard Darwin's recantation in his house, known as down house, was not present at any time during Darwin's illness.

3. Another erroneous argument for Creation stems from the national aeronautic and space administration's reported expectation of finding deep layers of dust on the moon, a discovery that would prove an ancient universe.

4. Actually, by 1969 evolutionists did not expect thick moon dust, and nasa knew that the early estimates of moon dust had been wrong; much of the public, however, still believed the early estimates.

5. Though some think that the great wall of china is visible to the naked eye from the Moon, astronauts reported that all they could see was clouds, ocean, and the occasional patch of desert or greenery.

6. A famous forged document was called the Donation of Constantine.

7. Some think that the first thanksgiving took place in late november; actually, it happened sometime between september 21 and november 11 and lasted three days.

8. Although the first written account of a possible Loch Ness monster episode occurred in ad 565, there is no substantial evidence to prove this supposed hoax.

9. In the information age, it seems that rumors and fabrications have only gotten worse.

10. The Democrats and the Republicans sometimes happily repeat untrue stories about each other, unaware that their information is faulty.

Underlining for Italics p. 337

Quotation Marks p. 330

Titles

Capitalize the first and last words in a title as well as all other important words. Do not capitalize an article, a coordinating conjunction, the *to* of the infinitive, or a preposition of fewer than five letters unless it is the first or last word in a title.

Titles	
Newspapers and magazines	*Washington Post* *Field and Stream*
Do not capitalize the word the *when referring to a newspaper.*	the *Atlanta Journal-Constitution*
Literary compositions (including books, essays, poems, and plays)	*Jane Eyre* "Prejudice and Intolerance" "The Road Not Taken" *Our Town*
Sections of a book or play	Chapter 12 Index Act 1
Some authorities do not capitalize the parts of a book or play unless they appear as a title.	The drama class performed a cutting of act 1 from *Macbeth*.
Musical compositions (including songs, operas, and instrumental music)	"Silent Night" *Aida* Adagio from the Fifth Symphony
Works of art (including drawings, paintings, and sculptures)	Ed Ruscha's *Self 1967* Baglione's *The Entombment of Christ* Michelangelo's *Pieta*
Television and radio programs	*Dateline NBC* *A Prarie Home Companion*
Specific courses of study	History of Civilization Algebra 1
Do not capitalize the common noun for a course.	Students must bring their textbooks to history class tomorrow.

282 Chapter 11 | Capitalization

11.7 PRACTICE the skill

Underline each word with a capitalization error.

1. In Act 3 of *as you like it*, Touchstone observes, "Honesty coupled to beauty is to have honey a sauce to sugar."

2. Forgery detection might be a good unit for an Art class!

3. In 1945, a painter named van Meegeren ran into serious trouble for his paintings, which included *Christ and the disciples at Emmaus.*

4. Van Meegeren, a native of the Netherlands, had faked Vermeer paintings and sold one, *Christ and the woman taken in adultery,* to the Nazi Hermann Göring.

5. When the war ended, the Dutch government wanted to try van meegeren for treason for selling national treasures to the enemy.

6. No one would believe that paintings like his *the last supper* were frauds, and van Meegeren finally had to paint another "Vermeer" in his cell to avoid conviction for treason.

7. Van Meegeren became a legend in the art world; Radnoti's book *the fake* discusses him, and in 2002, The *Casco Bay Weekly* ran an article referring to van Meegeren.

8. Violinist fritz Kreisler, on the other hand, was guilty of a backward kind of forgery.

9. Kreisler attributed his *tempo di minuetto* and *la précieuse,* as well as other works, to musicians such as Pugnani and Couperin, claiming to be only the arranger.

10. In the 1970s the Canadian Broadcasting Corporation's show *musicamera* presented a profile of this famous violinist.

View of Delft by Vermeer

11.8 REVIEW *the skill*

Write the letter of the choice that is capitalized correctly.

_____ 1. A. One hoax that was not meant to be taken seriously but shocked America concerned H. G. Wells's book *The War Of The Worlds*.
   B. One hoax that was not meant to be taken seriously but shocked America concerned H. G. Wells's book *The War of the Worlds*.

_____ 2. A. On October 30, 1938, the CBS radio Network broadcast *The War Of The Worlds*, a dramatized version of the book.
   B. On October 30, 1938, the CBS radio network broadcast *The War of the Worlds*, a dramatized version of the book.

_____ 3. A. The dramatization begins like any other program, with an orchestra playing music—in this case, "La Cumparsita."
   B. The dramatization begins like any other program, with an orchestra playing music—in this case, "La cumparsita."

_____ 4. A. Next in the show, a reporter interviews a man with great knowledge of astronomy about mysterious explosions on Mars.
   B. Next in the show, a reporter interviews a man with great knowledge of Astronomy about mysterious explosions on Mars.

_____ 5. A. This episode of *Mercury theatre on the air* continues in New Jersey with the attack of the Martians.
   B. This episode of *Mercury Theatre on the Air* continues in New Jersey with the attack of the Martians.

_____ 6. A. Worried inhabitants of Princeton, New Jersey, flooded the campus paper, the *daily Princetonian*, with calls.
   B. Worried inhabitants of Princeton, New Jersey, flooded the campus paper, the *Daily Princetonian*, with calls.

_____ 7. A. In Part two of the program, a man who thinks he is the lone survivor muses on the events.
   B. In Part Two of the program, a man who thinks he is the lone survivor muses on the events.

_____ 8. A. He discovers that the Martians have been killed by natural microbiology (bacteria present on Earth).
   B. He discovers that the Martians have been killed by natural Microbiology (bacteria present on earth).

_____ 9. A. The next day the *New York Times* ran a story on the panic that erupted.
   B. The next day *The New York Times* ran a story on the panic that erupted.

_____ 10. A. The American public could echo a line from *hamlet*, act 3, scene 1, and say, "We were the more deceived."
   B. The American public could echo a line from *Hamlet*, Act 3, Scene 1, and say, "We were the more deceived."

First Words & Single Letters

First word in a sentence	**T**he nativity scene was lighted beautifully.
Do not capitalize the first word of a sentence in parentheses within another sentence.	The nativity scene (**i**t is a new decoration this year) was lighted beautifully.
First word in a line of dialogue	Josh asked, "**W**ho is your favorite author?"
Do not capitalize the second part of a divided quotation unless the second part is the beginning of a new sentence.	"Dickens," Julie quickly responded, "**i**s definitely my favorite author." "He wrote many great novels," Julie continued. "**S**ometimes I have trouble deciding which is my favorite."
Do not capitalize quotations integrated into sentences of one's own.	"Do you really think that he wrote '**g**reat novels'?" inquired Josh.
First word in a line of poetry, whether formatted as a poem or quoted in a sentence	**I**n all this place of silence **T**here are no kindred spirits. (Edgar Lee Masters, "Flossie Cabanis") Do you know who wrote the lines "**I**n all this place of silence / **T**here are no kindred spirits"?
Do not capitalize a word that the poet does not capitalize. Many modern poets choose not to capitalize the first word of each line.	

First word (and any proper nouns or proper adjectives) in each item of a formal outline	I. **P**lanning a **C**hristmas party
	   A. **D**etermining a theme
	   B. **C**hoosing the main course
	   C. **D**eciding on the additional foods

First word in a formal statement or quotation following a colon	Those attending the trial gasped at the jury's verdict: "**W**e, the jury, find the defendant not guilty.
The first word of an explanatory statement following the colon is usually lowercased.	The neighborhood children learned a valuable lesson: **d**on't tease dogs unknown to you.
First word and all nouns in the greeting of a letter	**D**ear **F**ellow **S**tudents,
First word in the closing of a letter	**Y**ours truly,
Personal pronoun *I*	Joshua and **I** enjoyed playing board games after dinner.
Archaic address-form *O*	I will love thee, **O** Lord.

Commas in Letters
pp. 310–11

CONTINUED

First Words & Single Letters

Single letters used as words (including academic grades, vitamins, musical notes, and major musical keys)	James earned an **A** average during his first semester. Recent studies indicate that vitamin **K** is important for bone strength. During her practice time, she had difficulty with high **C**.
Letters used to clarify a following word	His **T**-shirt was hanging out from under his dress shirt. The **I**-formation is a popular football tactic.

PRACTICE *the skill*

Underline each word with a capitalization error.

1. Dear members of the Creation Science Society:

2. Yesterday's trip to the Natural History Museum was quite informative. The building is roughly t-shaped, with the entry in the top of the t.

3. When Daniel, Joanna, and i walked through the doors, the first thing we saw was a huge exhibit on the origins of life.

4. sections of the exhibit explained about the Big Bang, DNA, and mutation, and there was even a diagram of an evolutionary "tree." Other ideas were left out: certainly the biblical account got no space.

5. The exhibit credited Darwin with originating the concept of natural selection; Actually, natural selection was first suggested by a creationist twenty years before Darwin wrote.

6. Joanna gives the exhibit an a for graphics and layout and an f for impartiality.

7. Daniel was wearing his Creation Science Society t-shirt, and a man in the tour group asked him whether he really "Believes all that stuff."

8. Daniel replied, "not only do I believe it, but the weight of evidence is for it."

9. "But," the other man said, "How can you believe in Creation when mutation and change are all around?" Daniel pointed out that we know of no examples of mutation that add genetic information in the offspring.

10. In human experience, Mutation involves loss of genetic information in the offspring, which would not lead to a "higher" life form.

11.10 REVIEW *the skill*

Write the letter of the choice that is capitalized correctly.

_____ 1. A. In the meantime, Joanna and i were talking to the guide about evolution's basis of faith.
   B. In the meantime, Joanna and I were talking to the guide about evolution's basis of faith.

_____ 2. A. At one point, the guide said, "a proof for evolution is that all reputable scientists today believe it."
   B. At one point, the guide said, "A proof for evolution is that all reputable scientists today believe it."

_____ 3. A. Joanna commented that truth doesn't depend on who believes it: whether or not a person believes in gravity, it exists.
   B. Joanna commented that truth doesn't depend on who believes it: whether or not a person believes in Gravity, it exists.

_____ 4. A. Saying or hoping a thing doesn't make it true: I can say, "o king, live forever," but my words don't lengthen his life.
   B. Saying or hoping a thing doesn't make it true: I can say, "O king, live forever," but my words don't lengthen his life.

_____ 5. A. Next, the guide stated that the c-14 dating method proves the world to be ancient.
   B. Next, the guide stated that the C-14 dating method proves the world to be ancient.

_____ 6. A. However, the carbon-14 method loses much accuracy when the time span involved exceeds three thousand years.
   B. however, the carbon-14 method loses much accuracy when the time span involved exceeds three thousand years.

_____ 7. A. The guide finally admitted that her presuppositions (She called them "beliefs") have shaped her worldview.
   B. The guide finally admitted that her presuppositions (she called them "beliefs") have shaped her worldview.

_____ 8. A. As we left, I noticed a quotation from Shakespeare above the door: "Truth is truth / To the end of reckoning." How ironic.
   B. As we left, I noticed a quotation from Shakespeare above the door: "Truth is truth / to the end of reckoning." How ironic.

_____ 9. A. We might rather say, "truth is fallen in the street, and equity cannot enter" (Isa. 59:14).
   B. We might rather say, "Truth is fallen in the street, and equity cannot enter" (Isa. 59:14).

_____ 10. A. sincerely yours,
       Ginny Avery
   B. Sincerely yours,
       Ginny Avery

CUMULATIVE *review*

Rewrite the following paragraphs, correcting the fifteen errors from these categories: subject-verb agreement, pronoun-antecedent agreement, verb use, pronoun use, adjective and adverb use, and capitalization.

Literary frauds are produced for many reasons. Some people produce it solely for money and reputation, while others genuinely believe that their work is doing good. One example is W. D. Mahan, an American minister. In 1879, Mahan publishes a volume variously called *The Acts of Pilate, the Archko Volume,* or *A Correct Transcript of Pilate's Court.* Mahan claimed that he learned of the historical basis from a German guest. He said the guest (Whose name was Whydaman) later wrote from westphalia, Germany, to give more aid. Mahan supposedly then received documents from the Vatican concerning the trial of Jesus. Mahan later published more documents about Jesus and his life, saying him and other scholars had found additional information at Constantinople's Mosque of st. Sophia.

Unfortunately, the work is a fake. Mahan's claims about these most unique discoveries caused curiosity, and a contemporary attacked the book in the *Boonville Weekly advertiser* in 1885, pointing out various problems in their article. Mahan's church suspended him for a year because of his deception. The circumstances surrounding Mahan's claims are highly dubious. Twyman and McIntosh, the "great scholars" whom supposedly helped him find and translate the documents, is completely unknown. Historical details can be proved untrue: for example, he states that the historian Tacitus wrote a biography in AD 56, though Tacitus was born sometime around ad 55. These facts lead to a sad conclusion—the book by Mahan, though possibly a well-meaning attempt to support Christianity by adding archaeological evidence to the Bible, is a fabrication.

THINK ABOUT IT

Examine the Evidence!

Many of the hoaxes you have just read about were successful because the so-called evidence appeared to be sound even though it was not. Some hoaxes depended on the credentials or the apparent sincerity of the perpetrator of the hoax. When presented with something they hope to be true, people are often willing to suspend disbelief. They fail to examine the evidence or to question the soundness of the reasoning. They may believe whatever someone says if that person seems to be a sincere expert. A critical thinker, on the other hand, bases his or her decisions on sound reasoning and clear evidence.

Before you make a decision to accept or reject what someone else has proposed, first determine the bases for the statement. What reasons or evidence have been offered as support? Then examine that support, using the tools of critical thinking.

- Is the reasoning valid? Are the premises true?
- Is the evidence presented fact or opinion? If the evidence is merely opinion, is the opinion itself based on facts?
- From what sources is the evidence drawn? Does information come from primary sources, such as original documents or eyewitnesses? Or is the information borrowed from secondary sources, such as reviews of someone else's research or second-hand reports of events ("Mike says that Joyce saw it happen!")? As a general rule, primary sources tend to be the most reliable.
- Are the facts reasonable? Or is it unlikely that they could be true? For example, the claim that Tacitus wrote a biography in AD 56 is unreasonable to one who knows that Tacitus was probably born only a year earlier.

Of course, not all statements need to be tested by this kind of study. Remember that divine revelation is always trustworthy. When God says something in Scripture, we can accept it on His authority. Only human reasoning is subject to error.

Thinking It Through

Find an advertisement that uses what it claims to be facts or statistics to sell a product or a service. Evaluate the ad according to the criteria above. Then discuss your findings with someone and decide together whether you accept the claims.

Issue Analysis Essay | 292
Punctuation | 296
From the Written Word | 321

ISSUE ANALYSIS ESSAY Writing
PUNCTUATION Usage
12

Whenever there are two sides to an issue, careful thought is required of a person as he wades through the facts of the case and decides upon a course of action or a belief to be held. Issues abound—school vouchers, tax cuts, campaign financing, health benefits, food safety—the list is virtually endless. Many writers, mostly journalists, make a living writing opinion pieces in which they give their own opinions about topics or examine the opinions of others. The editors of Maclean's *magazine examine airport security measures in the United States and Canada and proposed changes to the process. They use facts, expert opinion, quotations, and some humor to make a serious point. In your issue analysis, you will write about a topic that interests (or irritates!) you.*

Bringing Some Sanity to Airport Security
by Peter Shawn Taylor

Line up. Liquids in a baggie. Toss your water. Wait. Stuff your jacket in a bin. Empty your pockets. Take off your belt. Wait some more. Walk through slowly. Raise your arms. Stand still.

Is there any modern activity more frustrating, time-consuming and humiliating than the airport security line? Improved vigilance against terrorism may be a necessity in our post–9/11 world. But does it have to be so awkward? And is that bottle of water really a threat to global security?

In what might be considered a welcome breath of fresh air for air travellers, the former head of U.S. airport security is calling for an end to many of the most outrageous and bothersome aspects of airport check-in: liquid of all sizes should be allowed as carry-on, bans on non-weapons such as lighters should be relaxed and, in the name of improved security, airlines should be forbidden from charging checked baggage fees. Could it really be possible to fly like it's 1999?

Kip Hawley was administrator of the U.S. Transportation Security Administration (TSA) from 2005 to 2009. During that time he was responsible for many of the decisions that turned air travel into such a grind, including restrictions on liquids. And that made him a frequent target of public outrage. In 2006, a Milwaukee man was detained by TSA staff when he wrote "Kip Hawley is an idiot" on the baggie holding his miniature vials of liquids at a security check. Hawley now appears to be trying to make amends.

Hawley's book *Permanent Emergency: Inside the TSA and the Fight for the Future of American Security* provides an insider's perspective on how to make airport security a less irritating experience without increasing overall risk. Given the high degree of co-operation between the TSA and the Canadian Air Transportation Security Authority, what Hawley says should resonate with put-upon Canadian flyers as well.

His most refreshing idea: allow passengers to bring liquids of all sizes in their carry-on luggage. Carry-on liquids and gels are currently limited to 100 ml in Canada and the U.S. But Hawley reports that airport scanners now have the ability to determine if a liquid is an explosive. He suggests specially designated lanes for passengers with "snow globes, beauty products, booze" or any other fluids they might wish to carry on. If you'd rather not buy a microscopic flask of mouthwash for every trip, you could simply pick the "liquids lane" at pre-boarding and bring your bottle from home.

Airline baggage fees should be outlawed as an impediment to security, argues Hawley. Charging for each piece of checked luggage has become commonplace among airlines eager for extra revenue. But this measure encourages passengers to stuff as much as physically possible into their carry-on bags, which are still free. This inevitably slows down pre-boarding inspections. While airlines would have to find other ways to squeeze money out of travellers, the result would be quicker and more thorough inspections.

And Hawley would eliminate the list of forbidden items, beyond the most obvious weapons such as knives and bombs. "Banning certain items gives terrorists a complete list of what not to use in their next attack," he explains in a *Wall Street Journal* column promoting his book. "Lighters are banned? The next attack will use an electric trigger." Both the Shoe Bomber and Underwear Bomber provide evidence of evolving terrorist ingenuity.

Finally, Hawley suggests wholesale reform of the philosophy behind airport security. Instead of rigid protocols, he would give individual officers greater flexibility and discretion to search for possible threats. He would also randomize detailed inspections and institute more interviews to keep terrorists off-balance.

Savvy travellers will recognize Hawley's last point as a modified version of the vaunted Israeli approach to air terrorism, which focuses on the risk posed by individual ticket holders through targeted behaviour recognition. The North American method of obsessing over each and every bag for potential terrorism paraphernalia, on the other hand, wastes everyone's time equally. While this may strike some as equitable, it's wholly illogical and represents a vast waste of resources. It's also worth noting that both the Shoe and Underwear Bombers were thwarted, not by security measures, but by the courageous and spontaneous reactions of passengers and crew. "In attempting to eliminate all risk from flying, we have made air travel an unending nightmare," says Hawley. "Terrorists are adaptive, we need to be adaptive too."

Without much difficulty, and without endangering security, we could return air travel to the modestly pleasurable activity it was 20 years ago. But getting there will require a whole new way of thinking about airport security.

Issue Analysis Essay

> Not that we are sufficient of ourselves to think any thing as of ourselves; but our sufficiency is of God.
> *2 Corinthians 3:5*

Being able to put in writing your thoughts and beliefs about an issue is an important skill—for both now and the future. A Christian writer will be called upon to analyze issues using God's Word as the basis for truth. Learn to think clearly about issues that affect you and your community and to put that thinking into written form.

Write a one- to two-page essay analyzing an issue approved by your teacher.

Planning

✔ **Look for an issue to analyze.** Issues, some important and some otherwise, are all around you. Consider some of the following sources as you decide what to write about.

- newspaper
- weekly magazine or journal
- local billboards or notices
- evening news
- sermons from your own pastor or others
- issues before your city or county council

✔ **Brainstorm with a partner.** Talk to your parents, friends, and teachers about issues that are important to them. Discuss varying sides of each issue to consider alternative points of view.

✔ **Make a list of points about your issue.** Answer the following questions to identify the areas you need to focus on in your analysis.

- What is the main point of your analysis?
- How will you support your main point?
- How do you want your readers to respond to your analysis? What action (if any) would you like them to take?
- Are there any objections to your main point? How will you address those?

✔ **Organize your points.** Use one of the methods discussed in Chapter 1 (see pages 14–17 for more information). Two of the five methods, cause-and-effect and order of importance, may be the most helpful as you write your analysis.

- Cause-and-Effect—explanation of a cause and its effects or vice versa
- Order of Importance—presentation of events from least to most or most to least important

✔ **Freewrite about a topic.** Set a time limit for yourself and write without stopping for that length of time. After you have finished, look at your writing for ideas that you need to develop further in order to present an effective analysis.

✔ **Interview an expert on the issue.** Talk to someone who knows a great deal about the subject or issue you want to write about. If possible, obtain permission to record the interview so that you can quote the expert on the record.

tip It is better to say more about less than to say less about more.

✔ **Narrow your topic.** Be sure that you can cover your topic fully within the length restrictions of your paper. Perhaps Taylor originally wanted to write about the difficulties of air travel in general; if so, he would have quickly found out that the topic was too broad for an article and would have chosen to examine current airport security policies instead. Ask yourself the following questions: *How long will my paper be? Is my topic too broad to be adequately covered in the assigned pages?* If you answer yes to the second, try focusing on just one aspect of your topic.

✔ **Consider your audience.** Analyzing your audience helps you to write the best piece possible for the reader. Taylor's essay is quite informal: it addresses readers directly as though they are passengers going through airport security. Later, it uses contractions and even some fragments instead of only formal sentences. Many journalists use informal language in order to appear to be on the same side as their audience. Use your judgment about how informal your analysis should be.

Thinking Biblically

Learning how to write persuasively is extremely important (Prov. 25:11, 15). To be effective, persuasive writing requires thoughtful, principle-based analysis, but people often fail to evaluate the issues against an objective standard. Instead, they simply choose a position they personally find most appealing. Truly good analysis, however, connects ultimate issues. For example, a debate about the use of excessive force by police raises issues about how much authority God has given to the state. A debate over racially charged issues—affirmative action, racial profiling, ethnic cleansing—is an opportunity to point readers to the only socially leveling force with any authority: the claim of Genesis that all people are made in God's image. As mentioned in Chapter 3, you need not quote a Bible verse every time the Republicans and Democrats disagree over a particular issue. But your reasoning should always return, ultimately, to the basic principles found in the Scriptures.

Topic Outlines
pp. 6–7

✔ **Outline your analysis.** Complete at least a topic outline before you begin drafting. This will help you identify the main points you hope to cover in your analysis. What follows is one student's attempt at an outline on the topic of year-round school (YRS).

    I. YRS and education
        A. Decreased "forgetting time"
        B. Increased review time
    II. YRS and economics
        A. Start-up/shut-down costs
        B. Cost of A/C in buildings/buses
    III. YRS and family, church, and community events
        A. Difficulty in scheduling events
        B. Extracurricular activities affected
    IV. YRS and teachers
        A. Burn-out
        B. Loss of summer education opportunities

Drafting

✔ **Write your thesis statement.** Your thesis should clearly identify a problem for analysis or present your position about your topic. Taylor's essay hints at its thesis in the second paragraph: "Is there any modern activity more frustrating, time-consuming and humiliating than the airport security line?" It states the thesis directly in the last paragraph: "Without much difficulty, and without endangering security, we could return air travel to the modestly pleasurable activity it was 20 years ago." Compose a thesis that you can support well.

Details
p. 367

✔ **Draft your analysis.** Use the ideas you developed in the planning stage to write your analysis. Make sure that your thesis statement is prominent near the opening of the piece. Include any concerns/objections you identified earlier.

✔ **Bolster your ideas with specifics.** Notice how many facts the editorial includes: names, dates, amounts. Your addition of details will make your analysis more credible. Look at these two sentences—the first a quotation from Taylor's piece and the second a rewrite taking out the specific examples. Notice how the first creates a picture that the second does not.

> If you'd rather not buy a microscopic flask of mouthwash for every trip, you could simply pick the "liquids lane" at pre-boarding and bring your bottle from home.

> If you'd rather not buy small containers of liquids for every trip, you could simply pick a special lane at pre-boarding and bring regular-sized containers.

✔ **Pay attention to your opening and closing paragraphs.** Do not forget the purposes of your introductory paragraph: to catch reader interest, to introduce the topic, and to draw attention to the main idea. Your conclusion should clinch the main idea, giving a sense of completeness. Taylor's essay does this effectively with its last paragraph. It states the thesis clearly and succinctly and then reminds the reader of what still needs to change: "But getting there will require a whole new way of thinking about airport security." Notice that the last sentence plays upon the travel theme by comparing new policies to a new location.

Revising

✔ **Step away from your paper.** Giving yourself time to think about your topic before revising is often a good idea. Get a good night's sleep and then look at your analysis again. Ask yourself whether your paper makes its point clearly and logically now that you're looking at it with fresh eyes.

✔ **Allow a peer to edit your paper.** Ask another writer to read your paper for you. Ask him to comment specifically on the following questions:
  - Is the thesis clear? Could you restate it?
  - Is there adequate support for the main points? Do you have any ideas for additional support?
  - Do you have any objections to the thesis not addressed in the paper?
  - Is there anything in the paper that needs further explanation?

✔ **Revise your paper for correctness.** After you incorporate the changes you have marked and make a fresh copy of your paper, read it over for grammar, mechanics, and usage errors. Use the spell-check feature on your computer but do not depend on it to catch all of your errors. Can you find the error in the sentence below? (The spellchecker cannot.)

> Outside, the lightening flashed.

The word *lightening* means "getting or making lighter." The writer probably wanted to use the word *lightning,* which refers to the flashing light in a stormy sky. Careful proofreading can help you catch such errors.

✔ **Choose wisely for variety and emphasis.** As you revise, look again at the various constructions you have chosen. You can improve your writing by making sure that you use the active voice in most instances and the passive voice only when justifiable. Look also at your use of indirect objects and prepositional phrases—do your choices reflect the proper emphasis?

Choosing Between Constructions pp. 361–62

Publishing

✔ **Submit your analysis to a journal or magazine.** Find a publication, either in print or online, that publishes articles on your topic. Research the guidelines for publication and, if necessary, revise your piece to reflect them.

✔ **Bind the class essays together.** Group the analyses by topic and bind them for display. Think of an appropriate title for the collection of essays.

✔ **Mail your essay to another student.** Exchange your essay with another student. Encourage him to comment on the issue you present.

✔ **Present your essay orally.** Read your essay aloud to a group of students and answer questions from your audience.

Some Ideas to Consider

Language
- Write about language changes (e.g., new spellings becoming acceptable, changes in punctuation rules, political correctness in language).

Government
- Analyze a local ordinance that is being considered by your county council.
- Examine efforts to remove the words "under God" from the Pledge of Allegiance.

Punctuation

Have you ever walked an unmarked trail in the dark? If you have, you probably remember wondering what you might be stepping on or what might be just ahead of you. On the other hand, you may have walked a well-marked, lighted path and been reassured about where you were stepping and where you were going. Punctuation marks used correctly guide both the writer and reader on a path of clear understanding.

Exclamation Point

Exclamatory Sentences p. 69

An exclamation point follows an exclamatory sentence, a brief exclamation, and some imperative sentences. Be sure to use the exclamation point sparingly.

EXCLAMATORY SENTENCE	There is a wasp nest under that step!
BRIEF EXCLAMATION	Oh, no!
IMPERATIVE SENTENCE	Go the other way!

Question Mark

Interrogative Sentences p. 69

A question mark comes at the end of a direct question. A polite request, however, is not usually punctuated with a question mark.

DIRECT QUESTION	Have you begun a family tradition at your home?
TAG QUESTION	You will begin a tradition soon, won't you?
ELLIPTICAL QUESTION	How many traditions do you intend to start each year? one? two?
POLITE REQUEST	Would you please consider beginning a patriotic tradition.

Declarative Sentences p. 69

Period

In Sentences

A period is used to indicate the end of declarative sentences, indirect questions, and imperative sentences that do not express strong emotion.

DECLARATIVE SENTENCE	A family tradition can be passed on to succeeding generations.
INDIRECT QUESTION	He asked us whether we had any family traditions.
MILD IMPERATIVE SENTENCE	Please begin a tradition in your family.

In English punctuation, all end marks (periods, question marks, and exclamation points) must follow the last word of the sentence immediately. Do not leave a space before those marks, but leave one or two spaces after them.

Similarly, use no space before a comma or a semicolon, but leave one space after either of these. For any other punctuation, observe the examples carefully. (Expect to use no space before any punctuation except for opening parentheses and opening quotation marks.)

tip

When the period of an abbreviation comes at the end of a sentence, that period also ends the sentence.

For Initials and Abbreviations

A period usually follows a person's initial and often follows an abbreviation.

Initials and Abbreviations	
Personal names and titles	Dr. George Allen Sr.
Periods are usually omitted after academic degrees following a name, after acronyms, and after most abbreviations of the names of governmental agencies, most organizations, and well-known businesses.	James Hall, MD PAC (Political Action Committee) FDA (Food and Drug Administration) USO (United Service Organizations) IBM (International Business Machines)
Parts of an address	Pearlman Dairy Rd. P.O. Box 69875
Periods do not follow state or province postal abbreviations; periods do not follow ZIP codes or other postal codes.	Snow Lake, AK 72379 BWI (British West Indies) Richmond Hill, ON L4B 1B4
Times and dates	10:00 p.m.
Periods are usually omitted in BC and AD.	607 BC; AD 1483
Measurements	6 ft. 3 in. 190 lb.
Periods are not used with metric measurements.	25 km 80 mg

In Outlines and Lists

A period follows each number or letter division of an outline.

    I. Problems building the Panama Canal
        A. Hostile neighbors
        B. Inadequate engineering knowledge
        C. Tropical disease
        D. Topographical elements
            1. Mountainous terrain
            2. Excessive vegetation
            3. Landslides
    II. Functions of the Panama Canal
        A. Providing a passageway between the Atlantic and Pacific Oceans
        B. Improving trade routes

A period follows each number or letter that precedes an item in a vertical list.

1. Determine the number of guests
2. Plan the menu
3. Purchase the groceries
4. Set the table
5. Prepare the food

A period does not follow the number or letter that precedes an item in a list within a sentence. Use pairs of parentheses instead of periods.

In preparation for the Thanksgiving dinner, we must (1) determine the number of guests, (2) plan the menu, (3) purchase the groceries, (4) set the table, and (5) prepare the food.

For Decimals

A period functions as a decimal point in numerical expressions.

$75.00

10.5 feet

94.5° F

12.1 PRACTICE *the skill*

Write the letter of the correctly punctuated sentence.

_____ 1. A. Our geography teacher, Dr. McGuire, asked us whether we understand the significance of worldwide tourism?

B. Our geography teacher, Dr. McGuire, asked us whether we understand the significance of worldwide tourism.

_____ 2. A. Would you look at the chart on page 212. There you'll find some statistics from the United Nations World Tourism Organization (UNWTO), which monitors tourism around the globe.

B. Would you look at the chart on page 212? There you'll find some statistics from the United Nations World Tourism Organization (UNWTO), which monitors tourism around the globe.

_____ 3. A. Wow! During 2010, countries around the world hosted almost 940 million people who crossed their borders as tourists.

B. Wow. During 2010, countries around the world hosted almost 940 million people who crossed their borders as tourists.

_____ 4. A. Please note the next figure as well. It says that tourists in 2010 spent over $919 billion.

B. Please note the next figure as well! It says that tourists in 2010 spent over 919 billion.

_____ 5. A. That total means each tourist spent an average of $977.66, doesn't it? Yes, but that's in U.S. dollars.

B. That total means each tourist spent an average of $977.66, doesn't it. Yes, but that's in U.S. dollars.

_____ 6. A. I think these numbers are staggering, don't you!

B. I think these numbers are staggering, don't you?

_____ 7. A. Here's a list of the fifteen most-visited countries. Which country is first, second, third?
       B. Here's a list of the fifteen most-visited countries. Which country is first? second? third?

_____ 8. A. Well, traditionally, the top three nations for attracting tourists are 1. France, 2. the United States, and 3. Spain.
       B. Well, traditionally, the top three nations for attracting tourists are (1) France, (2) the United States, and (3) Spain.

_____ 9. A. I learned a lot about world tourism. My notes look like this:
           I. Countries spending the most money as tourists
              A Germany
              B United States
              C China
           II. Countries receiving the most money from tourists
              A United States
              B Spain
              C France
       B. I learned a lot about world tourism. My notes look like this:
           I. Countries spending the most money as tourists
              A. Germany
              B. United States
              C. China
           II. Countries receiving the most money from tourists
              A. United States
              B. Spain
              C. France

_____ 10. A. I took a lot of notes on Dr. McGuire's fascinating lecture. In fact, my notebook probably weighed an extra 5 lb when class ended.
        B. I took a lot of notes on Dr. McGuire's fascinating lecture. In fact, my notebook probably weighed an extra 5 lb. when class ended.

Punctuation | Chapter 12 **299**

12.2 REVIEW *the skill*

Rewrite the following sentences, adding or deleting periods, decimal points, question marks, and exclamation points as necessary.

1. Mont-Saint-Michel is a popular tourist attraction in France, isn't it

2. Yes, this site is popular for several reasons:
   A Beautiful architecture
   B Rich history
   C Picturesque landscape

3. Mont-Saint-Michel comprises an abbey and a village mounted atop an enormous rock island with a height of more than 80 m., or 262 ft.

4. Listen while I tell you how the first building on this island began in AD 708

5. Did you know that Saint Aubert, a bishop from Avranches, claimed the archangel Michael appeared and told him to build a chapel

6. I wonder why people use the term *La Merveille,* "The Marvel," to speak of Mont-Saint-Michel

7. How many tourists do you think Mont-Saint-Michel brings to France each year 400,000

8. The local AAA might have some brochures about France that would tell us; the nearest agency is located at 56 E Antrim Dr

9. This view is spectacular

10. Quick, get the camera

Comma

The comma is the most frequently used mark of punctuation and probably the most frequently misused. Commas that are correctly placed can guide the reader to a clear understanding of the text. Incorrect commas, on the other hand, can create uncertainty. Understanding the following rules will help you write clearly.

In a Series

Commas separate words, phrases, or clauses that appear in a series.

Series of Three or More Items

In a series of three or more items joined by a conjunction, a comma follows each item of the series (except the last item). In less formal writing, such as journalistic writing, the comma before the last item in the series is omitted. In academic writing, however, the comma before the conjunction is expected.

Compound Sentences p. 132

We have chosen Jerry**,** Tom**,** and Mark to be the committee chairmen.

Inviting the guests**,** planning the program**,** and delegating food preparation responsibilities will be a part of the chairmen's job.

Coordinate Adjectives in a Series

A comma separates coordinate adjectives (adjectives that modify a noun separately), but a comma does not separate cumulative adjectives (adjectives that build on one another to modify a noun jointly).

Clauses pp. 116–28

COORDINATE	The *howling, swirling* wind whipped through the trees.
	Fall leaves of *vibrant, brilliant* hues began to fall to the ground.
CUMULATIVE	Leaves from the *tall old oak* tree covered the lawn.
	Long green blades of grass poked through the carpet of leaves.

Adjectives p. 48

Participial Phrases pp. 92–94

Punctuation | Chapter 12 **301**

Independent Clauses p. 116

Compound Sentences p. 132

Two or More Independent Clauses

In a compound sentence, a comma separates the first independent clause from the conjunction. A comma is not used between compound predicates.

> During the storm the night sky filled with dark clouds, and the wind blew violently through the trees.
>
> Did the thunder awaken you, or did you sleep through the storm?
>
> Lightning flashed through the night sky and illuminated the darkness.

Two independent clauses that are very short and closely related in meaning do not require a comma before the conjunction.

> The wind blew and the thunder roared.
>
> The baby cried and the dog barked.

If a compound sentence has three or more short independent clauses, a comma follows each clause except the last one.

> The rain stopped, the sky became clear, and the moon appeared overhead.
>
> The children returned to their beds, the dog stopped barking, and I collapsed into bed.

12.3 PRACTICE *the skill*

Insert any missing commas. If the sentence is already correct, write C in the blank.

_____ 1. The greatest feat of tourism ever imagined might be attributed to Phileas Fogg, the determined, daring hero of Jules Verne's classic story *Around the World in Eighty Days*.

_____ 2. Phileas Fogg is a reserved English gentleman who lives out his existence obsessed with adhering to a predictable punctual routine.

_____ 3. His daily activities consist of maintaining a respectable personal appearance taking his meals at the Reform Club reading the daily papers and playing whist with his friends at the club.

_____ 4. During a game at the Reform Club, Fogg and his friends begin discussing a recent bank robbery but a disagreement soon arises.

_____ 5. Mr. Stuart says the robber can certainly escape capture because the world is so big, and he takes issue with Fogg when the latter asserts that a man could travel around the whole world in a mere eighty days.

_____ 6. To win a wager and protect his word of honor, Fogg sets out to travel the world in eighty days, taking only his French valet Passepartout, a few articles of clothing, Bradshaw's book of train and steamship schedules and a carpetbag filled with £20,000.

_____ 7. On their journey they save an Indian princess from a suttee, they are attacked by Sioux Indians, and they are chased by a detective from England.

_____ 8. Detective Fix believes that Fogg has stolen £55,000 from the Bank of England and Fix is determined to bring Fogg to justice and win the reward.

_____ 9. Phileas Fogg Passepartout and Princess Aouda eventually arrive back in London at the Reform Club just in time to win the wager.

_____ 10. Phileas Fogg falls in love with Aouda and he marries her.

12.4 REVIEW *the skill*

Insert the ten missing commas in the following paragraph.

When planning a trip, a traveler should think ahead and pack wisely. He needs to determine what the weather will probably be and bring appropriate clothes. Some essentials to remember are an umbrella a light raincoat and comfortable shoes. Sample-size bottles of shampoo, conditioner, and hair spray are wonderful space savers. The hotel may have very dry air and leaving a few wet hand towels around the room at night will allow a traveler to sleep much more comfortably. Clothespins hold hotel curtains shut detergent wipes are great for stain removal and hand sanitizer protects from germs. The traveler should always remember to seal liquids and creams in plastic bags and he shouldn't forget to bring extra bags. A small portable first-aid kit can be a great help. Other handy useful items include folding scissors needle and thread safety pins and a flashlight with batteries.

After Introductory Elements

A comma follows certain introductory grammatical elements.

Introductory Participles and Participial Phrases

Use a comma after an introductory participle or participial phrase.

Participial Phrase
pp. 92–94

> Glistening, the snow lay undisturbed on the fields.
>
> Seizing the sled from its place in the garage, we headed to the slope.

Long Introductory Prepositional Phrases

Use a comma after a long introductory prepositional phrase (usually five words or more) or after multiple introductory prepositional phrases.

Prepositional Phrase
p. 88

> In spite of the bitter temperature, the children played in the snow.
>
> By the side of the old barn, the children built a large snowman.

Introductory Sequencing Words

A comma often follows an introductory sequencing word such as *first, second, next, finally,* or *last.* This comma is optional, but all such words should be treated alike. However, a comma never follows *then* when the word is used in this way.

> First, the youngest child chose a floppy wool hat for the snowman.
>
> Next, my brothers created his face.
>
> Last, I wrapped a red plaid scarf around his neck.

Introductory Adverb Clauses

Use a comma after an introductory adverb clause.

Adverb Clauses
pp. 122–23

> When the snowman was completed, neighbor children came to see the creation.
>
> After everyone had played in the snow for an hour, Mother served hot chocolate and cookies.

Other Introductory Elements

Use a comma after an element that modifies the sentence as a whole.

> To be sure, the children enjoyed their hours of playing outside.

Use a comma after an introductory element that contains a verbal, even if a comma would not otherwise be necessary.

Prepositional Phrases with Gerund
pp. 96–97

> Before coming inside, the children rode their sled down the slope for a final time.

12.5 PRACTICE *the skill*

Insert any missing commas. If the sentence is already correct, write C in the blank.

_____ 1. Lying above the river Tauber in northern Bavaria, Rothenburg ob der Tauber remains a medieval city.

_____ 2. Surrounding the city fully restored and preserved medieval walls create an atmosphere of the Middle Ages.

_____ 3. To be sure there are modern elements to Rothenburg; it accommodates thousands of tourists yearly.

_____ 4. Among the city's many attractions the Kriminalmuseum (Criminal Museum) is a collection of medieval punishments; it contains shame flutes for bad musicians, cages for bad bakers, an iron maiden, and an executioner's cloak and ax.

_____ 5. Built in 1395 and later remodeled the Kriminalmuseum is the only baroque building in the town.

_____ 6. In the dim, dark cellar of the Kriminalmuseum, one can find a torture rack.

_____ 7. Next the tourist should visit Käthe Wohlfahrt's Christmas Village.

_____ 8. Open year round the shop houses a permanent winter wonderland display of Christmas decorations.

_____ 9. Throughout this entire little city, the feeling of a walk back through time captivates the visitor.

_____ 10. In the twenty-first century Rothenburg offers both historical and modern cultural opportunities.

12.6 REVIEW *the skill*

Insert any missing commas. If the sentence is already correct, write C in the blank.

_____ 1. While enjoying a trip many people keep a record of their experiences through photographs.

_____ 2. Before leaving home the traveler should ensure that each camera he brings with him is in good working order.

_____ 3. By keeping a journal of pictures taken the tourist can identify each picture later.

_____ 4. If the traveler keeps a journal, he can use it as a record of when he visited each place and took each picture.

_____ 5. Of course one way to record information about tourist sites is to take pictures of informative signs on the premises.

_____ 6. To get the best photos possible the traveler should plan each picture for maximum dramatic effect.

_____ 7. Using people in the foreground to demonstrate scale, a traveler can take pictures that reflect the true size of objects.

_____ 8. By stocking up on memory cards and batteries in America an international traveler can likely save money. Such materials are typically more expensive elsewhere.

_____ 9. Finally a traveler should make sure that he is included in some of his snapshots.

_____ 10. As reminders of wonderful experiences, photographs are some of the best souvenirs.

To Set Off Elements

Commas separate certain words or groups of words from the rest of the sentence. Words or groups of words that come at the beginning of the sentence or at the end of the sentence use only one comma. A pair of commas encloses words or groups of words when they appear in the middle of the sentence.

Nouns of Direct Address

Use commas to separate or enclose a noun of direct address, the name or title of the person being spoken to, from the rest of the sentence.

> *Josh,* did you see the trail through the woods?
>
> I don't know, *Son,* that you should go that far into the woods.

Parenthetical Expressions

Use commas to set off a parenthetical expression, a word or phrase that could be left out of the sentence without damaging its meaning.

> The trail, *as you well know,* is not marked clearly.
>
> *As you well know,* the trail is not marked clearly.
>
> The trail is not marked clearly, *as you well know.*

Adverb Clauses pp. 122–23

Interjections

Use commas to separate a mild interjection from the rest of the sentence.

> *Sure,* there is time to shop for warm clothes.
>
> Be sure to buy a really warm jacket, *please.*

Phrases That Show Contrast

Use commas to set off phrases that show contrast, especially when the phrase begins with a negative word such as *not* or *never.*

> We will be sure to shop tomorrow, *not today.*
>
> A warm coat, *never just a sweater,* is necessary for subzero weather.

Appositives

Use commas to enclose most appositives.

> Jordan, *the boy next door,* wants to sled on the big hill.
>
> He chose the fastest sled, *the one with shiny metal runners.*

A restrictive appositive appears without commas. These short appositives are more specific and more important than the noun before them because they are necessary to identify that noun.

> Have you talked with my brother *Will?*
>
> He recently read J. R. R. Tolkien's novel *The Hobbit.*

Adjectives after a Noun

Use commas to set off a compound adjective or participle that appears after the noun it modifies.

> The children, *tired and cold,* came inside and enjoyed cider.
>
> They quickly gulped the cider, *spicy and warm.*

Participial Phrases pp. 92–94

Tag Questions

Use a comma to separate a tag question from the statement that precedes it.

> You enjoyed the cookies, *didn't you?*
>
> We are going to bake more, *aren't we?*

Adjective and Adverb Use pp. 243–44

Compound Sentences p. 132

Conjunctive Adverbs

Use commas to set off a conjunctive adverb from the rest of the sentence.

The chef, *however*, refuses to use prepackaged materials.

Therefore, all of the ingredients for the recipe are fresh.

When the conjunctive adverb appears between two independent clauses, use a period or a semicolon after the first independent clause. Then use a comma after the conjunctive adverb.

The chocolate layered dessert was quite tasty; *however*, it had too many calories for my diet.

The chocolate layered dessert was quite tasty. *However*, it had too many calories for my diet.

Restrictive and Nonrestrictive Elements

Adjective and Adverb Use pp. 243–44

A nonrestrictive modifier gives additional information that is not necessary to identify the thing being modified. The nonrestrictive element is set off from the rest of the sentence with a comma or a pair of commas. A restrictive modifier is necessary for identification; therefore, it is not set off by commas.

Nonrestrictive Adjective Clause	Walt Disney World, *which is located in Florida*, is a popular vacation spot.
Restrictive Adjective Clause	The Disney park *that he likes best* is Walt Disney World.
Nonrestrictive Phrase	Space Mountain, *with its dark tunnels*, brings smiles to many children's faces.
Restrictive Phrase	The roller-coaster ride *with dark surroundings* is Space Mountain.
Nonrestrictive Appositive	Big Thunder Mountain Railroad, *another roller coaster*, takes its riders through an old mining town.
Restrictive Appositive ("Close Appositive")	The roller coaster *Big Thunder Mountain Railroad* is in the Frontierland section of the park.
Nonrestrictive Adverb Clause	The children enjoyed other rides at the park, *although the roller coasters were their favorites*.
Restrictive Adverb Clause	Sometimes they would get in line again *after they had ridden the roller coaster*.

12.7 PRACTICE *the skill*

Write the letter of the correctly punctuated sentence.

_____ 1. A. Our trip to Beijing, as I may have told you, was very exciting.
   B. Our trip to Beijing as I may have told you was very exciting.

_____ 2. A. Tori did you prefer the Forbidden City or the Temple of Heaven?
   B. Tori, did you prefer the Forbidden City or the Temple of Heaven?

_____ 3. A. We decided that this year, not next year, would be the best time to visit the country.
   B. We decided that this year not next year would be the best time to visit the country.

_____ 4. A. Martyn, Tori's brother, wanted to climb the Great Wall of China.
       B. Martyn Tori's brother wanted to climb the Great Wall of China.

_____ 5. A. Oh, the Great Wall has a lot of steps!
       B. Oh the Great Wall has a lot of steps!

_____ 6. A. The Wall massive and gray can be very hot in the summertime.
       B. The Wall, massive and gray, can be very hot in the summertime.

_____ 7. A. Jacinta wanted to buy a pearl necklace, didn't she?
       B. Jacinta wanted to buy a pearl necklace didn't she?

_____ 8. A. However we didn't have time to stop by the marketplace.
       B. However, we didn't have time to stop by the marketplace.

_____ 9. A. The site, that was my favorite, was Tiananmen Square.
       B. The site that was my favorite was Tiananmen Square.

_____ 10. A. Were you aware that the Forbidden City, ancient and grand, opens directly onto Tiananmen Square?
        B. Were you aware that the Forbidden City ancient and grand opens directly onto Tiananmen Square?

12.8 REVIEW *the skill*

Insert any missing commas and cross out any unnecessary commas. If the sentence is already correct, write *C* in the blank.

_____ 1. When planning a trip, that includes travel abroad, a potential traveler should ensure that he has a valid passport.

_____ 2. A passport as many are aware can take several weeks to obtain.

_____ 3. Well the process begins at a passport acceptance facility.

_____ 4. Passport acceptance facilities include many courts, post offices, and libraries, don't they?

_____ 5. For the application process which can last some time the applicant should have proof of U.S. citizenship.

_____ 6. The applicant must also prove his identity, before he can be granted a passport. A driver's license not a Social Security card, is adequate proof.

_____ 7. However a previous passport or a naturalization certificate among other documents also suffices to demonstrate identity.

_____ 8. Another necessity, for the applicant, is a pair of passport photographs, pictures of the applicant that are about two inches square.

_____ 9. The passport must be processed; therefore the applicant must pay a fee.

_____ 10. The passport, small but powerful, is the prerequisite for travel abroad.

In Letters and with Quotations, Dates, and Addresses

Commas appear in certain locations within letters, dates, and addresses.

Salutations and Closings

Use a comma after the salutation of a friendly letter.

Dear Aunt Jenny and Uncle George,   Dear Charles,

Use a comma after the closing of a friendly letter or business letter.

Yours truly,   Sincerely,
Aunt Elizabeth   John D. Rockman

Quotation Marks
pp. 329–30

Direct Quotations

A comma or a pair of commas sets off a quotation tag from the quotation. The comma always appears before the quotation marks—inside closing quotation marks but outside opening quotation marks. A question mark or an exclamation point replaces the comma in sentences such as the third one below.

My brother said, "Let's get in line to ride the roller coaster again."

"I can't," I answered, "until I finish my ice cream."

"Will you please hurry!" he pleaded.

Dates

Use a comma to separate the day from the year in a date of month-day-year order and use one after the year when the date appears within a sentence.

Joshua and Jordan visited Florida on October 15, 2012.

On March 15, 2013, they visited California.

No comma is necessary when the date appears in day-month-year order.

Walt Disney was born 5 December 1901.

Addresses

Commas separate the elements in an address. If the address appears in the middle of a sentence, use a comma after the last element to separate the address from the remainder of the sentence.

Our vacation travels continued from Nags Head, North Carolina, to the picturesque city of Williamsburg, Virginia.

Do not insert a comma between the state, province, or territory and the ZIP code or another postal code.

The old address is 16 South Frederick Street, Evansville, Indiana 47714.

An address on an envelope uses the standard two-letter abbreviation for the state, province, or territory with no punctuation before or after it and no periods within it.

> Miss Christina Jackson
> 8609 Montebello Road
> Charlotte NC 28226

To Signal Special Constructions

Commas can appear in a sentence to signal that the writer has used an unusual sentence construction. These commas do not separate; they alert the reader and prevent misreading.

Transposed Words and Phrases

Use commas to indicate words or phrases that are out of their normal order.

> Most of the food at the party was too exotic. *The chocolate cake and pecan pie,* I really liked.

Commas in Place of Omitted Words

Use a comma to indicate the omission of what would otherwise be a repeated word in a parallel construction.

> The chef collected wonderful recipes; the maitre d', beautiful menus.
>
> The Hansons enjoyed a round of golf; the Baxters, a day at the museum.

Notice that the comma in the second clause replaces the *verb* of the first clause.

Commas with Certain Additions to Names

Use commas to enclose an abbreviated degree. Do not use a comma before numerals that follow a name.

> Jackson Coleman, MD, began his practice in a small rural town.
>
> His brother Dawson Coleman III, MD, joined the practice a year later.

A comma is optional between a name and the abbreviations *Jr.* and *Sr.* If you use a comma between the name and the abbreviation, be sure to use one between the abbreviation and whatever follows as well.

TRADITIONAL PRACTICE	Kenneth C. Roberts, Jr., is our new neighbor.
RECENT PRACTICE	Kenneth C. Roberts Jr. is our new neighbor.

Incorrect Commas

Commas that are in the wrong places are distracting and can cause confusion. Avoid these comma errors in your writing.

Before a Conjunction Joining Only Two Elements

Avoid using a comma when only two words, phrases, or dependent clauses are joined by a conjunction.

WRONG	Brent, and John are coming for the family reunion.
RIGHT	Brent and John are coming for the family reunion.

After a Conjunction

Do not use a comma after a conjunction unless the comma is necessary for some other reason.

WRONG	Brent arrived by plane this morning, and, John will arrive by train tomorrow.
RIGHT	Brent arrived by plane this morning, and John will arrive by train tomorrow.

Between a Subject and a Verb

Do not use a comma to separate a subject and a verb. A pair of commas, however, may set off nonrestrictive elements between the subject and the verb.

Wrong | In the late nineteenth century, a Japanese man named Jigoro Kano, developed judo, a sport similar to wrestling.

Right | In the late nineteenth century, a Japanese man named Jigoro Kano developed judo, a sport similar to wrestling.

Avoid using a comma to salvage a sentence that has a long, awkward subject; rewrite the sentence instead.

Poor | That Jigoro Kano studied techniques from many schools of martial art and incorporated them into his judo, is an interesting fact.

Better | An interesting fact is that Jigoro Kano studied techniques from many schools of martial art and incorporated them into his judo.

Integrated Quotations

Do not use a comma to set off a quotation that functions as the subject or predicate noun of a sentence.

Subject | "The sands of time are sinking" is the beginning of a hymn.

Predicate Noun | A favorite invitation hymn is "Just As I Am."

Like other restrictive appositives, a quotation that functions as a restrictive appositive is not enclosed by commas.

The motto "In God We Trust" is stamped on our coins.

Dates

Do not set off a year with commas when it appears with only a month (no date).

Wrong | In May, 2013, James and Susan visited missionaries in Cambodia.

Right | In May 2013 James and Susan visited missionaries in Cambodia.

12.9 PRACTICE *the skill*

Rewrite the following letter, adding any missing commas and omitting any unnecessary commas.

Dear Crispin

Greetings from the beautiful city of Venice Italy! Tradition says the city was founded on March 25 421. Jean and I are quite thrilled with the atmosphere of romance that fills the hot and busy streets. She actually said "I think we should come back here someday," a statement that is quite encouraging, considering that travel is not always her favorite occupation. I spend my time gazing at scenery and people; my sister at a map and travel brochures. She and I are going to visit Saint Mark's Square tomorrow, and possibly take a gondola ride. Almost everything here is just thrilling! (The humidity I could do without.)

Yesterday we visited the Rialto. I could almost hear that character in *The Merchant of Venice* saying, "What news on the Rialto?" as we walked across. And do you remember how Frank Griswold, MD used to say that the world is being taken over by tourists? Today the famous bridge is covered with stores, mostly souvenir shops. Nonetheless, Jean, and I are thoroughly enjoying our stay.

Sincerely

Gwendolyn

12.10 REVIEW *the skill*

Rewrite the following paragraph, omitting any unnecessary commas and adding any missing end marks and commas. There are ten errors.

The history of modern tourism, reaches back several centuries. In Europe it was traditional in the late eighteenth century, and in the nineteenth century for an upper-class young man to tour the Continent upon completing his studies. "Travel . . . is a part of education," was the rationale, as Francis Bacon put it. The Germans called this a *Wanderjahr,* or travel year; the British referred to it as the Grand Tour. As time went on, people began to travel to gain experience, to broaden their knowledge, and to see the world. With the arrival of World War I in June, 1914, many American soldiers found themselves overseas and later took their families to visit the same places. From that point on, there has been no turning back. People have come to love travel. Inexpensive it is not; today the tourism industry grosses about $104 billion yearly for the United States alone, and, Americans spend about $76 billion per year on tourism themselves. Some travel to visit family and friends; others to see new places. Perhaps some travelers feel as R. L. Stevenson did when he said "For my part, I travel not to go anywhere, but to go. I travel for travel's sake"

Semicolon

Use a semicolon to join equal units that require a mark of punctuation stronger than a comma but weaker than a period.

Between Two Independent Clauses

Use a semicolon between two closely related independent clauses not joined by a coordinating conjunction. The second clause often reinforces the first. A transitional word often appears within the second independent clause. When the second clause is introduced by a conjunctive adverb, place a semicolon before the conjunctive adverb and a comma after it.

Compound Sentences p. 132

> The high school cooking class prepared several varieties of pizzas for the reception; pepperoni pizza will probably be everyone's favorite.
>
> The girls in the class assumed many of the preparation duties; the boys, however, also assisted.
>
> The girls in the class assumed many of the preparation duties; however, the boys also assisted.

Independent Clauses p. 116

Before a Conjunction in a Long Compound Sentence

Use a semicolon instead of a comma before a coordinating conjunction that joins two independent clauses when the clauses have interior commas.

> One cookie recipe required a variety of ingredients, including two cups of flour, four eggs, and two cups of chocolate chips; but we had only three eggs.

Comma with Conjunctive Adverb p. 308

Between Word Groups Containing Commas

Use a semicolon to separate a series of coordinate phrases when any of the phrases contain internal commas.

> In the cooking class were the senior class president, Cindy Stormer; the junior class vice president, Jim Meadows; and the junior class treasurer, Adam Miller.

Use semicolons instead of commas when a list is introduced by a colon and has entries that are somewhat long.

> Preparations for the school-wide reception were delegated to a number of people: freshmen and sophomore students made plans and decorated the gymnasium; juniors designed and printed the invitations and decorated the food tables; and seniors planned and prepared the food.

Use a semicolon to separate Bible references whenever a new chapter is mentioned.

> A recent chapel speaker spoke from Titus 2:1–8, 12; and 3:8.

Colon

A colon separates elements almost as definitely as the period. A colon emphasizes what follows as important, explanatory, or more specific. Except in certain expressions, such as Bible references, a complete independent clause must precede the colon.

Punctuation | Chapter 12 **315**

In Bible References and Expressions of Time

Use a colon between the chapter and verse in a Bible reference and between the hour and minutes in an expression of time. Do not put a space after the colon in either case.

1 Timothy 4:12

10:00 p.m.

After a Salutation of a Business Letter

Use a colon after the salutation of a business letter.

Dear Senator Graham:

Underlining for Italics p. 337

Between a Book Title and a Subtitle

When you refer to a book by both its title and its subtitle, use a colon followed by a space between the title and its subtitle even if no punctuation appears on the title page of the book itself.

Children of the Storm: The Autobiography of Natasha Vins

Before a Series at the End of a Sentence

Use a colon to introduce a series that follows a complete independent clause. Do not use a colon when the series is a part of the basic sentence structure, such as a complement or the object of a preposition.

WRONG	The senior class trip will include: the Library of Congress, the Lincoln Memorial, and the Washington Monument.
RIGHT	The senior class trip will include the Library of Congress, the Lincoln Memorial, and the Washington Monument.
RIGHT	The senior class trip will include these popular sites: the Library of Congress, the Lincoln Memorial, and the Washington Monument.
RIGHT	The senior class trip will include the following: the Library of Congress, the Lincoln Memorial, and the Washington Monument.

The words *such as, for example,* and *including* should not be followed by a colon.

They also hope to visit some other interesting places, such as the Smithsonian Institution, the Bureau of Engraving, and the National Archives Building.

Use a colon for emphasis to introduce a single appositive at the end of a sentence.

One of the most interesting exhibits in the Smithsonian Institution's gem section is also one of its most beautiful: the blue Hope diamond.

Before a Long or Formal Direct Quotation

Use a colon before a long or formal direct quotation if the introduction is a formal statement and if the quotation appears at the end of the sentence.

The guidance counselor reiterated the words of Thomas Paine: "Reputation is what men and women think of us; character is what God and angels know of us."

Between Two Independent Clauses

Use a colon between two independent clauses without a coordinating conjunction when the second clause is an explanation of the first independent clause.

The students showed great interest in the Revolutionary War era of America: they chose to read Thomas Paine's *Common Sense*.

316 Chapter 12 | Punctuation

12.11 PRACTICE *the skill*

Write the letter of the sentence that exhibits correct use (or better use) of semicolons and colons.

_____ 1. A. Dear Travel Light Travel Agency;
       B. Dear Travel Light Travel Agency:

_____ 2. A. I am writing to inquire about your international services for the following reason; my family is planning a trip to Australia.
       B. I am writing to inquire about your international services for the following reason: my family is planning a trip to Australia.

_____ 3. A. The following is a list of our desires for the trip: we would like to stay three weeks in Australia and Tasmania; we wish to stay in comfortable hotels that provide breakfast, a swimming pool, and a hotel safe; and we want to experience as much as possible of Australia's beauty and culture.
       B. The following is a list of our desires for the trip; we would like to stay three weeks in Australia and Tasmania, we wish to stay in comfortable hotels that provide breakfast, a swimming pool, and a hotel safe, and we want to experience as much as possible of Australia's beauty and culture.

_____ 4. A. My wife hopes to see some examples of native crafts; she is especially interested in aboriginal art.
       B. My wife hopes to see some examples of native crafts: she is especially interested in aboriginal art.

_____ 5. A. I understand from the book *Antipodean Splendor, The Wonders of Australia* that Ayers Rock, or Uluru, is a place not to miss: this spectacular red monolith is 9.4 kilometers in circumference.
       B. I understand from the book *Antipodean Splendor: The Wonders of Australia* that Ayers Rock, or Uluru, is a place not to miss: this spectacular red monolith is 9.4 kilometers in circumference.

_____ 6. A. Do tours of Uluru begin as early as 7:00 a.m.?
       B. Do tours of Uluru begin as early as 7 : 00 a.m.?

_____ 7. A. We would also like to visit Shipwreck Coast and see the stones called the Twelve Apostles; however, if that is impossible, we will gladly spend some time on Kangaroo Island.
       B. We would also like to visit Shipwreck Coast and see the stones called the Twelve Apostles: however, if that is impossible, we will gladly spend some time on Kangaroo Island.

The Twelve Apostles

_____ 8. A. During our visit to Tasmania, we hope to see Cradle Mountain-Lake St. Clair National Park, which contains both ancient rainforests and alpine territory; or we could visit Lake St. Clair itself.

B. During our visit to Tasmania, we hope to see Cradle Mountain-Lake St. Clair National Park, which contains both ancient rainforests and alpine territory, or we could visit Lake St. Clair itself.

_____ 9. A. We plan two specific activities in Sydney, attending a performance at the architecturally wondrous Opera House and climbing the Sydney Harbour Bridge.

B. We plan two specific activities in Sydney: attending a performance at the architecturally wondrous Opera House and climbing the Sydney Harbour Bridge.

_____ 10. A. For our last stop before leaving the Land Down Under, my family would like to spend a few days sailing and scuba diving in the region of the Great Barrier Reef, diving at the reef has long been a dream of ours.

B. For our last stop before leaving the Land Down Under, my family would like to spend a few days sailing and scuba diving in the region of the Great Barrier Reef: diving at the reef has long been a dream of ours.

12.12 REVIEW *the skill*

Insert any necessary semicolons and colons. If the sentence is correct, write C in the blank.

_____ 1. Travel is not only for sightseeing; it can also be a way of serving the Lord.

_____ 2. The Bible includes several instances in which God commanded His servants to travel to spread His Word Jonah went to Nineveh to deliver God's warning the young prophet of 1 Kings 13 1–34 came to Jeroboam to prophesy judgment and Philip went south to Gaza to speak with the Ethiopian eunuch.

_____ 3. According to tradition, Thomas went quite far in his efforts to preach Christ crucified the tradition says that he arrived in India in AD 52 and preached to some of the leading Brahmin families.

_____ 4. Many examples of biblical missionaries exist however, the apostle Paul's ministry is probably the most obvious example of traveling to spread the gospel.

_____ 5. In Acts 13:46–47 18:6 and 19:21, Paul expresses his desire and intent to go and preach the gospel among the Gentiles.

_____ 6. And in 1 Corinthians 9 16, he makes a dramatic statement about his calling "Woe is unto me, if I preach not the gospel!"

_____ 7. On his first three missionary journeys, Paul visited—respectively—Salamis, Paphos, and Iconium; Syria, Cilicia, and Lystra; and Ephesus, Asia, and Troas.

_____ 8. He also employed several methods of travel by foot, by ship, and by basket.

_____ 9. Paul even preached during his last recorded journey when in a shipwreck on the way to Rome, he testified of God's power to the sailors and soldiers.

_____ 10. No matter where or how he was traveling, Paul never lost an opportunity to spread the gospel to everyone around.

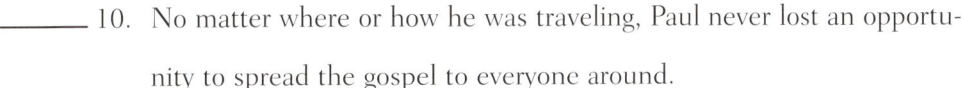

12.13 CUMULATIVE *review*

Correct the twenty errors in the following paragraphs by crossing out any incorrectly capitalized words and writing the correction above and by inserting any missing end marks, commas, semicolons, and colons.

In Matthew 28 19–20 the Lord commands "Go ye therefore and teach all nations." The greek participle for *go* carries the idea of "having gone"; in other words Christ was telling his disciples and, by extension, all Christians, "Having gone into all the world, preach." It is assumed one has already gone therefore, in one sense a person does not need to take an explicit missionary trip in order to be a missionary. The International traveler regularly comes into contact with various unsaved people. Before leaving home, the traveler can prepare for the trip spiritually one way to prepare is to gather tracts in the language of the country of destination. Becoming familiar with the culture and language shows the tourist's genuine concern for the people, customs, and nationality of the country and it often makes citizens more willing to talk to foreigners. Even just letting people know that one is a Christian and behaving in a Christlike manner is a witness. A thoughtful sensitive traveler will bear in mind the country's customs and laws as he seeks to be a witness for Christ.

but what kinds of travel include an obligation to witness Foreign only No, travel within one's own country also provides opportunities to share the gospel. A seatmate on an airplane a waitress in a Restaurant and a person in line at a store or amusement park all need to hear God's Word. Other avenues of witness include the following a bus, taxi, or shuttle driver the attendant at a gas station where a traveler fills up and the cashier at a scenic attraction's gift shop Whether traveling domestically or abroad, whether for a week or a year, any Christian anywhere can and should reflect to the world the glory of his Lord.

FROM THE WRITTEN WORD

Developing a Plan

Everyone has at some time analyzed a problem or a course of action. If you have spent time in a kitchen producing a chocolate creation that would please any chef only to have the cake fall flat, you were faced with a problem that needed to be analyzed before it could be corrected.

Perhaps you have explained why a particular football play or basketball defense has worked—or not worked—as it was intended. Perhaps you explained why your team tried unsuccessfully to gain possession of the football with an onside kick at the end of the game. Maybe you have explained the success of a box-in-one defense for a basketball game. In either case you were showing how that particular part of the game fit with the other parts of the game.

Analysis seeks to divide a topic or study into its parts and to show how and why these parts contribute to success or failure. By analyzing 2 Chronicles 31, you can discover why Hezekiah was successful as a king.

> And thus did Hezekiah throughout all Judah, and wrought that which was good and right and truth before the Lord his God. And in every work that he began in the service of the house of God, and in the law, and in the commandments, to seek his God, he did it with all his heart, and prospered. (2 Chron. 31:20–21)

How did Hezekiah achieve such success? Why did he do the things that he did? The *why* is explained in a single statement: Hezekiah sought to do that which was right in the sight of the Lord. The *how* involved several ideas. Read carefully 2 Chronicles 31. Then analyze how Hezekiah achieved his purpose.

Personal Response

Read Proverbs 3:1–12. The writer admonishes his son to obey. The Scriptures are for our admonition as well. The *why* in Proverbs 3:1–2 is the promise of a peaceful, long life. What, then, are the *how*'s? Based on this passage, write a paragraph that shows how you would secure this promise.

Response to Dramatic Scene	324
More Punctuation	329
Think About It	353

Response to Dramatic Scene Writing
More Punctuation Usage

When you see a play, many elements demand your attention: the sets, the costumes, the actors' voices, the music, the action, perhaps even some smells. Reading a dramatic scene can be a very different experience—no lights or sound cues to pull you in. You, the reader, must respond to the words and ideas themselves. That response can reveal something about you. The following piece was written by a student after a reading of the sleepwalking scene from Macbeth *by William Shakespeare. Notice how the author inserts her own beliefs about Lady Macbeth and her tormented sleep into the response. Later you will respond to a dramatic scene that has made an impression on you.*

Infected Minds *by Lachelle Berkins*

Near the end of Shakespeare's *Macbeth,* Lady Macbeth is awakened by guilt for her part in King Duncan's murder. Her nocturnal wanderings provide some of Shakespeare's most memorable scenes, for who has read her pleas for the removal of the bloodstains and envisioned the wringing of her hands without also feeling the tug of his own conscience for prior deeds? Shakespeare takes pains to make Lady Macbeth's sleepwalking scene especially meaningful. The significance of the scene is found in its use of sensory details, the fitness of the judgment to the crime, and the reminder for the reader that no one can escape the effects of conscience.

Sensory details used throughout make the scene significant: all of the senses but taste are used. Sight imagery—or a lack of sight—is an important part of the sleepwalking scene. Lady Macbeth demands that a light be near her all the time (5.1.20), and she carries a candle, even though she does not see (21–22). The reader watches her rise and write and return to bed through the words of the gentlewoman. Lady Macbeth's voice is the major sound in the scene. One can almost hear the pathos of her haunting "Yet here's a spot" and "Out, I say!" (5.1.26, 29). As Lady Macbeth repeatedly rubs her hands, we both hear and feel the action of the wringing. Her requests for water also seem to force the reader to feel the scouring. The perceived smell of blood on her hands makes Lady Macbeth cry, "All the perfumes of Arabia / will not sweeten this little hand" (5.1.42–43).

Second, I find Lady Macbeth's sleepwalking appropriate to her crime because she has disrupted the sleep of others. In the play sleep represents a respite from worldly cares: Macbeth describes sleep as "innocent" (2.2.33) and "knit[ting] up the ravell'd sleave of care" (2.2.34) and as the "balm of hurt minds" (2.2.36). Banquo, Duncan, and the two attendants—the innocents—all seek sleep or are sleeping in Act 2 before the murder. After Macbeth announces that he has "done the deed" (2.2.14), that is, murdered Duncan as he slept, he predicts that "Macbeth shall sleep no more" (2.2.40). The couple fears the sleepy servants, and Lady Macbeth takes the daggers

Thinking Biblically

Have you ever watched a movie, stage play, or musical and wondered afterwards, "What did that mean?" Sometimes valuable insights and profound themes in a creative work can be difficult to discern. A movie, for instance, may seem merely dark and cynical or hopeful and encouraging on the surface but, when inspected more closely, be complex and full of rich meaning. By examining a creative work closely, critics are able to produce very insightful writing that enhances a reader's understanding. The skill of critical analysis, like any other, requires practice. The Christian critic should be especially interested in developing his abilities because the Bible is a literary work full of dramatic scenes, profound themes, complex characters, and significant symbols. The Bible is not fictional drama, of course, but if "all the world's a stage," Christians know who the Playwright is. And His stories are rich with meaning. The story of Esther, for example, never mentions God by name—but a skilled reader will examine the details that point to Him.

to besmirch them with blood. Lady Macbeth is initially unmoved by the actions of the evening and rebukes her husband for his "brainsickly" thoughts (2.2.43) about the murder. She further determines that "a little water clears us of this deed" (2.2.64). For her part in the king's murder, Lady Macbeth is condemned to "slumb'ry / agitation" (5.1.9–10). And though she pleads with an unseen conversant, "To bed, to bed, to bed" (5.1.58), she will receive no profit from repose.

Lastly, the sleepwalking scene effectively reminds the reader that no one escapes the effects of a guilty conscience. Lady Macbeth seems fearful—of the darkness, of the blood ("who would have thought the old man to have had so much / blood in him?" [5.1.33–34]), of their unmerited royal positions, of her husband's guilty reactions, and of dead Banquo. Guilt for her deed makes her attempt to escape the delusive knocking near the end of the scene ("Come, come, / come, come, give me your hand" [5.1.56–57]), for guilty persons "flee when no man pursueth" (Prov. 28:1). Guilt makes her seek sleep, for there she believes she may "discharge [her] secrets" (5.1.63). But sleep will be as elusive to her as to any other guilty person. Perhaps most effective—and most disturbing for the reader—is the realization that a guilty person is blind to the obviousness of his guilty actions. Lady Macbeth walks in darkness, but she is seen by others in the light. The gentlewoman and the doctor observe her easily and remark openly about her condition. This resembles the guilty person who thinks that no one but he knows what he has done. The Bible comments on man's deeds being seen when it states that "all things are naked and opened unto the eyes of him with whom we have to do" (Heb. 4:13).

Shakespeare's extraordinary deftness with detail and his knowledge of human behavior make him a master storyteller. Our senses are stirred, our demand for justice aroused, and our consciences prodded as we watch Lady Macbeth's nocturnal pacings. Perhaps Shakespeare gave us Lady Macbeth to help us understand what comes from trying to cover up our sin.

Response to Dramatic Scene

> For the word of God is quick, and powerful, and sharper than any two-edged sword, piercing even to the dividing asunder of soul and spirit, and of the joints and marrow, and is a discerner of the thoughts and intents of the heart.
>
> *Hebrews 4:12*

It's one thing to say that you like something. It's another to be able to say why. And it is important to be able to say why. We should be able to defend our opinions and to make good judgments, judgments based on reason and knowledge as well as emotion. Articulating positions well using textual evidence as support is an important skill not only in writing but also in life. The piece you will write for this chapter will force you to analyze your response to a piece of drama and to support that response from the text of the dramatic scene.

Choose a scene from a play and write a thoughtful response to it. You may choose to respond to the scene from David Burke's "This Same Jesus," found in Chapter 6, or you may respond to part of another play.

Planning

✓ **Choose your scene.** Start with a play you enjoy or are familiar with. Then look for a key moment in the play or a moment that you find especially interesting. The sleepwalking scene from *Macbeth* is a good choice for students who have read the play because of the scene's universal theme and striking imagery.

> **tip**
> Make a copy (for personal use only) that you can mark up. Then write impressions and questions in the margins. Underline or circle important images or themes that you notice as you read.

✓ **Re-read the scene.** If you have time, re-read the whole play to set the scene in context. Read the scene itself at least twice: once for flow and again for details. Read as many times as necessary to become familiar with the wording and details.

✓ **Take notes.** As you read, mark or write down anything that stands out to you. In preparing to write her essay on Lady Macbeth, Lachelle Berkins might have noted that Lady Macbeth keeps a candle with her all the time, acts as though she is washing her hands, and speaks of blood. In her notes, then, she could see how many times and in what ways Shakespeare appeals to the senses in the scene.

✓ **Select an aspect to analyze.** Now that you've read the scene several times and taken notes of your impressions, look for common threads among your reflections. One student noticed the significance of windows—both literal [stained glass] and figurative [a person's testimony] in "This Same Jesus" and decided to write about how the scene establishes man as a window to those around him. Think about what you learned in Chapter 6 about characters, conflict and resolution, plot, and setting. Ask yourself about each element: Is there anything unusual or repeated about one or more of these elements? Are any names—places or people—meaningful on a figurative level? What about the various elements might be considered universal? In addition, examine the theme of the piece and decide how the author reveals the theme in that scene. Look at the following notes about the window idea mentioned above.

> Windows:
> - The whole focus of this scene (and the whole play) is Adonis's fixing the windows. He's just finishing up as the scene starts.
> - Both Dan & Adonis admire them.
> - comment on storm's passing/getting sun soon
> - wife looked out
> - noticed windows every time he visited her grave
> - Adonis talked to his wife about the windows he was working on.
> - uses phrase "restorations in churches"—SIGNIFICANT?

✓ **Decide on a thesis.** Your thesis must state something about the scene that would not be readily apparent to the casual reader. For example, the point this thesis makes may not be obvious to everyone: "The significance of the [sleepwalking] scene is based on its use of sensory details, the fitness of the judgment to the crime, and the reminder for the reader that no one can escape the effects of conscience." On the other hand, a thesis like the following would be so easy to prove that no one would want to read the paper: "Lady Macbeth is guilty of

murder." Anyone who has seen or read the play would certainly yawn at that opening. Your thesis will probably do one of the following:
- analyze a problem in the text
- support an arguable position from the text
- examine a personal view of the text

Outlining pp. 6–8

✔ **Develop an outline.** Look again at your notes. Organize the details into categories of related items. Look at the items within each group. How are they connected? Express those connections in a phrase or a sentence. These ideas will become your topic sentences.

✔ **Write out your thesis and topic sentences.** They should be complete, declarative sentences. The content of the thesis and the topic sentences should be the main ideas of the paper and the paragraphs.

Lachelle Berkins went through several drafts of her thesis before deciding on the one you see above. First, she wrote,

> There are a lot of senses used in the sleepwalking scene, and the judgment fits the crime exactly since Lady Macbeth interrupted the sleep of others, and no one can escape their own conscience.

She decided that the wording of her thesis was weak and that she was presenting some of the information that belonged in the body of the paper too early. She then drafted the following statement:

> The significance of the sleepwalking scene is found in its use of sensory details, the fitness of the judgment to the crime, and reminding the reader that no one can escape the effects of conscience.

After reading her revised thesis, Berkins realized that all that was needed was to make the three points parallel. Her final thesis became

> The significance of the [sleepwalking] scene is found in its use of sensory details, the fitness of the judgment to the crime, and the reminder for the reader that no one can escape the effects of conscience.

✔ **Organize your topic sentences.** Use this strategy: put your strongest point last, your second strongest point first, and any other points between those. You want your paper to end with convincing power. Why do you think Lachelle Berkins chose the order she did for her paper?

✔ **Fill in the outline with supporting details.** Use specifics from the scene. Remember that for your conclusion you will also need a clear restatement of your thesis.

tip
Make your restatement a true restatement—not a simple repeat of the thesis. You can emphasize the purpose of your paper with an effective restatement.

Drafting

✔ **Use your outline to write a rough draft.** Berkins unified her paragraphs by keeping the topic sentences always in mind. She did not add unnecessary details or comments but rather kept directing her proofs and explanations back to the point at hand. Likewise, you should link your sentences together logically, drawing the reader's attention from point to point, adding proof as you go.

✔ **Include information from your notes.** The notes you took in the planning stage will be useful now. If you wrote directly on a copy of the text, consult those notes for quotations and ideas you want to include in your response.

✓ **Integrate quotations into your response.** To bolster your arguments or analysis, you will need to include direct quotations from your dramatic scene. To do so correctly, you must incorporate the quotation seamlessly into your own text. Look at the following possible use of a quotation.

> Lady Macbeth is initially unmoved by the actions of the evening and rebukes her husband by saying, "Why, worthy thane, / You do unbend your noble strength, to think / So brainsickly of things" (2.2.41–43).

Although technically correct, the incorporated quotation is cumbersome and includes more than Berkins wanted to highlight. Berkins's quotation below takes only the pertinent information—in this case one word—and blends it directly into the text.

> Lady Macbeth is initially unmoved by the actions of the evening and rebukes her husband for his "brainsickly" thoughts (2.2.43) about the murder.

Berkins's first quotation above does show the proper way to quote lines of poetry. (Most of the text of Shakespeare's plays is written in verse.) When quoting lines of poetry (three or fewer) that are incorporated into a paragraph, use a slash mark with a space before and after it to represent line division. The word following a slash mark should be capitalized or lowercased as it appears in the original. For longer quotations (four or more lines), indent the entire quotation and omit the quotation marks. Remember, too, that any changes made to a direct quotation must be noted by brackets.

> There she believes she may "discharge [her] secrets" (5.1.63).

(The original is "discharge their secrets.")

Quotation Marks, Ellipses, and Brackets pp. 329, 335–36

✓ **Include biblical allusions.** Berkins quotes from Hebrews 4:13 in her comments about guilty consciences. An appropriate Bible verse used in context often encapsulates a complex theme and forces the reader to think beyond the actual text.

✓ **Beware of textual distortion.** It is tempting to take quotations and information about the text out of context just to prove a favorite point. Integrity demands that you deal honestly with the text and with the author's intent. Be careful not to twist meanings as you write. Additionally, never take credit for work that is not your own—either in idea or in wording. Doing so makes one guilty of **plagiarism,** a serious offense that is considered to be stealing another's work.

✓ **Write a good opening paragraph.** Notice how Berkins started her paper close to the point she wanted to make. She did not give a summary of the whole play or speak of guilt in general. She began with Lady Macbeth's sleeplessness and referred only to background pertinent to the scene. The opening also engages the reader, giving him reason to read on.

Introductions and Conclusions pp. 10–13

tip
Include in your introduction the title and the author of the piece you will discuss.

✓ **Write a solid closing paragraph.** Do not let the last paragraph be a simple mirror image of the first. The reader no longer needs background; he now needs to understand how this new perspective benefits him. Berkins implies for the reader that, like Lady Macbeth, everyone will be accountable for his sins.

Revising

✔ **Read over your rough draft.** Do you notice any places where the proof or the explanation is missing or weak? Rewrite these passages, making your arguments precise and well supported. You may need to add more details from the scene to prove your points, or you may need to make the explanation clearer or more logical.

Here is the rough draft of Berkins's second paragraph.

> There are lots of sensory details used throughout to make the scene significant: all of the senses but taste are used in abundance. Sight images—or lack of them—are throughout. Lady Macbeth demands that a light be near her all the time (5.1.20), and she carries a candle (5.1.21–22). The reader watches her get up and write on a paper and go back to bed along with the gentlewoman of the scene. The sound of Lady Macbeth's voice is the major sound in the scene. And her words are haunting when she keeps referring to the spot. Lady Macbeth repeatedly rubs her hands, and it seems as though we both hear and feel the action of the wringing. Her repeated requests for water to wash her hands with. The smell of blood on her hands makes Lady Macbeth cry, "All the perfumes of Arabia will not sweeten this little hand. O, O, O!" (5.1.42–43).

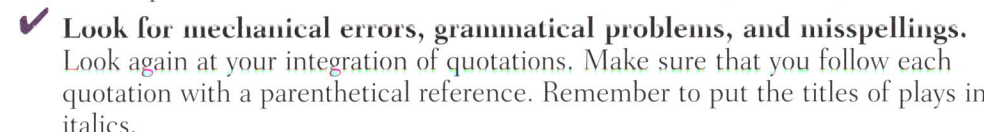

Berkins does not give enough explanation of her points to show the reader how the sensory details of the scene are significant. In her second draft she also corrects several problems of redundancy and lack of precision. Look again at the final draft:

> Sensory details used throughout make the scene significant: all of the senses but taste are used. Sight imagery—or a lack of sight— is an important part of the sleepwalking scene. Lady Macbeth demands that a light be near her all the time (5.1.20), and she carries a candle, even though she does not see (21–22). The reader watches her rise and write and return to bed through the words of the gentlewoman. Lady Macbeth's voice is the major sound in the scene. One can almost hear the pathos of her haunting "Yet here's a spot" and "Out, I say!" (5.1.29). As Lady Macbeth repeatedly rubs her hands, we both hear and feel the action of the wringing. Her requests for water also seem to force the reader to feel the scouring. The perceived smell of blood on her hands makes Lady Macbeth cry, "All the perfumes of Arabia / will not sweeten this little hand" (5.1.42–43).

Quotation Marks and Underlining for Italics pp. 329–30, 337

✔ **Look for mechanical errors, grammatical problems, and misspellings.** Look again at your integration of quotations. Make sure that you follow each quotation with a parenthetical reference. Remember to put the titles of plays in italics.

Publishing

✔ **Title your work.** For this type of essay, the best title ideas often come from the work being studied. Think about your thesis and the message of your response. Then look for a quotation or part of a quotation from the scene that corroborates your message.

✔ **Share your essay with your class.** If possible, obtain a visual recording of a performance of the drama you have discussed and play your topic scene for the class. Following the scene, read your critical response to it.

✔ **Display your essay on a bulletin board.** If your school has a speech and drama room, ask for permission to display your class responses in that room. Near the display, leave a pile of blank note cards and an empty box with a note inviting other students who use the room to read your responses and to write their own comments about particular essays. These comments provide feedback to help you see whether your arguments were convincing to someone else.

Some Ideas to Consider

History
- Find a play review from the late 1800s or early 1900s. Compare the style and content to what you might write today.

Journalism
- Write a review of a play for the Arts section of the newspaper.

MORE PUNCTUATION

End marks and commas, the most frequently used marks of punctuation, aid us in understanding the meanings of sentences. In addition to these, other marks of punctuation further help to clarify meaning for the reader and the writer. Without these additional markers, clear understanding would be difficult.

Quotation Marks

Direct Quotations

Quotation marks indicate the exact words of a speaker or writer. Do not use quotation marks for indirect quotations, words that report the idea of the speaker or writer but not the exact words. Quotation marks always occur in pairs.

DIRECT	Sunday's sermon text was Philippians 2:25: "Yet I supposed it necessary to send to you Epaphroditus, my brother, and companion in labour, and fellowsoldier."
	I commented as we left, "I had never thought about these ideas before."
	"Yes, Paul must have valued Epaphroditus's friendship greatly," my brother said.
INDIRECT	Philippians tells us the kind of person that Epaphroditus was.
	I said that I had never thought about these ideas before.
	My brother said that Paul must have valued Epaphroditus's friendship greatly.

tip Remember to be accurate and honest when you are quoting another person's work. Place direct quotations in quotation marks. If you are summarizing or paraphrasing, use your own words, your own organization, and your own sentence structure without quotation marks. (See also page 266.)

Writer's Toolbox

When the dialogue tag appears in the interior of a sentence, enclose the tag with commas, not with quotation marks. Use quotation marks to enclose the two parts of the quoted material.

> "You can read further about Epaphroditus," the preacher said, "in Philippians chapter four."

Well-known proverbs (including certain biblical sayings) are often not enclosed with quotation marks.

> Jerry remembered his grandmother's admonition to waste not, want not.

tip

A prose quotation that is more than four typed lines or a poetry quotation of more than three lines is not enclosed in quotation marks. Instead, the quotation begins on a new line and is indented one inch. The parenthetical citation occurs at the end of the quotation. If you choose to use one of these long quotations, be sure that the quotation is relevant and fits smoothly into the text of your paper.

Dialogue

Use quotation marks to enclose the words of each speaker and begin a new paragraph whenever the speaker changes.

> Johanna asked, "Did you purchase all the ingredients that we need for the cookies?"
>
> "I bought everything that I thought we might need," Sheila answered.

Do not use quotation marks for the speeches of characters within a play when the speeches are formatted as a script.

BANQUO	How goes the night, boy?
FLEANCE	The moon is down; I have not heard the clock.
BANQUO	And she goes down at twelve.
FLEANCE	I take't, 'tis later, sir.

William Shakespeare, *Macbeth*, Act 2, Scene 1

Titles of Short Works

Titles
p. 282

Use quotation marks to enclose the titles of short works. A work is considered a short work if it would not stand alone as a published work. Examples of short works are articles, chapters of a book, short stories, essays, songs, and most poems. Use quotation marks for the titles of individual episodes of radio or television programs.

> "Give of Your Best" is an article that challenged me to be more unselfish.
>
> Edgar Allan Poe wrote "The Cask of Amontillado."
>
> John Newton's "Amazing Grace" is a favorite song of many Christians.

Quotation marks are not used to indicate the major subdivisions of the Bible.

> The Sunday morning sermon was from the thirty-second chapter of Genesis in the Old Testament.

The titles of historical or political documents such as the Constitution and the Gettysburg Address are not enclosed in quotation marks. In addition, quotation marks are not used with a title when the title stands as the heading of the work itself.

> **tip**
> Do not put the title of your own paper in quotation marks on the title page or on the first page of the paper.

Words Used in a Special Sense

Occasionally, it is permissible to use quotation marks to indicate that a word is used in a special sense. It is better, however, to revise the sentence to clarify the meaning. (Do not use quotation marks around a word that is used in its normal sense.)

ACCEPTABLE	My favorite "low-calorie" chocolate milk shake was on sale this afternoon.
BETTER	My favorite chocolate milk shake made with skim milk was on sale this afternoon.

Quotation marks may be used to indicate words or expressions that are noticeably more formal or more informal than the rest of the passage. Although an occasional use of a slang word may seem effective, it is better to avoid slang expressions and maintain a consistent level of usage.

ACCEPTABLE	The exhausted college student felt like an "airhead" after a late night of studying.
BETTER	The college student was mentally exhausted after a late night of studying.

Quotation Marks and Other Punctuation

In American usage commas and periods appear before adjacent quotation marks, but colons and semicolons appear after closing quotation marks.

"The players are meeting for an important practice session," the principal announced.

He then said, "The student council will meet as well."

The cheerleaders composed a new closing line for the school song "Fighting Swordsmen": "Give it all your might!"

The student council wrote "Swordsmen Are on the Top"; the new cheer will be introduced at the championship game.

End Marks
pp. 296–98

Commas
pp. 301–12

Semicolon and Colon
pp. 315–16

Question marks and exclamation points may appear inside or outside closing quotation marks, depending upon the meaning of the sentence. If the quotation itself is a question or an exclamation, the mark of punctuation goes inside the closing quotation marks. If the entire sentence, but not the quotation itself, is a question or an exclamation, the mark of punctuation appears outside the closing quotation marks.

Have you read Abraham Lincoln's "Thanksgiving Proclamation"?

"Wasn't Lincoln's thankful spirit during the time of war unusual?" asked the young history student.

"Oh, look at our Thanksgiving dinner!" squealed the child.

Look carefully at the examples. If a question word (*who, when, where,* etc.) or a subject-verb inversion (*Have you, Was he,* etc.) is inside the quotation marks, then the question mark should also be inside the quotation marks.

> **tip**
> The placement of the dash in relation to quotation marks follows the same guidelines as given for the question mark and exclamation point.

Only one mark of punctuation appears at a time with quotation marks. When a speaker tag, for example, follows a question, the question mark alone—without a comma—separates the question from the tag.

> **ESL** When a quotation tag follows the quotation, it is spoken with the same rise or fall as the quoted sentence. (See page 70.)
>
> | | |
> |---|---|
> | **QUOTED STATEMENT** | "Thanksgiving is a time to thank God for His blessing," ↓ she said. ↓ |
> | **QUOTED QUESTION-WORD QUESTION** | "When did it begin?" ↓ I asked. ↓ |
> | **QUOTED YES/NO QUESTION** | "Is it always in November?" ↑ I asked. ↑ |

Single Quotation Marks

Use single quotation marks when quotation marks are necessary within other quotation marks. The rules that govern other marks of punctuation in relation to double quotation marks apply to single quotation marks also.

"Did you hear Brittany say, 'What song should we sing?'" asked Austin.

"Could we sing 'We Gather Together' for our Thanksgiving program?" the children asked.

"Yes, it will fit well with our theme from 1 Thessalonians 5:18: 'In every thing give thanks,'" the teacher answered.

13.1 PRACTICE *the skill*

Write the letter of the sentence that is correctly punctuated.

_____ 1. A. "Come, join us; the banquet is prepared," the rich count announced to his guests.
B. "Come, join us; the banquet is prepared", the rich count announced to his guests.

_____ 2. A. "The table," he exclaimed, "is spread with hundreds of dishes and bowls of fresh fruits"!
B. "The table," he exclaimed, "is spread with hundreds of dishes and bowls of fresh fruits!"

_____ 3. A. My brother said that he was not sure whether he would thoroughly enjoy a meal without potatoes.
B. My brother said that "he was not sure whether he would thoroughly enjoy a meal without potatoes."

_____ 4. A. "Loaded" Elizabethans dined twice a day: breakfast at eleven or twelve and supper at five or six.
B. Wealthy Elizabethans dined twice a day: breakfast at eleven or twelve and supper at five or six.

_____ 5. A. "My, my," shouted the guest at a water performance, "look at the actor riding the dolphin"!
       B. "My, my," shouted the guest at a water performance, "look at the actor riding the dolphin!"

_____ 6. A. Singers who sang Rose, Rose, Rose Red and Queen's Round might have provided entertainment for the feasts.
       B. Singers who sang "Rose, Rose, Rose Red" and "Queen's Round" might have provided entertainment for the feasts.

_____ 7. A. Meals of the common man were not nearly as elaborate.
       B. Meals of the "common" man were not nearly as elaborate.

_____ 8. A. "Did you hear the count ask, 'And when do you eat?" asked the servant.
       B. "Did you hear the count ask, 'And when do you eat?'" asked the servant.

_____ 9. A. "Elizabethan noblemen," I read, "loved hospitality and had guests on a regular basis."
       B. "Elizabethan noblemen," I read, "loved hospitality and had guests on a regular basis".

_____ 10. A. The nobleman commanded, "Give the leftovers first to the servants and then to the poor people outside the gates!"
        B. The nobleman commanded, "Give the leftovers first to the servants and then to the poor people outside the gates"!

More Punctuation | Chapter 13

13.2 REVIEW *the skill*

Insert any missing single quotation marks or double quotation marks. Circle any unnecessary quotation marks. Use the transpose symbol (∩) to indicate the correct placement of any misplaced periods, commas, question marks, exclamation points, colons, and semicolons.

1. "Have you ever thought about the kinds of snack foods that existed in Elizabethan England"? the lecturer asked.

2. "Was it John who said, 'They probably didn't have any?" I asked.

3. I think that chocolate, a thin and bitter drink at the time, had only "medicinal" purposes.

4. The lecturer continued by saying "that at this time the Swiss had not yet added milk and sugar to chocolate."

5. He also said, The English had delicious marzipan, fruit pies, and puddings.

6. "Did you know that the English enjoyed a cheesecake dessert"? I asked.

7. One student commented, "I can't believe that the English enjoyed, of all things, pretzels and bagels"!

8. "Vanilla was not a flavoring of that time", the lecturer explained, but almond flavoring was very common."

9. Another student asked, "Was sugar available"?

10. The lecturer answered, "Yes, it was available;" then he explained that it was more expensive than honey.

Ellipses

Ellipsis marks, or points, either indicate the omission of something in a quoted passage or signal halting or unfinished speech. Use three spaced dots or periods with a space before the first and after the last.

Omission of Words in a Quotation

Use ellipses to indicate the omission of one or more words from a quoted passage. Be careful not to change the meaning of the passage when you omit the words.

ORIGINAL	"Know ye that the Lord he is God: it is he that hath made us, and not we ourselves; we are his people, and the sheep of his pasture. Enter into his gates with thanksgiving, and into his courts with praise: be thankful unto him, and bless his name." (Ps. 100:3–4)
WITH OMISSIONS	"Know ye that . . . we are his people, and the sheep of his pasture."

When you are quoting from multiple sentences, use a period followed by three spaced dots to indicate the omission of the end of the preceding sentence or the omission of the beginning of the following sentence. The new quotation must be a complete thought, and the first word of the second sentence must be capitalized, regardless of whether it was capitalized in the original.

> The psalmist wrote, "Know ye that the Lord he is God. . . . Be thankful unto him, and bless his name."

Use a full line of spaced dots to indicate the omission of one or more lines of poetry when the poem is formatted in stanzas.

ORIGINAL	The King of love my Shepherd is, Whose goodness faileth never; I nothing lack if I am His And He is mine forever.
WITH OMISSIONS	The King of love my Shepherd is, ... I nothing lack if I am His And He is mine forever. From "The King of Love My Shepherd Is" by Henry W. Baker

Halting or Unfinished Speech

Use ellipses to indicate hesitant pauses in speech. Use a period followed by ellipses to indicate unfinished speech that trails off gradually.

> The young child began his part in the program: "'Make a joyful noise unto the Lord' . . . oh . . . I can't remember the next. . . ."

Brackets

Brackets may resemble parentheses in appearance, but brackets cannot be used interchangeably with parentheses. Brackets indicate an addition to a quotation or a change in a quotation.

Dashes
p. 347

Insertion or Replacement in a Quotation

The reader must be able to distinguish your words from the words of the person being quoted. Use brackets to indicate your own words whether they add to, replace, or correct the quoted material.

ORIGINAL	"Many of those who became settlers had been frustrated when the Church of England embraced aspects of the Reformation while continuing several Roman Catholic practices. Christians quickly discovered that their king was not interested in fully implementing the work of the Reformation. As a result, they looked on the New World as a haven where they could establish communities and complete the Reformation. This reason for settlement distinguished the colonial heritage of the United States from that of new colonies established in other regions." from UNITED STATES HISTORY, Fourth Edition, by Timothy Keesee and Mark Sidwell (BJU Press, 2012) [p. 25]
ADDITION	"Christians quickly discovered that their king was not interested in fully implementing the work of the [Protestant] Reformation."
REPLACEMENT	Keesee and Sidwell write, "As a result, [settlers] looked on [America] as a haven where they could establish communities and complete the Reformation."

Replacing Parentheses Inside Other Parentheses

Though seldom needed, brackets are used as parentheses inside other parentheses. It is better, however, to rewrite the sentence or to give the additional information in a footnote or endnote.

> In the early sixteenth century, Europe saw changes in established religion (the Roman church departed further from some of its basic doctrines [one being the authority of Scripture]) and experienced a spiritual depression.

Error in Original

At times you may find it necessary to quote a passage that contains an error or some unconventional usage. In order to identify the error or the unconventional usage, you have two options. You may replace the error with your own correction enclosed in brackets or add the Latin word *sic* ("thus" or "such") enclosed in brackets immediately after the word or phrase in question to indicate that you have quoted the text accurately. (Although the word *sic* [a foreign word] has become common in English, documentation standards require it to be italicized.)

Underlining for Italics
p. 337

INDICATION OF ERROR	"Each believer should read their [sic] Bible daily."
	"The report identified numerous problems between you and md [sic]."
CORRECTION	"Each believer should read [his] Bible daily."
	"The report identified numerous problems between you and m[e]."

Underlining for Italics

Use italic print to indicate the titles of books or other long works and for other specialized uses. In a handwritten paper, underlining indicates that a word should be italicized.

HANDWRITTEN	<u>Free Indeed</u> presents biographical sketches of notable black American ministers.
PRINTED	*Free Indeed* presents biographical sketches of notable black American ministers.

Titles of Long Works

Use italics for the titles of long literary or musical works.

Titles
p. 282

BOOKS	My sister enjoyed reading *Suncatchers* by Jamie Langston Turner.
PERIODICALS	What was today's lead article in the *Wall Street Journal*?
NEWSPAPERS	The *Los Angeles Times* reported the newest presidential candidate's bid for the presidency.
MUSICAL COMPOSITIONS	Donizetti's opera *Lucia di Lammermoor* will be presented at the local university next month.
TELEVISION OR RADIO SERIES	Do you remember the radio program *The Lone Ranger*?
EPIC POEMS	The British Library in London houses the epic poem *Beowulf*.
PLAYS	Does Shakespeare's *Richard III* reveal the problems of England at that time?

Works of Art

Use italics for the names of visual works of art.

The sculpture *Pieta* by Michelangelo can be seen in St. Peter's Basilica in Rome.

Giuseppe Chiari's painting *The Return from the Flight into Egypt* is part of the museum's collection.

Large Vehicles

Use italics for the names of specific large vehicles, but not for a class of vehicles.

Transportation
p. 274

SHIPS	A visit to the USS *Yorktown* will provide historical insights into the Battle of the Pacific.
AIRCRAFT	The first B-2 or stealth bomber was the *Spirit of Missouri*.
TRAINS	The *Crescent Limited* follows a route from New York City to New Orleans.
SPACECRAFT	*Endeavour* has traveled on a mission to the space station.

Words, Letters, and Numerals Being Discussed

Use italics for words, letters, and numerals that you are discussing as words.

The British spelling adds the *a* in *paediatrician*.

Be sure to cross all of your *t*'s to avoid spelling mistakes.

The children practiced dividing by *12*s during math class last week.

Foreign Words and Phrases

Use italics for unfamiliar foreign words or phrases in an English sentence. If the foreign word or phrase is an entry in an English-language dictionary, it does not need italics. Use quotation marks instead of italics if the entire sentence is written in a foreign language.

NO ITALICS	Chef Schopf was a bona fide master in his field.
ITALICS	Some toddlers are the epitome of an *enfant terrible*.
QUOTATION MARKS	During Sunday school the Spanish children enjoyed singing, "Cristo me ama, me ama a mí."

Special Emphasis

Use italics only occasionally to emphasize a particular word or phrase. It is generally better to achieve emphasis by placing the word or phrase at the end of the sentence.

>Many people *think* that politics is a necessary evil.

>The idea that politics is a necessary evil has become a part of people's thinking.

PRACTICE *the skill*

Insert any missing ellipses or brackets in each numbered item. If the item is already punctuated correctly, write C in the blank.

From the Reformation until the eighteenth century, English Protestants did not use hymns in their church services. Instead, they sang rhymed settings of the Psalms, believing that church music should be drawn directly from Scripture. Many of these psalm settings, however, were poorly written and hard to sing. Determined to improve the music in his own congregation, a minister named Isaac Watts (1674–1748) began to write hymns. Although at first many Protestants of all denominations rejected this "innovation," Watts persevered in his efforts. He is known today as the Father of English Hymnody.

Churchgoers in the early eighteenth century did not have hymnals; therefore, the pastor or someone else had to read the lines of the psalm or hymn aloud. After each line was read, the congregation would sing it, and then the reader would proceed to the next line. Therefore, Watts ensured that each line of his hymns made sense when read by itself.

>Joy to the world! the Lord is come;
>Let earth receive her King;
>Let every heart prepare him room,
>And heaven and nature sing.

adapted from *World History*, Fourth Edition, by Dennis Bollinger (BJU Press, 2013)

_____ 1. "From the Reformation until the eighteenth century, English Protestants did not use hymns in their church services."

_____ 2. "Instead English Protestants sang rhymed settings of the Psalms."

_____ 3. "They believed that church music should be drawn directly from Scripture."

_____ 4. "Determined to improve the music in his own congregation, Isaac Watts (1674–1748) began to write hymns."

_____ 5. "Although at first many Protestants rejected [his hymns], Watts persevered in his efforts."

_____ 6. "[Isaac Watts] is known . . . as the Father of English Hymnody."

_____ 7. "Churchgoers in the early eighteenth century did not have hymnals After each line was read, the congregation would sing it."

_____ 8. "The congregation would sing [one line], and then the reader would proceed to the next line."

_____ 9. "Each line of Watts's hymns made sense when read by itself."

_____ 10. "Joy to the world! the Lord is come;
. . . .
Let every heart prepare him room,
And heaven and nature sing."

13.4 PRACTICE *the skill*

Underline each word that should be italicized. If the sentence is already correct, write *C* in the blank.

_____ 1. The Enlightenment, or Aufklärung, encouraged widespread learning in England.

_____ 2. The eighteenth century Royal Navy consisted of merchant ships that had been equipped for war.

_____ 3. One such ship, HMS Northumberland, transported Napoleon into exile on St. Helena.

_____ 4. Periodicals such as The Tatler by Richard Steele had an appeal to both men and women and contained essays on various topics.

_____ 5. In 1702 the Daily Courant became London's first daily newspaper.

_____ 6. In addition to these publications that focused on news events, other writing was also popular in England.

_____ 7. John Dryden's first play, The Wild Gallant, was a failure, but Dryden soon became a successful writer.

_____ 8. John Locke was one of many oil portraits by Sir Godfrey Kneller.

_____ 9. In England many arts flourished during the eighteenth century.

_____ 10. Did you by any chance watch the educational television special entitled The Life of William Shakespeare?

John Locke

13.5 REVIEW *the skill*

Write the letter of the sentence that is punctuated correctly.

_____ 1. A. My brother enjoys listening to "The Lone Ranger" radio program.
B. My brother enjoys listening to *The Lone Ranger* radio program.

_____ 2. A. Did you know the man who played "Brutus" in Shakespeare's *Julius Caesar*?
B. Did you know the man who played Brutus in Shakespeare's *Julius Caesar*?

_____ 3. A. In Paris, France, my family enjoyed seeing the *Mona Lisa* in the Louvre Gallery.
B. In Paris, France, my family enjoyed seeing the Mona Lisa in the *Louvre Gallery*.

_____ 4. A. While we were eating at "Brewster's Bagels," we saw a man reading the *New York Post*.
B. While we were eating at Brewster's Bagels, we saw a man reading the *New York Post*.

_____ 5. A. The Cub Scouts visited "Patriot's Point," where the aircraft carrier *Yorktown* is located.
B. The Cub Scouts visited Patriot's Point, where the aircraft carrier *Yorktown* is located.

_____ 6. A. The famous oratorio *Messiah* is often performed during the Christmas season.
B. The famous oratorio "Messiah" is often performed during the Christmas season.

_____ 7. A. It is sometimes difficult to remember to include the correct number of *s*'s in Mississippi.
B. It is sometimes difficult to remember to include the correct number of *s*'s in Mississippi.

_____ 8. A. The professor stood before the class and said, "Tomorrow we will continue. . . . oh, let's go on to another topic."
B. The professor stood before the class and said, "Tomorrow we will continue . . . oh, let's go on to another topic."

_____ 9. A. The theme of "Great Expectations," a novel by Charles Dickens, is that love and loyalty are more important than self and ambition.
B. The theme of *Great Expectations*, a novel by Charles Dickens, is that love and loyalty are more important than self and ambition.

_____ 10. A. "Traditional Home" magazine has many useful and cost-effective tips for home decorating.
B. *Traditional Home* magazine has many useful and cost-effective tips for home decorating.

Apostrophe

Use apostrophes to indicate omissions, possessives, and plurals.

Omission

Use an apostrophe to indicate the omission of letters and numbers in contractions or other shortened forms of words or phrases.

I will — I'll
have not — haven't
class of 2007 — class of '07

Be careful to distinguish between the possessive pronoun *its* and the contraction *it's* (for *it is* or *it has*).

POSSESSIVE | The new bicycle is not roadworthy; its tire is flat.
CONTRACTION | The new bicycle has a flat tire; it's not roadworthy.

ESL

Some contractions with **not** change the spelling of the main word slightly.
will + not = **won't**
can + not = **can't**

Some words, such as *may* and *ought*, are rarely contracted with *not*. The contractions would be understood by a native English speaker, but they would sound formal or old-fashioned. Avoid *mayn't* and perhaps *oughtn't*.

Possession

Add the *'s* to show possession for most singular nouns and indefinite pronouns. (Use only the apostrophe after the traditional exceptions *Jesus* and *Moses*.)

Possessive Nouns p. 35

Terry's motorcycle helmet has a design different from the design on his brother's helmet.

Someone's motorcycle helmet was left in the parking lot of the gymnasium.

Several members of the motorcycle club enjoy reading Dickens's writings.

Add an apostrophe to plural nouns ending in *s* or *es*.

The motorcycle riders' goal was to collect one thousand toys that day.

Several businesses' goal was to help distribute the toys to needy children.

For plural nouns that do not end in *s*, add an *'s*.

Several motorcycle riders saw the children's response of gratitude.

Jessica worked many long hours to prepare the women's part for the program.

More Punctuation | Chapter 13

To indicate that two or more people own something together, add 's to the last noun. To indicate separate possession, an 's should be added to each noun or pronoun.

> Organizing the distribution of the toys was Mark and John**'s** responsibility.
>
> Brian**'s** and Stephen**'s** ideas for gifts were quite different.

Special Plurals

Plural Nouns
pp. 35–36

Although regular nouns do not use an apostrophe to indicate plurals, *'s* is used for the plural of an italicized letter or word being discussed. An apostrophe is not necessary to form the plurals of numbers, symbols, and dates.

> All the children shouted repeated *yes***'s** to the teacher's suggestion that they have a party.
>
> During the late 1990**s** stock prices advanced.

Hyphen

Use the hyphen to join parts of a word or to join separate words.

Omission of Connecting Words

Use a hyphen in place of a single connecting word to replace words such as *to* or *through*. Do not use a hyphen to replace one of a pair of connecting words such as *from* and *to* or *between* and *and*.

WRONG	This series of messages on Philippians 3:1-7 will last **from** September-November.
RIGHT	This series of messages on Philippians 3:1-7 will last September**-**November.
	This series of messages on Philippians 3:1-7 will last **from** September **to** November.
WRONG	Pastor Brooks will change the theme of his messages **between** December 1-December 31.
RIGHT	Pastor Brooks will change the theme of his messages December 1-December 31.
	Pastor Brooks will change the theme of his messages **between** December 1 **and** December 31.

Word Division at the End of a Line

Use a hyphen to divide a word at the end of a line. The hyphen appears at the end of the line, not at the beginning of the next line. Do not divide the word unless you can meet all three of these guidelines.

1. Divide a word only between syllables. If the word does not have at least two pronounced syllables, do not divide it.
2. Leave at least two letters and the hyphen on the first line.
3. Carry over at least three letters to the second line.

> Listening intently to Pastor Brooks's message, Charles felt deep conviction in his heart.

Compound Constructions

Use a hyphen in **multiword numbers** from twenty-one through ninety-nine when they are spelled out.

> Luther's *Ninety-Five Theses* challenged the sale of indulgences, calling their sale a corrupt practice.

> One hundred sixty-five dollars was the amount on the check.

Use a hyphen in spelled-out **fractions** unless either the numerator or the denominator already contains a hyphen.

> Nearly three-fourths of the team became ill with the flu virus.

> Three and one-half cups of flour are necessary for the cake recipe.

Use a hyphen when a **prefix** such as *all-*, *ex-* (meaning "former"), *half-*, or *self-* is added to a word. Prefixes such as *non-* and *anti-* are permissible in either style; however, the trend is toward making these words solid.

> Matthew 28 reveals the all-inclusive task for believers.

> Hamilton was an ex-waiter who became the restaurant manager.

Use a hyphen when a prefix comes before a number, a proper adjective, or a proper noun.

> The pre-2002 stock market showed consistent gains.

> The post-Christmas day sales offered many desirable bargains.

Hyphens are also necessary to distinguish a word with a prefix from another that is spelled similarly.

> The re-creation of the housing committee made everyone happy.

> The recreation building will be completed within six months.

Use a hyphen in certain **compound words**.

> John's father-in-law provided him numerous power tools to aid in building the addition.

> The three-year-old tried to act more like his older brother.

Compound Nouns p. 36

Use a hyphen in **multiword modifiers**. When two or more words function as a single unit to modify a following noun, hyphenate the temporary compound.

> His all-or-nothing approach to the game gave him an added competitive edge.

> Her tea-length dress was quite appropriate for the reception.

Words with a Common Element

If two or more hyphenated words have the same final element, that element should be omitted from all but the last word. Hyphenate and space the words as follows:

> The fans attended all the pre- and post-game events.

> The soccer team hopes to have a first- or second-place finish.

13.6 PRACTICE the skill

Underline each word that contains a mistake in the use of apostrophes or hyphens.

1. Hugh Latimer (c. 1492 1555), a brilliant preacher of the Tudor Renaissance Era, possessed an all consuming desire to proclaim Christ in an England that was still suffering the effects of pre Reformation darkness.

2. It wasnt until Latimer was a thirty year old that he became truly convinced of the theological positions of the Reformers: His Bachelor of Divinity thesis, an anti Reformation treatise, had attacked the doctrines of a prominent reformer named Philip Melanchthon.

3. However, Latimers thesis prompted a godly individual named Thomas Bilney to diligently share the gospels truth with Latimer.

4. Thomas Bilney and Hugh Latimers doctrinal beliefs differed significantly initially; however, Bilneys repeated "What saith the Scripture?" gradually brought Latimer to a full understanding of the gospel.

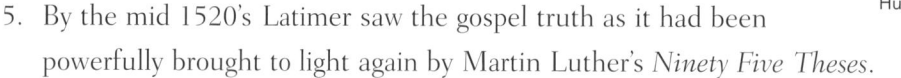
Hugh Latimer

5. By the mid 1520's Latimer saw the gospel truth as it had been powerfully brought to light again by Martin Luther's *Ninety Five Theses*.

6. Perhaps youve heard of Latimers famous homily entitled "Sermon of the Plough": it's text from 1 Peter 5:8 warns all believers of the devils self evident strategy—seeking whomever he may devour.

7. Ephesians 6:10 18 provides the believer with the spiritual weapons needed not only during Satans attacks but also in pre and post trial living.

8. Latimers work to promote an English translation of the Bible gained him the common citizens's appreciation yet Cardinal Thomas Wolseys censure.

9. In light of the fact that he served under monarch's Henry VIII, Edward VI, and Mary I, its amazing that Latimer never forgot that having Jesus' approval mattered far more than having theirs.

10. Such a strong stance for gospel truth resulted in Latimers imprisonment on various occasions and his eventual martyrs death, but it was because of God's all sufficient might that Latimer endured his tribulations and passed on into glory.

PRACTICE *the skill*

Insert any missing apostrophes or hyphens. If the sentence is already correct, write C in the blank.

_____ 1. During the Tudor period, the sermons literary merit increased drastically.

_____ 2. As language and thought developed in this period, so did mans ability to use that language.

_____ 3. Though this time period brought great development to the sermon, it brought with it great persecution.

_____ 4. Robert Barness sermon against Cardinal Wolsey earned Barnes a conference with Wolsey.

_____ 5. Barnes was persuaded to recant but escaped to Germany 2 3 years later.

_____ 6. With the support of Henry VIII, Barnes traveled freely between Germany and England pre-1540 until he was executed as a heretic.

_____ 7. Others in the same movement also were outspoken against the pa pacy.

_____ 8. Hugh Latimer thundered against such vile blasphemies as the venera tion of images and the practice of indulgences.

_____ 9. He was eventually tried, and he stood powerfully on Gods word.

_____ 10. There are several stories of the Reformation and pre Reformation similar to this one, many written with great power and truth.

Cardinal Wolsey

REVIEW *the skill*

Rewrite the paragraph, correcting the ten errors in the use of apostrophes and hyphens.

The tourists couldnt believe that English kitchens had changed very little from the fifteenth-seventeenth centuries. Castle kitchens had any number of unfamiliar cooking utensils or cooking locations. Noblemen had well equipped kitchens, and their's were filled with brass and copper utensils. In the kitchen, most likely, was a posnet, a three legged container with a metal handle, used for boiling. A gridiron was a utensil of parallel metal bars for broiling fresh fish over a fire. Additional rooms were part of the kitchen area. A pastry room had a kneading trough and a baking oven that may have been one half the size of the room. An additional area called the bolting house was a place for sifting bran or coarse meal. The meat room contained ovens with spits for roasting deer, pheasant, wild boar, or rabbit. In addition to the meat-room, there may have been a larder, a closet sized room for storing meat. Some cooking utensils would be familiar to us today. Chafing dishes, graters, mortars and pestles, knives, and frying pans are among the many items in pre and post Elizabethan kitchens.

Dash

The dash—about twice as long as the hyphen—is used to separate, to emphasize, and to indicate an abrupt change in thought. The dash is a rather informal, yet strong, mark and should be used sparingly.

Certain Sentence Elements

Use a pair of dashes to separate an **interrupting phrase or clause** from the remainder of the sentence.

> Her chocolate cake creation—with three kinds of chocolate—won first prize in the baking contest.
>
> A beautiful sight—and I mean beautiful—is the colorful mountain leaves during the fall season.

Commas with Nonrestrictive Elements
p. 308

Use a pair of dashes to separate an **internal appositive series** from the remainder of the sentence. When an appositive series contains three or more elements that are separated from each other by commas, a pair of dashes is necessary to signal the beginning and the ending of the appositive.

> My brother's favorite sundae toppings—hot fudge sauce, nuts, and whipped cream—are available at the dessert bar.
>
> Other dessert possibilities—peach pie, sugar cookies, and butterscotch pudding—are also available.

Use a dash to connect an **introductory list** to a grammatically complete **summary statement** after it.

> Hot fudge sauce, nuts, and whipped cream—all are delicious sundae toppings.
>
> Peach pie, sugar cookies, and butterscotch pudding—these are not temptations for me.

Colon Before a Series
p. 316

tip

Remember that you do not use a period or comma next to a dash.

Emphasis

On occasion you can use a dash to give special emphasis to a phrase or clause that appears at the end of a sentence. Use dashes sparingly to emphasize material so that they will not lose their effectiveness.

NORMAL PUNCTUATION	My uncle's car is a new production car, a car with style, class, and speed.
EMPHATIC	My uncle's car is a new production car—a car with style, class, and speed.

Interrupted Speech

Use a dash or pair of dashes to indicate various speech interruptions.

FALTERING SPEECH	"Dad, I didn't mean—um—I mean—I will try to do better in the future."
ABRUPT BREAKING OFF OF A SENTENCE	"Son, you must try harder—if you want to use the car," his father said.
	"But, Dad, I—" the young son implored.
ABRUPT CHANGE OF THOUGHT	Looking carefully through his wallet, James said, "But officer, I thought—oh, here, I found it."

Ellipses
p. 335

Parentheses

Like quotation marks, parentheses appear in pairs. Parentheses enclose additional information that is relatively unimportant.

Supplementary Elements

Use a pair of parentheses to enclose additional, or explanatory, information.

His next sermon (the third in the soulwinning series) will be tomorrow.

His last message was his best. (He seemed to reach the hearts of the students.)

Placement of Other Punctuation with Parentheses

Usually end marks, commas, semicolons, and colons go outside parentheses. If the material enclosed by parentheses is a complete thought, the period goes inside the closing parenthesis. If the parenthetical material itself is a question or an exclamation, the question mark or exclamation point goes inside the closing parenthesis.

Tax returns were reviewed by the Internal Revenue Service (IRS).

Our last tax return (did you do yours?) seems to be without error.

We have a refund (how wonderful!) coming this year.

> **tip**
> A parenthetical sentence that is not enclosed within another sentence should begin with a capital letter and should have end punctuation inside the final parenthesis.

A parenthetical source note in a paragraph follows the general rules because it is considered to be part of its sentence. However, if the quotation itself is a question or an exclamation, punctuate the quotation appropriately and then place a period after the parenthetical source note.

The preacher reminded us again to "go . . . into all the world, and preach the gospel to every creature" (Mark 16:15).

At Christ's trial before Pilate, Pilate asked, "Shall I crucify your King?" (John 19:15).

Numbers or Letters That Identify Divisions

Use a pair of parentheses to enclose numbers or letters that indicate divisions within a sentence.

Your exercise program should include (1) the warm-up, (2) the workout, and (3) the cooldown.

You should participate in one of the following exercise programs: (a) water aerobics, (b) walking, or (c) low-impact aerobics.

> **tip**
> Be sure to separate the items of the list within the sentence with commas or semicolons.

Comparison of Parentheses with Pairs of Commas and Dashes

Pairs of commas, dashes, and parentheses set off extra information in a sentence. **Commas**, the normal, neutral punctuation, set off short phrases and clauses. **Dashes**, though less formal, indicate to the reader that the enclosed material is important. On the other hand, **parentheses** show the reader that the enclosed material is relatively unimportant. The writer can achieve a particular emphasis by using these marks of punctuation appropriately.

Maintaining good health, as I said yesterday, requires an exercise program.

Maintaining good health—as I said yesterday—requires an exercise program.

Maintaining good health (as I said yesterday) requires an exercise program.

Periods with Lists
p. 297

Commas
pp. 301–2

Semicolons and Colons
pp. 315–16

Commas with Restrictive, Nonrestrictive Elements
p. 308

13.9 PRACTICE *the skill*

Insert any missing parentheses or dashes.

1. Hampton Court Palace it has enclosed tennis courts, a famous garden maze, and paintings from the Royal Collection has a fascinating history.

2. When Cardinal Wolsey built Hampton Court Palace for himself in 1525, he spared no expenses expenses paid out of King Henry VIII's coffers.

3. In response to Henry VIII's grumbling that Wolsey lived better than he, Wolsey stammered something like "Of course uh all these lands belong to thee, O King."

4. Henry VIII took Wolsey at his word and confiscated Hampton Court Palace. It came with 500 employees and 1,000 rooms.

5. Catherine of Aragon, Anne Boleyn, Jane Seymour, Catherine Howard, and Catherine Parr all lived at one time or another at Hampton Court Palace.

6. Inspired by France's Versailles and Louvre, Sir Christopher Wren have you heard of him? remodeled Hampton Court Palace in the late 1600s.

7. The works of various master painters Holbein, Lely, and Tintoretto may now be viewed at Hampton Court, thanks to a more recent addition to the palace: air-conditioned galleries.

8. A turn about the gardens of Hampton Court may provide more horticultural delight than you bargained for sixty acres' worth!

9. Henry VIII's unique clock displaying the hours, days, months, lunar phases, and tides at London Bridge remains a popular attraction at Hampton Court.

10. Although Hampton Court displays some of the finest craftsmanship ever to belong to men, we must remember Scripture's admonition: "For what shall it profit a man, if he shall gain the whole world, and lose his own soul?" Mark 8:36.

13.10 REVIEW *the skill*

Combine the following sets of sentences by using commas, parentheses, or dashes. You may reword the sentences slightly and incorporate other punctuation if necessary.

1. Much of the music of the Baroque period has an almost dancelike sound to it. It is light, and it is often played on a harpsichord.

   _____
   _____
   _____
   _____
   _____

2. The major musicians of the Baroque period include Johann Sebastian Bach, Arcangelo Corelli, and Antonio Vivaldi. They all composed in the Baroque style with different emphases.

   _____
   _____
   _____
   _____
   _____

3. Many instruments were played during the Baroque period that are not played often today. These include the lute, sackbutt, viol, and harpsichord.

   _____
   _____
   _____
   _____
   _____

4. The lute is a stringed instrument, similar to the guitar. It is plucked by the player's fingers.

   _____
   _____
   _____
   _____
   _____

5. The sackbutt is a brass instrument. Although it is similar to the trombone, it produces a softer sound that beautifully complements the harpsichord.

6. The viol is an instrument similar in some respects to the cello, but in many other ways very different. It rests not on the floor but on the knees of the instrumentalist.

7. The viol emits a clear, penetrating sound when it is played. The bow of the viol is convex, not concave.

8. Another instrument of the Baroque period is the harpsichord. In appearance, the harpsichord is very similar to the piano.

9. The strings of the harpsichord are plucked when the keys are pressed. The result is a clear note that can be heard above the other instruments, producing a beautiful effect.

10. The music of the Baroque period utilizes many unfamiliar instruments. The music remains some of the most popular in the world.

13.11 CUMULATIVE *review*

Rewrite the following paragraph, correcting the twenty errors in capitalization and punctuation. (Punctuation marks used as a pair are counted as a single error.)

Catherine Parr the last wife of Henry VIII was possibly the strongest in character of all his wives. She was first offered in marriage to Lord Scropes noble son when she was only twelve years old. However a condition was discovered in the will of her father that prevented her ever marrying him. Eventually she married Edward Lord Borough of Gainsborough but did not live with him until she was fourteen He died in 1529 however, and she returned to the royal court of Henry VIII. She met with her second husband at court functions, and they were married he at the age of forty two and she at the age of nineteen. He was John Neville, lord latimer. The two of them came under suspicion and were almost executed during the controversy over anne Boleyn and Thomas Cromwell. after Neville died, she entered into a relationship with Thomas seymour, brother of the late Queen. This relationship was ended by Henry VIII, who then began his courtship of catherine. Eventually they were married, and Catherine became more like a nurse to the King than a wife for he was by then quite old. She was instrumental in the presentation of the royal family as a strong family; this strength impressed foreign ambassadors when they came to the court. Her great interest in protestantism almost cost her dearly, when she was accused of having ties with heresy. However she avoided prosecution as a heretic by her behavior at a public court function. Of all of Henrys wives, she was perhaps his most loved, and at his death she became a wealthy dowager queen.

THINK ABOUT IT

Problem Solving

By now you know much about critical thinking. You know the difference between what to think and how to think. You know how to analyze information to discern the author's or speaker's purpose and message. You can tell the difference between subjective and objective viewpoints and between fact and opinion. You know to evaluate the logic of an argument and to examine the evidence before making a decision. But a critical thinker must do more than just analyze the statements of others. A critical thinker should be able to solve problems in everyday situations.

The ability to solve problems is a skill that relies on the mastery of other thinking skills. Everything you know, every fact you have learned, every skill you have mastered, every talent that you possess—all of these are valuable tools to assist you in your problem-solving efforts.

A key factor in problem solving is the ability to think inductively. The logic problems that we analyzed in an earlier chapter rely on deduction: making a particular application from general principles. Induction, on the other hand, draws a general principle from particular instances. Inductive thinkers begin with what they already know and form principles from that knowledge. For example, scientists employ induction when they draw conclusions (general principles) from the results of observation and experimentation (particular instances).

Likewise, a critical thinker can form a hypothesis and predict what is likely to happen in a given situation. A hypothesis, of course, is more than just a guess; it is an informed opinion, an "educated guess" based on previous observation and experience or knowledge of universal principles. If you know that you usually need thirty minutes to get ready in the morning, you will not arrange your schedule to allow only twenty minutes of preparation. Your experience allows you to predict that twenty minutes will likely be inadequate.

When you are presented with a problem to solve or alternatives from which to choose, consider the situation carefully. What information do you already have about the possible solutions? Are any events from your past similar to the current situation? What universal principles apply? What does Scripture say about the issue? When your analysis is complete, take the information that you have gathered, form a hypothesis for each alternative, and predict the likely outcomes for those alternatives. Then you will be ready to make an informed decision.

Thinking It Through

Are you a critical thinker? Consider a recent decision you have made or a problem you have solved. Analyze the strategies that you used in that situation. Are you satisfied with the outcome? Should you have handled the situation differently? Write about your findings.

Writing Strategies | 355
History of the English Language | 393

WRITING STRATEGIES Composition   14

By now you are familiar with the four stages of the writing process. You have written a number of pieces in which you focused on specific writing strategies to help make your writing stronger. In this chapter you will study further the sometimes difficult ideas of variety, emphasis, and logic. Strategies such as these will separate extraordinary writing from that which is ordinary. As you study each topic, take time to look back at the various literary models in Chapters 2–13. Note how each author manipulates words and sentences to make each say exactly what is intended. You too can use language to your advantage when you follow certain guidelines.

Sentence Variety and Emphasis

As a writer, you have the opportunity to create sentences that emphasize (or de-emphasize) whatever you wish and that engage your readers from beginning to end. This chapter will instruct you in methods of manipulating words, phrases, clauses, and sentence types to ensure variety and to achieve emphasis.

Achieving Emphasis

The following general guidelines for achieving emphasis are ordered from least important to most important.

- **Use vivid verbs and strong nouns.** Do not rely on prepositions, adjectives, and adverbs to enliven your writing.

    | WEAK | Martin's shirt had a garlicky smell. |
    | STRONGER | Martin's shirt reeked of garlic. |

Parts of Speech p. 35

- **Place a short sentence before or after a series of longer sentences.** A reader can tire of reading long, complicated sentences, and too many of them in a row can distract him from your message. Brief sentences achieve emphasis. Unusual types of sentences can serve the same purpose. (See page 356.)

    > Gioacchino Rossini's version of the Cinderella story places the mistreated Cinderella in the household of a greedy stepfather and two pretentious half sisters. Cinderella is made to clean the ashes from the hearth and attend to the vain wishes of each member of the Magnifico family. When she hears of the Prince's upcoming ball, Cinderella begs her stepfather for leave to go, but he refuses her request. Then enters Alidoro. Disguised as a poor beggar, Alidoro, the Prince's own tutor, discovers the kind and beautiful Cinderella and promises her that she will indeed attend the ball.

Thinking Biblically

When Paul preached the gospel, he used both rhetorical flourishes and carefully constructed syntax—but he did not trust in these techniques to persuade his hearers (see Rom. 11:36). Paul's letters are full of beautiful, powerful, and often very personal writing. So why did Paul say, "Christ sent me . . . to preach the gospel: not with wisdom of words [or not with words of eloquent wisdom]"? He tells us why himself: "lest the cross of Christ should be made of none effect" (1 Cor. 1:17). Paul recognized that the power of the gospel does not depend upon man's words, no matter how eloquent. No, the gospel itself is powerful—because it is the Word of God. The gospel is His powerful message, which He has given man to deliver. To spread God's message effectively—with clarity and memorability—Christians should practice good writing and speaking, as Paul did. Man's words can be powerful when used well, but only God's Word holds supreme power—the power to save!

Inverted Subject and Predicate p. 71

Fragment pp. 135–37

- **Place the important word or phrase at the end of the sentence for natural emphasis.** Since these are the last words the reader will see, they are the words that he will remember the longest. A writer may accomplish this emphasis by moving phrases and adding clauses to place important ideas in strong positions.

EMPHASIS ON FILM VERSION	Rossini's *La Cenerentola* differs greatly from the Cinderella story made popular in the children's film version.
EMPHASIS ON *LA CENERENTOLA*	The Cinderella story made popular in the children's film version differs greatly from Rossini's *La Cenerentola*.
NORMAL EMPHASIS	The opera *Barbiere di Siviglia* was a great success for Rossini.
EMPHASIS ON *BARBIERE DI SIVIGLIA*	The opera that was a great success for Rossini was *Barbiere di Siviglia*.

Moving an idea other than the subject to the beginning of the sentence or clause gives a certain amount of emphasis also, albeit to a lesser degree.

> The singer saw the conductor, but the falling curtain she missed.
>
> Singing with her eyes closed, the soprano narrowly missed being hit by the weighted curtain.

tip

Do not overuse emphasis strategies: too much emphasis is as tiring as listening to someone shouting all of the time.

- **Include unusual types of sentences in your writing.** The following sentence types should be used only occasionally for effect and emphasis.

Sentence Type	Use	Example Sentence
Inverted sentence	Places a complement or a verb at the front of the sentence	A world-class golfer he was definitely not.
Periodic sentence	Fairly long sentence in which the main idea is not complete until the end	One may find in Prague, in addition to its quaint architecture, soaring cathedrals, numerous bridges, and final resting place of the legendary King Wenceslas, a city truly alive with history.
Rhetorical question	Question not meant to receive an answer	Who would want to eat liver? I prefer a thick, juicy steak.
Short fragment	Expresses emphasis or ironic afterthought	Everyone assumed that Maria knew the way back to the meeting place. Bad assumption.

tip

Avoid using an inverted sentence when the main verb is too far from the rest of the predicate.

14.1 PRACTICE *the skill*

Using the guidelines in parentheses, rewrite each sentence to improve emphasis.

1. Poodles come in colors other than the typical white, black, gray, and brown. Poodles' coats sometimes have peach or blue tints to them. *(rhetorical question)*

2. Poodles can perform a variety of tasks. They often served as water retrievers during the sixteenth century. *(important information at the end)*

3. The "Continental" style is the one you may automatically think of when you hear the word *poodle*. In this cut the dog's coat is immaculately styled with little muffs around the legs and the tip of the tail. *(periodic sentence)*

4. Many first-time poodle buyers wrongly suppose that smaller poodles, such as the miniature and toy varieties, have friendlier personalities than larger poodles. *(fragment)*

5. This variety of dog may weigh anywhere from three to sixty pounds. *(vivid verbs and strong nouns)*

14.2 USE the skill

Using the guidelines for proper emphasis, write a paragraph that answers this question: What type of animal makes the best pet?

_____
_____
_____
_____
_____
_____
_____
_____
_____

Varying Sentence Length and Complexity

Professional writers use a variety of short, medium, and long sentences to make reading their works easier and more interesting. Often, this strategy involves varying sentence complexity by using simple, compound, complex, and compound-complex sentences.

> Who invented and popularized some of America's favorite icons? Who designed the cartoons of Santa Claus, Uncle Sam, the Democratic donkey, and the Republican elephant? The answer may surprise you. One artist created all of these caricatures. Thomas Nast (1840–1902) was the son of German immigrants. He demonstrated remarkable artistic skill as a young man. He landed his first illustrator's position at the age of fifteen. Nast enjoyed a long and productive career of designing cartoons. This cartoonist was very effective in portraying his political messages. President Abraham Lincoln dubbed Nast the Union's "best recruiting sergeant" during the Civil War. Nast's pictures convey strong impressions. His images continue to communicate distinct messages today.

Though the first paragraph communicates the information, this second paragraph, implementing greater sentence variety, is much easier to read.

> Have you ever wondered who invented and popularized some of America's favorite icons? Consider famous cartoons such as the jolly, stout Santa Claus, the tall tailcoat-wearing Uncle Sam, or the quintessential Democratic donkey and Republican elephant. It may strike you as surprising, but one artist created all of these caricatures. Thomas Nast (1840–1902), the son of German immigrants, demonstrated remarkable artistic skill as a young man and even landed his first illustrator's position at the age of fifteen. Thus began Nast's long and productive career of designing patriotic, whimsical, and even scathing political cartoons. In fact, so effective was this cartoonist in portraying his message that President Abraham Lincoln dubbed Nast the Union's "best recruiting sergeant" during the Civil War. Nast's pictures convey strong impressions that continue to communicate distinct messages today.

Varying Sentence Patterns

What is true of grammatical sentence types is also true for sentence patterns: too much of one type makes for monotonous reading. Use a variety of sentence patterns as you write.

> In the years following World War II, Bette Nesmith Graham was an executive secretary during the heyday of electric typewriters. The trouble with these typewriters was their greater sensitivity to touch than the old manual typewriters. The secretaries were the creators of unsightly company documents covered with erasures. This woman was an amateur painter. She invented a shade of paint that matched her boss's stationery. She began painting over her typing errors with a fluid she dubbed "Mistake Out." The word among the secretaries in Graham's office was that Graham had a new invention. Soon Graham became the supplier for her time- and document-saving invention. She even became the founder of her own Liquid Paper company. She was the one to begin producing and marketing the product. Graham's business became a multimillion-dollar one. Had it not been for her practical problem-solving skills, people would not be the beneficiaries of those handy bottles, pens, and tape dispensers of white correction fluid.

Again, this second paragraph integrates a wider variety of sentence patterns, thereby achieving greater fluidity.

> In the years following World War II, Bette Nesmith Graham worked as an executive secretary during the heyday of electric typewriters. These typewriters had a greater sensitivity to touch than the old manual typewriters had. As a result, the secretaries kept producing unsightly company documents covered with erasures. Graham, an inventive woman and an amateur painter, simply mixed a shade of paint that matched her boss's stationery and began painting over her typing errors with a fluid she dubbed "Mistake Out." Word spread among the secretaries in Graham's office, and soon Graham began supplying orders of her time- and document-saving invention. In time, she even began her own Liquid Paper company to produce and market her product. What began as one woman's creative solution to a typewriter problem became a multimillion-dollar business. Had it not been for one woman's practical skills, people would not have the benefit of those handy bottles, pens, and tape dispensers of white correction fluid.

Sentence Patterns pp. 74–77

Varying Sentence Beginnings

Check your writing for the ways in which you begin your sentences and experiment with changing some of the beginnings for variety and effectiveness.

Phrases pp. 92–102

Clauses pp. 116–28

Possible beginning	Example sentence
Adverb modifiers	*Suddenly* and *noiselessly*, the gate shut.
Prepositional phrase	*Without warning*, a loud buzzing began.
Other phrases	*Trembling at the thought of being seen*, Jason tried to slip through the fence. (participial phrase)
	Knees knocking, he stared down the barrel of a flashlight. (absolute phrase)
Dependent clauses	*After the laughing stopped*, Jason realized he'd been caught still holding the "Happy Birthday" sign he'd meant to leave on the front door.

14.3 PRACTICE *the skill*

Rewrite the following paragraph, following the suggestions below.

¹Marian Anderson was a pioneer in the field of female music performance. ²She was African American by birth. ³Marian Anderson began her musical career by playing the violin. ⁴She soon focused on singing. ⁵She applied to a music school in order to develop her ability but was denied admission because of her race. ⁶With the encouragement and support of a local church, she was able to study under a professional teacher. ⁷Her career in the United States met with some disappointments. ⁸In 1925 she went to England and then to Europe. ⁹During the next ten years she developed into an accomplished performer. ¹⁰She returned to the United States. ¹¹She became a major box office draw. ¹²She, however, continued to meet opposition because of her race. ¹³The media's focus on her ability and not on her race was accomplished by her concert on the steps of the Lincoln Memorial in 1939. ¹⁴She eventually became the first African American to sing for the Metropolitan Opera. ¹⁵She is most often remembered for her rich contralto renditions of black spirituals. ¹⁶Dignity and perseverance characterized her career. ¹⁷She was a role model for succeeding generations.

1. Combine sentences 3 and 4 to add complexity.

   _____
   _____
   _____

2. Vary the beginning of sentence 5.

   _____
   _____

3. Combine sentences 7 and 8 for complexity.

   _____
   _____

4. Combine sentences 10 and 11 to show coordination of ideas.

   _____
   _____

5. Change the sentence pattern of sentence 13 to S-TrV-DO.

   _____
   _____
   _____

14.4 USE *the skill*

Write an original paragraph on your own paper. Vary your sentence patterns, sentence beginnings, and the length and complexity of the sentences. When you finish writing, answer the following questions about your paragraph.

1. How many sentences did you write? _____

2. Write down the number of times you used the following sentence patterns.

S-InV _____	S-LV-PA _____
S-TrV-DO _____	S-LV-PN _____
S-TrV-IO-DO _____	S-be-AdvI _____
S-TrV-DO-OC _____	

3. Write down the number of times you used each of the following sentence types.

simple _____	compound _____
complex _____	compound-complex _____

4. List the types of structures that begin your sentences. _____
   _____

5. How many different beginning structures did you use? _____

Choosing Between Constructions

As you look at a piece of writing, you may wish to make changes to improve variety or to change emphasis.

Active and Passive Voice pp. 187–89

Active or Passive

Active sentences are stronger and more direct than passive sentences. Where possible, eliminate unnecessary passive verbs from your writing.

TOO MANY PASSIVES | The first-place medal was awarded to Anja Bronner, whose entry, a pair of ceramic candlesticks, had been sculpted by hand.

BETTER | Anja Bronner won the first-place medal for her pair of ceramic candlesticks that she had sculpted by hand.

In certain instances (as in the following examples), the passive voice may be a better choice than the active. Know the situation and choose accordingly.

Situation	Active Sentence	Passive Sentence
Unknown or unimportant doer of action	Someone tested the water for harmful bacteria.	The water was tested for harmful bacteria.
Inconsistent subjects	The water technician asked how often the manager of the resort checks the pool's pH level. The manager told him that the employees check the pH level weekly.	The water technician was informed by the resort manager that the pool's pH level is checked weekly.
Awkwardly long subjects	Chlorine, chemical test kits, water clarifier, and algae treatments keep pools clean.	Pools are kept clean by chlorine, chemical test kits, water clarifier, and algae treatments.
New or important information not in position of emphasis	The lifeguards quickly noticed and rescued the floundering swimmer.	The floundering swimmer was quickly noticed and rescued by the lifeguards.

Sentence Pattern
S-TrV-IO-DO
p. 76

tip An occasional passive is permissible, and in some cases desirable. But when in doubt, use active voice.

Indirect Object or Prepositional Phrase

Any sentence containing an indirect object can be reworded to include a prepositional phrase. Note the change in emphasis between the two sentences.

WITH INDIRECT OBJECT	Lonnie gave the orphanage two bicycles.
WITH PREPOSITIONAL PHRASE	Lonnie gave two bicycles to the orphanage.

Prepositional Phrases
p. 88

Interchange these equivalent structures to put last the object that is longer or that you wish to emphasize.

14.5 PRACTICE *the skill*

Rewrite each sentence to give the emphasis indicated in parentheses.

1. A visit to the Shedd Aquarium in Chicago will be enjoyed by most families. (*Use active.*)

   _____

   _____

2. Built in 1929, the Shedd Aquarium offers visitors of every age many updated exhibits. (*Use a prepositional phrase to emphasize the visitors.*)

   _____

   _____

3. The Caribbean Reef, a 90,000-gallon aquarium, is inhabited by more than seventy species of animals, including sharks and stingrays. (*Use active instead of passive.*)

_____

_____

4. To the enjoyment of the many observers, skilled divers enter the aquarium and feed the fish five times a day. (*Use passive to eliminate the doer of the action.*)

_____

_____

5. As the divers feed the fish, the fish swim close to the observation portholes. (*Use passive to have consistent subjects.*)

_____

_____

14.6 USE *the skill*

Write an original paragraph on your own paper, using active and passive voice, indirect objects, and prepositional phrases appropriately for variety. Answer this question: What was your favorite family vacation and why?

Using Coordination and Subordination

The purpose of coordination and subordination is to show how ideas are related to one another within a sentence or paragraph. Proper use of these two strategies results in logical and effective writing.

Coordination

Using equal structure, **coordination** joins ideas that are equal in importance. There are several ways to show that ideas are equal within a sentence: a coordinating conjunction, correlative conjunctions, and a semicolon with a conjunctive adverb.

Coordinating Conjunctions p. 54

ORIGINAL SENTENCES	Alfred, Lord Tennyson became England's poet laureate. He became the unofficial spokesman for Victorian England.
COORDINATED SENTENCE	Alfred, Lord Tennyson became England's poet laureate, and he became the unofficial spokesman for Victorian England.
COORDINATED COMPLEMENT	Alfred, Lord Tennyson became England's poet laureate and the unofficial spokesman for Victorian England.

Successful coordination requires that ideas be equal in importance and type and that they be separate. Mixing facts that are unequal or joining statements in which one expands upon the other results in **faulty coordination** of ideas.

FAULTY COORDINATION	Tennyson's *In Memoriam* met with almost instant success, and Tennyson himself compared the structure of this work to Dante's *Divina Commedia*.
REVISED FOR COORDINATION	Tennyson's *In Memoriam* documents the speaker's journey from despair to elation, and Tennyson himself compared this work's climactic structure to Dante's *Divina Commedia*.

FAULTY COORDINATION	At the age of twelve, Tennyson was engrossed in writing an epic, and he wrote a lengthy narrative poem in formal language.
REVISED FOR LOGIC (NOT COORDINATE)	At the age of twelve, Tennyson was engrossed in writing an epic, a lengthy narrative poem in formal language.

Coordination also requires that the parts be similar grammatically.

FAULTY COORDINATION	An excursion to the Pyrenees provided Tennyson with inspiring landscapes for his later poems, a fascination with the isolated village of Cauteretz, and motivating him to return to this location throughout his lifetime.
CORRECT COORDINATION	An excursion to the Pyrenees provided Tennyson with inspiring landscapes for his later poems, a fascination with the isolated village of Cauteretz, and the motivation to return to this location throughout his lifetime.

Subordination

Subordinating Conjunctions p. 55

Using unequal structure (structure that emphasizes one idea over another), **subordination** joins ideas that are unequal in importance. In a sentence that evidences appropriate subordination, one idea is less important than another. Subordinate ideas usually appear in dependent clauses or in phrases.

ORIGINAL SENTENCES	Tanzanite is a valuable gemstone. It was unknown to the world until 1967.
SUBORDINATED (DEPENDENT CLAUSE)	Tanzanite, which is a valuable gemstone, was unknown to the world until 1967.
SUBORDINATED (APPOSITIVE PHRASE)	Tanzanite, a valuable gemstone, was unknown to the world until 1967.

tip When subordinating ideas, try to place at least part of the important idea at the end of the sentence, the position of strength.

Effective subordination joins ideas in such a way that the reader can easily tell which is the more important idea and how it is related to the subordinate idea.

FAULTY COORDINATION	Manuel d' Sousa was a tailor turned prospector, and he became the first to register his discovery of Tanzania's blue sapphire-looking stone.
APPROPRIATE SUBORDINATION	Manuel d' Sousa, a tailor turned prospector, became the first to register his discovery of Tanzania's blue sapphire-looking stone.

Notice that the information in the appositive phrase is included as an added detail. The more important information, however, is found in the sentence's independent clause.

Errors in subordination often occur when unequal ideas are joined as if they are equal (faulty coordination) or when the less important idea is emphasized over the more important one (faulty subordination). The less important idea should always be located in the dependent (subordinate) clause or in a phrase.

Dependent Clauses and Complex Sentences pp. 116, 132–33

NO SUBORDINATION	The bluish gemstone discovered in 1967 could be found only in Tanzania, and Tiffany and Company jewelers named the stone "Tanzanite."

364 Chapter 14 | Writing Strategies

FAULTY SUBORDINATION	Since Tiffany and Company jewelers named the bluish gemstone "Tanzanite," we can guess that this stone discovered in 1967 could be found only in Tanzania.
BETTER SUBORDINATION	Because the bluish gemstone discovered in 1967 could be found only in Tanzania, Tiffany and Company jewelers named the stone "Tanzanite."

PRACTICE *the skill*

Rewrite each sentence, correcting any faulty coordination or subordination. If the sentence is already correct, write C in the blank.

1. The Empress Hotel in Victoria, British Columbia, called "The Jewel of the Pacific," is a fine hotel, and people visit throughout the year.

2. Built in the Edwardian style, the 460-room hotel offers the visitor quite an historical stay. The hotel was designed by Francis Rattenbury in 1908. Today the hotel continues to be a landmark on Victoria Island.

3. More than 75,000 people per year enjoy the Empress's afternoon tea that includes berries, scones, crumpets, pastries, and sandwiches; and, of course, people drink tea.

4. In 1989 a $45 million project modernized the hotel, but interested parties made sure the hotel retained its historical significance.

5. Past guests to the hotel include members of the monarchy and international leaders, and many famous Americans have stayed there.

14.8 REVIEW *the skill*

Correctly combine the following groups of words according to the instructions in parentheses.

1. Big Ben is one of London's most famous landmarks. It was named for member of Parliament Sir Benjamin Hall. *(Subordinate one sentence to the other.)*

2. The bell tower is most impressive after dark. Each clock is twenty-three feet square. At night the four faces are illuminated. *(Combine the ideas into one sentence.)*

3. The minute hand on each dial is fourteen feet long. The figures on each clock face are two feet high. *(Coordinate the sentences.)*

4. Big Ben is actually the thirteen-ton bell inside the clock tower. Whitechapel Foundry was responsible for casting the bell. *(Combine the ideas into one clause focusing on the casting.)*

5. The clock tower survived the bombs of World War II. The continued ringing of Big Ben offered hope to the entire world. *(Coordinate the sentences.)*

Sentence Energy

The words you use make your writing either come alive or fall flat. Vivid verbs, interesting details, strict accuracy, and figurative language infuse your writing with energy.

Action Verbs

Where you can, edit out state-of-being verbs (verbs that show no outward action, e.g., *be, become, seem*), replacing them with strong action verbs.

STATE-OF-BEING VERB	After two hours of snowboarding, Denijer seemed tired.
ACTION VERB	After two hours of snowboarding, Denijer threw himself on top of a snowbank to rest.

Details

Interesting details give the reader the information needed to imagine a situation.

FEW DETAILS	The rain was turning into sleet.
MORE DETAILS ADDED	Raindrops pummeled my umbrella for several minutes before I detected faint crunching sounds underfoot.

Accuracy

Pay strict attention to accuracy as you write. Inaccurate words, phrasing, and connotation reflect poorly on the writer and make understanding difficult for the reader. There are four categories of accuracy that you should be aware of as you write.

Dictionaries and Thesauruses pp. 404–5

- **Accurate Words**—Choose words carefully. A thesaurus will give you ideas for similar words, and a dictionary will help you determine shades of meaning and differentiate among words with similar meanings.

WRONG WORD	A statue of Józef Bem in Budapest, Hungary, bears an *epitaph* recounting the general's motivational words to his troops at Piski.
CORRECTION	A statue of Józef Bem in Budapest, Hungary, bears an *epigraph* recounting the general's motivational words to his troops at Piski.

- **Accurate Phrasing**—Use phrases accurately and idiomatically. Misstated and misused phrases often cause the reader to lose the focus of the message.

INACCURATE PHRASING	As a general *thumb rule* one should not wear plaids and stripes simultaneously.
CORRECTION	As a *rule of thumb,* one should not wear plaids and stripes simultaneously.

- **Appropriate Connotation**—Check the **connotation,** or associated meaning, of a word or phrase when you write. Often the connotation is as important as the **denotation,** what the word names or describes.

INAPPROPRIATE CONNOTATION	The *odor* coming from Mom's cooking was amazing!
APPROPRIATE CONNOTATION	The *aroma* coming from Mom's cooking was amazing!

- **Specific, Concrete Words**—Use specific words instead of general or abstract ones where possible.

ABSTRACT	Everyone agreed that the stray cat needed *attention.*
SPECIFIC	Everyone agreed that the stray cat needed *warm milk, a soft bed, and plenty of stroking.*
GENERAL	Martin was the kind of man whose wardrobe consisted mostly of *work clothes.*
SPECIFIC	Martin was the kind of man whose wardrobe consisted mostly of *jeans and T-shirts.*

Pauses for Breath

Long sentences can leave a reader tired and confused. Break a stringy sentence into two or more sentences.

Stringy	In 1824, in order to construct the first rubber balloon, Michael Faraday, a lecturer at the Royal Institution in London, cut and laid out two large sections of rubber sheets that he placed one atop the other before bonding the edges together and dusting the interior with flour to prevent the rubber from sticking and ruining his attempts to fill the balloonlike bag with air and an experimental substance called hydrogen.
Split into Four Sentences	In 1824, in order to construct the first rubber balloon, Michael Faraday, a lecturer at the Royal Institution in London, cut and laid out two large sections of rubber sheets. He then placed one sheet atop the other and bonded the edges together. Next he dusted the interior of the balloon with flour to prevent the rubber from sticking and ruining his experiment. Faraday then filled this rubber balloon with air and an experimental substance called hydrogen.

Figurative Language

Describing one thing in terms of another is called **metaphor**. Metaphors may be stated or implied comparisons.

Stated Comparison	The name of the Lord is a *strong tower*: the righteous runneth into it, and is safe. (Prov. 18:10)
Implied Comparison	For in the time of trouble He shall hide me in His pavilion: in the secret of His tabernacle shall he hide me; he shall set me up upon a rock. (Ps. 27:5)

In Psalm 27 David compares God's comforting nearness during times of trouble to a sheltering pavilion from the blasting heat and other perils of the desert. Further, David likens God's nearness to being protected in God's own dwelling place, His tabernacle. Finally, David compares his stability in the Lord to the security of standing on a block of stone.

A **simile** is a comparison that uses *like* or *as* in the statement of comparison.

And the staff of [Goliath's] spear was **like** a weaver's beam. (1 Sam. 17:7)

---

tip

Overuse of figurative language can be distracting or annoying to a reader. Use metaphors and similes in moderation.

Mixed metaphors and stretched metaphors often plague the writing of novices (and some professionals!). In a **mixed metaphor** the writer uses two or more metaphors together illogically.

Mixed Metaphor	Having mined the riches of her creativity, Raven reaped a harvest of awards with the publication of her novel.

The phrase "mined the riches" evokes an image of miners working to obtain precious metals from the earth. The phrase "reaped a harvest," on the other hand, is an agricultural description that does not fit logically with the previous metaphor.

MIXED METAPHOR	As Ed watched the video advertisement, his interest took flight with no sign of running aground.
POSSIBLE IMPROVEMENT	As Ed watched the video advertisement, his interest set sail with no sign of running aground.

The overly elaborate metaphor also troubles writers. Attempting to apply a metaphor too fully can stretch a metaphor beyond the bounds of proper comparison. In the example below, the basic comparison works well enough, but the comparison begins to break down as the writer continues to use it.

STRETCHED METAPHOR	It does not take a weathered voice coach to tell you that putting a bit of sunshine in your voice goes a long way in cultivating communication. Genuine warmth radiating from your voice can instantly brighten your listener's day, thaw many tensions, and help the friendship to blossom and grow.
IMPROVED	It does not take a voice coach to tell you that putting a bit of sunshine in your voice goes a long way in furthering communication and fostering friendship.

Do not allow your metaphors to hinder your message; avoid stretching them too far.

14.9 PRACTICE *the skill*

Revise each sentence according to the instructions in parentheses. Research the subject and restructure the sentence if necessary.

1. Squash is a game played with a racquet and a ball. (*Use more details.*)

2. The racquet is almost as long as a tennis racket, but lighter in weight. (*Use an action verb.*)

3. Since the squash ball is smaller than a golf ball, the squash player should choose approximate eye guards. (*Use an accurate word in place of* approximate.)

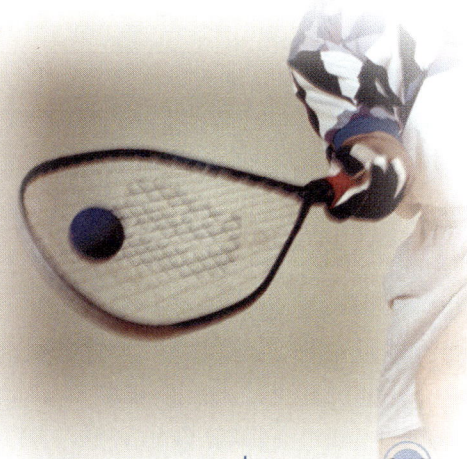

4. The server is the only one to score a point in a game, and the winner is the first one with nine points and a two-point margin. (*Use action verbs.*)

5. Persons of all years can enjoy playing squash. (*Use an accurate and idiomatic phrase.*)

14.10 REVIEW *the skill*

Revise the following paragraph to add action verbs, details, accuracy, and figurative language. If necessary, research the subject.

Have you ever visited a national cemetery? Although there are many cemeteries, the most beautiful may be the National Memorial Cemetery of the Pacific. The location itself is odd: Puowaina Crater near Honolulu, Hawaii. Many people who fought in different wars are buried in this cemetery. For some visitors, however, it is most closely associated with World War II. Dedicated on September 2, 1949, the cemetery is the resting place for victims of the attacks on Pearl Harbor.

Sentence Expansion and Reduction

You should be aware of two essential techniques as you draft and edit your work. Should you find that you have written simple sentence after simple sentence or only very lengthy sentences, the following expansion and reduction techniques will help you to develop or combine your thoughts logically.

Expansion of Sentences

Sentence expansion shows connections between ideas and makes your sentences more interesting. Expansion techniques also increase the amount of information that can be contained in a sentence and can change the rhythm of a piece of writing. By adding descriptive clauses and/or phrases, a writer adds interest and meaning to sentences that might otherwise be flat or dull.

Benjamin Harrison

Using Clauses

Add adjective, adverb, or noun clauses to increase the variety, clarity, and sophistication of your writing.

Type of Clause	Function	Example Sentence
Adjective	modifies a noun or pronoun	President Benjamin Harrison, **who was our twenty-third president**, held Bible studies in the White House.
Adverb	most often modifies a verb but can modify an adjective or adverb	**Although he was criticized for doing so**, John Ashcroft, attorney general under George W. Bush, held daily Bible studies at the Justice Department.
Noun	functions as a noun (subject, direct object, predicate noun, etc.)	Christians know **that the Bible is the basis of all truth**.

Clauses pp. 116–28

Using Phrases

Descriptive phrases—prepositional and verbal—add complexity of meaning and richness of detail to your sentences.

Original Sentence	Phrase(s) Added	Revised Sentence
Benjamin Harrison requested prayer.	prepositional	In a letter to his wife, Benjamin Harrison requested prayer for himself and for his Civil War regiment.
Harrison regularly shared the gospel.	verbal	Devoted to personal soul-winning, Harrison regularly shared the gospel.

Phrases pp. 88–102

Beware of adding too many descriptive phrases to your writing. The resulting sentences may become stringy and complicated rather than interesting.

After sticking the brightly colored plastic figurine into the driver's seat of the toy dump truck and cradling his latest acquisition from his Aunt Hazel, two-year-old Braydon squealed with excitement and told everyone what he had decided to name the little construction man included with his new toy: "Me."

14.11 PRACTICE *the skill*

Combine each pair of sentences by making one of the sentences a dependent clause.

1. The Maginot Line was to be a protective barrier between France and Germany. The construction of the Maginot Line took place after World War I in France.

2. Some historians have called the Maginot Line a fiasco. The Line was a technological success.

3. The Line, a series of forts and blockhouses, was buried one hundred feet or more in the earth. Access to the forts and blockhouses was by trolleys.

4. The Maginot Line was a military success. Germany's invasion of France in World War II brought Germany around the line, not through it.

5. Reading history reveals an interesting fact. The Line surrendered, but it was not taken militarily.

14.12 REVIEW *the skill*

Expand each sentence by adding a clause or phrase to the independent clause provided. You may need to research the subject.

1. The Sistine Chapel is most often associated with Michelangelo.

2. In 1508 Michelangelo was commissioned to repaint the star-covered ceiling.

3. Before Michelangelo began his work, famous artists such as Botticelli, Signorelli, and others had painted frescoes.

4. These fresco cycles portray the lives of Moses and Christ.

5. The side walls show continuity.

Reduction of Sentences

Sentence reduction tightens your writing and makes it less complicated. Although it is often desirable to use sentence expansion, sometimes the result is a sentence that is very complicated or lengthy. A writer might then use sentence reduction techniques to make the writing tighter and more understandable. One common way to reduce sentences is to make a compound sentence into a simple sentence with a compound part such as a compound predicate or subject.

COMPOUND SENTENCE	James M. Barrie lived during the peak of the Victorian Era, and he incorporated all the literary conventions of his age into his writings.
COMPOUND PREDICATE	James M. Barrie lived during the peak of the Victorian Era and incorporated all the literary conventions of his age into his writings.
COMPOUND SENTENCE	James M. Barrie used much fantasy in his plays, and W. S. Gilbert of the Gilbert and Sullivan duo did too.
COMPOUND SUBJECT	James M. Barrie and W. S. Gilbert of the Gilbert and Sullivan duo used much fantasy in their plays.

Often, a writer will practice reduction naturally by eliminating words that he knows will be understood by the reader. This process is called **ellipsis**. Ellipsis often results in a simple sentence with a compound part.

> James Barrie gained an appreciation for literature from his mother and [he] vowed to make writing his career.

But sometimes the result is a compound sentence in which some of the words are understood. The sentence below contains an elliptical independent clause.

> People most often associate James Barrie with his play *Peter Pan*, but [they do] not [associate him] with his forty or so other works.

Writer's Toolbox

Reducing Adjective Clauses

Some clauses can be reduced to a brief phrase or a single word. When the subject of an adjective clause is a relative pronoun, you can usually reduce the clause to one of the following:

Adjective Clause to Prepositional Phrase

An adjective clause that consists of a relative pronoun, a form of *be*, and a prepositional phrase can be reduced to just the prepositional phrase.

Adjective Clauses pp. 117–18

> Many characters ~~which are~~ in *Peter Pan* were modeled after the author's experiences while vacationing with the Davies family.

> Many characters in *Peter Pan* were modeled after the author's experiences while vacationing with the Davies family.

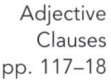
Prepositional Phrases p. 88

Adjective Clause to Participle or Participial Phrase

An adjective clause can often be reduced to a simple participle or a participial phrase.

> Students ~~who are~~ seeking additional information should stay after the meeting.

> Students seeking additional information should stay after the meeting.

Notice that an adjective clause with an active verb produces a present participle. An adjective clause with a passive verb produces a past participle (more accurately called a "passive participle") as in the sentence below.

> The meeting ~~that was~~ scheduled for tomorrow has been cancelled.

> The meeting scheduled for tomorrow has been cancelled.

So far the phrases we have looked at have remained after the nouns they modify. However, when all that remains of a clause is a simple participle, the participle may move to a position before the noun (much like a regular adjective).

Participles and Participial Phrases pp. 92–94

> No one recognized the importance of the meeting ~~that was~~ cancelled.

> No one recognized the importance of the cancelled meeting.

Note that an entire participial phrase could not be moved; that is, we would not say "*The scheduled for tomorrow meeting* has been cancelled." However, a participle modified only by a preceding adverb can usually be moved.

> No one recognized the importance of the meeting ~~that was~~ suddenly cancelled.

> No one recognized the importance of the suddenly cancelled meeting.

Although it seems that a clause must have a form of *be* in it to be a candidate for reduction, in actuality certain clauses without *be* can be reduced by changing the main verb to a present participle. Note the example below.

students who seek information → students seeking information

Adjective Clause to Single Adjective or Appositive

When an adjective clause contains a relative-pronoun subject and a form of *be* followed by a predicate adjective, that clause can be reduced to the adjective alone.

Jonathan swam in the relay that was arduous.

Jonathan swam in the arduous relay.

An adjective clause that contains a predicate noun after a relative-pronoun subject and a form of the linking verb *be* can be reduced to an appositive or appositive phrase.

Mandy's aunt, who is a doctor, specializes in pediatric medicine.

Mandy's aunt, a doctor, specializes in pediatric medicine.

Reducing Adverb Clauses

Some adverb clauses can be reduced to simpler structures, such as prepositional phrases, verbal phrases, absolute phrases, or elliptical adverb clauses.

Adverb Clause to Prepositional Phrase

Certain adverb clauses can be reduced to prepositional phrases.

After there are rainstorms, the beach looks fresh, smooth, and ready for new footprints and sandcastles.

After rainstorms, the beach looks fresh, smooth, and ready for new footprints and sandcastles.

When the adverb clause does not contain a noun that can become the object of the preposition, sometimes a noun can be made from another part of speech.

When it is cold outside, few people stroll casually along the beach.

During cold weather few people stroll casually along the beach.

Adverb Clause to Verbal Phrase

If an adverb clause has the same subject as the main clause and expresses time, cause, or condition, it may be reduced to a participial phrase.

Because you are so tactful, you have been chosen to break the news to the second-place team.

Being so tactful, you have been chosen to break the news to the second-place team.

Note that when reducing a time clause, you use a present participle to indicate the same time as in the main clause. To express prior time, use a perfect participle.

After they finished the game, Chad's team reviewed the video.

Having finished the game, Chad's team reviewed the video.

An adverb clause expressing purpose can often be reduced to an infinitive phrase if the adverb clause has the same subject as the main clause.

> Eden is going to Camp Hope this weekend ~~so that she can~~ baby-sit the children of those attending the couples' retreat.

> Eden is going to Camp Hope this weekend to baby-sit the children of those attending the couple's retreat.

Absolute Phrase
pp. 88–89

Adverb Clause to Absolute Phrase

If the subject of the adverb clause is different from that of the main clause, you may be able to turn the adverb clause into an absolute phrase.

> being
> ~~Since~~ her group ~~was~~ late, Sharon decided not to stop for a snack.

> Her group being late, Sharon decided not to stop for a snack.

Reduce a clause to an absolute phrase by dropping the subordinating conjunction and changing the verb to a participle. What remains is a typical absolute phrase.

In the example above, the present participle *being* indicates approximately the same time as the verb in the main clause. Note that the reduction could be taken a step further—to a prepositional phrase: "With her group late."

Adverb Clause to Elliptical Adverb Clause

Another way to reduce an adverb clause is to keep the subordinating conjunction and simply drop one or more other words that can be understood from context.

Elliptical Adverb Clause
p. 123

> Unless ~~he is~~ late for class, Cliff empties the trash cans in the morning.

> Unless late for class, Cliff empties the trash cans in the morning.

Because the subordinating conjunction remains in sentence two above, the origin of the word group as an adverb clause is still clear, and we call it an "elliptical clause." Note that an elliptical clause has the same function in the sentence as a full adverb clause.

Elliptical adverb clauses can also include participles, reduced from verbs.

> If ~~we are~~ told in advance, our group can bring refreshments.

> While ~~she was~~ circling the track, she felt a cramp in her foot.

Elliptical clauses are often used for comparison.

> Reena is taller than Jordan is ~~tall~~.

> Reena is taller than Jordan ~~is tall~~.

Dangling Modifiers
p. 251

---

tip

Never reduce an adverb clause whose subject is different from that of the main clause. (The result is a dangling modifier.)

ADVERB CLAUSE	Because we arrived early, the hostess was not ready yet.
DANGLING MODIFIER	Arriving early, the hostess was not ready yet.

376 Chapter 14 | Writing Strategies

Reducing Noun Clauses

Many noun clauses cannot be reduced to any simpler construction. When it is possible, though, reducing a noun clause can result in a tighter sentence.

Noun Clause to Verbal Phrase

Noun clauses can sometimes be reduced to gerund phrases or infinitive phrases.

NOUN CLAUSE	My choice is *that I would invest the money.*
GERUND	My choice is *investing the money.*
INFINITIVE	My choice is *to invest the money.*

Noun Clause
pp. 126-28

Verbal Phrases
pp. 92–102

Of the last two sentences above, the infinitive may be preferable, since the gerund could possibly be misread as part of a progressive verb ("is investing"). The last sentence could also be made more concise:

I choose *to invest the money.*

I choose *investing the money.*

Notice how the sentence changes when the subject of the noun clause and the subject of the main clause are different:

      S   TrV   DO

My mother learned that I invested the money wisely.

My mother learned about my investing the money wisely. (*gerund OP*)

In this case (two subjects or actors are different—*mother* and *I*), the subject of the noun clause cannot just be dropped. Instead, it appears as a possessive modifier (*my*).

When you reduce a noun clause to an infinitive, the subject of the noun clause becomes the "subject" of the infinitive phrase, usually after *for*. If the subject of the noun clause was a personal pronoun, the "subject" of the infinitive must be an objective-case pronoun.

      S LV PN

The manager's idea is that we participate in the book sale.

The manager's idea is for us to participate in the book sale. (*infinitive PN*)

Noun Clause to Noun Phrase

Sometimes a noun clause can be reduced to a noun and its modifiers (a noun phrase). Usually this reduction is possible only when there exists a noun that is closely related in meaning to the verb of the noun clause.

CLAUSE	I know that he worked as a personal trainer for a time.
PHRASE	I know about his vocation as a personal trainer.
CLAUSE	Whom he associates himself with is unknown.
PHRASE	His associates are unknown.

Reducing Complex Sentences

Certain complex sentences with predicate adjectives can be reduced to simple sentences containing adverbs as sentence modifiers. Notice that the reduced sentence is both shorter and more to the point.

It was providential that no one was hurt in the accident.

Providentially, no one was hurt in the accident.

14.13 PRACTICE *the skill*

Rewrite each sentence to reduce the italicized clause to the shorter construction indicated in parentheses.

1. The Western Wall, *which is often called the Wailing Wall*, is located in the old city of Jerusalem. *(participial phrase)*

2. The Western Wall dates from about the first century, *and the wall is the only remains of the second temple of Jerusalem. (appositive phrase)*

3. *Because the wall is a sacred place to Jewish people*, prayer and worship often take place at the wall. *(absolute phrase)*

4. The Western Wall is also a place *where some participate in Jewish religious or military ceremonies. (infinitive phrase)*

5. Jews *who are mourning* come to the Wailing Place, a part of the Western Wall. *(participle)*

14.14 REVIEW *the skill*

Reduce each sentence, using the techniques discussed in this section.

1. Because Hadrian wanted to mark the northern boundary of his empire, the Romans built Hadrian's Wall in northern Britain.

   _____
   _____

2. The stone wall, which is considered one of the Roman Empire's greatest engineering feats, is seventy-three modern miles long.

   _____
   _____

3. During Hadrian's time, a mile castle was located at every Roman mile measurement, and eight soldiers guarded the castle.

   _____
   _____

4. Additional soldiers guarded from turrets that were located equal distances between the mile castles.

   _____
   _____

5. After the decline of the Roman Empire, parts of Hadrian's Wall were stolen, and they appeared in houses, churches, and other walls.

   _____
   _____

Parallelism

Joining sentence elements of similar form is called **parallelism**. Parallel structures have the same grammatical form and are most often joined by a coordinating conjunction. Effective parallelism shows the relationship between ideas and makes writing flow more smoothly.

ACCEPTABLE	The fisherman says his special today is halibut. He also says there is a special buy on salmon. Additionally, he has a promotional offer on trout.
IMPROVED WITH PARALLELISM	The fisherman's specials today include halibut, salmon, and trout.

Writing Strategies | Chapter 14

Using Parallelism Only for Parallel Ideas

Parallelism in writing should be reserved for ideas that are truly of the same type.

ILLOGICAL PARALLELISM	While assessing the Shanghai facility, we noted favorable marketing opportunities, solid first quarter earnings, and *delightful seaport cuisine.*
CORRECTION	While assessing the Shanghai facility, we noted favorable marketing opportunities and solid first quarter earnings.

---tip

Make sure that one item in the parallel structure is not more general or less general than the others. For example, write, "We bought seeds for lettuce, carrots, and other garden vegetables," not "for lettuce, carrots, and garden vegetables."

Using the Same Part of Speech

Parts of Speech
p. 35

Parallel structures joined by coordinating conjunctions should be of the same grammatical type and part of speech.

NOT PARALLEL	Most first-time home buyers want residences with good resale value, room for an expanding family, and *conveniently located.*
PARALLEL	Most first-time home buyers want residences with good resale value, room for an expanding family, and *a convenient location.*

Using the Same Type of Structure

Making parallel sentences involves using the same kinds of words, phrases, verbals, or clauses.

Kinds of Words or Phrases

Verbals p. 92

Although verbals function as nouns, adjectives, and adverbs, verbals should not appear in parallel structures with those parts of speech.

NOT PARALLEL	New home buyers often purchase personalized home accessories such as cabinet fixtures, wall hangings, and *installing window treatments.*
PARALLEL	New home buyers often purchase personalized home accessories such as cabinet fixtures, wall hangings, and *window treatments.*

Prepositional phrases are preferably not mixed with other constructions as in the sentence below.

NOT FULLY PARALLEL	Meg finds this project more fulfilling, *of greater importance,* and less stressful.
PARALLEL	Meg finds this project more fulfilling, *more important,* and less stressful.

Kinds of Verbals

Gerunds, participles, and infinitives should not be mixed in the same construction.

NOT PARALLEL	Research tasks will include *touring* an upholstery manufacturing facility and *to test* product samples for flammability.
PARALLEL	Research tasks will include *touring* an upholstery manufacturing facility and *testing* product samples for flammability.

Phrases and Clauses

A phrase and a clause should not be joined with a coordinating conjunction. Rather, make the phrase into a clause or the clause into a phrase.

Conjunctions
pp. 54–55

NOT PARALLEL	The interior designer asked *for our color preferences* and *whether we had a project budget*.
PARALLEL	The interior designer asked *whether we had color preferences* and *whether we had a project budget*.
EVEN BETTER	The interior designer asked *for our color preferences* and *for our project budget*.

With correlative conjunctions (*both—and, neither—nor*), the same type of structure should follow each of the two words.

NOT PARALLEL	Those making matching donations **both** boosted the number of charitable gifts **and** the individual amounts contributed.
PARALLEL	Those making matching donations boosted **both** the number of charitable gifts **and** the individual amounts contributed.

Sometimes adding a subject and an auxiliary makes the two parts parallel.

NOT PARALLEL	**Not only** has the Christian radio station made its fundraising goal **but also** received enough money to build a better radio tower.
PARALLEL	**Not only** has the Christian radio station made its fundraising goal, **but** it has **also** received enough money to build a better radio tower.

Kinds of Clauses

A dependent clause and an independent clause should not be joined by a coordinating conjunction.

NOT PARALLEL	All employees must view the safety video, *but when they are not regularly scheduled to work*.
PARALLEL	All employees must view the safety video, *but they must watch it when they are not regularly scheduled to work*.
ALSO GOOD	All employees must view the safety video *when they are not regularly scheduled to work*.

Clarifying Parallelism

A writer may employ several methods to make clear to a reader which sentence parts are intended to be parallel. The methods are listed in the chart below.

Method of Clarification	Example Sentence
Use correlative conjunctions correctly.	Our swim team will compete in freestyle and butterfly or backstroke categories. *(confusing)*
	Our swim team will compete in either freestyle and butterfly or the backstroke category.
	Our swim team will compete in the freestyle and either the butterfly or backstroke categories.

CONTINUED

Repeat a key word.	The advanced swimming course offers instruction in interpreting a pace clock, flip turns, and technique drills. *(interpreting flip turns and technique drills?)*
	The advanced swimming course offers instruction in interpreting a pace clock, in flip turns, and in technical drills.
Reorder joined elements.	The pool's mechanically controlled floor depth and lifeguard staff make this facility an ideal choice for parents with young children. *(mechanically controlled lifeguard staff?)*
	The pool's lifeguard staff and mechanically controlled floor depth make this facility an ideal choice for parents with young children.

14.15 PRACTICE *the skill*

Rewrite each sentence, correcting any illogical or incorrect parallelism. If the sentence is already correct, write C in the blank.

1. The Shunammite woman of 2 Kings 4 was a woman of hospitality, perception, and she was content.

2. Elisha and his servant, Gehazi, visited the woman and her husband on several occasions and when they traveled in that part of Israel.

3. God directed the Shunammite family not only to build a chamber but also they invited Elisha to use the chamber.

4. In the chamber were items necessary for Elisha: a bed, a table, a stool, and there was a candlestick.

5. God blessed the Shunammite woman for taking care of both the prophet and the prophet's servant.

14.16 USE *the skill*

Write an original sentence using the listed items in parallel ways. Omit or modify items that do not fit with the others logically. Be efficient and logical in word types and constructions.

1. high school graduation / going to college / get a job

   _____
   _____
   _____

2. to work at a summer camp / going on a mission trip / help in Bible school at her church

   _____
   _____
   _____

3. the payment for her first year in college / to help her sister in need / being her father's assistant in the business

   _____
   _____

4. praying daily / read God's word / Janie sought wise counsel.

   _____
   _____

5. the desire to know God's will / wants to obey God's will

   _____
   _____

Sentence Logic

You have no doubt read articles or listened to speeches that caused you to wonder about the logic of the writer or speaker. Sometimes grammatical constructions or meanings do not fit together correctly, and the resulting sentences seem illogical. This section identifies common logic problems and suggests ways to correct them.

Writer's Toolbox

Saying Things Directly

Determine to deliver your message in as few words as possible. Look for "built nouns" in your writing—nouns that are formed from simpler words. For example, the noun *separation* comes from the verb *separate; happiness* comes from the adjective *happy*. Many sentences can be simplified by using words in their original part of speech.

TOO WORDY (DENSE)	To enforce their *warning* that a hurricane was making its *approach*, lifeguards ordered an *evacuation* of the beach.
REVISED	Lifeguards *warned* that a hurricane was *approaching* and then *evacuated* the beach.

Saying What You Mean

Avoid making your reader unsure of your meaning. Say precisely what you mean by using logical predication and by making sure that your examples are truly examples.

- Make your subjects and verbs work together logically.

ILLOGICAL PREDICATION	Lifeguards desiring to take the advanced water safety course will be available next semester.
CORRECTION	Lifeguards who desire advanced training in water safety may take a course next semester.

- Make your examples actual examples. The phrases *for example* and *such as* notify the reader that examples will follow; therefore, the examples should be the main words after those phrases.

ILLOGICAL EXEMPLIFICATION	This swimming course emphasizes more advanced skills such as *practicing* diving and rotary breathing.
CORRECTION	This swimming course emphasizes more advanced skills such as *diving* and *rotary breathing*.

Saying Things Consistently

When writing, avoid the tendency to begin a sentence with one construction and mistakenly end with a different one.

MIXED CONSTRUCTIONS	When William S. Gilbert wrote the librettos of numerous comic operas were based on plot and character ideas from his earlier contributions to a magazine.
	From studying logic as a law student may have influenced W. S. Gilbert's ability to satirize Victorian England.
POSSIBLE CORRECTIONS	William S. Gilbert, the librettist of numerous comic operas, drew many plot and character ideas from his earlier contributions to a magazine.
	W. S. Gilbert's ability to satirize Victorian England may have stemmed from his training in logic while a student of law.

Making Clear and Logical Comparisons

When comparing two or more things, state the comparison clearly and logically.

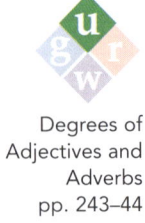

Degrees of Adjectives and Adverbs pp. 243–44

Logical Comparisons

- Things being compared must be separate; one cannot be part of another.

FAULTY COMPARISON	Robert made higher SAT scores than anyone in his senior class. (*Robert is part of the senior class, so he cannot be compared with himself.*)
CORRECTION	Robert made higher SAT scores than anyone *else* in his senior class.

- Things being compared must also be of the same type.

FAULTY COMPARISON	The landscapes of the Hudson River artists are more realistic than most modern painters. (*Landscapes are compared with painters.*)
CORRECTION	The landscapes of the Hudson River artists are more realistic than the landscapes of most modern painters. (*Here landscapes are compared with other landscapes.*)

Peace and Plenty by George Inness

FAULTY COMPARISON	Robert's SAT scores were higher than anyone else in his senior class. (*Scores are compared with people.*)
CORRECTION	Robert's SAT scores were higher than those of anyone else in his senior class. (*Scores are compared with other scores.*)

Clear Comparisons

Sometimes the last part of a comparison will be understood from the context.

Jamison has studied longer than Brad. (longer than Brad *has studied*)

He studies chemistry more than physics. (more than *he studies* physics)

Although it is acceptable, even advisable, to leave out the part that will be understood, never leave out anything that is needed for clarity.

UNCLEAR	The teacher heard Ben as well as Liz. (*Is Liz the subject of an understood clause? Or is Liz the direct object of the understood verb* heard?)
POSSIBLE CORRECTIONS	The teacher heard Ben as well as Liz did.
	The teacher heard Ben as well as she heard Liz.

> Notice the use of *did* in the first "possible correction" above. If a comparison clause (beginning with *than* or *as*) compares subjects of the same verb, English speakers often repeat the first auxiliary in the comparison clause. If there is no auxiliary or *be* verb present, they use the appropriate form of the auxiliary *do*.
>
> | FIRST AUXILIARY | Jamie has been studying as long as Brad **has**. |
> | --- | --- |
> | BE VERB | I am as tall as he **is**. |
> | FORM OF DO | I finished my homework faster than you **did**. |
> | | He likes drawing more than I **do**. |

Completing the Construction Before Or

Some comparisons state that one of the things may be either equivalent or superior with regard to some quality. In such a construction with *or*, *as* is needed before *or*.

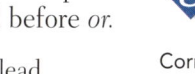

Correlative Conjunctions p. 55

INCOMPLETE CONSTRUCTION	Joanie sings this aria *as well* or better than the lead soprano does.
CORRECTIONS	Joanie sings this aria *as well as* or better than the lead soprano does.
	Joanie sings this aria *as well as* the lead soprano does, or better.
INCOMPLETE CONSTRUCTION	When Dad hears of Joanie's success, he will be *as happy* or happier than she.
CORRECTIONS	When Dad hears of Joanie's success, he will be *as happy as* or happier than she.
	When Dad hears of Joanie's success, he will be *as happy as* she is, or happier.

> Statements of equivalence use an *as . . . as* construction with an adjective or an adverb in the middle.
>
> | WITH ADJECTIVE | Dad is *as happy as* Joanie (is). |
> | --- | --- |
> | WITH ADVERB | Joanie sings *as well as* the lead soprano (does). |

Using Noun Clauses When Needed

Using the wrong type of clause may throw a sentence off course. Learn to use noun clauses correctly.

Clauses
pp. 122–28

Noun Clause, Not Adverb Clause

Do not use an adverb clause when a noun or noun clause is required. Either replace the adverb clause with a noun clause or recast the sentence to allow for the original adverb clause.

ADVERB CLAUSE AS SUBJECT	Because a country signs a treaty is no guarantee it will honor its word.
CORRECTION	That a country signs a treaty is no guarantee that it will honor its word.
ADVERB CLAUSE AS PN	The time I need to sleep is whenever I'm tired.
CORRECTION	I need to sleep whenever I'm tired.

tip

An adverb clause can never function as a noun: subject, direct object, predicate noun, and so on.

Dependent (Noun) Clause, Not Independent Clause

Never use an independent clause as the subject of a sentence. Rather, convert the independent clause to a noun clause (or noun equivalent) or revise the sentence completely.

INDEPENDENT CLAUSE AS SUBJECT	Spring has come at last was our motive for putting out the patio chairs.
POSSIBLE CORRECTIONS	The arrival of spring was our motive for putting out the chairs.
	Spring has come at last, so we decided to put out the patio chairs.
	We decided to put out the patio chairs because spring has come at last.

Similarly, a direct question must be changed to an indirect question if it is to be used as a noun clause.

DIRECT QUESTION AS SUBJECT	How do Christians respond to trial is an important question.
CORRECTIONS	How Christians respond to trial is an important question.
	An important question is this: How do Christians respond to trial?

Indirect questions do not have subject-verb inversion.

DIRECT QUESTION	She asked, "How do Christians respond to trial?"
INDIRECT QUESTION	She asked how Christians respond to trial.

Placing Words in the Sentence

Create a natural flow from one sentence to another by placing elements strategically at the beginnings and ends of sentences.

Word Placement
p. 356

Managing Subjects Within the Sentence

Subjects of sentences or clauses within a paragraph should fit together well. Avoid needless shifting of topics.

Subjects
p. 70

Paragraph with Subject Shifts

Shoes with exaggeratedly high soles pass into and out of fashion, but Japan's traditional *geta* shoes existed long before modern platform shoes. During the Heian Period (794–1192) the Japanese developed wooden-soled shoes that rested upon two narrow wooden blocks called *ha*. The word *ha* actually means "teeth." Although *ha* raised the shoe only one or two inches off the ground, the shoes' elevation prevented people from soiling their long kimonos in the dust of the road. The kimono is the traditional formal dress garment of the Japanese. Additionally, on rainy days, people could even wear *geta* water shoes with significantly higher wooden blocks. Another item of traditional Japanese footwear is the *zori*, a sandal made of rush matting or woven brocade. *Geta* are held on the foot by the *hanao*, or "thongs." *Hanao* traditionally come in two colors, red for women and black for men, although more recently, *hanao* have taken on many different colors. In the summer of 1997, *geta* again became popular as a fashion item in Japan.

Improved

Shoes with exaggeratedly high soles pass into and out of fashion, but Japan's traditional *geta* shoes existed long before modern platform shoes. *Geta* are wooden-soled shoes that rest on two narrow wooden blocks. Although the blocks, known as *ha* ("teeth") raised the shoe only one or two inches off the ground, the shoes' elevation prevented people from soiling their kimonos in the dirt. *Geta* are held on the foot by *hanao* or "thongs." *Hanao* traditionally come in two colors, red for women and black for men. In the summer of 1997, *geta* shoes again became a popular fashion item.

Notice that the revised paragraph sticks to the topic and does not stray from it. The first paragraph includes several diversions from the original topic, such as the references to kimonos and *zori*. Concise, clear writing depends on the writer's sticking to the topic instead of leading the reader away from the main idea with sentences unrelated to the theme.

Ending in Strength

Final impressions are lasting impressions; therefore, end your sentences with strength.

Important Information

Because we learn inductively (by drawing conclusions from what we already know), it is natural within a sentence or paragraph to progress from familiar information to new information. Good writers take advantage of this natural progression by putting the important information last in their writing. Study the strategies below under "Linking with New Information" for ways to move important information to the end of the sentence.

Solid Words

Just as we expect sentences to end with important information, we expect sentences to end with "solid" words. Weak wording dilutes an otherwise strong idea.

WEAK	Even if the Victorian Era is not your forte, Gilbert and Sullivan's operettas contain many timeless situations that you will find humor in.
STRONG	Even if the Victorian Era is not your forte, Gilbert and Sullivan's operettas contain many timeless and humorous situations.
ADEQUATE	Arthur Sullivan composed masterfully.
STRONG	Arthur Sullivan composed with mastery.

Compared with the solid word *situations*, the preposition *in* is a weak word. The noun *mastery* communicates a stronger message than the adverb derived from it. The chart below shows how some parts of speech rank according to their relative strengths.

Strong				**Weak**
nouns	verbs	adjectives, adverbs		prepositions, adverbs that sound like prepositions (such as *in*), pronouns

Not all sentences can or should be manipulated to end with a strong word. Use solid-word endings for your most important information.

Linking with New Information

The end of a sentence is not only the place to put important information but also the place to put information that links ideas together. Good paragraphs contain sentences that lead naturally into one another, often by repeating in one sentence an idea that was introduced briefly in the sentence before. Although this kind of link is not always possible, it is sometimes a good way to tie sentences together. The chart below lists several ways to get new information to the end of the sentence.

Method	Original Sentences	Revised Sentences
Reverse the subject and the predicate noun.	Coins have been made from nonmetals such as porcelain and plastic, as well as from silver, nickel, platinum, and **gold**. By the nineteenth century the worldwide standard was **gold**.	Coins have been made from nonmetals such as porcelain and plastic, as well as from silver, nickel, platinum, and **gold**. **Gold** was the worldwide standard by the nineteenth century.
Move items out of the way at the sentence end.	The United States first used **nickel** to mint coins in 1865. **It** was used to produce a three-cent piece.	In 1865 the United States first minted coins from **nickel**. **It** was used to produce a three-cent piece.
Change active to passive or vice versa.	**Lead** was used by the American colonies to make the continental dollar. Today counterfeiters use **lead** to produce phony coins.	The American colonies made the continental dollar from **lead**. **Lead** is used today by counterfeiters to produce phony coins.

Certainly not every pair of sentences should be tied together in this way. However, used effectively, this technique will provide the link needed to strengthen your writing.

14.17 PRACTICE *the skill*

Rewrite each sentence, correcting any sentence logic problems. If the sentence is already correct, write C in the blank.

1. The reason for the introduction of the Union Pacific Big Boy steam locomotive was because the railroad company needed an engine that could pull a heavy load over a difficult track without assistance.

2. In the 1930s problems of transporting goods by railroad in the far West were greater than previous years.

3. Because their engines were too small is why other trains could not navigate the steep grades of the western mountains of Utah.

4. From 1941 to 1944 twenty-five Big Boy engines were built is the reason trains could cross the Wasatch Mountains.

5. Until their retirement in 1962 Big Boys averaged over one million miles per engine.

14.18 USE the skill

Rewrite the following paragraph to reduce the number of subject shifts and to end sentences with strength.

Guion "Guy" Bluford was the first African American NASA astronaut. In 1979 the desire to be an astronaut became a reality. We read that he traveled on four space flights from 1983 to 1992. The first flight began in August 1983 at Kennedy Space Center in Florida. The last flight landed in December 1992 at Edwards Air Force Base in California. During the four space flights, his participation in a number of scientific experiments was crucial. Dr. Bluford paved the way for future space exploration.

___

Biased Language

A Christian's communication must avoid giving unnecessary offense to listeners or readers. Though commanded in Ephesians to "[speak] the truth," Christians are to speak that truth "in love" (4:15). **Stereotypes**, a common vehicle for offense, are oversimplified generalizations about persons or events based on carelessness, ignorance, or even malice, and they often perpetuate inaccurate and unreasonable prejudices against groups of people. Usually a stereotype emphasizes one feature of a person while disregarding other features. Some stereotypes are universally recognized to be negative. Other stereotypes are simplistic or thoughtless statements posing as neutral statements. Offensive generalizations based solely on age, cultural or ethnic background, gender, physical characteristics, or race have no place in the Christian's spoken or written communication.

Today's society increasingly demands strict "political correctness" in all forms of communication. At times, the effort to please everyone ends in sacrifices of accuracy, clarity, or precision. For the informed and thoughtful communicator, three basic guidelines may help as he attempts to balance his writing:

- **If possible, use terms preferred by the group or person that you are writing about.** Many Native Americans prefer being referred to by a specific tribal designation (e.g., *Dakota, Cherokee*).
- **Concentrate on a person's positive qualities or strengths.** Referring to someone as *the girl who runs using a prosthesis* sounds better than *the one-legged runner* or *a prosthesis-wearing runner*.
- **Remember the person foremost and the condition second.** Consider saying *a boy who is blind* instead of *the blind boy* or *the woman using a wheelchair* not *who is wheelchair-bound*.

Many corrections can be made by simply deleting the biased word or phrase or by changing the placement of a given word or phrase. Notice the examples below.

STEREOTYPE	The blond woman driver ignored the stop sign and proceeded through the intersection. *(Failure to stop at a stop sign has nothing to do with the driver's gender or hair color.)*
CORRECTION	The motorist ignored the stop sign and proceeded through the intersection.
STEREOTYPE	Immigrants should attend language school in order to learn the language of their new country. *(Many already know the language of their new country.)*
CORRECTION	Anyone desiring additional language instruction should be able to attend language school.
STEREOTYPE	Just like a typical teenager, he cannot be counted on to mow the grass each week. *(His being a teenager is irrelevant to his choice to be irresponsible.)*
CORRECTION	He cannot be counted on to mow the grass each week.

Inflammatory language reflects poorly on the communicator—it shows that he has not considered the sensitivities of his audience.

14.19 PRACTICE *the skill*

Underline the biased language in the following paragraph. Then rewrite the paragraph, correcting the bias and overall tone.

Welcome to Riverdale Driving Academy, our community's leading provider of quality driving instruction. We serve everyone from insecure teenagers to older folks needing a review of state driving rules. For the past twenty-five years our company has led the upstate in making affordable driving instruction available to all. We provide a range of services, including our English- and Spanish-speaking instructors for immigrants, vehicles accessible to the wheelchair-bound, and remedial instruction for the quintessential blond. Please take a moment to examine our brochure and register for the next available class. We thank you in advance for your business.

_____
_____
_____
_____
_____
_____
_____
_____

14.20 CUMULATIVE *review*

Revise the following paragraph, using all the skills discussed in this chapter.

Buying an automobile for the first time is an exciting event for a teenager. Prior to purchasing an automobile, however, a written driver's test and a road test must be passed and received his driver's license. Don't be afraid to consider several things before you purchase a vehicle. First decide whether you can afford to purchase a new vehicle or a used vehicle. For most teenagers a used car is the better choice. People can often find a very good deal on a used car. Consult the newspaper or a reputable used car dealer. Next you need to consider if you want a truck, a van, or if you want a car that is full-size or compact. There are several additional considerations to be made about the prospective vehicle. What will this vehicle be used for? Some teenagers are buying their first car as a status symbol. Others are buying their first car for transportation to and from work and school. Others are buying their first car just for fun. Then you must consider some other things. Before the car is purchased, a mechanic with good skills and a sound reputation should inspect the car for mechanical problems. How many miles are on the odometer? Has the vehicle been wrecked at any time? Is there any rust on the body of the vehicle? The seats and dashboard should be in good shape with no tears, worn places, or soil marks. Maybe the color of the vehicle is very important to you. Now you are ready to fulfill your dream of purchasing your first vehicle.

HISTORY OF THE ENGLISH LANGUAGE

Continual Small Changes

You have read that spoken languages are always changing. Little by little the sounds change, the words change, and even some of the grammar changes. You can see some of these language changes in the Greek examples on pages 26–27 and in the English examples given again below. You would notice even more changes if you heard these translations of John 1:1 pronounced.

Old English (Anglo-Saxon)
On frymthe wæs Word, and thæt Word wæs mid Gode, and God wæs thæt Word.

Middle English
In the bygynnynge was the worde (that is goddis sone) and the worde was at god, and god was the worde.

Early Modern English
In the beginning was the Word, and the Word was with God, and the Word was God.

The examples of Latin and its daughter languages (p. 26, 2.1–2.4) show how one language can slowly split into several languages. Latin, the common language of most of the Roman Empire, was still being spoken in the time of Christ. Although scholars continued to read it and write it in about the same way for centuries, the common people all over Europe spoke it in their own local ways.

After a few hundred years, Latin had changed significantly, with different changes in different parts of Europe. The changes became so great that people from one area could not understand people from another area. When that happens, we say that they speak different languages. In this case, the local varieties of Latin ended up as the languages of Spanish, French, Italian, and so on. Here, then, we see an example of the second reason for language differences: languages are always changing, and a language spoken long enough and over a broad enough area will eventually split into different languages. This same process has occurred all over the world.

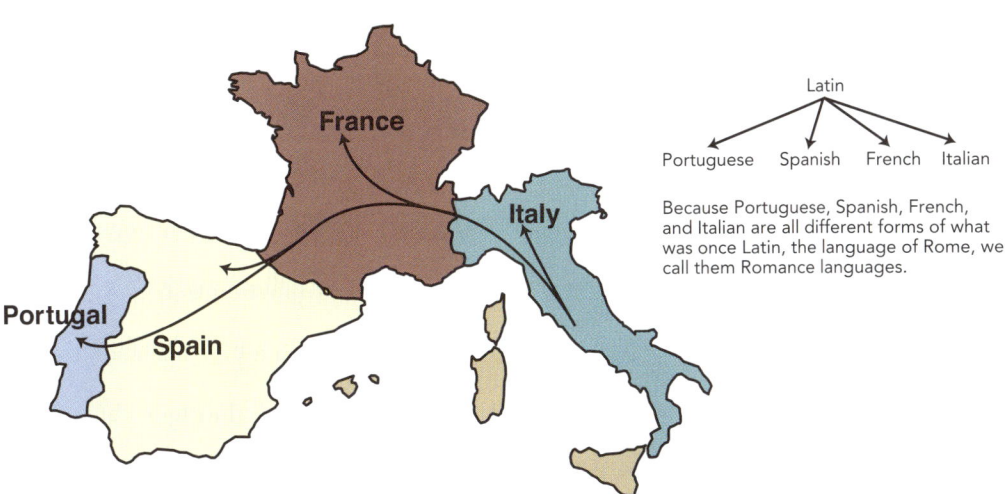

Because Portuguese, Spanish, French, and Italian are all different forms of what was once Latin, the language of Rome, we call them Romance languages.

Library Skills | 395
History of the English Language | 407

LIBRARY SKILLS Reference

15

Our English word *library* comes to us from a Latin word meaning "of books." That connotation was an appropriate one for thousands of years. Over the past several decades, however, libraries have expanded their holdings to include not only books but also magazines, newspapers, audio-visual recordings, and even artwork. Today's library is a rich depository of valuable resources for education and entertainment.

The Arrangement of Library Materials

In order to use the library to its fullest potential, you need to find the answers to two basic questions. First, how is the library arranged? In other words, what sections or special rooms does it include and where are they located? If the library is small, you can probably figure out the floor plan easily on your own. If the library is large, look for a posted floor plan or ask a library staff member for help. Pay attention to the labels that the library uses to identify its sections and materials. Each item in the library probably carries a label that indicates the room or section to which it belongs.

Kind of Material	Examples	Possible Label
Books	fiction and nonfiction, both hardcover and paperback	FIC, NFIC, PB *(paperback)*, LP or LT *(large print or large type)*
Periodicals	newspapers, magazines, journals	PER
Audio-Visual Materials	audiocassettes, CDs, DVDs, videocassettes, filmstrips, works of art	AV, CD, DVD, VHS, CAS *(cassette)*
Reference	encyclopedias and other noncirculating materials that can be used only in the library	R *or* REF
Children / Young Adult	books, periodicals, and audio-visual materials designed especially for children or teens	J *or* JUV *(juvenile) or* YA
Special Collections	local interests, genealogy records, rare books	

The second question to answer is this: How are the materials themselves arranged? Finding the fiction or nonfiction section is not enough; you also need to find the specific item that you want. Knowing how the library classifies its materials will save you valuable time as you search for the resources you need. Follow the general principles explained in this chapter. Then look for posted explanations or ask a library staff member if you need further assistance.

Fiction

Fiction books are arranged on the shelf alphabetically according to the authors' last names. If two authors share the same last name, their novels are arranged alphabetically by their first names. If an author has written more than one novel, his books are arranged alphabetically by title, ignoring any initial articles.

No Vacation for Maigret by Georges Simenon

The Manor by Isaac Bashevis Singer

Joy in the Morning by Betty Smith

A Tree Grows in Brooklyn by Betty Smith

The Hundred and One Dalmatians by Dodie Smith

Specialized fiction books might be shelved separately from general fiction. Books in these genres usually carry an extra label that indicates the section to which they belong, such as *MYS* for mystery fiction. Short story collections may be shelved either alphabetically with the novels, in a special section of fiction shelves just for short stories, or in the nonfiction section with other books about literature.

Nonfiction

Nonfiction books are arranged by topic. Most libraries use one of two common classification systems to arrange nonfiction books: the Dewey decimal system and the Library of Congress system. Each book carries a label with the book's **call number**, which represents the subject category to which the book has been assigned. The label might also include a **Cutter number**, which represents the author of the book and may include one or more letters of the author's name or perhaps one or more letters of the title.

Dewey Decimal System

The **Dewey decimal system** is based on units of ten. A three-digit number signifies three levels of division: main category, subcategory, and a further subcategory. Decimal numbers after the three-digit number represent further division into even more specific categories.

Number	Category	Examples
000–099	Computer science, information and general works	encyclopedias, general reference works, computing, journalism
100–199	Philosophy and psychology	metaphysics, logic, ethics
200–299	Religion	Bible, theology, church history
300–399	Social sciences	political science, communications, folklore
400–499	Language	grammar, linguistics
500–599	Science	physics, paleontology, zoology
600–699	Technology	agriculture, chemical engineering, manufacturing

CONTINUED

700–799	Arts and recreation	sculpture, music, sports, theater
800–899	Literature	novels, short stories, plays, literary essays
900–999	History and geography	travel, biography, genealogy

Most libraries arrange biographies within the 920 section alphabetically by the last names of the subjects. A capital letter *B* may be added to the call number to indicate that the book is a biography or an autobiography. However, some libraries shelve biographies with the appropriate subject area, such as the 780s (music) for a biography of a musician.

Library of Congress System

The **Library of Congress system** uses a combination of letters and numbers. There are twenty-one basic categories, each represented by a letter. These categories can be further subdivided several times. A typical call number usually consists of one or two letters followed by a series of numbers.

A	General works	M	Music and books on music
B	Philosophy, psychology, religion	N	Fine arts
C	Auxiliary sciences of history (such as archaeology, genealogy, biography)	P	Language and literature
D	World history	Q	Science
E	History of the Americas	R	Medicine
F	History of the Americas	S	Agriculture
G	Geography, anthropology, recreation	T	Technology
H	Social sciences	U	Military science
J	Political science	V	Naval science
K	Law	Z	Bibliography, library science, information resources
L	Education		

15.1 PRACTICE *the skill*

Considering the main areas of the library, identify the section in which you would expect to find each item.

1. In which section of the library would you find a novel?

2. What identifying label would a library use for an encyclopedia?

3. In which library section would you find copies of the *New York Times*?

4. What identifying label might you find on a biography of Margaret Thatcher?

5. A compact disc recording entitled *Gettysburg* would be in what section?
   _____

6. A large print Bible might have what identifying label?
   _____

7. Dr. Seuss's *The Cat in the Hat* would be in what section?
   _____

8. In what section of the library would you find a collection of historical records of your city?
   _____

9. Some libraries allow patrons to check out works of art. In what section would you find these?
   _____

10. In what section would you find materials with an indication of "Library Use Only"?
    _____

15.2 PRACTICE *the skill*

Number the following fiction books in the order in which they would appear on a library shelf.

_____ 1. Milne, A. A. *The Red House Mystery*

_____ 2. MacInnes, Helen. *Above Suspicion*

_____ 3. MacDonald, Betty. *Nancy and Plum*

_____ 4. Milne, A. A. *Now We Are Six*

_____ 5. MacDonald, George. *The Baronet's Song*

Using the Dewey decimal chart on pages 396–97, identify the number range of the correct category for each item.

_____ 6. *Spanish Made Easy*

_____ 7. *Cayman Islands: A Visitor's Guide*

_____ 8. *Applied Psychology*

_____ 9. *101 Best Sports Stories*

_____ 10. *A Study in Systematic Theology*

Using the Library of Congress chart on page 397, identify the letter of the correct category for each item.

_____ 11. *Watercolor Painting Techniques*

_____ 12. *Heart Disease Diagnosis and Therapy: A Practical Approach*

_____ 13. *Archaeology in Old Testament Lands*

_____ 14. *A Compliance Guide to the Family Medical Leave Act*

_____ 15. *Transit: When Planets Cross the Sun*

Search Tools and Strategies

Gathering Information p. 5

Knowing how the library materials are arranged on the shelves is important. But knowing how to search the library's holdings to find exactly the right item you need is important too. Use the following search tools and strategies to find the materials that interest you most or address your research topic best.

Library Website

Use the **library website** to plan your library visit before you leave home. Most library websites include the library's hours of operation, its branch locations, its policies, announcements of special activities, information about available resources, and access to the library's online catalog. Patrons can use this access to search the catalog for the materials they need and to check on the availability of those materials. Some online catalogs also allow patrons to reserve or renew library materials, to request materials from interlibrary loan, or to contact the library staff by e-mail for further help or for answers to reference questions.

Library Stacks

Browsing the library stacks—the shelves of circulating materials—is an often-overlooked strategy that may lead you to something that you would never have thought to search for otherwise. Start by using the catalog to find a book about your topic and then browse the shelf where it is located to find additional helpful books. Or simply check the classification table that your library uses and then find the shelves labeled with the number or letter that signals your topic.

tip

Should you ever judge a book by its cover? Sometimes the condition of a book's cover can be a clue that the book is old, perhaps containing out-of-date information. Check the copyright page to find out when a book was first published.

Library Catalog

The library's catalog is a versatile search tool with information about each item that the library owns. Most libraries have online catalogs, sometimes called OPAC (online public access catalog). An **online catalog** allows library patrons to search electronic records that list information about all the library materials. Each electronic record includes the title, the author, the call number, and publication information for that item. Some records also include a summary of the item's contents and a description of the item's physical characteristics, such as the number of pages that the book contains. Most online catalogs also report the status of each item: available, reserved for another patron, or already checked out (and when the book is due to be returned).

Although online catalogs differ somewhat, they generally allow the patron to search the catalog by typing in whatever search criteria the patron has. You can search by author's name, by title, by subject matter, and sometimes by call number or kind of material. The catalog will then display a list of records that match the criteria you typed into it. In addition, some catalogs will allow you to sort the results according to selected criteria (such as publication date or author's name) or to view more detailed information about a particular item by selecting that item from the list.

Some smaller libraries still use card catalogs instead of online catalogs. A **card catalog** is a file of alphabetized cards housed in a cabinet with small drawers. Each item in the library's collection is usually represented by at least three cards: an author card, a title card, and a subject card. Each type of card lists all the basic information for a particular item (author, title, publication information, and call number), but the order of information differs. The author card lists the author's name on the top line, the title card displays the title of the work at the top, and the top line of the subject card shows the subject classification for that item.

Specialized Indexes

The library catalog usually lists only the books, periodicals, and other materials that a library has available but not the various chapters, articles, or stories in those resources. To find a specific article or several articles on a specific topic, use an index or a bibliography. Many of these tools are available in both printed and electronic formats. Consult a librarian for more information about the particular resources available at your library.

Periodical Indexes

Consult a **periodical index** to find a specific article from a newspaper, a magazine, or a professional journal. The most popular periodical index is the ***Readers' Guide to Periodical Literature***, which lists articles from over two hundred magazines by subject and by author. The index is updated regularly throughout the year. Soon after publication, articles are listed in one of the paperback volumes issued during the year. At the end of each year, these volumes are combined and reissued in a single large volume. An online version of the *Readers' Guide* is also available.

To find an article about a particular subject, look up a keyword for your topic. Directly under the subject heading, you may find "see also" entries that suggest related subject headings. The article entries are listed next, sometimes grouped under subheadings. (Some articles may be listed under more than one subheading.) Each individual entry includes the article's subject, its title, its author, the magazine in which it appears, the volume number or date of the magazine, and the page numbers of the article. If the article has illustrations, the entry will include that information too. The listings use several abbreviations explained in the front of each volume.

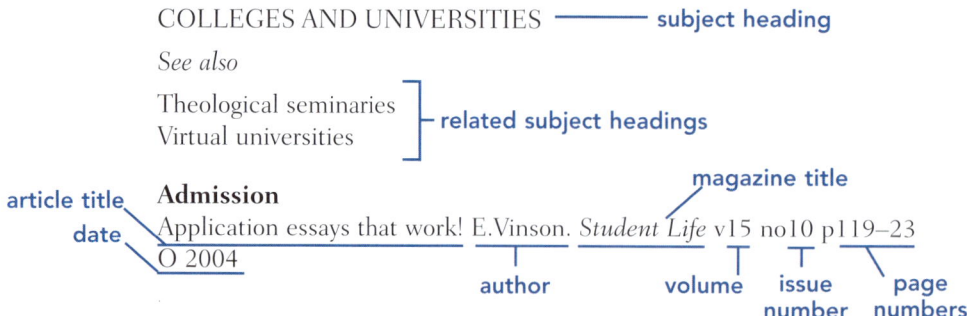

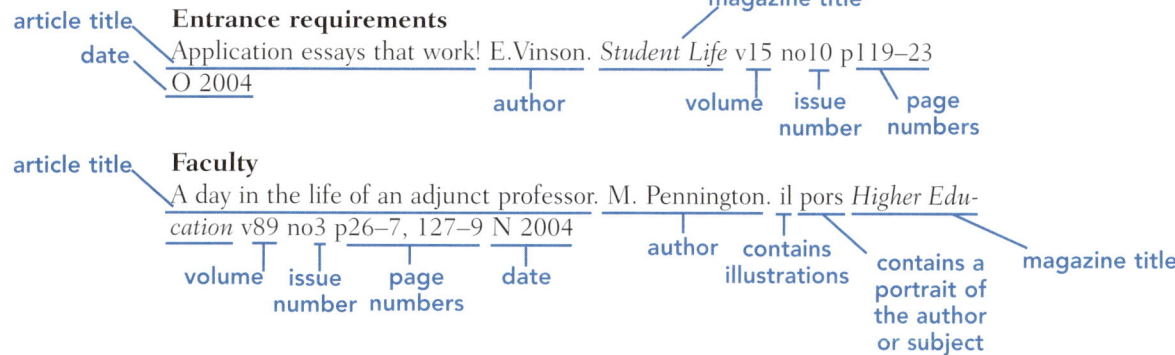

The **New York Times Index**, which is available in both print and electronic versions, lists articles that have appeared in that newspaper only. However, by helping you discover the dates of newsworthy events, it can assist your search for information in back issues of other newspapers as well. Some local newspapers also publish indexes, and many newspapers offer searchable archives on their websites.

Consult a **subject index** if you need to find up-to-date scholarly information about your topic. A subject index is more selective than a general periodical index; it usually focuses on detailed articles from scholarly journals. Examples include the *Social Sciences Index* and the *Humanities Index.*

Libraries today carry many electronic databases to index and search encyclopedias, newspapers, periodicals, and books, often giving full texts of newspapers and periodicals. Because these databases select information from reliable sources, they may contain more valuable information than an unknown source accessed through the Internet.

Literary Indexes

Consult a **literary index** to find a particular short work (such as a poem or short story) included in an anthology. A literary index is more useful than the library catalog because the catalog entry for an anthology will often list only partial contents or none at all. A literary index allows you to look up the short work itself for a list of the collections in which it appears. *Granger's Index to Poetry* (also known as *Columbia Granger's World of Poetry* in its electronic format) is especially helpful because it allows you to look up a poem by its title, its author, or its first line. Other useful literary indexes include *Short Story Index, Play Index,* and *Essay and General Literature Index.*

Bibliographies

A valuable source of information that researchers sometimes overlook is a **bibliography**. A bibliography section in the back of a book about your topic can be helpful because it will point you to other sources of information about your subject. Even more helpful may be a book-length bibliography. Many of these longer works (usually compiled by scholars who specialize in the field covered by the bibliography) include annotations for each source listed. The annotation usually includes a summary of the work and a comment on its usefulness or accuracy. After you identify the sources that look most promising, check the library catalog to see which of them are available from your library. If a particular book or article is not available, you may be able to request it through interlibrary loan.

Parts of a Book
pp. 410–11

15.3 USE *the skill*

Use the library's catalog to find at least five books and five nonprint items (audio-visual or electronic format) about a topic of your choice. List the title, author, and call number for each item.

1. _____
2. _____
3. _____
4. _____
5. _____
6. _____
7. _____
8. _____
9. _____
10. _____

15.4 USE *the skill*

Use the *Readers' Guide to Periodical Literature* to find five articles about a topic of your choice. List the title, author, periodical, and date for each article.

1. _____
2. _____
3. _____
4. _____
5. _____

Use the *New York Times Index* or another newspaper index to find five articles about a topic of your choice. List the title, author, newspaper, and date for each article.

6. _____
7. _____
8. _____
9. _____
10. _____

15.5 USE the skill

Use an appropriate literary index to answer each question.

1. From what short story is this opening line: "Let us hurry to the walls"?
   _____

2. What is the first line of Percy B. Shelley's "Ozymandias"?
   _____
   _____

3. From what play is "Neither a borrower nor a lender be"? Who is the author?
   _____
   _____

4. "Jabberwocky" by Lewis Carroll is part of what larger work?
   _____
   _____

5. Who wrote the short story "The Business Man"?
   _____

Reference Works

General reference works provide an overview of the topics they discuss—and perhaps some detailed information as well—making them excellent sources for someone beginning to research a topic. In addition to the traditional printed reference books, some works are available in microform (such as microfilm or microfiche) or in an electronic format (such as a CD-ROM or an online website). The electronic version makes searching for information fast and easy; some even allow you to print entire articles. Check with a librarian to find out what reference works are available in your library.

Almanacs and Yearbooks

An **almanac** is a yearly publication that includes tables of weights and measures, lists of sports statistics, names of award winners, information about government agencies and programs, summaries of recent events, and other facts. You can find the information you need by looking in the index of the almanac, which may appear at the front of the book like a table of contents.

A **yearbook** is also published annually. It gives current information, such as statistics and events, about a specific subject. Examples include *American Law Yearbook* and *The Shakespearean International Yearbook.*

Atlases and Gazetteers

An **atlas** is a book of collected maps. Most atlases also contain information about weather, geography, population, and other statistics. The index lists the page number for each map in the collection. A **gazetteer** is an index of place names. Some gazetteers include additional information, such as elevation or population, for each place listed.

 **Thinking Biblically**

Reference works attempt to be objective, reporting the facts without mixing in opinions. Encyclopedia editors gather experts who are known for their careful work on any given historical, scientific, linguistic, mathematical, or other topic. Even the online community behind Wikipedia aims at what they call NPOV, a neutral point of view. Since many writers—from journalists to authors of pulp fiction—can be deeply and unfairly biased, any effort at evenhanded objectivity is commendable. But Christians must recognize that no one is neutral in the ultimate sense. All truth and all good belong on one side. All lies and all evil belong on the other. Each man retains some good because he is made in God's image; evil nonetheless touches every part of man because of Adam's Fall. The "facts" of a case are always interpreted through a person's worldview; no one is truly neutral. Our goal ought to be to seek GPOV—God's point of view.

Bible Commentaries and Concordances

A **Bible commentary** is a verse-by-verse or section-by-section explanation of Scripture. Some commentaries cover individual books of the Bible; longer works cover the entire Bible.

A **Bible concordance** is an alphabetical index to the words of the Bible, helpful for locating a passage and sometimes for studying a subject through the Bible. Some concordances include the Hebrew or Greek word from which the English word was translated. When you can remember only part of a verse, look up an important word from the verse in the alphabetical list. If the particular passage you want is not listed, try another keyword. Not all keywords or passages will appear in every concordance.

Spelling
p. 426

Biographical Sources

A number of sources provide concise biographical information about prominent people. (For more detailed information, check a book-length biography.) To research someone living today (or just recently deceased), check a current **biographical dictionary**, such as *Current Biography, Contemporary Authors,* or the various *Who's Who* publications. To find information about someone who is no longer living, check an older edition of these works or a source such as the *American National Biography* or the British *Oxford Dictionary of National Biography*. Most of these sources are arranged alphabetically by the subjects' last names; some of the multivolume works may be arranged alphabetically within chronologically arranged sections. Check the index to find the pages that discuss the person you are researching. The index for a multivolume work might be a separate volume.

Hyphens
pp. 342–43

Capitalization
pp. 270–86

Dictionaries

Dictionaries contain a wealth of helpful information about words and languages. A typical dictionary entry includes the word's correct spelling (and any acceptable variant spellings), pronunciation, part of speech, inflected forms, definitions, and etymology. Some entries also include labels or notes that indicate proper usage.

A large **unabridged dictionary** contains several hundred thousand words. An abridged dictionary, or **desk dictionary**, is much shorter, but even it contains thousands of words, usually all the words we use on a regular basis. **Special-purpose dictionaries** include Bible dictionaries, dictionaries of synonyms, foreign language dictionaries, dictionaries of English as a second language ("ESL" dictionaries), and dictionaries of subjects like sports, the sciences, and professions such as medicine and law.

History of the English Language
p. 407

 If English is not your first language, you would benefit from having and using an ESL dictionary. In an ESL dictionary, the definitions are easier to understand, and every word meaning has a sample sentence so that you can see the word in use. An ESL dictionary also gives more grammatical information to help you use words correctly. (Ask your teacher to help you understand the features of your ESL dictionary, especially by going through the introductory pages with you.)

Encyclopedias

Encyclopedias contain articles that give brief introductions to many subjects. Electronic versions usually offer keyword-searching options. Printed encyclopedias usually consist of several volumes, each labeled with one or more letters and a numeral. The articles are arranged alphabetically. Guide words at the top of the page tell you the topic of the first article on that page. Information on some subjects may be included in several different articles. The index lists all the pages that contain information on a particular subject. Some encyclopedias have an index in each volume; others have a separate volume (usually the last volume) that is the index for the entire set. Many encyclopedia articles list cross-references to other related articles under a heading such as "See also."

Literary Sources

A variety of sources are available to those who are researching literary topics. In-depth research requires more specific information, but these sources can provide an introduction or an overview to those who need only basic information. Both *The Oxford Companion to English Literature* and *The Oxford Companion to American Literature* contain short articles about authors, plots, characters, and related subjects. The *Cyclopedia of Literary Characters* contains brief "biographical" descriptions of characters from famous literary works. *Book Review Index* provides bibliographic entries and excerpts of book reviews that appeared in newspapers, magazines, and journals. A quotation index, such as *Bartlett's Familiar Quotations* or *Columbia World of Quotations,* allows you to find a famous quotation by looking up its author, a keyword, or the topic. Most quotation indexes also list each quotation's source and date.

Thesauruses

Useful with a dictionary is a **thesaurus**, a treasury of synonyms and antonyms. Some thesauruses list the main words alphabetically, and others group all words by meaning, directing you to the meaning groups from a detailed index in the back. In either case, you choose a synonym (or antonym) from the words you find listed. A dictionary and a thesaurus are often used together—the thesaurus to help you think of a word and the dictionary to confirm that the word is in fact the one you need.

15.6 PRACTICE *the skill*

Identify the reference tool that would be most useful for finding the answer to each question.

1. What is the population of Cheyenne, Wyoming?

2. What was the first published work of the American novelist Sarah Orne Jewett?

3. Describe the character Mr. Bounderby in Charles Dickens's *Hard Times.*

4. What did the critics say about Peggy Noonan's book *When Character Was King: A Story of Ronald Reagan*, published in November of 2001?

5. Who wrote, "No stile [sic] of writing is so delightful as that which is all pith, which never omits a necessary word, nor uses an unnecessary one"?

6. How do electric motors work?

7. Where would I find a section-by-section explanation of the Bible's book of Job?

8. Who won the Nobel Peace Prize in the year in which you were born?

9. Did the International Langland Society hold any sessions in your state last year?

10. Where exactly is Londonderry in England?

15.7 USE *the skill*

Using standard reference tools, answer the following questions.

1. What is the population of Kingston, Jamaica?

2. What types of energy sources does Uruguay possess?

3. When was the prophecy of Ezekiel 31 pronounced in relation to the fall of Jerusalem?

4. List two Old Testament references for uses of the word *leaf*.

5. Who coined the phrase "the great silent majority"?

6. What is the area code in Coventry, Connecticut?

7. How would one pronounce and define the word *outré*?

8. What is the elevation of Great Salt Lake in Utah?
   _____

9. In what year did Queen Victoria of England marry Prince Albert, and how many children did they have?
   _____

10. What novel contains a character named Peggotty?
    _____

HISTORY OF THE ENGLISH LANGUAGE

Great Vowel Shift

The American English that you speak today developed from Early Modern English, the language of Queen Elizabeth I, of William Shakespeare, and of the King James Version of the Bible. Late in the Middle English period (in the 1400s), a phenomenon known as the Great Vowel Shift (GVS) began to alter greatly the vowel system of English. Because the GVS was a gradual, multistep process, scholars vary on the exact dates of the shift, but most agree that the changes occurred mainly in the fifteenth and sixteenth centuries.

This "shift" in vowels refers to the area of the mouth where English vowels are articulated. Today when you say the vowel sound of the word *feet* (the so-called long /ē/ sound), your tongue is high and forward in your mouth. Now say *foam* (long /ō/ sound): your tongue lowers and moves ("shifts") to the back of your mouth. In Old and Middle English, however, the sounds indicated by the same spellings were somewhat different. For example, the word *feet* probably sounded much more like the long /ā/ of today's *fate*. Therefore, the GVS refers to changes in the long vowels of English. It affected only the vowels that were literally long (held out longer). In the GVS most long vowels were raised in the mouth, one was also fronted, and some became diphthongs. We still call these our "long vowels," even though the term does not apply literally today.

We can thank the GVS for many of the complexities of and exceptions to our English spelling and pronunciation. Have you ever wondered why words spelled with *ea* can be pronounced with a long /ē/ (*glean, leaf, speak*) or a long /ā/ (*break, great, steak*)? Blame the Great Vowel Shift!

Study Skills | 409
History of the English Language | 425

Study Skills Reference

Success in both personal and academic achievements depends upon the ability to set and accomplish goals. Most students find it easy to set goals, but many find it very difficult to accomplish the goals they have set. How many times have you set a goal and within a very short time failed in your efforts to reach that goal? Perhaps you set a personal goal to read your Bible each day and have a specific prayer time. For the first few days, you did well. But then you found that one day you were too involved in other activities to read your Bible and pray. You failed to accomplish the goal, and your first inclination might have been to give up rather than to put the single failure behind you and continue to pursue your goal.

The same may be true for you in academics. You may have tried to do all of your homework, to read all of the outside reading, or to make a passing grade on a test. However, music lessons, basketball practice, work at a fast-food eatery, or myriad other activities took the time you needed for schoolwork. How can you improve this situation? You must learn to set priorities, use time wisely, and develop helpful study skills.

Developing Good Study Skills

Determine a time and place to study. Choose a specific time to study when you plan your daily schedule. Yes, even the weekend should include planned study time. Before you begin studying, pray: ask the Lord for guidance and help for your study time. You may find that fifteen-minute periods of concentrated study may be more effective than a long period of concentrated effort. In addition to a specific time, determine a specific place to study. Your study area should be quiet, well lighted, and free of distractions such as a telephone or television. A computer or tablet can be a highly useful tool for studying; however, limit your use of these devices to academic purposes during your study time. Left unchecked, they too can become distractions.

Organize your study materials. Whether in a notebook or in computer folders as digital files, organized study materials are essential. To organize a multi-subject notebook, designate one division for each subject and use a pocket page to store assignments and related class work. To organize digital files, name them by assignment and sort them into folders named for each subject. In addition to your organized notebook (or computer or tablet), be sure to have other necessary materials, including textbooks, other resource books, and a daily planning calendar (or planning software).

Assess the assignments. Record daily homework assignments in a specific place in your notebook, in a specific assignment notebook, or on planning software. As you evaluate the assignments, designate them as long-term (taking more than a day) or short-term (taking a day or less) and mark them by the day, the week, or the month. Using a calendar to record dates for tests and assignments will give you an overview of times when you will be particularly busy.

Thinking Biblically

Developing good study skills requires self-control—a trait that none of us possesses naturally. Naturally, we seek to please ourselves, to avoid work for less demanding activities. In fact, self-control, as the Scriptures remind us, is one of the fruits of the Spirit, the result of a life yielded to Christ (Gal. 5:22–23). In other words, the Holy Spirit is able to empower us to overcome our selfish desires. But the change from selfish to self-controlled does not happen instantly. As the apostle Paul describes, obtaining self-control requires consistent practice (1 Cor. 9:24–27).

Take notes. As you read your assignments, take notes on the material, even if you do not think you will use the notes. Putting ideas that you have read into your own words will help you retain the ideas. Be alert to phrases such as *most important*, *for example*, and *to review*. Develop a personal abbreviation list for frequently used words or ideas; use these abbreviations to save time as you take notes. At this point, you need to review the notes that you took in class, organize them according to main ideas, and place them in the specific subject area in your notebook or in the appropriate folders on your computer.

Develop study aids. Using vocabulary cards can help you learn vocabulary words and their definitions more quickly. Using cards for Bible verse location and memorization is also helpful. For each subject area, use a different-colored card.

Proofread your work. For written assignments that you will be submitting for a class, allow yourself time to proofread and to review your work several times. As you proofread, be alert to grammatical errors, misspelled words, and inaccurate documentation.

Take personal responsibility for studying. You must remember that no one else can study or take tests for you. It is your responsibility to complete the work independently and punctually. Developing good study habits and using study helps can aid you in reaching your goals. Always precede your study time, your writing endeavors, and your test-taking experiences with prayer for clarity of thought and for God's presence with you.

Using the Parts of a Book

Textbooks and other nonfiction books include information that can help you locate and use information in the book. The chart below gives a summary of features found in a book.

Part of Book	Useful Information
Title Page	Title of book Name of author or editor Name of publisher Place of publication *Look here when you are creating a bibliography.*
Copyright Page	Year of publication Name of copyright holder *A copyright is the legal right to a book—no one can reprint any part of the book without permission from the copyright owner.*
Table of Contents	Main topics Organization of topics *Unit divisions appear in numerical order with page numbers.*
Acknowledgments	Names of people the author or editor wishes to thank for their assistance or contribution
List of Illustrations	Location and sequence of pictures
Introduction or Preface	Purpose of the book or important background information

CONTINUED

Text	The main part of the book, usually divided into units or chapters
Bibliography	List of sources that the author used in writing or that would provide additional information about the subject
Appendix	Section of additional information related to the text (may include charts, diagrams, long lists, and notes of explanation)
Glossary	Type of appendix: definitions of important vocabulary in the text
Index	Alphabetical list of key words and phrases in the text with page numbers

PRACTICE *the skill*

Write the name of the book section that would provide the information necessary to answer each question. (Answers may be used more than once.)

_____ 1. Does this book discuss a certain issue or idea?

_____ 2. On what page does a particular photograph appear?

_____ 3. Has a certain book been used as a reference in this book?

_____ 4. Where was this book published?

_____ 5. When was the book published?

_____ 6. Whom does the author thank?

_____ 7. What does this unfamiliar term mean?

_____ 8. Where can I find more information about the topic of this book?

_____ 9. On what page does the third chapter begin?

_____ 10. What is the author's purpose for this book?

16.2 REVIEW *the skill*

Use the sample table of contents and index pages from *CHEMISTRY*, Third Edition, by Brad R. Batdorf and Rachel Santopietro (BJU Press, 2009) to answer each of these questions.

_____ 1. In which chapter could you learn about analog instruments?

_____ 2. On what pages would you find information about Jons Jakob Berzelius?

_____ 3. Which chapter discusses the states of matter?

_____ 4. Would you find information about the atomic theory in Chapter 4?

_____ 5. On which page does the introduction start?

_____ 6. Is Chapter 6 the only chapter that includes information about the Apollo Space program?

_____ 7. On what page does the discussion of types of chemical bonds begin?

_____ 8. On which page would you learn about the properties of acid?

_____ 9. In which chapter section would you first find out about absolute zero?

_____ 10. In which chapter might you find a definition of chemical studies?

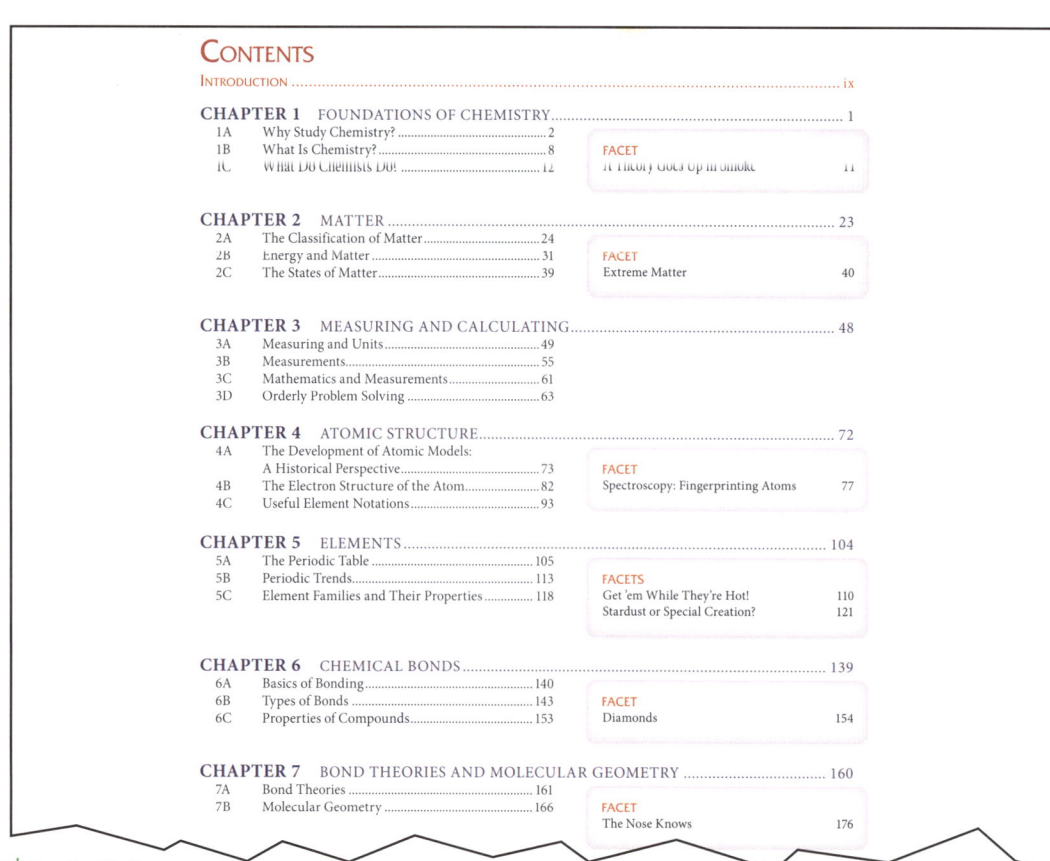

412 Chapter 16 | Study Skills

Index

A

absolute zero, 37, 339
absorption, 359, 365
accuracy, 55, 68
acid: Arrhenius, 398; binary, 194; boric, 408–9; Brønsted-Lowry, 399, 410; citric, 459; conjugate, 400; hydrochloric, 414–15; Lewis, 401; phosphoric, 227; properties of, 397; sulfuric, 215, 236; ternary, 194
acid-base reactions, 402
acidic solution, 403
acid-ionization constant (K_a), 407
acid reflux, 414–15
actinide series, 112, 124
activated complex, 355
activation energy (E_a), 355
active site, 360
activity series, 205
actual yield, 235
addition polymers, 485
addition reaction, 464
adenine, 471–72
adhesion, 287
aerosol, 320
airbag, 267
alchemy, 10
alcohol, 291, 310, 419, 456
aldehyde, 458
aliphatic compound, 447

amorphous solid, 280
amphoteric substance, 410
analog instrument, 57
analytical chemist, 262, 281
anesthetist, 274
angular momentum equations, 83
anhydrous, 194
anion, 98, 432
anode, 434, 436
antacid, 414–15
antibonding orbital, 165
antifreeze, 317, 457
antimony, 129
Apollo space program, 139, 238
apothecary, 9
applied science, 12
Arabic science, 10
area, 51
argon, 133, 269
Aristotle, 10
aromatic compound, 447, 452–53
array, 29
Arrhenius acid, 398
Arrhenius model, 398, 400
Arrhenius, Svante, 398
arsenic, 129
artificial elements, 107
aryl group, 455
aryl halide, 455
astatine, 131
asthma, 48, 57

base: Arrhenius, 398; Brønsted-Lowry, 399, 410; conjugate, 400; Lewis, 401; properties of, 397–98
base-ionization constant (K_b), 407
base unit, 50
basic solution, 404
battery, 436, 438–40
becquerel (Bq), 504
Becquerel, Henri, 501
bent molecule, 170, 174
benzene, 280, 452–53
Berzelius, Jons Jakob, 129, 484
beta decay, 506
beta particle (β), 503
bias, 5, 19
big bang, 121
binary acid, 194
binary covalent compound, 188
binary ionic compound, 189–90
binding energy, 517
biochemistry, 11, 126, 445, 465
biopolymer, 494
bleach, 427
blood, 417–18
blood alcohol content (BAC), 419
Bohr, Niels, 78
Bohr's atomic model, 78, 80
boiling, 25, 289
boiling point, 290
boiling-point elevation (ΔT_b), 313
bond: chemical, 337–38; covalent, 141,

Improving Reading Comprehension

As you progress in your academic career, reading will become one of the major contributors to your learning. A good reader takes time nearly every day for recreational reading, such as the newspaper, a trade magazine, or a novel. You will find that recreational reading greatly improves your comprehension, speed, and vocabulary. In the academic realm, the teacher is no longer the primary provider of knowledge. Instead, the student has learned to "dig out" important principles, facts, or truths from the assignments. As you anticipate being a college student, you must realize the importance of improving your reading skills.

Context Clues

Paying attention to the words and sentences that surround an unfamiliar word can help you infer the meaning of that word. The following strategies may help you understand the meaning of an unfamiliar word.

Verbal Context

If the text does not give the meaning of the word, it may use other words from which you can determine the definition.

> Daniel answered in the presence of the king, and said, The secret which the king hath demanded cannot the wise men, the astrologers, the magicians, the *soothsayers*, shew unto the king. (Dan. 2:27)

Although you may not know that *soothsayers* are those who predict the future, you can infer its meaning from surrounding words such as *astrologers*.

An unfamiliar word is often followed immediately by an explanation or a synonym.

> After Daniel interpreted the dream, King Nebuchadnezzar sought to honor Daniel by an *oblation*, the act of offering something to a deity.

From the context you can conclude that an *oblation* was a presentation showing good will to someone who had godlike qualities.

The unfamiliar word in the context may be in a cause-and-effect relationship.

> Because the three Hebrew men would not bow to the golden image, King Nebuchadnezzar became very angry and his *visage* changed toward the men.

When you realize that the king was very angry because the Hebrew men disobeyed his order, you can surmise that *his visage* probably refers to the king's face or appearance.

An unfamiliar word may be compared or contrasted with familiar words.

COMPARISON	The Hebrew men's allegiance to God under King Nebuchadnezzar parallels Daniel's continued *homage* to God under King Darius.
CONTRAST	After learning that Daniel had survived the den of lions unharmed, Darius's *lament* changed to a cry of praise to God.

Were you able to determine that *homage* means a public expression of loyalty and that *lament* is a mournful expression of grief?

ESL Try all of these strategies and use the ones that are most helpful for you.
- Look at title, chapter, and heading names to discover the topic of the reading.
- Try to read each paragraph or short section without using your dictionary. After reading through the material once, look up any words that keep you from understanding the meaning of the paragraph or short section.
- Do **not** look up in a dictionary every word that you do not know.
- Read a paragraph, write a few words beside it in the margin to summarize it, and keep reading. You can use your marginal words to help you review your reading.
- Do not read everything at once. Read for thirty minutes. Use five minutes to stand up, walk around, or drink some water. Then continue reading for another thirty minutes. Repeat this cycle until you finish your reading.

Grammatical Context

An unfamiliar word may be clarified by the grammatical structure in which it occurs. Look for words that are familiar to you. For example, if a word appears in a series of words, then it probably has something in common with the words in the series.

> Then these men were bound in their coats, their *hosen*, and their hats, and their other garments, and were cast into the midst of the burning fiery furnace. (Dan. 3:21)

Although *hosen* may be an unfamiliar word, you can guess that it must be some article of clothing since it is listed with other articles of clothing.

Word Parts

Roots, prefixes, and suffixes can help you to determine the meaning of an unfamiliar word. The root is the main part of the word. Common roots appear in many different words. The root *voc* means "to call." You will find this root in many familiar words including *vocal, vocation, vocabulary.* An extension of this root is the word *voice.* An unfamiliar word such as *vocative* becomes easy to understand because you know the meaning of the root word. You can probably guess that *vocative* means "pertaining to or having reference to calling."

Dictionaries
p. 404

Prefixes are word parts added to the beginning of a word. The prefix *re-* means "backward or back." To *revoke* means to "call back." Your understanding of both the root word and prefix helps you to determine the meaning of the word. You must remember, however, that some words include more than one prefix. The word *irrevocable* adds an additional prefix to *revoke.* The new prefix means "not," and the new word means "not able to be called back" or "impossible to call back." Using your knowledge of prefix meanings will help you to understand unfamiliar words and to build your working vocabulary.

Suffixes are word parts added to the end of a word. The suffix *-al* means "relating to or characterized by" and is used to form adjectives. The word *vocal* then means "relating to or characterized by calling" or "relating to the voice." The common suffix *-ion* forms nouns; *vocation* then is a person's "calling" or "occupation." *Vocabulary* is the words in a language. By consulting your dictionary, you can trace the etymology of *vocabulary* to the root word *voc.*

Adding Suffixes
pp. 429–30

16.3 PRACTICE *the skill*

Write the letter of the word or phrase that most closely matches the meaning of the italicized word. Be prepared to explain what context clues you used.

_____ 1. The clown entertained the children with feats of *prestidigitation* such as pulling a rabbit from a hat.
    A. amusement or entertainment
    B. magic or conjuring

_____ 2. Before the builders can begin the new structure, they must *raze* the abandoned building already on the site.
    A. to demolish
    B. to renovate

_____ 3. Troy hurried into the conference room, apparently unaware that his tie was *askew* from the wind outside.
    A. crooked
    B. flimsy

_____ 4. That clerk has behaved so badly that his coworkers *ostracize* him, failing even to invite him to eat lunch with them.
    A. exclude
    B. reject

_____ 5. Young athletes in training often try to *emulate* successful older athletes.
    A. admire
    B. imitate

Considering the context of the sentence, write a definition of the italicized word. Be prepared to explain what context clues you used.

6. Melanie found the lavishly decorated office very different from the *austere* façade of the municipal building.

   _____

   _____

7. The careless student's paper was *replete* with errors.

   _____

   _____

8. We all admired the *sylvan* setting of the cottage, entirely surrounded by tall trees.

   _____

   _____

9. The *stentorian* tones of the speaker, rising above the noise of the crowd, reminded us of a foghorn.

   _____

   _____

10. In his new suit, shirt, and tie, Thomas was the picture of *sartorial* splendor.

    _____

    _____

16.4 REVIEW *the skill*

Use a dictionary to find the meaning of each root, prefix, or suffix. Then write a word that uses the root, prefix, or suffix.

1. de- _____   _____
2. post- _____   _____
3. anim _____   _____
4. tract _____   _____
5. in- _____   _____
6. -hood _____   _____
7. voc _____   _____
8. arch _____   _____
9. circum- _____   _____
10. struct _____   _____

Using Memory Techniques

Successful memorization depends upon many factors. One of the most important factors is having confidence in yourself and your ability to memorize. You must realize that the material before you is important, that there is a need for the material, and that you can learn the material.

Read through your notes each day. Regular review will be much more effective than a long study session the night before a test. As you study, make a list of key items you need to remember or mark the most important facts in your notes and review that information daily.

Break down large chunks of information. When studying a large amount of material, try to organize the material into smaller, more manageable units. If you have a long list of items to memorize, separate them into categories and focus on learning one category at a time. If you need to learn facts from maps, charts, or graphs, study only one section at a time, working your way through each section in a regular pattern so that you do not miss any information.

Make flash cards from your notes. Flash cards allow you to quiz yourself or to enlist the help of a family member or friend to quiz you. Write a question on one side of each card and the answer on the other. Note which questions you are unable to answer quickly and then spend extra time studying those flashcards. Digital flashcard programs are also available online.

Create a quiz for yourself as you study. Write down important questions on one sheet of paper and the answers on another. Try to answer the questions a few days later. This strategy will help you know what you need to study more thoroughly.

Use mnemonic [ni-mon´ik] devices to memorize a list. Rhymes, acronyms, and acrostics are convenient ways to remember lists of information. An acronym is a word in which each letter stands for another word. An acrostic is a phrase in which each initial letter stands for a different word or phrase.

Taking Tests

Classroom Tests

Although each test is unique, certain strategies will help you do your best on each test you take. Use these techniques to demonstrate what you have learned.

Arrive early. Be in the classroom and in your seat prior to the beginning of the test. Avoid rushing in at the last minute. Having time to get settled and to arrange your materials for the test will help calm your spirit.

Look over the entire test to determine the number and types of questions. If you are told to write a lengthy essay at the end, you do not want to spend too much time on the first part of the test. Throughout the test, check your watch or a clock to keep track of how much time you have left.

Read all directions carefully and listen for any additional instructions from the teacher. You may be tempted to skim the directions and to start right away answering questions, but you can needlessly miss several points by simply failing to follow the exact directions. Don't forget to check the board for additional written instructions. Talk to your teacher if you do not completely understand all of the directions.

Write down from memory any equations, formulas, or rules that you will need. Unless you are allowed to use your textbook or your notes, all of the helps you need to complete the test should be committed to memory. Before you begin answering questions, transfer those helps from your memory to a separate sheet of paper or the margin of the test. Then refer to your jottings as you work through the questions.

Use your time wisely, working through the test in one of three ways:

- **Start at the beginning of the test and keep going.** Answer the questions that you know or that you are reasonably confident about. Mark the questions that you do not know or that you need more time to consider. Then go back to those questions later. Occasionally information in a later part of the test will help you recall other points.
- **Scan the test for the easier questions first and answer them quickly.** Then spend the rest of the time on the difficult questions.
- **Begin by completing the more difficult section of the test.** This strategy is helpful if the difficult questions are worth more credit because it ensures that you will have time to answer those questions before you answer those that will earn you less credit. However, be careful to save enough time to answer the easier questions whose answers you know.

Try to answer every question, even if you have to guess at some.

Think carefully and be selective about what you write. It is better to write a little about what you know than to write a lot about what you do not know.

Allow yourself time to recheck your work. As you review your work, look for any questions that you may have accidentally overlooked. Check for correct spelling and grammar. Careless errors are often identified during this rechecking time.

Write neatly. Correct answers will not count if your teacher cannot read what you have written.

 Your teachers want to help you learn. When you ask your teacher for help, ask specific questions. For example, do not just say, "I don't understand. Can you help me?" You should ask questions like "I do not understand what I must do. Can you explain the directions to me?" or "I do not understand my homework. Can you show me how to do this part?"

Essay Tests

Essays pp. 19–20

Answering an essay question requires more than simply answering an objective test question. An essay question usually asks you to do more than merely list facts; it gives you an opportunity to demonstrate what you know about the topic and to show connections between ideas. Use these techniques to hone your essay-writing skills.

Read the directions carefully. If you have a list of essay questions to choose from, choose the one you are best prepared to answer.

- **Focus on the main verb in the directions.** Common verbs found in essay questions include *analyze, compare, contrast, discuss, evaluate,* and *explain.* If the question asks you to analyze a situation, merely describing the facts would be insufficient.
- **Notice the important nouns in the question.** If the question asks you to explain how Wyatt and Surrey contributed to the development of the Elizabethan sonnet, you should avoid discussing the sonnets of Shakespeare and Petrarch or the ballads and quatrains of other poets.
- **Understand what format you are to use.** If the directions are unclear, ask the teacher to clarify whether you are to write one well-developed paragraph or a multiparagraph essay, with or without separate introduction and conclusion paragraphs.

On a separate sheet of paper, jot down all the facts you know that are related to the topic. Include names, dates, and important points that you do not want to leave out.

Organize your ideas. Decide which facts are of primary importance and which are subordinate to others. Then group related facts to create a rough outline. To save time, don't write out a formal outline but use arrows and other markings on your idea list instead.

Write a thesis statement. A thesis statement gives the purpose and often indicates the organization of your essay. One useful strategy is to restate the question as a thesis statement.

ESSAY QUESTION	Contrast the positions promoted by Lincoln and Douglas in their famous debates.
THESIS	The positions promoted by Abraham Lincoln and Stephen A. Douglas in their famous debates differed in three key respects.

Write a topic sentence for each main point in your answer. In a short essay (1–3 paragraphs), limit the number of main points to three or four. Be sure that each topic sentence directly supports your thesis statement.

Support each topic sentence with specific detail. Provide sufficient proof for each statement but avoid "padding" your essay with interesting but irrelevant information that does not directly support the topic sentence.

Write a conclusion that restates your thesis. A simple rewording of the thesis is usually a sufficient conclusion for a short essay.

Quickly proofread your essay. Correct any factual, grammatical, or mechanical errors and add any necessary clarification. Clearly rewrite any illegible passages.

Standardized Tests

As you finish high school and prepare for college, you will probably be required to take a standardized test. Since these tests are often different in format from a classroom test, it is important for you to understand the various question formats. Also, be aware that you may not be allowed to write or mark on the test paper but only on an answer sheet.

Reading Comprehension

The reading comprehension section asks you to read a passage and then answer a question or questions about that passage. (If there is just one question, you might read the question first to determine what to look for as you read.)

> After the terrorist attacks of September 11, 2001, U.S. President George W. Bush launched a war on terror. The United States government sent troops to several sensitive locations. Some troops assumed strategic positions in the Persian Gulf. Others found themselves in the mountainous regions of Pakistan and Afghanistan. In the Far East, troops were located in the semideserted island areas.

Example: __C__   The main topic of the passage is
- A. places in the world.
- B. military troops.
- C. a global war on terrorism.
- D. the president's desire for peace.

Vocabulary

Standardized tests usually contain a vocabulary section. You may be asked to determine the meaning of a word that you do not know. In this case, use the context to help you determine your choice.

Example: __B__   United States military troops participate in a number of public operations, but they also execute many **clandestine** operations.
- A. daily
- B. secretive
- C. similar
- D. peaceful

Another type of vocabulary question will give a word in a sentence and then ask you to identify another sentence in which the word is used in the same way.

Example: __D__   The unusual print on Jessica's scarf is quite striking.
- A. The blurred print made the letter difficult to decipher.
- B. The investigators were unable to match the suspect's prints to those on the weapon.
- C. Keegan has several new prints on display at the art gallery.
- D. Does the designer plan to reproduce the original wallpaper print for the restoration project?

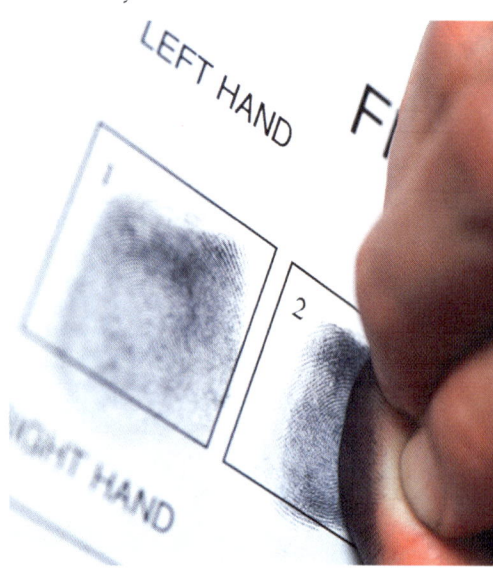

Analogy

An analogy is a comparison that shows the similarities or the relationship between two things. Analogy questions ask you to find the relationship between two words by identifying another group of two words that shows the same relationship. The two words in a set are usually separated by a colon that stands for the phrase "is to"; the two sets of words are separated by a double colon that means "as."

Example: __A__   artist : brush ::

    A. dentist : drill
    B. police officer : hat
    C. firefighter : fire station
    D. commander : flag

Grammar, Usage, and Mechanics

Standardized English tests also include a section on grammar, usage, and mechanics (spelling, capitalization, and punctuation). One type of question will show a sentence with several parts underlined. You are to identify the underlined part that contains an error.

Example: __D__   <u>Military personnel</u> <u>were responsible</u>
                       A   B
to organize <u>their equipment</u> in an
                C
orderly fashion. <u>No error</u>
                   D

Another type of question will give a sentence with one part underlined. You must choose a replacement part that will make the sentence correct.

Example: __C__   The platoon gave <u>lieutenant Johnson's wife</u> a gift for her birthday.

    A. lieutenant Johnsons wife
    B. Lieutenant Johnsons wife
    C. Lieutenant Johnson's wife
    D. correct as is

Some tests will divide a sentence into several parts with each part on a separate line. You must choose the line that contains the error in mechanics.

Example: __B__   A. General Thompson invited Tom,
               B. Jim, and me, to attend the
               C. staff meeting on Friday.
               D. no mistakes

16.5 PRACTICE *the skill*

Reading Comprehension: Read the paragraph and answer the questions that follow it. Write the letter of the best answer.

If you have experienced God's saving grace, you have insight many experienced chemists lack. We cannot properly study chemistry unless we approach it from a Christian perspective. To many people, that statement sounds controversial—even nonsensical. After all, what does Scripture have to do with chemistry? What Bible verses explain the structure of atoms or the nature of chemical bonds?

True, the Bible is not a chemistry textbook. But the Bible confronts humans with a distinct worldview, a perspective from which to see and interpret all of life. Like a corrective lens, the Bible brings into focus every part of the world, including chemistry. As we look at chemistry through the lens of Scripture, we find that the best reasons to study chemistry are biblical ones.

(from CHEMISTRY, Third Edition, by Brad R. Batdorf and Rachael Santopietro, BJU Press, 2009)

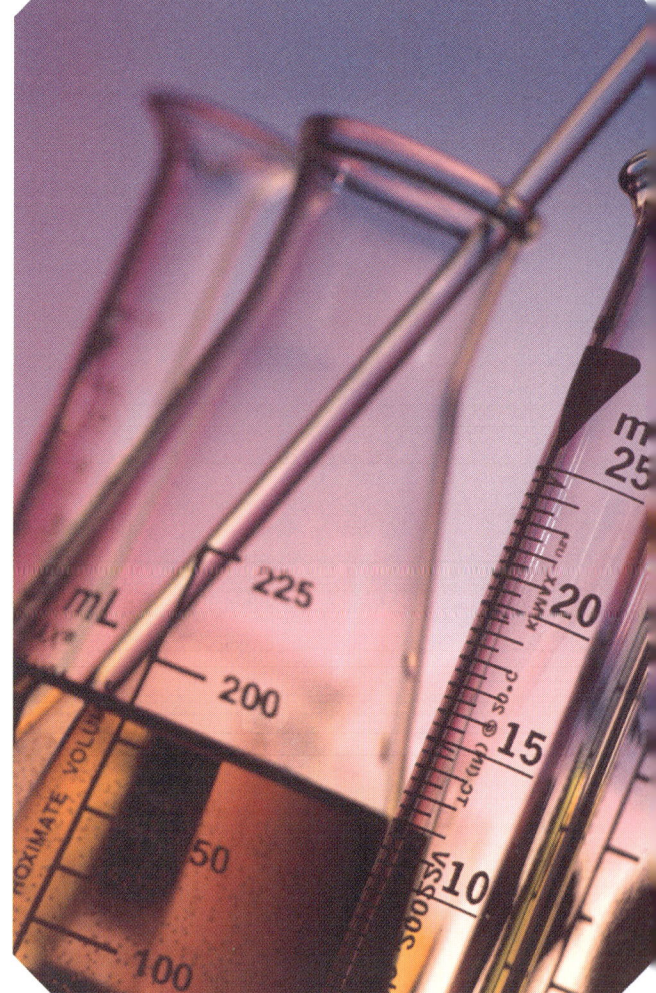

_____ 1. This passage is mainly about
   A. the biblical study of chemistry.
   B. the development and importance of chemistry.
   C. the philosophical foundations of scientific study.

_____ 2. According to this passage, the Bible
   A. can be used as a chemistry textbook.
   B. is universally accepted as useful.
   C. provides a necessary perspective for scientific study.

_____ 3. This passage does not mention
   A. the controversial nature of the biblical worldview.
   B. a justification for chemical study.
   C. the biblical account of Creation.

_____ 4. A good title for this passage would be
   A. The Development of the Science of Chemistry.
   B. A Definition of Chemistry.
   C. Chemistry in Biblical Focus.

_____ 5. In this passage the word *nature* means
   A. the physical world.
   B. the characteristics of something.
   C. the human condition without God's grace.

Vocabulary: Write the letter of the definition that most closely matches the word in bold print.

_____ 6. The knife's **keen** edge was useful for slicing tomatoes.
   A. sensitive
   B. sharp
   C. quick

_____ 7. The use of too much makeup may make a person look **ostentatious.**
   A. humorous
   B. fat
   C. showy

_____ 8. Based on **tenuous** foundations, his argument was unconvincing.
   A. flimsy
   B. strong
   C. wicked

Vocabulary: Write the letter of the sentence in which the definition of the underlined word more closely matches that of the underlined word in the first sentence.

_____ 9. Who will be giving this year's commencement address?
   A   Sheila receives her business mail at a separate address.
   B. The queen's address to the nation was broadcast live.

_____ 10. The coach's pep talk galvanized the team in the second half of the game.
   A. The editorial in today's newspaper failed to galvanize the council to make a decision.
   B. They galvanize both iron and steel at the shop.

16.6 PRACTICE *the skill*

Analogy: Write the letter of the pair of words whose relationship most closely matches the relationship of the original pair of words.

_____ 1. fur : dog ::
   A. dog : dish
   B. peel : orange
   C. fire : wood

_____ 2. island : ocean ::
   A. moon : space
   B. wind : rock
   C. sandpaper : wood

_____ 3. foot : shoe ::
   A. page : book
   B. nail : board
   C. hand : glove

_____ 4. keys : ignition ::
   A. time : clock
   B. fan : ceiling
   C. pick : lock

_____ 5. speak : word ::
   A. sing : song
   B. noise : sound
   C. scream : yell

Grammar, Usage, and Mechanics: Write the letter that corresponds to the error in the sentence.

_____ 6. Everything works together wondrously, yet people still believe that there
            A   B   C
is no God. No error
            D

_____ 7. According to Psalm 19, "The heavens declare the glory of God".
                     A   B   C
No error
D

Grammar, Usage, and Mechanics: Write the letter of the correct replacement for the underlined section of the sentence. If the sentence is correct, choose D.

_____ 8. My brothers enjoys playing the piano, and I often enjoy listening to them play.
   A. My brother's enjoys
   B. My brothers enjoy
   C. My brother's enjoy
   D. correct as is

424 Chapter 16 | Study Skills

Grammar, Usage, and Mechanics: Write the letter of the section that contains an error. If the sentence is correct, choose *D*.

_____ 9. A. Acting is one way
B. to overcome the fear,
C. of speaking to large groups.
D. no mistakes

_____ 10. A. Many high schools
B. and many colleges
C. offer acting classes.
D. no mistakes

HISTORY OF THE ENGLISH LANGUAGE

Rules for Modern English

The language of the Early Modern English period seemed free and strong, but in the later 1600s some people worried that it was too free. They began looking for rules to guide them as they used English. They already had rules for writing in Latin, and for good reason—for centuries no one had grown up speaking Latin, and so they had to learn it from books. So, they thought, why not also have rules for writing in English? Beginning about 1660, with especially high interest during the eighteenth century, more and more people wanted grammars and dictionaries to tell them how to write and speak. Some people even wanted to regulate the language itself.

People looking for authority tended to accept whatever rules the grammarians made. Some of the rules did describe what good English was like, and we follow most of them today. Other rules were based on Latin (instead of English) or on one person's idea of what English should be.

One example of this kind of rule is the notion that one should never end a sentence with a preposition. However, good English speakers routinely used sentences like the following: *What are you getting at? I don't know what you're talking about. Do you know what rules are for? They didn't know what they were up against.* Because Latin sentences never ended with a preposition, grammarians decided that English sentences should not either. And the rules are seemingly constantly in flux. Your teachers and parents have seen many changes in punctuation rules during their lifetime (e.g., dropping the comma after a short introductory prepositional phrase) as well as in rules of spelling and grammar (e.g., use of *shall* and *will*). It might be easier if we could just forget about all these rules, but some of them have become part of good English—especially formal English. The rules you are taught today reflect how English is used, informally and formally, by educated people in America.

Spelling

Good spelling is an essential writing skill. Whether you are writing a research paper or a personal letter, your message is communicated most clearly by using the right words and spelling them correctly. Use these spelling hints and master these rules so that you will be a competent writer.

Spelling Hints

Pay attention to the spelling of new words.

Make a point of focusing on the spelling of new or unfamiliar words. When you read, you certainly read for meaning; but an occasional focus on spelling can help you become a good speller. (Spell the word softly to yourself and try to learn it.)

Spell by syllables.

Dividing a word into its individual syllables will help you to spell it correctly. Think about prefixes, suffixes, and other word parts as you spell words by syllables.

mis + spell	misspell
over + react	overreact
over + eat	overeat
general + ly	generally

Use a dictionary.

Look up the spelling of words when you are unsure of the correct spelling. Keep a good dictionary available when you are writing. Although you might be unsure of a word's exact spelling, you probably know enough of the word to find it in the dictionary.

Dictionaries p. 404

Keep a list of words that are problems for you.

Whenever you misspell a word and then locate the correct spelling of that word, put it on your list of problem words. Study your list systematically. Begin by writing a word several times, concentrating on its appearance and pronunciation. Repeat this procedure on three or four different days of the next week. Then ask someone to quiz you. If you can write the word correctly without hesitation, transfer it to your "learned" list. If a problem remains, keep working on the word.

Look for possible groupings among your problem words.

If you find a group of similar words, try to formulate or find a rule for that group. For example, you may find that several of your problem words contain *ie* or *ei*. Learning the rules for *ie* and *ei* will allow you to spell an entire group of words correctly.

Compare related words.

The sound of a related word can be a clue to the spelling of an unclear vowel.

Unclear Vowel	Clear Vowel	Unclear Vowel	Clear Vowel
her*e*sy	her*e*tical	simil*a*r	simil*a*rity
exhib*i*t	exhib*i*tion	specif*y*	specif*i*c

However, certain related words are spelled differently. Check your dictionary if you are unsure of the spelling of any word.

Spelling Singular Present-Tense Verbs and Plural Nouns

General Principles

If the word ends in *ch, sh, s, x,* or *z,* add *es.*

touch	touch**es**
crash	crash**es**
pass	pass**es**
annex	annex**es**
waltz	waltz**es**

If the word ends in *y* preceded by a consonant, change the final *y* to *i* and add *es.*

| casualty | casual**ties** |
| deny | den**ies** |

If the word ends in *y* preceded by a vowel, add *s.*

| display | display**s** |
| enjoy | enjoy**s** |

If the word ends in *f* or *fe,* consult your dictionary. For most, add *s*; for others, change the *f* to *v* and add *es.*

gulf	gulf**s**
chafe	chafe**s**
cliff	cliff**s**
self	sel**ves**
life	li**ves**

Add *s* to most other words.

parka	parka**s**
due	due**s**
boycott	boycott**s**
eat	eat**s**

If the word ends in *o,* consult your dictionary. For most, add *es*; for others, add *s.*

| tomato | tomato**es** |
| archipelago | archipelago**s** |

Musical terms are more likely to require *s* than *es.*

| adagio | adagio**s** |
| piano | piano**s** |

Some nouns have irregular plural forms. Consult your dictionary for nouns with irregular plurals.

man	men
datum	data
parenthesis	parentheses

Plural Nouns pp. 35–37

Present Tense pp. 178–79

Plurals of Proper Nouns

The plurals of proper nouns are made by adding *s* or *es* according to the preceding rules but without any other spelling changes. Never use an apostrophe in making the plural of a proper name.

| the McDonoughs | the Gregorys | the Douglases | the Marches |

Some plurals of personal titles are irregular.

General or Formal	*General or Informal*
Messrs. Franklin and Firth	Mr. Franklin and Mr. Firth
Mmes. Proffit and Rood	Mrs. Proffit and Mrs. Rood
Misses Lucy Butler and Frieda Scholtze	Miss Lucy Butler and Miss Frieda Scholtze
Drs. Joseph Markham and Alice Kenney	Dr. Joseph Markham and Dr. Alice Kenney

A plural title can also be used when the same title applies to two or more persons with the same name.

Formal	*General or Informal*
the Misses Pelham	the Miss Pelhams
the Drs. Harvey	the Dr. Harveys

Plurals of Compounds

Attach *s* or *es* to the end of most compounds.

| snowboard | snowboards |
| homestretch | homestretches |

Pluralize the first element of certain compound nouns—those in which the first element is felt to be the most important part of the compound. When in doubt, consult your dictionary.

| secretary of state | secretaries of state |
| brother-in-law | brothers-in-law |

Pronunciation of Possessives, Plurals, and Singular Present-Tense Verbs

The same pronunciation rules apply to three English suffixes—the possessive suffix for nouns (spelled '*s*), the regular plural suffix for nouns (spelled *s* or *es*), and the third-person singular suffix for present-tense verbs (spelled *s* or *es*). The pronunciation of all of these suffixes depends on what kind of sound precedes the suffix.

- These suffixes are pronounced /əz/ after **s**, **z**, **sh**, **zh**, **ch**, and **j** sounds (sounds similar to the /s/ and /z/ sounds of the suffixes). These sounds include the **x** and **ge** spellings.

    classes, waxes, glazes, dishes, corsages, matches, badges

- The suffixes are pronounced /s/ after other voiceless consonant sounds (sounds that you form with your mouth but do not say with your vocal cords): **f**, voiceless **th**, **p**, **t**, and **k**.

    cuffs, moths, Kip's, Matt's, clocks

- The suffixes are pronounced /z/ after other voiced sounds (sounds that you both form with your mouth and say with your vocal cords): **v**, voiced **th**, **b**, **d**, **g**, **m**, **n**, **ng**, **l**, **r**, **w**, **y**, and all vowels.

    knives, clothes, Rob's, Todd's, dogs, hems, tunes, rings, Paul's, hours, tows, toys, fleas, copies, trios, Julia's

Spelling with *ie* and *ei*

When the sound is "long *e*," put *i* before *e* except after *c*.

i before *e*	except after *c*
bel**ie**ve	c**ei**ling
gr**ie**f	rec**ei**pt

Exceptions:

caffeine, leisure, protein, seize, sheik, weird; either and *neither,* in their more common American pronunciation, are also exceptions to this rule.

When the sound is "long *a*," put *e* before *i*.

v**ei**n	b**ei**ge

When the two vowels are pronounced separately, spell according to the pronunciation of the first vowel.

qu**ie**t	ath**ei**st

We call a vowel "long" when its pronunciation is the same as the name of the letter. For example, the vowel sound in *cake* is "long *a*."

Adding Suffixes

Doubling a Final Consonant

If a one-syllable word ends with a single consonant preceded by a single vowel, double the final consonant before adding a suffix that begins with a vowel.

plot	plot**ted**
stun	stun**ning**

Similarly, if a multisyllable word with its main accent on the final syllable ends with a single consonant preceded by a single vowel, double the final consonant before adding a suffix that begins with a vowel.

permit	permit**ted**
refer	refer**ring**

Exceptions:

The consonant does not double when the suffix causes the main accent to shift away from the final syllable: **con**ference vs. con**fer**ring.

The final *l* sometimes doubles regardless of the location of the main accent, especially in British usage: *counselor* or (mainly British) *counsellor.* Consult your dictionary.

If a word ends with a single consonant preceded by two vowels, do not double the final consonant before adding a suffix.

greet	greet**er**
wait	wait**ing**

Changing the Final *y* to *i*

If a word ends with a consonant and *y*, change the final *y* to *i* before adding a suffix.

| cleanly | clean**liness** |
| rely | rel**ied** |

However, if the suffix itself begins with *i*, do not change final *y* to *i*.

| supply | supply**ing** |
| baby | baby**ish** |

Exceptions:

Some words keep the *y*: *babyhood, shyness.*

In a few established spellings, the *y* has become *i* in spite of the preceding vowel: *daily, paid.*

Dropping the Final Silent *e*

Drop the final silent *e* that is preceded by a consonant before adding a suffix beginning with a vowel.

| advise | advis**able** |
| tune | tun**ing**, tun**ed** |

Keep the final silent *e* before adding a suffix beginning with a consonant.

| achieve | achieve**ment** |
| tune | tune**ful** |

Exceptions:

The *e* is kept to signal the "soft" pronunciation of *c* or *g* before a suffix beginning with *a* or *o*: *noticeable, courageous.*

A word ending in *ue* normally drops the *e* even when the suffix begins with a consonant: *truly, argument.*

Words ending in *dge* lose their *e* (in American English) before *ment*: *judgment, acknowledgment.*

A few other words are exceptions, some of them to distinguish homonyms: *dyeing* (vs. *dying*), *singeing* (vs. *singing*).

Chapter 2 Review: Parts of Speech

Nouns
Identify each italicized noun as *possessive, proper, compound, collective,* or *abstract*.

_____ 1. Hurricanes and typhoons are different names for strong tropical disturbances; the *majority* are often not extremely destructive.

_____ 2. The *truth* of the matter is that both of these can have heavy rain and strong winds.

_____ 3. Although all severe weather can be dangerous, hurricanes and typhoons usually cause more damage than *thunderstorms* do.

_____ 4. A number of years ago a Caribbean storm was often named for the *saint's* day on which the storm occurred.

_____ 5. Hurricane *Santa Ana* struck Puerto Rico in 1825.

Pronouns
Identify each italicized pronoun as *personal, indefinite, demonstrative, relative,* or *indefinite relative*.

_____ 6. Before the end of the nineteenth century, an Australian meteorologist began giving women's names to *most* of the tropical storms.

_____ 7. For a period of time storm names were given in alphabetical order, but *these* were different in other parts of the world.

_____ 8. In 1979 *whoever* was responsible for naming storms began to alternate men's and women's names for storms in the Western Hemisphere.

_____ 9. The name of a storm may be dropped from the list if *its* destruction is very deadly and costly.

_____ 10. The committee *that* determines the list of names for a storm season may remove a name and place another name on the list.

Identify each italicized pronoun as *interrogative, reflexive, intensive,* or *reciprocal*.

_____ 11. *Who* has ever heard of the 1954 hurricane called Hazel?

_____ 12. Hazel *herself* caused the deaths of one thousand people in Haiti.

_____ 13. As a category-four hurricane, Hazel devastated the North and South Carolina coastlines by *herself*.

_____ 14. *What* would be the result of such a destructive storm?

_____ 15. People asked *each other* whether their lives or property would ever be the same.

Verbs
Identify each italicized verb as *action*, *state-of-being*, or *auxiliary*.

_____ 16. Hazel's destructive wind and rain *killed* ninety-five people in the United States.

_____ 17. In the Toronto area, hurricane Hazel, accompanied by excessive rainfall, *was* responsible for eighty-one deaths.

_____ 18. An eighteen-foot storm surge *destroyed* a great part of the coastal region of North Carolina.

_____ 19. Because of the extreme destruction of this storm, the name Hazel *is* on the list of retired names.

_____ 20. The names Irene, Katrina, and Tomas, among others, *have* been retired as well.

Adjectives and Adverbs
Underline each adjective once and each adverb twice. Do not underline articles.

21. Tropical cyclones appear predominantly in the Southern Hemisphere, where they get energy from warm tropical oceans.

22. Clockwise winds of a tropical cyclone may whirl unceasingly in excess of 90 km, and storm gusts may exceed 260 km.

23. Very violent storm surges can cause the ocean to rise many feet above high tide.

24. Tropical cyclones may last for many days and follow unpredictable paths.

25. Excessively high winds are a destructive force to vessels at sea and in the harbors.

Prepositions, Conjunctions, and Interjections
Identify each italicized word as a preposition *(prep)*, a coordinating conjunction *(coord conj)*, a correlative conjunction *(correl conj)*, a subordinating conjunction *(sub conj)*, or an interjection *(interj)*.

_____ 26. *Not only* do tropical cyclones continue for many days, *but* they *also* follow very unpredictable paths.

_____ 27. High winds can destroy buildings *and* turn airborne debris into deadly missiles.

_____ 28. *Wow!* Did you see the huge pine tree that was blown over by the winds?

_____ 29. *If* tropical cyclones encounter land or cooler waters, their strength will diminish.

_____ 30. Pedestrians should seek substantial protection *during* a tropical cyclone.

Chapter 3 Review: Sentences

Kinds of Sentences

Identify each sentence as *declarative,* *exclamatory,* *imperative,* **or** *interrogative.* **Place the appropriate punctuation mark at the end of the sentence.**

_____ 1. Have you ever been outside the United States

_____ 2. International flights are often quite tiring

_____ 3. Once you arrive at your destination, you will most likely want to sleep

_____ 4. Visiting a foreign country can be a blast

_____ 5. If you ever have the opportunity to visit a foreign country, take it

Subjects and Predicates

Underline the simple subject once and the simple predicate twice in each independent clause.

6. Juan and Victor flew to Puerto Rico to visit their extended family.

7. As they traveled, they talked excitedly about the events of the upcoming week.

8. After landing, they exited the plane and made their way through the busy airport to the baggage claim area.

9. They claimed their luggage and met their relatives, who were very glad to see them.

10. After an exciting but tiring two weeks, they flew back to the United States with many memories of a different culture.

Underline each complete subject once and each complete predicate twice. If the subject is understood, write *you* **to the left of the number.**

11. Imagine how you would feel leaving your country to live in a foreign country for a long period of time.

12. There are some people who have had that experience.

13. Would you enjoy living outside the United States?

14. Many of the people living outside the country are missionaries.

15. These missionaries sacrifice life in their homeland, financial prosperity, and many other things to spread the gospel of Christ.

Sentence Patterns

Label the sentence pattern of each independent clause *S-InV*, *S-TrV-DO*, *S-TrV-IO-DO*, *S-TrV-DO-OC*, *S-LV-PN*, *S-LV-PA*, or *S-be-Advl*. If the adverbial is a prepositional phrase, underline it.

16. Missionary stories are often extremely exciting and thought provoking for children.

17. Part of the appeal of the missionary story is in its reality.

18. In addition to being factual, missionary stories teach children moral values and character qualities.

19. These stories often come from the missionary's personal experiences.

20. They may make the children more responsive to the needs of others.

21. Hearing vivid accounts of real needs instills in children a desire to spread the Word and to see God work in their own lives.

22. Many of the stories teach children the power of prayer.

23. Many young people attending a Bible club have not experienced answers to prayer in their lives.

24. Missionary stories are an interesting, attention-grabbing means of giving the gospel.

25. Teaching such a story to children is a wonderful ministry tool and a great responsibility.

Chapter 4 Review: Phrases

Prepositional Phrases
Place parentheses around each prepositional phrase and underline the simple object of each preposition. In the blank, write the word or words that each phrase modifies.

_____ 1. In 1767 the innovative John Webster advertised a new product that proved to be both decorative and practical: wooden blinds.

_____ 2. Their original name, Wooden Venetian Sun Shades, reveals their primary function in the home.

_____ 3. With the ability to open various degrees, wooden blinds simultaneously provide privacy and light.

_____ 4. At a time when window decoration relied primarily on architectural design, wooden blinds provided a welcome addition to the decorative repertoire.

_____ 5. Though today blinds are common, their versatility was a novelty in the 1700s.

Appositive Phrases
Underline each appositive phrase. In the blank write the word or words that the appositive renames.

_____ 6. In colonial times wooden blinds visible in the homes on Duke of Gloucester Street, a famous avenue in historic Williamsburg, indicated their popularity.

_____ 7. Thomas Jefferson, a most influential man of his day, reportedly had many wooden blinds in his residence.

_____ 8. Some classicists, such as Edith Wharton, a noted American author and interior decorator, preferred older forms of window coverings such as an inside shutter.

_____ 9. Wooden blinds are still popular in renovated buildings; those at the Lawn, the historic campus of the University of Virginia, add to the authenticity of the buildings.

_____ 10. More popular today are miniblinds, a cheaper alternative to wooden blinds.

Participial Phrases
Underline each participle or participial phrase. Then identify the word or phrase as *present, past,* or *perfect.*

_____ 11. Furniture craftsmen probably developed the first manufactured wooden blinds.

_____ 12. Boards left from furniture production became blinds.

_____ 13. Having studied Colonial decorating, historians have found that walnut wooden blinds were very prominent.

_____ 14. Having two-inch wooden slats, these blinds were easily incorporated into Georgian design.

_____ 15. Painting or staining the wood, manufacturers matched the color of the blind to the color of the room.

Gerund Phrases
Underline each gerund or gerund phrase. Identify its function as subject *(S)*, direct object *(DO)*, predicate noun *(PN)*, indirect object *(IO)*, or object of the preposition *(OP)*.

_____ 16. Decorating during the Federal Period focused on a classical style.

_____ 17. To match the light-colored stone popular in architecture during this period, decorators updated dark blinds by painting them white.

_____ 18. Occasionally, a decorator deviated from using the lighter colored blinds and painted them a dark green color instead.

_____ 19. Ladies enjoyed working with colorful fabrics and making frilly curtains.

_____ 20. These new choices gave decorating a more elegant tone.

Infinitive Phrases
Underline each infinitive and place parentheses around each infinitive phrase. Then identify its function as noun *(noun)*, adjective *(adj)*, or adverb *(adv)*.

_____ 21. To have elaborately decorated homes became popular during the Victorian Era.

_____ 22. Some decorators chose to replace wooden blinds with movable shutters.

_____ 23. The popularity of wooden blinds declined for a brief time; they became popular again because they are beautiful and easy to use.

_____ 24. Nearly three centuries have witnessed people's desire to ornament their windows with wooden blinds.

_____ 25. If you choose to hang these blinds in your home, you will continue a long-standing American tradition.

Chapter 5 Review: Clauses

Distinguishing Independent and Dependent clauses
Identify each italicized clause as independent (IC) or dependent (DC).

_____ 1. *What has been your experience with advertising*, if any?

_____ 2. You know *you are constantly the target of advertising*.

_____ 3. Whenever you see a billboard or a shop, *that is advertising*.

_____ 4. Almost everything *that we see* is sending us some sort of message, whether good or bad.

_____ 5. Christians must be wise *as they view commercials*; otherwise, they can fall prey to covetousness.

Adjective Clauses
Place parentheses around each adjective clause. In the blank, write the word it modifies. Underline each relative pronoun once; underline each relative adverb twice.

_____ 6. Often, a local church will have a need for advertising that you can help with.

_____ 7. Perhaps you could help write content for a website that the church uses for communication with its members and visitors.

_____ 8. Many churches have tract distribution programs, which aid in the spread of the gospel and acquaint people with the church.

_____ 9. Some churches have boards where service times and opportunities are listed.

_____ 10. You yourself are a form of advertisement, either good or bad, to any person with whom you speak about your church.

Adverb Clauses
Place parentheses around each adverb clause, including any elliptical adverb clause. In the blank, write the word or words it modifies. Underline each subordinating conjunction.

_____ 11. When advertising, keep your message clear and simple.

_____ 12. Before you prepare an advertisement, you must first settle on a target audience.

_____ 13. You will be glad for your preparation, for you cannot design an advertisement when you do not know the audience or the objective.

_____ 14. After you have prepared your advertisement, you can submit it to the media through which you wish to make it public.

_____ 15. If the message achieved its purpose, you will see the results.

Noun Clauses
Place parentheses around each noun clause. Identify the function of each noun clause as subject (S), predicate noun (PN), direct object (DO), indirect object (IO), object of the preposition (OP), or appositive (App). Underline each subordinating conjunction, indefinite relative pronoun, and indefinite relative adverb.

_____ 16. Where the pretzel comes from is a question some people may ask.

_____ 17. The question whether the pretzel, a creation of a young monk, originated in southern France or northern Italy became a matter of discussion.

_____ 18. After the monk prepared unleavened bread for the Catholic festival of Lent, he shaped small arms folded in prayer from what was left of the dough.

_____ 19. The recipient of the new pastry was whoever said his prayers.

_____ 20. We learned that the creation was named *pretiola*, Latin for "little reward."

Correcting Sentence Problems
Identify each group of words as a sentence (S), a fragment (F), a comma splice (CS), or a fused sentence (FS).

_____ 21. Volleyball originated in 1885 at the YMCA in Holyoke, Massachusetts.

_____ 22. A combination of basketball, baseball, tennis, and handball.

_____ 23. William Morgan, a businessman, wanted a game for everyone, people of his status could also play the game.

_____ 24. During a demonstration game, someone remarked about the volleying of the ball as a result, Morgan decided to call the game volleyball.

_____ 25. Since that time volleyball has become a major sport, second only to soccer.

Chapter 6 Review: Agreement

Subject-Verb Agreement

Subjects and Predicates

Underline the simple subject(s) of the verb in question. Then underline the correct verb from the choices in parentheses.

1. Although Americans may consider Henry Ford the inventor of the automobile, a study of the history of automobiles (*reveals, reveal*) a different origin.

2. Twenty-seven years (*is, are*) the period of time between Nikolaus Otto's invention and the beginning of the Ford Motor Company.

3. In 1876 neither Nikolaus Otto nor other Germans (*was, were*) aware of the importance of his invention, the gas motor engine.

4. In 1885 both planning and preparation (*was, were*) evidenced in a revolutionary car design.

5. Even today the work of German engineers (*continues, continue*) to bring innovations to the automotive industry.

Subject Identification

Underline the simple subject(s) of the verb in question. Then underline the correct verb from the choices in parentheses.

6. The facts about the German automobile industry (*is, are*) quite fascinating.

7. The invention of the first practical automobiles with internal-combustion engines (*begins, begin*) the story of Karl Benz's influence on the auto industry.

8. Benz's inventive accomplishments, not his skill in business, (*fascinates, fascinate*) anyone who reads about him.

9. In 1894 Benz's first production car, along with many others, (*was, were*) part of the Paris-Rouen Race, the first recorded car race.

10. In addition to his many other accomplishments (*was, were*) the first truck, built in 1895.

Problem Nouns and Pronouns

Underline the simple subject(s) of the verb in question. Then underline the correct verb from the choices in parentheses.

11. In the eyes of German people as well as others, thanks (*goes, go*) to Gottlieb Daimler for being the father of modern automobiles.

12. *The Beaulieu Encyclopedia of the Automobile* (*gives, give*) further information about Daimler.

Agreement | Chapter 6 Review **439**

13. All the finishing cars in the Paris-Rouen Race were powered by a Daimler engine, and each team in the race *(was, were)* made up of a driver and mechanic.

14. Germany's economics after World War I *(reveals, reveal)* many problems facing the country.

15. In 1919 twenty-five million marks *(was, were)* needed to purchase an automobile.

Correct any subject-verb disagreement by writing the correct form of the verb in italics. If the sentence is already correct, write C in the blank.

_____ 16. Few today *realizes* that Wilhelm Maybach contributed greatly to the auto industry.

_____ 17. He was one of the innovative designers who *were* thriving on the enthusiasm for automobiles.

_____ 18. In 1889 Maybach, along with Daimler, placed an engine into a carriage; many of the observers of that historical event *was* surprised that the carriage reached a speed of eleven miles per hour.

_____ 19. Most of those who study in this field *is* surprised that Maybach pioneered the building of the engine for the zeppelin airship.

_____ 20. Several of the accomplishments attributed to him *includes* an honorary doctorate and a place in the Automotive Hall of Fame.

Pronoun-Antecedent Agreement

Nouns as Antecedents and Compound Antecedents
Underline the correct pronoun from the choices in parentheses.

21. Do you know the person who spent the last years of *(his, their)* career developing dirigible balloons?

22. An individual named Count Ferdinand von Zeppelin spent *(his, its, their)* fortune in expensive experiments to develop an airship.

23. Private donations and contributions from the government made *(its, their)* impact on the further development of the airship.

24. From the earliest experiments until the airship was improved, the dirigible encountered several factors that contributed to *(his, its, their)* destruction.

25. The Germans used the dirigible in World War I to drop bombs on *(its, their)* enemies.

Collective Nouns and Indefinite Pronouns as Antecedents
Write an appropriate personal pronoun to complete each sentence.

_____ 26. Some of the early German dirigibles with ? awkward fuel systems met with failure.

_____ 27. Everyone was interested in ? opportunity to ride in Dr. Hugo Eckner's LZ-127 *Graf Zeppelin* equipped with ? own galley, dining area, and new fuel system.

_____ 28. The *Graf Zeppelin* was the most successful airship ever built; however, no one in Germany could afford to give enough of ? wealth to keep the ship in the air.

_____ 29. Dr. Eckner gained support from William Randolph Hearst, an American whose family had made ? wealth in the newspaper business.

_____ 30. Someone who makes dirigible history ? object of study will find that the *Graf Zeppelin* completed a round-the-world trip in the fastest time recorded up to that point.

Chapter 7 Review: Verb Use

Principal Parts and Tenses
Underline the complete verb of each independent clause. Then identify its tense.

_____ 1. Sam is visiting his Italian grandparents in Chicago this week.

_____ 2. He had been looking forward to this trip for several weeks.

_____ 3. His grandmother has been cooking Sam's favorite dishes for days.

_____ 4. The entire family has always eaten pasta at every family event.

_____ 5. The history of pasta dates back thousands of years.

_____ 6. Sources vary concerning the origin of pasta.

_____ 7. Italians, Chinese, or Arabs could have invented pasta.

_____ 8. During the American Civil War, macaroni and cheese was a popular dish.

_____ 9. Italian immigrants in the early 1900s brought with them the popular spaghetti dishes so familiar today.

_____ 10. Pasta, with its great taste and its variety, will continue to be a popular dish for years.

Consistency and Sequence of Tenses
Underline the verbs in incorrect tense. Write the correct word in the blank. If the sentence is already correct, write C in the blank.

_____ 11. Tracy sits nervously and tightly grips her pencil.

_____ 12. Trying to remember all that she studied, she is relieved that the precalculus test has not been too difficult.

_____ 13. She worked quietly and steadily, answering each question carefully.

_____ 14. A squirrel outside the window entertains Tracy briefly but did not distract her from the test.

_____ 15. The bell rings and she marked her final answers on the sheet before setting her pencil down.

Voice

Underline the verb in each independent clause. Then identify its voice as active (A) or passive (P). If the verb is passive, double underline any retained objects or subjective complements.

_____ 16. My first day at college, I was awakened by the sound of leaf blowers outside my window.

_____ 17. I soon learned the importance of cleaning the sidewalks every day.

_____ 18. The students whose job it is to clean the sidewalks must remove all debris from the sidewalks.

_____ 19. Other students would be shown a poor example if leaves or sticks were strewn on the sidewalks.

_____ 20. Leaf blowers can be ignored when I'm tired enough.

Mood

Identify the mood of each italicized verb as *indicative*, *imperative*, or *subjunctive*.

_____ 21. Macbeth *is* one of Shakespeare's darkest works.

_____ 22. Driven by intense ambition, Macbeth *dreams* of being king at any cost.

_____ 23. If he *had* not *committed* regicide to obtain the throne, he might still have become king one day.

_____ 24. *Notice* Shakespeare's masterful use of particular elements to enhance the mood of the play.

_____ 25. The night setting *presents* a dark mood and *represents* the darkness of the deeds of evil men.

_____ 26. The color red and the blood imagery *permeate* the play to further intensify the mood.

_____ 27. *See* the blood on the king, on the knife, on the hands of the killers, on Banquo, and on Macbeth as he is slain in the end.

_____ 28. If you *were wondering* about Shakespeare's source for this play, you would find that similar events actually took place in the year AD 1050.

_____ 29. *Observe* Shakespeare's adaptation of history; historically, Duncan's enemies, not Macbeth, killed Duncan.

_____ 30. Historically and in the play, Duncan's son Malcolm *returns* and *defeats* Macbeth, forcing him to relinquish the throne.

Chapter 8 Review: Pronoun Use

Pronoun Case
Provide an appropriate personal pronoun. Then identify it as subjective (S), objective (O), possessive (P), or independent possessive (IP).

_____ _____ 1. My brother's favorite geological features are geysers, but _?_ are volcanoes.

_____ _____ 2. While visiting Indonesia with our grandparents, _?_ learned of a volcanic island called Krakatau.

_____ _____ 3. According to _?_ tour guide, the volcanic explosions on Krakatau could be heard in Japan, Australia, and the Philippines!

_____ _____ 4. Sunsets after the Krakatau disaster were unusual; volcanic dust gave _?_ an eerily unnatural hue.

_____ _____ 5. People as far away as in England reported that _?_ too witnessed unusual sunsets.

_____ _____ 6. Following the seismic eruption on Krakatau, two-thirds of _?_ land area vanished into the sea.

_____ _____ 7. Additionally, the Indonesian guide told _?_ that thirty-six thousand people of Java perished as a result of the Krakatau disaster.

_____ _____ 8. Devastating tidal waves following the volcanic eruption buffeted the coast of Java and brought devastation to _?_ people.

_____ _____ 9. Some survivors wrote about their amazing experiences. One man survived by clinging to an uprooted banana tree floating amid debris from his village. _?_ was a thrilling story.

_____ _____ 10. To _?_, such an event as Krakatau's eruption serves as a reminder of humanity's absolute dependence on God for sustenance.

Appositives; Comparisons Using *Than* or *As*
Underline the correct pronoun from the choices in parentheses.

11. Reading about the European explorers' search for a route to the Indies caused several students—Takako, Sam, and *(I, me)*—to become curious about what exact land mass the explorers had in mind.

12. *(We, Us)* three learned that the Indies actually encompassed modern day Indonesia in addition to other countries.

13. We students—Takako, Sam, and *(I, me)*—learned that the Indies at one time extended from India to China.

Pronoun Use | Chapter 8 Review **445**

14. Takako knew better than *(I, me)* the history of western exploration in Japan.

15. A comparison of colonization attempts in India and Indonesia interested Sam as much as *(I, me)*.

"Subjects" and Objects of Verbals; Using *Who* and *Whom*
Underline the correct noun or pronoun from the choices in parentheses.

16. Have you ever heard of Sir Thomas Stamford Raffles (1781–1826), the politician and colonial official *(who, whom)* wrote the famous *History of Java*?

17. *(He, His)* being born into an English sea captain's family certainly did nothing to discourage the young lad's desire to see new lands.

18. When he was only twenty-three, the East India Company decided to send *(he, him)* to Penang, Malaysia.

19. *(Raffles, Raffles's)* learning the Malay language while traveling to Penang was especially astonishing and made him an invaluable employee to his company.

20. Thomas Raffles learned that it was he *(who, whom)* India's governor-general chose to be a trusted governor.

21. Raffles's wise and judicious social policies enabled *(he, him)* to become the lieutenant governor of Java and later the governor of modern-day Sumatra.

22. Thomas Raffles is also the one *(who, whom)* Singaporeans credit with founding their nation in 1819; they still admire his strong antislavery principles as well as his work to provide education and human rights to the region.

23. Have you heard about *(him, his)* hiring zoologists and botanists to document and study specimens from Java, Sumatra, and Singapore?

24. Often the financier of these costly studies had to be *(he, him)*: with his own savings he would sponsor the collection and study of regional plants and animals.

25. A native named Abdullah was the one *(who, whom)* Raffles relied upon to assist him in the Malay tongue and to manage the various collected plant and animal specimens.

Courtesy Order and Use of Reflexive and Intensive
Underline the correct pronoun or pronouns from the choices in parentheses.

26. Grandmother told (Kasan and me, *me and Kasan*) about her girlhood home in Indonesia.

27. She began with describing how all the men of her family labored many long days to construct a *kampong* for (*them*, themselves).

28. Between (you and me, *you and myself*) I had no idea that a *kampong* is a traditional multi-family housing unit in Indonesia.

29. Kasan and I asked (*us*, ourselves) whether we could imagine living in an elevated thatched-roof village with all of our extended family members.

30. Grandmother then explained how refreshingly cool and simple her girlhood home was and how her family planted (*theirselves*, themselves) beautiful fruit and palm trees around the *kampong*.

Pronoun Shift
Underline the correct word from the choices in parentheses.

31. If a tourist to Indonesia enjoys eating rice, (he, *you*) will certainly take pleasure in many of the authentic foods.

32. When comparing the quality of crops in Indonesia, anyone can tell that (he, *you*, they) will reap a much more bountiful harvest from lands near an active volcano, for ash in the soil aids the fruitfulness of the field.

33. Many of the people of Indonesia have chosen Java as (*his*, their) home.

34. Anyone interested in volcanoes must not forget (his, *your*, their) camera when visiting Indonesia; this archipelago contains at least sixty active volcanoes.

35. If you want to see a vast assortment of wildlife, (we, he, *you*) should study Indonesia's reptiles, mammals, marsupials, and birds, for they have both Asian and Australian origins.

Chapter 9 Review: Pronoun Reference

Ambiguous Reference and Remote Reference

Identify each sentence or group of sentences as having clear pronoun reference (C) or unclear pronoun reference (U).

_____ 1. Leonardo da Vinci began his trade as an apprentice to Andrea del Verrocchio; he eventually became arguably one of the paramount painters of the Italian Renaissance.

_____ 2. One distinctive innovation of da Vinci's was a painting technique called *sfumato*. In contrast with del Verrocchio's crisp, obvious lines, da Vinci experimented with shade. Its distinctive trademark is a purposeful blurring of the paint around an image's corners or where shadow is desired.

_____ 3. Interestingly, when applying for a position under the Duke of Milan, da Vinci told the Duke via letter that he was gifted chiefly in military and civil engineering.

_____ 4. This same letter closes with da Vinci's casually mentioning his own abilities in painting, sculpting, and architecture.

_____ 5. People credit da Vinci with helping to usher in the style of the High Renaissance, for he possessed remarkable creativity and was not afraid to try innovative methods. It is characterized by graceful painted images and contrasting areas of dark and light hues.

_____ 6. *The Last Supper* and *Mona Lisa,* both by da Vinci, possess worldwide eminence, but it has sparked much controversy and debate.

_____ 7. People still enjoy proposing and speculating about various possible models for *Mona Lisa.* They certainly are interesting.

_____ 8. *The Last Supper* and *Mona Lisa* paintings both show wear and tear, although it is covered with a lacquer, now turned yellow, designed to preserve the painting's beauty.

_____ 9. *The Last Supper* shows da Vinci's innovative nature. Another painter might have depicted this scene with a straight row of disciples, according to tradition; yet da Vinci grouped them and depicted their unique personalities.

_____ 10. Da Vinci also experimented with the mediums he used in conveying his pictures. For example, in painting *The Last Supper,* da Vinci abandoned the usual fresco method that required rapid painting. Instead, he mixed his own special wall coating that permitted slower, more detailed painting. This new medium, however, was not one of his successes.

Reference to an Implied Noun and to a Noun That Is a Modifier

Rewrite each sentence to correct any unclear pronoun reference. If the antecedent is already clear, write C in the blank.

11. While serving at the court in Milan, da Vinci honed his skills in architecture and designed Milan Cathedral's proposed dome; however, it never received da Vinci's architectural brainchild.

12. The Court of Milan's beautiful theatrical productions brought it great popularity.

13. Leonardo da Vinci himself designed the costumes, sets, and stage machinery for the productions, which were huge successes for the Court of Milan.

14. After the French attacked Milan, da Vinci sought work as a mapmaker, and they are still regarded as classic masterpieces of this profession.

15. During the golden age of High Renaissance art, da Vinci moved to Rome; however, they learned nothing from da Vinci, who chose to spend his days studying other branches of learning.

Indefinite Reference of Personal Pronouns and Reference to a Broad Idea
Identify each sentence as correct (C) or incorrect/informal (I).

_____ 16. What time is it in Italy?

_____ 17. Art aficionados say that da Vinci was exceedingly proficient as a bronze caster: in fact, this skill landed him his first job at the Court of Milan.

_____ 18. It says on this website that da Vinci used a technique called aerial perspective: this technique is especially visible in the background of his *Mona Lisa.*

_____ 19. In 1499, they used a huge clay model of da Vinci's for an archery target.

_____ 20. How often does it snow in Florence, Italy?

_____ 21. You should take the opportunity to view da Vinci's *Mona Lisa* should you ever visit Paris's Louvre Museum.

_____ 22. Da Vinci possessed a great affinity for mathematics, especially geometry, which greatly aided his paintings.

_____ 23. In fact, da Vinci himself stated that you must be a mathematical scholar to best appreciate his works.

_____ 24. In Giorgio Vasari's biography of da Vinci it says that the master painter possessed an uncommon assortment of gifts: da Vinci was both immensely handsome and a genius in every discipline to which he applied himself.

_____ 25. All his life da Vinci felt a great affinity for the natural world. It prompted him to purchase caged birds and then to release them into the wild.

Chapter 10 Review: Adjective and Adverb Use

Modifiers: Comparisons and Functions

Underline each adjective, including the correct adjective choice from the adjectives in parentheses. Double underline each adverb that modifies a noun.

1. While driving toward the historic area of Alexandria, Virginia, one passes (*lower-income, more lower-income*) government housing projects and is suddenly transported back in time with the sight of cobblestone streets and red brick Federal Period buildings.

2. One historic townhouse on Oronoco Street bears (*significant, more significant, most significant*) historical import than all the other traditional red brick residences.

3. The boyhood home of Robert E. Lee was a rather (*unassuming, most unassuming*) dwelling at 607 Oronoco Street.

4. In fact, a (*large, larger*) nursery wing is where Robert's mother cared for her five children: Carter, Ann, Smith, Robert, and Mildred.

5. Before the Lee family's residency here, the previous owners experienced the (*great, greatest*) honor of serving George Washington in their home.

Underline each adverb. Double underline each noun or noun phrase that modifies a verb.

6. My family actually visited Robert E. Lee's boyhood home last year as part of our family vacation.

7. Upon entering the house's foyer, we immediately noticed a gorgeous drawing room now referred to as the Lafayette Room: here the greatly esteemed Revolutionary War general Lafayette had once come to pay his respects to the Lee family.

8. I will always recall feeling somewhat awed as we prepared to ascend the stairs, for five chronological paintings of Robert E. Lee hang majestically along the wall of the staircase.

9. I also learned that day a fact I had not known before: Robert E. Lee's father was the enormously famous General "Light Horse Harry" from the Revolutionary War.

10. My family and I spent the morning leisurely touring Robert E. Lee's boyhood home and totally absorbing ourselves in the period décor and furniture.

Problems with Modifiers
Underline each incorrect adjective or adverb. Write a suitable correction in the blank. If the sentence is already correct, write C in the blank.

_____ 11. Henry Lee (1756–1818), Robert E. Lee's father, seemed to naturally possess most perfect military abilities.

_____ 12. The advent of the Revolutionary War permanently interrupted Henry Lee's plans for law school yet introduced a military career for which he was more better suited.

_____ 13. One of America's first cavalry soldiers, Henry Lee early proved himself an indispensable leader and arguably became one of George Washington's most trusted military leaders.

_____ 14. After the Revolutionary War, Lee still enjoyed a close friendship with the commander in chief: Washington even called Lee away from his governing duties in Virginia to quell the Whiskey Rebellion in Texas.

_____ 15. We do not possess no better epitaph on George Washington than the one penned by Henry Lee: "First in war, first in peace, and first in the hearts of his countrymen."

Placement of Modifiers
Rewrite each sentence, making the modifiers clear or correct. If the sentence is already correct, write C in the blank.

16. Robert E. Lee most likely almost read all the classic works accessible to him in the original languages, for on his West Point application he mentions his skill in reading classic works in Latin and Greek.

_____

_____

_____

17. Following the death of his father, Henry Lee, young Robert E. Lee took upon himself the duties of caring for his frail mother, who greatly needed individual care.

_____

_____

_____

18. Family finances that were depleted drastically dictated the employment of every cost-cutting measure Mrs. Lee could devise.

19. Robert opted to selflessly receive his higher education at West Point rather than reduce the family finances further by attending a costly university.

20. Attending West Point, not a single demerit blotted his record.

21. Robert E. Lee graduated with the second highest grade average of his class, which demonstrated his unusual discipline and intelligence.

22. A soldier and engineer at Fort Monroe, Virginia, Mary Anna Randolph Custis married Robert E. Lee in her beautiful home called Arlington.

23. Only one of Robert and Mary Lee's children was born somewhere other than the family home at Arlington.

24. Visitors who observe the Arlington House in detail describe several original oil paintings by the first owner of the home, George Washington Parke Custis.

25. Touring Arlington House, a gorgeous view of the skyline of Washington, D.C., is a memorable sight for visitors.

Chapter 11 Review: Capitalization

Personal Names, Religions, and Nationalities
Underline each word that contains a capitalization error.

1. My <u>Grandmother</u> graduated from Central <u>academy</u>.
2. The principal, Horatio Davis, <u>phd</u>, expanded the language program of his school to include <u>german</u>, <u>french</u>, and <u>spanish</u>.
3. At the beginning of each day, <u>dr.</u> Davis led the students in <u>bible</u> reading and prayer.
4. Both my uncle and aunt worked during the <u>Winter</u> as helpers at the school.
5. Neither <u>mother</u> nor uncle Joe graduated from the <u>High</u> <u>School</u> where Grandmother went to school.

Place Names, Transportation, and Astronomy Terms
Underline each word that contains a capitalization error.

6. A trip to Australia aboard a <u>qantas</u> airliner would take the traveler thirty-six hours from <u>san</u> <u>diego</u> to <u>sydney</u>, with much of his flight being over the <u>pacific</u> <u>ocean</u>.
7. After arriving there, the visitor might see a beautiful print of the HMAS <u>geelong</u>, a minesweeper built in 1918.
8. A part of a relaxing vacation in <u>australia</u> might include a viewing of the night sky constellations such as the <u>tarantula</u>, which is similar to <u>orion</u> but much larger.
9. Snorkeling north of <u>queensland</u>, a swimmer might see a small jellyfish called an Irukandji.
10. The <u>great</u> <u>barrier</u> <u>reef</u> off the coast of Australia provides some of the most incredible underwater sights in the world.

Businesses and Organizations, Cultural and Historical Terms
Underline each capitalization error. If the sentence is correct, write *C* in the blank.

_____ 11. The <u>spanish</u> club will meet on the Saturday before the fifth of <u>may</u>.

_____ 12. Celebrated primarily as a <u>Regional</u> <u>Holiday</u> in the area of Puebla, that day was chosen to celebrate Mexico's declaration to be independent from Spain.

_____ 13. Mexico's Independence Day is celebrated later in the calendar year.

_____ 14. Celebrations commemorate Mexico's victories over Spain and other conflicts, including the Mexican civil war.

_____ 15. The hacienda restaurant, where we ate, is a member of the local restaurant owner's association.

Titles, First Words, and Single Letters
Underline each word that contains a capitalization error. If the sentence or phrase is correct, write C in the blank.

_____ 16. Dear aunt Betty and uncle George,
Very Truly Yours,

_____ 17. Next school year I plan to attend the music seminar "A study in hymnology" with Dr. Alan Albert, speaker.

_____ 18. In Dr. Albert's office, I left a piece of sheet music on the t-shaped table.

_____ 19. "There is a fountain filled with blood
drawn from Immanuel's veins;
And sinners, plunged beneath that flood,
lose all their guilty stains."

_____ 20. The male quartet plans to sing "Since I have been Redeemed" and "Rise Up, O Men Of God" next Sunday morning.

_____ 21. Guests on the redeemed radio program are my pastor and youth pastor.

_____ 22. Even our labrador retriever enjoys listening to us practice our music.

_____ 23. Fanny Crosby (She is one of my favorite hymn writers) played the organ at the Bowery Mission in New York City.

_____ 24. I. The Early Life Of Fanny Crosby
  A. Hymn Writer at Age Eight
  B. School Admission at Age Eleven

_____ 25. On Fanny Crosby's gravestone are the words of a familiar hymn: "Blessed Assurance, Jesus Is Mine! / Oh, what a Foretaste of Glory Divine!"

Chapter 12 Review: Punctuation

End Marks and Other Uses of the Period
Add the correct end mark to each sentence and insert any missing periods or decimal points.

1. How many years does it take to earn a doctoral degree two five

2. Our friend William A Hindt, MD, earned his degree from the Medical University of South Carolina, known as MUSC, after four years of study

3. We often asked when he would be done with school

4. Only family members attended the commencement ceremony, which began at 9:00 am

5. Now he must work as a resident in a hospital—for three more years

Commas in a Series and After Introductory Elements
Insert any missing commas.

6. To begin meal preparation a cook should read the entire recipe carefully, assemble all the supplies and measure all the ingredients.

7. When the diligent efficient cook has everything ready ahead of time the meal preparation itself should be easy.

8. Anticipating a delicious meal the dinner guests may arrive early but the host should also be prepared for some latecomers.

9. After its time in the oven a cut of meat may continue to rise in temperature for a few minutes.

10. Finally the meal is served and the dinner begins.

Commas to Separate
Insert any missing commas.

11. I enjoy studying history don't you?

12. The study of history in my opinion is both useful and enjoyable.

13. Leila have you ever thought about the benefits of studying history?

14. History teaches us the follies of others; consequently we are better prepared to avoid their mistakes.

15. One example of failing to learn from others' mistakes happened during World War II when Hitler attempted to invade Russia.

16. Napoleon Bonaparte once the emperor of France had attempted the same thing over a century earlier.

17. Both Napoleon and Hitler however failed in their attempts.

18. The Russian winter cold and severe was the enemy that defeated them.

19. History teaches lessons relating to almost every field of study not just warfare.

20. Remind me to finish my history report after dinner please.

Commas in Letters, Quotations, Dates, Addresses, and Special Constructions
Insert any missing commas.

21. George Bernard Shaw has been credited with saying "England and America are two countries separated by the same language."

22. Americans have been developing their own expressions and dialect for centuries—even before July 4 1776.

23. Some words have different meanings in America than they have in Britain. The meanings of *boot* and *bonnet* I sometimes confuse.

24. Americans call a large four-wheeled vehicle a *truck*; the British a *lorry*.

25. "We [English] have really everything in common with America these days" Oscar Wilde wrote, "except, of course, language."

26–30. Insert any missing commas in the following letter.

Dear Joyce and Robert

　　Thank you so much for hosting the farewell party honoring my sister and me. We have really enjoyed our visit with you and our other cousins these past few weeks. We will visit Uncle Jeff in Portland Maine next month. Neither of us has seen him since his graduation from law school; I am still surprised when I think of him as Jeffrey Statz JD. Theresa and I would love to see you again, and so would Mom and Dad. Perhaps you can come to see us next summer. Thanks again for your hospitality.

Yours truly

Gary

Incorrect Commas
Circle any incorrect commas. If the sentence is already correct, write C in the blank.

_____ 31. Learning how to fish, and learning how to ski are common goals.

_____ 32. People can fish and ski in summer and winter, but, I prefer the summer versions.

_____ 33. Before our last fishing trip, my brother and I tried unsuccessfully to buy some supplies.

_____ 34. The slogan "Gone Fishing," was posted on the door of the store.

_____ 35. Ralph Samuelson invented water skiing in July, 1922, on Lake Pepin, Minnesota.

Semicolons and Colons

Insert any missing semicolons or colons. If the sentence is already correct, write *C* in the blank.

_____ 36. Did you attend the lecture about Maxwell Perkins at 400 yesterday?

_____ 37. The biography *Max Perkins Editor of Genius* by A. Scott Berg describes how Perkins helped several famous authors of the early twentieth century.

_____ 38. Perkins, a former newspaper reporter, was an editor at Charles Scribner's Sons he worked with authors such as F. Scott Fitzgerald, Ernest Hemingway, and Marjorie Kinnan Rawlings.

_____ 39. He died before the publication of Hemingway's book *The Old Man and the Sea*; nevertheless, the author dedicated it to the memory of his friend.

_____ 40. Perkins's ancestors were illustrious too Roger Sherman, a signer of the Declaration of Independence; William Maxwell Evarts, a United States Senator and Charles Callahan Perkins, a friend of Browning and Longfellow.

Chapter 13 Review: More Punctuation

Quotation Marks, Ellipses, and Brackets

Read the following paragraph and then determine whether the quotations, ellipses, and brackets in the following items are correct. Identify each item as correct (C) or incorrect (I).

    A pioneer is someone who launches into the unknown. He might be a settler clearing a wilderness, or he might be a scientist seeking a cure for a deadly disease through a new line of research. In Christian history, a pioneer is one who carries the gospel to an area where the name of Jesus Christ is little known or to a people who are being ignored by the rest of the Christian world. George Liele was a true Christian pioneer. Relatively early in his Christian life, he helped found one of the first black churches in America. Then, forced by necessity to leave his home, he went to Jamaica as a missionary more than ten years before Englishman William Carey launched the modern foreign missions movement.
from *Free Indeed: Heroes of Black Christian History* by Mark Sidwell (BJU Press, 2001)

_____ 1. "A pioneer . . . launches into the unknown."

_____ 2. "In Christian history, a pioneer is one who carries the gospel. . . . George Liele was a true Christian pioneer."

_____ 3. "George Liele found[ed] one of the first black churches in America."

_____ 4. "Forced by necessity to leave his home, [Liele] went to Jamaica as a missionary."

_____ 5. "[Liele became] a missionary more than ten years before William Carey, 'the Father of the Modern Missionary Movement,' launched the modern foreign missions movement."

Quotation Marks and Underlining for Italics

Insert any missing quotation marks. Circle any unnecessary quotation marks. Use a transpose sign (∩) to indicate the correct placement for any misplaced periods, commas, question marks, colons, and semicolons. Underline any words that should be italicized.

6. James entered the classroom, put his books on his desk, and said, I have finished reading the novel The Scarlet Letter.

7. Why did you read an entire book? asked a classmate; I read Poe's short story The Pit and the Pendulum.

8. According to Miss Stevens, who said, You may read either two short stories or one novel', you could do either for the book report, Lauren said.

9. I thought she told us that 'we needed to read just one short story,' replied Jack, so I read only Hawthorne's The Minister's Black Veil.

10. Lauren remarked in a quiet tone, Maybe next time you will listen more carefully".

Apostrophes and Hyphens
Insert any missing apostrophes and hyphens.

11. Preparing ones testimony for presentation at a foreign missions conference requires careful thought and planning.

12. Life verses such as Proverbs 3:5 6 should be a part of the testimony.

13. In addition to someones life verses, Gods direction in leading that person to the mission field should also be a part of the testimony.

14. Its encouraging to others to learn about the problems and blessings associated with preparing to go to the mission field.

15. In the mid 1980s a missionary family, the Moores, left Fairmont, West Virginia, for Fortelaza, Brazil. Their self sacrificing spirit was an encouragement to many from their home church.

Dashes and Parentheses
Insert any missing dashes or parentheses.

16. "Did you know that no one at least none that I have talked to has ever heard of the dessert white fungus with white sugar?" Jacob inquired.

17. "Do you mean oh, I can't remember the name yes, tremella, also known as white mushrooms?" Sheila asked.

18. "Yes, the Oriental Cuisine Society OCS includes this dessert in their cookbook," chimed in Sylvia.

19. "I'm not sure that you mean you boil them first? I would be able to eat mushrooms with sugar," added Jared.

20. "If you want to make the dessert, you have to 1 boil the mushrooms, 2 dry the mushrooms, and 3 mix them with a sugar syrup," said Sylvia.

INDEX

a/an, 49
absolute phrase. *See* phrase
abstract noun, 37
academic mode of writing, 9
accuracy in writing, 367
action verb. *See* verb
active voice. *See* verb, voice
adjective
    article
        definite *(the)*, 49
        definition of, 49
        indefinite *(a/an)*, 49
    comparison, showing
        absolute, 244
        degrees of, 243
        irregular comparison of, 244
        regular comparison of, 244
    coordinate, punctuation of, 301
    correct usage of, 243–52
    cumulative, punctuation of, 301
    definition of, 48
    determiner
        article, 49
        demonstrative, 49
        indefinite, 49
        interrogative, 49
        possessive, 49
    independent possessive, 49
    irregular comparison of. *See* adjective, comparison
    modifier, 243
    modifying noun, 50
    positions of, 48
    predicate adjective, 44, 48, 75–76
    prepositional phrase as, 88
    problems with
        dangling, 252
        double comparison, 247
        misplaced, 250
        modifiers that cannot be compared, 247
        two-way, 251
    proper, 50
    regular comparison of. *See* adjective, comparison
adjective clause
    definition of, 116
    function of, 116
    punctuation of, 308
    reduction of, 374–75
    relative adverb with, 118–19
    relative pronoun with, 117
    use in writing, 371, 374–75
adverb
    comparison, showing
        degrees of, 243
        irregular comparison of, 244
        regular comparison of, 244
    conjunctive, 51
    correct usage of, 243–52
    definition of, 50
    interrogative, 51
    modifier, 243
    position of, 50
    prepositional phrase as, 88
    problems with
        dangling, 252
        double comparisons, 247
        double negatives, 247
        misplaced, 250
        modifiers that cannot be compared, 247
        split infinitives, 251
        two-way, 251
    qualifier, 50
    relative, 51, 118–19
    relative, indefinite, 51, 128
    verb-adverb combination, 45
adverb clause
    definition of, 122
    elliptical, 123
    function of, 122
    punctuation of, 304, 308
    reduction of, 375–76
    subordinating conjunction with, 126–27
    use in writing, 371, 375–76
adverbial, 76
adverbial noun, 243
agreement. *See* pronoun-antecedent; subject-verb
almanac. *See* reference works
analogy, 421
antagonist, definition of, 146
antecedent
    agreement of pronoun with, 164
    clear reference, 226, 229, 232–33
    collective noun, 166
    compound, 164
    definition of, 37
    indefinite pronoun, 167
apostrophe
    contractions, 341
    omissions, 341
    possession, 341–42
    possession, joint, 341–42
    special plurals, 342
appositive, 89, 206
appositive noun, 206–7
appositive phrase, 89
article. *See* adjective
atlas. *See* reference works
audience, considering your. *See* writing process, planning
auxiliary
    definition of, 44
    examples of, 44
    modal, 44

be, forms of, 149
biased language, 390–91
Bible commentary. *See* reference works
Bible concordance. *See* reference works
bibliography. *See* book, parts of a
biographical source. *See* reference works
biography, library classification of, 397
block arrangement, 16
book, parts of a
    acknowledgments, 410
    appendix, 411
    bibliography, 401, 411
    copyright page, 410
    glossary, 411
    index, 411
    introduction (preface), 410
    list of illustrations, 410
    table of contents, 410
    text, 411
    title page, 410
brackets
    error in original, 336

insertion or replacement in a quotation, 336
parentheses inside parentheses, 336
brainstorming, 2–3

Capitalization
abbreviations, 277–78
academic courses, 282
art, works of, 282
astronomical terms, 274
book, sections of, 282
brand names, 277
buildings, monuments, 278
businesses, 277
calendar items, 278
cultural terms, 277–78
descriptive substitutes for proper nouns, 270
ethnic groups, 271
first words, 285–86
geographical names, 274
God (words for), 270
governmental departments, 278
historical terms, 278
I, personal pronoun, 285
languages, 270
letters used as words, 286
letters used for musical notes, grades, etc., 286
letters used to clarify a following word, 286
literary works, 282
magazines, 282
musical compositions, 282
nationalities, 270
newspapers, 282
O, archaic address form, 285
organizations, 278
outlines, 285
personal names, 270
personal titles, 270
personifications, 270
place names, 274
poetry, 285
proper adjectives, 50, 271
proper nouns, 270
radio and television programs, 282
religions and related terms, 270
schools, 278
titles of works (artistic, literary, musical), 282
transportation, 274
card catalog. See library
case. See pronoun

cause-and-effect. See order, paragraph writing
chronological order. See order, paragraph writing
citations, parenthetical, 268
clarity of purpose, 20
clause. See also adjective clause; adverb clause; noun clause
definition of, 116
dependent, definition of, 116, 386
independent, definition of, 116
in sentence types, 132–33
nonrestrictive, 118, 308
problems with, 250–51
restrictive, 118, 308
use in sentences, 371–78, 386
coherence, 23–24
collective noun
definition of, 37
pronoun-antecedent agreement, 166
subject-verb agreement, 154
college application essay, 222–25
colon
Bible references, 316
business letter, salutation of, 316
independent clauses, 316
quotation, long or formal direct, 316
series at the end of a sentence, 316
subtitle, book, 316
time, expressions of, 316
comma
addition to name, 311
address, 310
adjective after a noun, 307
appositive, 307
compound sentence, 302
conjunction, with, 311
conjunctive adverb, 308
contrast, phrase that shows, 307
coordinate adjectives, 301
date, 312
incorrect use of, 311–12
independent clauses, two or more, 302
interjection, 307
introductory elements, 304
letter, 310
nonrestrictive element, 308
noun of direct address, 307
omitted words, 311
parenthetical expression, 307
quotation, direct, 310

quotation, integrated, 312
restrictive, 308
series, three or more items in a, 301
tag question, 307
transposed, words and phrases, 311
comma splice. See sentence problems
commentary, Bible. See reference works
common noun. See noun
comparative degree of modifiers, 243–44
comparison-and-contrast. See order, paragraph writing
comparisons
after than or as, case of pronoun, 206
clear, 384–85
implied, 368
logical, 384–85
modifiers, with. See adjective, modifier; adverb, modifier
stated, 368–69
complement
definition of, 74
See adverbial; direct object; indirect object; objective complement; predicate adjective; predicate noun
complete predicate, 70
complete subject, 70
complex sentence. See sentence, types of
compound
noun, 36
predicate, 71
pronoun. See pronoun, intensive; pronoun, reflexive
sentence. See sentence, types of
subject, 71
compound-complex sentence. See sentence, types of
compound words
plural, 428
punctuation of. See hyphen
conciseness, 22
concluding paragraph. See writing process, drafting
concluding sentence. See writing process, drafting
concordance, Bible. See reference works
concrete noun. See noun
conjunction
coordinating, 54
correlative, 55
definition of, 54

466 Index

subordinating, 55, 122, 126–27
conjunctive adverb, 51
connotation, 367
context clues for reading comprehension, 413
contractions. *See* apostrophe
coordinating conjunction. *See* conjunction
coordination, 363–64
correctness, revising for, 23
correlative conjunction. *See* conjunction
count noun. *See* noun
couplet, 240–41
courtesy order, 213
creative mode of writing, 9
critical thinker, 80–81, 141, 196–97, 237, 289, 353

D

dangling modifier, 251
dash
    emphasis, 347
    internal appositive series, 347
    interrupted speech, 347
    interrupting phrase or clause, 347
    introductory list, 347
    summarizing statement after a list, 347
declarative sentence. *See* sentence, types of
degrees of comparison, 243
demonstrative determiner. *See* adjective, determiner
demonstrative pronoun. *See* pronoun
denotation, 367
dependent clause. *See* clause
descriptive mode of writing, 9
details, in writing, 367
determiner. *See* adjective
Dewey decimal system. *See* library
dialogue
    definition of, 144
    punctuation of. *See* quotation marks
dictionary. *See* reference works
direct object, 44, 76
double comparisons, 247
double negatives, 247
drafting. *See* writing process
drama, 143–48
dramatic scene, response to, 324–29

E

ellipses (mark of punctuation)
    halting or unfinished speech, 335
    omission of words in quotation, 335
ellipsis, 374
elliptical adverb clause, 123
elliptical *to*, infinitive phrase, 102
emphasis
    revising for, 22
    sentence, 355–59
encyclopedia. *See* reference works
end marks. *See* exclamation point; period; question mark
energy, sentence. *See* sentence
ESL notes
    adjectives, no plurals of, 48
    articles, use of *a/an*, 49
    as . . . as in comparisons, 386
    be-passive distinguished from *get*-passive (idiomatic), 190
    collective noun, agreement with (American usage distinguished from British usage), 154
    collective nouns, made from adjectives or participles, 37
    collective nouns, plural verbs, 154
    common or proper noun, 278
    compound nouns vs. adjective plus noun, 36
    count and noncount nouns, 36
    dependent clause, contrast or concession, 123
    dependent clause, identifying, 116
    determiner, 36
    did in clear comparisons, 385
    either–or distinguished from *neither–nor*, 164
    end punctuation, position of, 278
    ESL dictionary, 404
    fragment, 136
    freewriting, 3
    gerund as object of preposition, 98
    good writing in English, 11
    if-clause or time clause, expression of future time, 180
    imperative distinguished from request, 69
    implied comparison, pronoun usage, 207
    indefinite pronouns distinguished from nouns, 39
    independent possessives, 205
    indirect question, no inversion, 386
    intonation (quotation tag), 332
    intonation (types of sentences), 70
    inverted order to form a question, 71
    long vowels, definition, 429
    misplaced modifiers, 251
    modal auxiliaries, 45
    not, spelling of in contractions, 341
    objective complement, 77
    or, meaning of with *not*, 164
    order, subject and verb, 70
    personal pronoun, avoid additional, 164
    possessives, plurals, and singular verbs, pronunciation of, 428
    possessives, relationships expressed by, 204
    present perfect tense, 179
    principal parts of *be, have,* and *do,* 179
    progressive verb distinguished from participle, 93
    proper adjective used as a noun, 271
    question mark with quotation marks, 331
    reading comprehension, verbal context, 414
    relative adverbs, use of adjective clauses introduced by, 119
    relative pronoun distinguished from interrogative pronoun, 117
    relative pronoun *that* after a comma, 118
    some distinguished from *any,* 247
    subjunctive mood, 193
    subordinating conjunction distinguished from preposition, 55, 122
    tense, when to shift, 185
    test taking, asking questions, 418
    that clause, subjunctive, 192
    the, use of with superlative, 243
    to of the infinitive distinguished from preposition *to,* 101
    verb-adverb combination, 45
    verbs followed by gerunds distinguished from verbs followed by infinitives, 103

video report, 201
who/whom, case of, 211
word order in a clause (subject before verb), 70
you, subject of a command, 71
essay
   basics, 19–20
   comparison-and-contrast, 61–68
   descriptive, 29–34
   extemporaneous, 173–77
   issue analysis, 291–95
   persuasive, 109–15
essay tests, 419
exclamation point, 296
exclamatory sentence. *See* sentence, types of
expansion of sentences, 371–72
expletive, 76, 127
expository mode of writing, 9

F

faulty coordination, 363
fiction books, 395–96
figurative language, 368–69
flashback, 15
fragment. *See* sentence problems
freewriting, 3
fresh words (in writing), 22
fused sentence. *See* sentence problems
future perfect tense, 179
future tense, 179

G

gazetteer. *See* reference works
gender of personal pronouns, 37–38
gerund
   definition of, 96
   function of, 96
   passive, 98
   perfect, 98
   perfect passive, 98
   present, 98
   present passive, 98
   "subject" and object of, 209–10
gerund phrase
   definition of, 97
   function of, 97
   use in writing, 377
   with complements, 97
   with modifiers, 97

H

have, forms of, 179
helping verb. *See* auxiliary
history of the English language, 26–27, 393, 425
hyphen
   compound words, 343
   multiword modifiers, 343
   numbers and fractions, 343
   omission of connecting word, 342
   prefixes, 343
   word division, 342
   words with a common element, 343

I

ideas, revising for. *See* writing process
imperative mood. *See* verb, mood
imperative sentence. *See* sentence, types of
importance, order of. *See* order, paragraph writing
indefinite determiner. *See* adjective, determiner
indefinite pronoun. *See* pronoun
indefinite relative adverb. *See* adverb
indefinite relative pronoun. *See* pronoun
independent clause. *See* clause
independent possessive. *See* adjective
index
   bibliography, 401
   literary, 401
   periodical, 400
   quotation, 405
   subject, 401
   use of, 400–401
indicative mood. *See* verb, mood
indirect object, 44, 76, 362
indirect quotation, 329
infinitive
   definition of, 101
   distinguished from prepositional phrase, 101
   functions of, 101
   passive, 102
   perfect, 102
   perfect passive, 102
   progressive, 102
   simple, 101
   split, 251
   "subject" and object of, 210
infinitive phrase
   definition of, 101
   elliptical *to,* 102
   function of, 101
   split, problems with, 251
   use in writing, 377
   with complements; with modifiers, 101
infinitive vs. preposition, 101
information, gathering. *See* writing process, planning
intensive pronoun. *See* pronoun
interest (in writing), 20
interior monologue, 84–87
interjection, 55
Internet
   library websites, 399
   websites as sources, 5
interrogative adverb. *See* adverb
interrogative determiner. *See* adjective, determiner
interrogative pronoun. *See* pronoun
interrogative sentence. *See* sentence, types of
intransitive verb. *See* verb
introductory paragraph. *See* paragraph
inverted word order
   for emphasis, 356
   for questions, 71
   problems with, 150–51
   with *there* or *here,* 71
isolate. *See* interjection
it
   expletive, 127
   idiomatic use of, 232
   indefinite use of, 232
italics
   art, works of, 337
   foreign words and phrases, 337
   special emphasis, 338
   titles of long works, 337
   vehicles, large, 337
   words, letters, numbers being discussed, 337

L

language
   biased, 390–91
   figurative, 368–69
library
   bibliographies, 401
   books, arrangement of
      fiction, 395–96
      nonfiction, 395–96
   call number, 396
   card catalog, 400
   Cutter number, 396
   Dewey decimal system, 396

Library of Congress system, 397
online catalog (OPAC), 399
periodical section/materials, 400
reference section/materials/tools, 403–5
special indexes, 400
special reference works, 403–5
stacks, 399
website, 399
Library of Congress system. *See* library
linking verb. *See* verb
list of illustrations. *See* book, parts of a
listing, 2
literary index, 401
literary sources, 405
logic. *See* sentence, logic
    deductive, 353
    inductive, 353

memory techniques, 417
metaphor, 368–69
misplaced modifier, 250–51
mixed metaphor, 368–69
mnemonic device, 417
modal auxiliary. *See* auxiliary
mode, choosing a. *See* writing process, drafting
Modern English, rules for, 425
modifier. *See also* adjective; adverb
    dangling, 252
    misplaced, 250–51
    two-way, 251
    with split infinitives, 251
modifying noun, 50
mood (of verbs). *See* verb

narrative mode of writing, 9
New York Times Index, 401
noncount noun. *See* noun
nonfiction, 395–96
nonrestrictive clause. *See* clause
nonrestrictive modifier, 308
nonverbal phrases, 88–89
noun
    abstract, 37
    adverbial, 243
    collective, 37, 154
    collective, antecedent, 166
    common, 35–36
    compound, 36
    concrete, 37

count, 36
definition of, 35
formation of compounds, 36
functions of
    appositive, 89
    direct address, 307
    direct object, 44
    indirect object, 44
    objective complement, 44
    object of the preposition, 53
    predicate noun, 44
    subject, 35, 66, 69
irregular plural, 427
modifying, 50
noncount, 36
plural, 35, 428
possessive, 49
proper, 35–36, 428
singular, 35
noun clause
definition of, 126
function of, 126
indefinite relative adverbs with, 128
indefinite relative pronouns with, 127–28
reduction of, 377
subordinating conjunctions with, 126–27
use in writing, 371, 377, 386
number
of indefinite pronouns, 157–58
of nouns, 153–54
of personal pronouns, 37–38
numbers
a number distinguished from *the number,* 158–59
apostrophes with, 342
hyphens with, 343
italics for, 337
omission of, 342
parentheses with, 348
period following, 297
plurals of, 343

objective case. *See* pronoun, case
objective complement, 44, 48, 77
object of the preposition, 53
order, paragraph writing
    cause-and-effect, 16
    chronological, 15
    comparison-and-contrast, 16–17
    importance, 16
    spatial, 15
organization, paragraph, 14

outline
    sentence, 7
    tentative, 6
    topic, 6–7
outlining, *See* writing process, planning

Paragraph
    concluding, 13, 19
    development, 11
    introductory, 10–11
    organization, 14–17
    supporting sentences, 12
    topic sentence, 11
parallelism
    clarification, 381–82
    definition of, 379
    illogical, 380
    of parts of speech, 380
    of structures, 380–81
paraphrasing, 264, 266
parentheses
    comma and dash pairs, compared, 348
    numbers/letters that identify divisions, 348
    placement with other punctuation, 348
    supplementary elements, 348
parenthetical citations, 268, 348
participial phrase
    dangling, 252
    definition of, 92–93
    misplaced, 250–51
    use in writing, 371–72, 374–75
    with complements; with modifiers, 92
participle
    definition of, 92
    function of, 92
    past, 94
    perfect, 94
    progressive passive, 94
    perfect passive, 94
    present, 93
parts of speech. *See* adjective; adverb; conjunction; interjection; noun; preposition; pronoun; verb
passive infinitive. *See* infinitive
passive voice. *See* verb, voice
past participle. *See* participle
past perfect tense, 179
past tense, 179
pauses for breath, 368
perfect gerund. *See* gerund
perfect infinitive. *See* infinitive

Index 469

perfect participle. *See* participle
perfect passive infinitive. *See* infinitive
perfect tense. *See* verb, tense
period
    abbreviations, 297
    decimals, 298
    initials, 297
    lists, 297
    outlines, 297
    sentences, 296
periodical index, 400
periodicals, 400–401
personal mode of writing, 9
personal pronoun. *See* pronoun
personifications, capitalization of, 270
persuasive mode of writing, 9
phrase
    absolute, 88–89
    appositive, 89
    definition of, 88
    gerund, 96–98
    infinitive, 101–2
    nonrestrictive, 308
    participial, 92–94
    prepositional, 88
    problems with, 250–52
    restrictive, 308
    use in writing, 371–72, 374–75
plagiarism, 266, 268
planning. *See* writing process, planning
plurals, 35, 342, 428
point-by-point arrangement, 17
positive degree of modifiers, 243–44
possession, joint. *See* apostrophe
possessive case. *See* pronoun, case
possessive determiner. *See* adjective, determiner
possessive, independent. *See* adjective
possessive noun. *See* noun
possessive phrase, 49
possessive pronoun. *See* pronoun, case
precise words, 22, 367
predicate
    complete, 70
    compound, 70
    definition of, 69–70
    simple, 70
predicate adjective, 44, 48, 75–76
predicate noun, 44, 75
predication, logical, 384
prefixes, 415

preposition
    definition of, 53
    idiomatic use of, 54
prepositional phrase, 53, 88, 362
present perfect tense, 179
present tense, 178–79
principal parts of verbs. *See* verb
progressive infinitive. *See* infinitive
progressive tense. *See* verb, tense
pronoun
    case
        correct use of, 37–38, 203–16
        for appositives, 206
        for comparisons using *than* or *as*, 206
        independent possessive, 204
        objective, 38, 204, 210
        possessive, 38, 204, 209
        subjective, 38, 204, 210
    compound. *See* pronoun, intensive *and* pronoun, reflexive
    courtesy order, 213
    definition of, 37
    demonstrative, 39
    gender, 37–38
    indefinite, 38–39, 123, 157, 167
    indefinite relative, 39, 123
    intensive, 40, 216
    interrogative, 40, 47
    number, 37–38
    person, 37–38
    personal, 37–38, 203–16
    reciprocal, 40
    reference. *See* pronoun reference
    reflexive, 40, 213
    relative, 39, 117–18, 159, 210–11
    relative, indefinite, 39, 123
    shift
        number, 216
        person, 216
    usage, *who* and *whom*, 210–11
pronoun-antecedent agreement
    with compound antecedents, 164–65
    with indefinite pronouns, 167
    with number and gender, 163–64
pronoun reference
    ambiguous, 226
    indefinite, of personal pronouns, 232
    remote, 226
    to a broad idea, 233

    to an implied noun, 229
    to a noun that is not a modifier, 229
proofreading, 23–24
proper adjective. *See* adjective
proper noun. *See* noun
protagonist, definition of, 146
publishing. *See* writing process
punctuation marks. *See* apostrophe; colon; comma; dash; ellipsis; exclamation point; hyphen; italics; parentheses; period; period, decimals; question mark; quotation marks; semicolon
purpose, determining a. *See* writing process, planning

qualifier. *See* adverb
question. *See also* sentence, types of, interrogative
    indirect, 296
    inverted order with, 71, 150–51
    rhetorical, 356
    tag, 307
questioning, 2
question mark, 296
quotation index. *See* index
quotation marks,
    dialogue, 330
    direct quotations, 329–30
    indirect quotations, 330
    other punctuation, use with, 331
    single quotation marks, 332
    titles, short works, 330
    words used in a special sense, 331

Readers' Guide to Periodical Literature, 400
reading comprehension, improving
    context clues, 413–14
    word parts, 415
reciprocal pronoun. *See* pronoun
reduction of sentences, 373–78
redundancy, 22
reference, pronoun. *See* pronoun reference
reference works
    almanac, 403
    atlas, 403
    biographical source, 404
    commentary, Bible, 404
    concordance, Bible, 404
    dictionary, 404
    encyclopedia, 404–5

gazetteer, 403
index, 400–401
thesaurus, 405
yearbook, 403
reflexive pronoun. *See* pronoun
relative adverb. *See* adverb
relative adverb, indefinite. *See* adverb
relative pronoun. *See* pronoun
relative pronoun, indefinite. *See* pronoun
research
    interviewing, 3–4
    notes, taking, 264
    sources
        documenting, 264, 268
        evaluating, 5, 263
        finding, 263
        primary and secondary, 263
research report, 259–69
restatement, thesis, 19
restrictive clause, 118, 308
restrictive modifier, 308
retained object, 189
revising. *See* writing process
rhetorical question, 356
roots, 415
run-on. *See* sentence problems, comma splice; sentence problems, fused sentence

semicolon
    Bible references, to separate, 315
    commas, between word groups containing, 315
    compound sentence, in a long, 315
    conjunction, before a, 315
    independent clauses, between two, 315
sentence
    beginnings, 359
    choosing constructions, 361–62
    complexity, 358
    definition of, 69
    ellipsis, 374
    emphasis, 355–56
    energy, 366–69
    expansion of, 371–72
    length, 358
    logic, 383–85
    reduction of, 373–78
    types of
        complex, 132, 365
        compound, 132
        compound-complex, 133
        declarative, 69
        exclamatory, 69
        imperative, 69
        interrogative, 69
        simple, 132
    variety, 355–65
    word order, 356, 359, 361–62, 387–88
sentence patterns
    S-*be*-Advl, 76
    S-InV, 75
    S-LV-PA, 75–76
    S-LV-PN, 75
    S-TrV-DO, 76
    S-TrV-DO-OC, 76
    S-TrV-IO-DO, 76
sentence problems
    comma splice, 137
    fragment, 135–37
    fused sentence, 137
    run-on. *See* sentence problems, comma splice; sentence problems, fused sentence
sentence variety and emphasis, 355–66
    energy, 366–69
    expansion of sentence, 371–72
    inverted, 356
    periodic, 356
    reduction of sentence, 373–78
    rhetorical question, 356
    short fragment, 356
sequence of subjects within a paragraph, 387
sestet, 240
shift in person and number, 216
shift of subjects within a paragraph, 387
simile, 368
simple sentence, 132
simple subject, 70
smoothness (in writing), 22
sonnet, 239–42
spatial order. *See* order, paragraph writing
spelling
    adding suffixes, 429–30
    by syllables, 426
    changing *y* to *i*, 427, 430
    doubling a final consonant, 415
    dropping final silent *e*, 430
    ie and *ei*, 429
    plural forms of nouns, 427–28
    possessive forms of nouns, 341–42, 428
    pronunciation of possessives, plurals, and certain verbs, 428
    verbs, third-person singular present-tense, 427
split infinitive, 251
squinting modifier. *See* modifier, two-way
standardized tests, taking of, 420–21
state-of-being verb, 42–43
stereotype, 390–91
stream of consciousness, 84
study skills, 409–21. *See also* book, parts of a; index, use of; memory techniques; reading comprehension, improving; test-taking strategies
style, revising for. *See* writing process, revising
subject
    complete, 70
    compound, 71
    definition of, 70, 74
    simple, 70
    understood *you*, 70
subjective case, 38, 204, 210
subjective complement. *See* predicate adjective; predicate noun
subjective complement, passive verb, 189
subject-verb agreement
    amounts, 155
    auxiliaries, 149
    collective nouns, 154
    compound subjects, 161–62
    forms of *be*, 149
    indefinite pronouns, 157–58
    intervening phrases, 150
    inverted order, 150
    predicate nouns, 150
    problem nouns, 153
    quoted word or phrase, 155
    relative pronouns, 159
    titles, quotations, and amounts, 155
subjunctive mood
    condition contrary to fact, 193
    definition of, 192
    doubtful future condition, 193
    expression of obligation or recommendation, 193
subordinating conjunction. *See* conjunction
subordination, 364–65
suffixes, 415. *See also* spelling, adding suffixes
superlative degree of modifiers, 243–44
syllables, spelling by. *See* spelling
synonyms, 405

T

tag question, 307
tense, verb. *See* verb
test-taking strategies
    classroom tests, 417–18
    essay questions, 419
    standardized tests, 420–21
theme (literary), 325, 327
thesaurus, 405
thesis restatement, 19
thesis statement. *See* writing process, drafting
they, indefinite use of, 232
Think About It, 80–81, 141, 196–97, 237, 289, 353
title of a paper, choosing a. *See* writing process, publishing
title of a work
    capitalization of, 282
    colon before subtitle, 316
    italics for, 337
    quotation marks for short works, 330
topic, choosing. *See* writing process, planning
topic, narrowing. *See* writing process, planning
topic sentence, 11
transitional expression, 20
transitive verb, 44
two-way modifier, 251

U

underlining for italics, 336–38
understood *you. See* subject
unity of ideas, 20
universal truth, 184

V

variety, sentence, 355–65
verb
    action, 42, 366
    as simple predicate, 70
    auxiliary, 44
    be, 44, 75–76
    complete, 44, 70
    definition of, 42
    do, 44, 179
    have, 179–80
    intransitive, 43
    irregular, 178
    linking, 44
    mood
        imperative, 43, 192
        indicative, 43, 192
        subjunctive, 43, 192
    number, 43
    person, 43
    principal parts
        past, 178
        past participle, 178
        present, 178
    regular, 178
    shall, 179
    spelling of third-person singular present-tense verbs. *See* spelling
    state-of-being, 42
    tense
        consistency and sequence of, 184–85
        perfect, 179
        progressive, 180
        simple, 178–79
        time, 43
    transitive, 44
    voice
        active, 43, 187–89, 361–62
        passive, 43, 187–89, 361–62
        usage, 361–62
verb-adverb combination, 45
verbal. *See also* gerund; infinitive; participle
    definition of, 92
    objects of verbals, 210
    "subjects" of verbals, 209–10
verbal phrase. *See* gerund phrase; infinitive phrase; participial phrase
video report, 200–203
villain, definition of, 146
voice. *See* verb

W

website
    evaluating a, 5
    library, 399
word order
    in writing, 356
    placement, 387–88
word parts, 415
Written Word, From the, 59, 107, 171, 219, 257, 321
words, specific and concrete, 355, 366–67
works-cited list, 268
World Wide Web. *See* Internet
writing process
    drafting
        concluding paragraph, 19
        concluding sentence, 13
        essays, 19–20, 33, 66–67, 112–14, 175–76, 294
        introductory paragraphs, 10–11
        mode, choosing a, 9
        paragraph development, 11
        paragraph organization, 14–17
        thesis statement, 10, 19, 66, 112, 175, 294
        topic sentence, 11
    planning
        audience, considering your, 4
        information, gathering, 5
        outlining, 6–8
        purpose, determining, 4
        topic
            choosing, 1–4
            narrowing, 4
    publishing
        neat copy, making a, 24
        title, choosing a, 24
    revising
        for correctness (proofreading), 23–24
        for ideas, 20–21
        for style, 22
writing strategies. *See specific topic*

Y

yearbook, 403
you
    indefinite use of, 232–33
    understood, 70